Matches in Dispatches
Seventy-five of the Greatest and Most Significant Games in the History of St Johnstone FC

By Alastair Blair and Brian Doyle

Matches in Dispatches
Published by thePotentMix,
Newmilns, Ayrshire, November 2023

Cover by Skep Design

Acknowledgements

Thank you to all the following, who contributed in ways great and small, but without whom we would not have been able to put together such a comprehensive array of reminiscences. Any errors are, of course, our responsibility.

Dave Anderson, Maggie Anderson, Steven Anderson, Kenny Aird, Gordon Bannerman, David Begg, Steve Bright, John Brogan, Ian Brown, Graeme Buchan, Zander Clark, John Connolly, Stuart Cosgrove, Liam Craig, Ian Crockatt, Nick Dasovic, Callum Davidson, Jimmy Donaldson, Liam Doris, Philip Doyle, Jack Findlay, Scott Findlay, Ally Forbes, Matt Gallagher, Roddy Grant, Helen Green, Danny Griffin, Henry Hall, Stan Harris, Ian Heddle, Kevin Heller, Eddie Henderson, Linda Henderson, Jason Kerr, John Litster, Alistair Lowe, Anne Mailer, Bryan Malcolm, Alan Mannus, Jim Masson, Bev Mayer, Ali McCann, Jim Mackintosh, Derek McIntosh, Robert McIntosh, Colin McCredie, Stewart McKinnon, Ian McLaren, Tom McLaughlan, Alastair Mitchell, Derek Mitchell, Jim Morton, Gordon Muir, Ian Munro, Gordon Murdoch, Eric Nicolson, Donald Paton, David McPhee, Donald McPhee, Derek O'Connor, Jim Pearson, John Pelosi, Bill Powrie, Allan Preston, John Robertson, Shaun Rooney, Philip Scott, Keith Sievwright, Ian Slater, Gregor Sleith, Gordon Small, Charles Smith, Iain Smith, Paul Smith, David Somers, Bill Taylor, Andrew Tulloch, Steven Watt, Gordon Whitelaw, David Wotherspoon, Tommy Wright and the staff at the Local History Department of the AK Bell Library in Perth. Apologies to anyone we have missed off this list.

Notes:

We have tried, wherever possible, to give the name of the publication or online medium from which we have taken our quotes and descriptions of these games. Our sources covered a wide range of different media in order to gain as good an impression of each match and any additional details as possible. These include: the British Newspaper Archive, the Perthshire Constitutional, the Perthshire Courier, the Perthshire Advertiser, the Scottish Referee, The (Dundee) Courier, The Sporting Post, The Sunday Post, the (Dundee) Evening Telegraph, The Press and Journal, the Aberdeen Evening Express, the Daily Record, The Scotsman, the Edinburgh Evening News, the Montrose Advertiser, the Arbroath Herald, the Airdrie and Coatbridge Advertiser, the Coatbridge Express, The (Glasgow) Herald, the BBC, the Daily Telegraph and The Guardian. If no name is given to a quotation, the source is invariably the Perthshire Advertiser.

Where available, we have given the Saints' team lines for each match along with the attendance. The line-up is given in the format in which it was reported at the time. For example, up to the 1960s it was invariably punctuated as a 2-3-5 formation and in more recent years simply as a list, beginning with the goalkeeper and trying to follow what appeared to be the formation used on the day.

Finally, the occasionally quirky chapter headings are invariably taken from a contemporary match report, although they are not always referenced in the text of each chapter. We hope you enjoy them!

Dedication

To the two men who managed St Johnstone Football Club to victory in the Scottish Cup Finals of 2014 and 2021and the League Cup Final of 2021.

Tommy Wright and Callum Davidson

Foreword, by Liam Craig

Give them something to attack

That's the thought going through my head as I stand over a corner at Ibrox on the 25th April 2021. It was the 122nd minute, and we were trailing 1-0 to Rangers in the Scottish Cup quarter final.

Seconds later...my favourite moment in arguably my favourite game in a St Johnstone strip...the corner is heading into the middle of the six-yard box; now I am thinking, someone attack it.

Little did I think that someone was going to be our goalkeeper, Zander Clark, who would head the ball down for Kano to turn it into Allan McGregor's goal to equalise, send the game to penalty kicks and ultimately to a win that would be the only domestic loss for Rangers at Ibrox in a season in which they would be crowned SPFL Premier League champions.

The significance of that corner would be laid bare in the months that would follow as we added the Scottish Cup to the League Cup, which already sat proudly in the McDiarmid Park trophy room.

A domestic Cup Double! An unbelievable achievement by a group of players and staff that made a dream become a reality for a unique club and its fantastic supporters.

As I write, I am privileged to have retired as the leading appearance holder for this special club.

I have been lucky enough to play for St Johnstone during the most successful period in our history, accompanied along the way by some great characters amongst the playing squad, the backroom staff and the directors.

I have had so many special moments that I could talk about, but I'd like to mention just one more that stands out. It was in Istanbul, against a superb team that has been a giant of European football over many years. Jason Kerr, our Double-Cup winning captain, scores a penalty to put us in front against the background of a stadium filled with Turkish noise and colour. The Galatasaray fans fall silent and I look up to the scoreboard to see, 'Galatasaray 0-1 St Johnstone.' Back home at McDiarmid Park, the flag, 'Underestimated since 1884' flies high once again.

When speaking to the authors about the book, one thing we agreed was that the great games, moments of excitement and the order they would appear in the book will cause debate, arguments and maybe confusion amongst supporters. This is what makes being a St Johnstone fan so special: we have had so many great moments throughout our history. The Scottish Cup win in 2014 and the Cup Double in 2021 are arguably the standouts, but, like me, every supporter has their own personal memories and stories to tell, some of which appear in the pages below.

Enjoy the book and never forget: this club has achieved things other clubs will only ever dream about.

Liam Craig

Contents

Introduction

POEM – Through City Veins, by Jim Mackintosh

PART I - Milestones

Part II - Significant Games

1. (Glasgow) Thistle, 1st January 1886
2. Tulloch, 17th September 1887
3. Our Boys Blairgowrie, 21st December 1889
4. Arbroath Wanderers, 23rd December 1893
5. Clydebank, 14th April 1923
6. Dundee United, 17th April 1926
7. Arsenal, 26th September 1932
8. Berwick Rangers, 27th April 1960
9. Rangers, 21st December 1963
10. Hibernian, 24th December 1966
11. Clyde, 10th April 1971
12. Celtic, 26th April 1975
13. Ayr United, 28th April 1990
14. Rangers, 29th November 1998
15. Dunfermline Athletic, 25th November 2007
16. Aberdeen, 13th April 2014
17. Kilmarnock, 4th December 2019
18. Inverness Caledonian Thistle, 23rd May 2022

Part III - The Greatest Games

30. St Johnstone 7, Leith Athletic 3, 28th January 1950
29. St Johnstone 1, Dundee 0, 23rd May 1999
28. Partick Thistle 1, St Johnstone 8, 16th August 1969
27. St Johnstone 2, Airdrie 2, 4th December 1954
26. Fair City Athletic 4, St Johnstone 9, 16th November 1895
25. Rangers 0, St Johnstone 2, 8th November 2006
24. Dundee 3, St Johnstone 4, 2nd January 1978
23. St Johnstone, 3 Rangers 3, 14th February 1981
22. Hamilton 3, St Johnstone 4, 28th April 2007
21. Rangers 1, St Johnstone 1, (2-4 on penalties), 25th April 2021
20. Celtic 0, St Johnstone 1, 16th August 1961
19. St Johnstone 2, Celtic 0, 30th August 1961
18. St Johnstone 2, Celtic 0, 12th August 1981
17. St Johnstone 10, Brechin City 1, 6th December 1919
16. Rosenborg 0, St Johnstone 1, 18th July 2013
15. St Johnstone 3, Celtic 2, 22nd December 1990
14. St Johnstone 4, Partick Thistle 3, 2nd September 1961
13. St Johnstone 9, Albion Rovers 0, 9th March 1946
12. St Johnstone 3, Hearts 0, 27th October 1998
11. St Johnstone 3, Monaco 3, 30th September 1999
10. St Johnstone 1, Livingston 0, 28th February 2021
9. Galatasaray 1, St Johnstone 1, 5th August 2021
8. St Johnstone 1, Hibernian 0, 22nd May 2021
7. Celtic 2, St Johnstone 2, 30th August 1969
6. St Johnstone 7, Dundee 2, 1st January 1997
5. St Johnstone 5, Aberdeen 0, 29th September 1990
4. St Johnstone 2, Dundee United 0, 17th May 2014
3. Stenhousemuir 5, St Johnstone 5, 22nd September 1962
2. St Johnstone 3, Airdrie 1, 31st March 1990
1. St Johnstone 3, SV Hamburg 0, 29th September 1971

INTRODUCTION

Since the club's foundation on Tuesday, 24th February, 1885, to the end of the 2022-23 season, St Johnstone have played 5,777 matches. The club's first game, in March 1885, resulted in a win. This was the first of the 2,397 matches we have won since then, with a further 1,215 drawn and 2,165 lost, with 10,476 goals scored and 9,647 conceded. Along the way, there have been many other firsts of course – the first ever trophy, the first game in the Scottish League, the first game at Muirton, the first game at McDiarmid, a first national Cup final, a first League Championship and a first (but not last) game in European competition. Interspersed with these significant milestones, there are many other games which created an indelible impression on everyone who witnessed them. Some of these were, naturally, deep in the past with no-one still alive to recall what happened, while others are still as fresh in the mind as the day they occurred. Each fan will have their own particular favourites and while we cannot please everyone, what follows is, in our view, a definitive compendium of the key games in St Johnstone's history.

Many of you opening this book will have witnessed some, possibly many, of these matches. If you are young, you'll have a fund of recent memories to grow old with, or, if you are nearer the other end of life's journey, you'll be able to look back upon these with immense fondness, remembering the thrill of living through moments of great joy and excitement. This has particularly been the case in the twenty-first century; unarguably the greatest period of success in St Johnstone's history. Yet that success was dependent on so many men (and the occasional woman) who, over the last 138 years, overcame trials and hurdles that would, in other hands, have led to St Johnstone becoming an also-ran in Scottish football history and even, as with some others, a footnote recording a club that no longer exists. There are several examples of the latter and it's instructive – and, we would argue, essential for the club's custodians – to recall that many other clubs have had their great decades, Cup finals and Cup wins, but then faded from the scene and now struggle to re-capture past glories.

For all these reasons and more, it's important, in our view, to include not just recent victories, but also games from the distant past. Obviously, we are dependent on reports from the newspapers for the earlier matches, but as we approach the present, reminiscences from fans add colour, personal analysis and perspective to the match descriptions from the media. The inclusion of games from long-ago and the personal recollections of our fans all serve to emphasise (not that it should really need such emphasis) that many people of Perth and district, plus those 'ex-pat' supporters spread across the UK and indeed the globe, have always carried St Johnstone in their hearts and taken joy from the team's successes and pain from its failures. Whether it's the soldiers of the Black Watch, writing home from the front during the First World War to seek news of Perthshire Cup scores, or the far-flung individuals who some hundred years later crossed continents to see the club win its first major trophy in 2014, the ties that bind Perth, Perthshire and St Johnstone run deep and true. Generations yet unborn will, we trust, come to share our affection and commitment to the wee team from Craigie that developed into a significant force in Scottish football and today commands respect on and off the field for its football prowess and the administrative excellence that underpins it. We owe it to both the current generation and our predecessors that St Johnstone's achievements are remembered and celebrated and, in this book, we hope to have made a small contribution to that end.

Alastair Blair and Brian Doyle, November, 2023

THROUGH CITY VEINS

I am there now. I see the town, St Leonard's across the Inch,
prison walls threaten dark behind me but can't hold me back.
I am born, free to think, to play the game. I can feel the grass.
I can hear them circling above, curious gulls mocking us.
We, this odd bunch of men in shorts – students of football.

The cricket bats in a bag, in a shed for another day
for another team, for now, spurred on – I am St Johnstone.
I am born to reach out across the Inch, to run slick
through city veins, bubble up through the mouths
of honest grafters, to soothe the toil of blistered lives.

I was uncertain of everything – the rules, the tactics
the opposition's learnings matching mine – unsettling
the stumbling steps of my newly found rhythm
but my mind was sure of this – defeat would not kill me.
It would nourish me. I was born St Johnstone.

I am my own flesh and grow beyond your shifting lives.
My blood would spill, soak into the soil of foreign fields
for King and Country. I left myself there yet returned
in shelled parts to be born again. I would breathe again,
because you would breathe with me. I am St Johnstone.

I am there now. I see the Stand, the Ice Rink, the steel
barriers, the Ormond boys, the Muirton aces. Signal
letters – DRYBROUGHS rippling across corrugation
bold, brainwashing, echoing around chimney stacks
through the clag of industry summoning the faithful

the curious, the rich men, poor men, big men,
wee men, fair maids, old maids and the etceteras
who pumped their blood into me. We ran together.
We stood up together, became more than our yesterdays.
I lived on beyond your narrow days. I am St Johnstone.

Then *He* found me in the slump. Not dead but tired,
bruised, bleached where the juice had been sucked
from my bones. *He* lifted me up, nurtured me,
took me to the green fields, built me a new home.
I am there now. In the four Stands, the fancy Suites

the weave of tartan. I am the grass, the cotton,
the blue, the white, the zipped up effort of youth.
Its brittle edge and fiery stew of energy where my
tomorrows will flourish. The gulls circle yet no
longer mock. I bristle with possibilities. I am St Johnstone.

8

I am St Johnstone until I die but why should I care
of death when I am re-born every day? I am the smudge
on the engraved curves of envied silver. Three times born
again in the blue ribboned hands of my captains from
an open top bus, the ghost buses in our lockdown disbelief.

I have spun the roulette wheel in Monaco's casinos,
walked to the edge of the Arctic Circle, dipped my
toes in glacial blue waters and sang by alpine shores.
Every day, I reach the far side of this earth, secure
in kinship hearts. Every day, I am St Johnstone.

I am there now. In dressed shop windows, memory
laden bar shelves to the right of the busy optics.
I am in the queue at the checkout, at the bus stop,
on the oak lined road to the next departure
from the Crematorium. I am all the Lotto numbers.

I am the spare peg in the dressing room, every blade
of grass, the first goal, the last point, the air in the nets,
the corner flag flutter of every game, the bait hook of
every word in every column inch. I am there now. I am
the echo of studs in the tunnel and the last floodlight fading.

I am St Johnstone. I'm in the checked-in holiday baggage.
I'm on Sugar Loaf, Table Top and every postcard sent home.
I'm on the walk down from Letham, the bus up from Muirton.
I'm the anticipation of early arrivers, the slouch of early leavers.
I'm the ramble of East Stand opinions, the choir of joy-song

the bounce of bare chested unity. I'm all your beating hearts.
I'm players not yet legend, dreams not yet imagined,
adventures not yet planned. I'm your manifest destiny.
I will breathe tomorrow if you will breathe with me
for we are all St Johnstone - forever.

Jim Mackintosh

PART 1

MILESTONES

This section of the book covers those matches that were important milestones in St Johnstone's history. In the main, these are events such as the first and last games at the various grounds the club has occupied since 1885, as well as notable firsts such as the first Cup win of any kind, the first Scottish League match, the first match against European opposition, etc. Some of these matches are well-known to the present generation of Saints' fans: others, by virtue of the decades that have passed, less so.

While the era in which these early games took place is long gone, they all had significance, not just for the supporters of the day but for the club itself as it struggled to make its mark in Perthshire and then in the wider Scottish game beyond. The fact that today it is St Johnstone FC that garners headlines in the top flight of Scottish football and not, say, Fair City Athletic, is testimony to the unstinting efforts of all the early administrators, directors and, most importantly, those pioneering players who first decided that kicking a ball around after cricket practice was a good idea.

No. 1.
In the beginning…

The first match
St Johnstone 1, Caledonian 0, Friendly match,
South Inch, Perth, Saturday, 7th March 1885

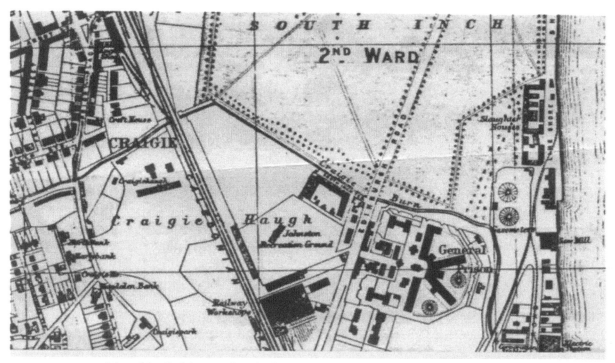

Map of the Craigie area of Perth, showing the location of the Recreation Grounds.
Saints first games were played on the area where the words '2nd Ward' are printed.

After St Johnstone Football Club came into being on 24th February 1885, the members of the new club were keen to organise a game and so St Johnstone's first ever match took place just a few weeks later. It was against Caledonian, a club formed by local employees of the eponymous railway company. There are only three reports of this contest, all of which are brief and in the style of the day…

"Teams representing these clubs met for the first time on the South Inch on Saturday and the game resulted in a victory for the St Johnstone by 1 goal, their opponents failing to score."
Perthshire Constitutional and Journal, Monday, 9th March 1885.

"The St Johnstone encountered for their first match the Caledonian on the South Inch on Saturday.
The St Johnstone from the first pressed their opponents hard and Gordon had to use his hands frequently to save his goal from disaster. For the St Johnstone team Lorimer and W. Thomson at back played a hard game and Scobie as centre worked hard. Gordon at goal for the Caledonian played well; and McDiarmid on the right wing played hard but he had a tendency to be rather rough.
Victory resulted in favour of the St Johnstone team by 1 goal to nothing."
Perthshire Advertiser, Monday, 9th March 1885.

"The St Johnstone encountered for their first match the Caledonian on the South Inch on Saturday and it resulted in a win for them by one goal to nothing."
Dundee Advertiser
Monday, 9th March 1885.

The other source of information about this first match is Peter Baxter's seminal book, *"Football in Perthshire,"* which was published in 1898. Although written more than a decade after the events and containing a number of unfortunate errors (the most egregious being his wrongly dating St Johnstone's formation to 1884), he did provide a team line-up for the game against Caledonian, which he erroneously believed was Saints' second match, not their first. Consequently, we believe that Saints first ever team line-up almost certainly included most of the men listed by Baxter, viz: Charles Thomson; W Thomson, F Lorimer, Dunn, Lambert, Colbron, Wood, Imrie, Wilson, Stuart and Scott. However, as you can see from the local press reports here, it seems that an additional player, Scobie, took part, so we can never be certain just who had the honour of appearing in that first ever St Johnstone team.

That said, one man who we are (fairly) sure will have played was the club captain, Daniel Scott. He was elected to that position at the meeting on 24th February 1885 when the club was formed. Although he had played football for Fair City Athletic, who were formed in 1884, he had also been a member of St Johnstone Cricket Club and when the cricketers formed St Johnstone FC his footballing allegiance passed from Fair City to Saints. He played at outside right and was described as being fast on the ball and possessed of a good shot. Amongst the many other things we don't know is what kit these men wore, although from what we can gather, they simply took to the field in the white shirts they used for cricket. However, we also know that Harper Wood and D M Stuart took part in the match after walking to the South Inch from the North Inch, where they had been playing rugby and they played football in their rugby kit. It's also worth noting that until 1909 there was no requirement for a distinguishing jersey for the goalkeeper. Another distinction from today's game is that the goalkeeper was allowed to handle the ball anywhere on the pitch (in 1887 this was changed so he could only handle it in his own half and then in 1912 only within his penalty area).

One thing that would have been common to all the players though was the type of footwear used. The pitches in those days were much rougher and less well maintained than the bowling-green surfaces we have today and the pioneering Saints' team's boots would have been sturdy (and *very* heavy) leather items compared to today's lithe, ultra-modern, multi-coloured football shoes.

As noted in the updated version of the club's official history, we previously believed this first ever match was played on the Lesser South Inch; that strip of grass nearest the river Tay on the far side of the Edinburgh Road. Subsequent research showed that in fact it was played on the western side of the Inch. More specifically, we believe the actual area of the Inch that was used for this game is that which borders South Inch Terrace (described as the 2nd Ward on the map here), which in turn overlooked (in the other direction) the area outside the Inch and across the road from Perth Prison that was to become the St Johnstone Recreation Grounds later that same year (also as shown on the map). On a corner of South Inch Terrace there are still the remains of a painted sign which probably dates back to Recreation Ground days, although after all this time it's impossible to make out what it originally said, although the word *"Johnstone"* is discernible. The picture here (courtesy of Graeme Buchan) shows all that's left of this sign.

We know these early games were organised between the rival football clubs that were springing up in Perth and Perthshire during the mid-1880s, almost all of whose members will have known each other from playing in other sports, principally cricket and rugby. However, unlike today when football and rugby pitches – with their associated markings, posts and bars - are part and parcel of the landscape of both the North and South Inches, in those days clubs had to buy their own posts and take them to each game. We know that St Johnstone did this and we can presume they also had a crossbar as well as posts. We can infer this because, two years earlier, in 1883, the laws of the game were changed to require a solid crossbar. We also know (see next chapter), that they had a crossbar by November 1885. Prior to this a tape was used and so it is not impossible that some local clubs, who were in effect learning as they went along, made do with a tape initially.

Similarly, we don't know who was responsible for marking out the pitches, which, of course, were not laid out in the same way as they are today. It wasn't until 1883 that there was a requirement for a continuous touchline around the pitch. This was usually made using a solution of chalk and mud, or alternatively was just a furrow in the ground. There were no goal areas or penalty areas, no centre circle and no penalty mark – simply the touchlines, four corner flags and the goalposts (but no goal-nets). The various incarnations of the goal area/line and penalty area/line were not introduced until later in the nineteenth century and were mostly not altered to their current configuration until the early twentieth century.

The ball itself would have been far removed from the modern football. For a start, it was slightly lighter, being 13-15oz as opposed to the modern ball (since 1937) of 14-16oz. In addition, it was not exactly spherical, being made of a brown leather outer casing surrounding a bladder of vulcanised rubber and secured by a lace that was stitched into a series of holes in the leather that surrounded the slit through which the bladder was then inserted into the casing.

It may not have been football as we know it today, but one thing is certain: this match in 1885 was the humble beginning from which St Johnstone FC has grown and developed to its current position, recognised as a major team in Scottish football and (at the time of writing) firmly established in the upper echelon of the game here.

No. 2
He confessed that he had been playing in Dundee that season…

The first competitive match
St Johnstone 1, Our Boys Blairgowrie 0, Perthshire Cup, First Round,
Recreation Grounds, Saturday, 14th November 1885

Following on from their first ever match, St Johnstone continued to play friendlies, using the South Inch as their 'home' turf until the summer of 1885. Over that summer, the Recreation Grounds were built and the official opening saw a challenge match between the almighty Queen's Park, then almost certainly the best team in Britain, and Dundee Our Boys. Dundee Our Boys were one of the two teams (the other being Dundee East End) who merged to form Dundee FC and the latter adopted the Our Boys dark blue jerseys. It's slightly ironic that Saints' first ground was hanselled with a match involving a club that would go on to be our greatest rival.

There was no league competition available at this time so St Johnstone continued to play friendly matches until November, when they were tested in competitive football for the first time ever, in a Perthshire Cup tie against Our Boys of Blairgowrie. The Perthshire Football Association had only been formed the previous season and therefore 1885-86 was the first year in which the Perthshire Cup was contested.

There are three reports of this match available in the local press. The PA's report is short, but fairly informative…

OUR BOYS (BLAIRGOWRIE V.
ST JOHNSTONE (PERTH) – CUP TIE
"These clubs met in the first round of the Perthshire cup ties on the ground of the latter in presence of about 300 spectators. The Boys kicked off, with a slight breeze in their favour. During the first half the game was very equal, and somewhat slow. Two or three times the St Johnstone looked like

scoring, but the shots rebounded from the crossbar and upright. The Blair lads had also a look in once or twice, but their shooting was wide. Half time sounded and the first period was a blank. A good part of the second half had gone and the game continued of a give and take nature. The visitors' centres got hold of the sphere and ran it well up, and passed to the right wing, who sent it spinning through, but the point was disallowed, owing to a clear case of off-side. The Saints in turn paid a visit to the Our Boys citadel, and the ball was well returned, but McLaren was at hand, and sent in a long and sure shot, and amid cheers scored the only point of the match. The game ended – St Johnstone 1; Our Boys 0."
Perthshire Advertiser,
Monday, 16th November 1885.

Interestingly, the Courier's report is, with just one, crucial exception, word for word the same as the PA's, suggesting that the practice of using a 'stringer' to report for more than one paper was established a long time ago (and we'll see other examples of this in some of the match reports of subsequent games in the chapters below).

The crucial exception is in identity of Saints' goalscorer. The Courier gives this as "McLean," not "McLaren" as in the PA. To make matters more complicated, John Litster's records of Scottish players do not list either man at St Johnstone that season, although a McLean is listed as playing for Saints in season 1888-89. However, another source, (Peter Baxter's book *"Football in Perthshire"*) cites McLean as the scorer – so that's the name we're going with!

From the Blairgowrie perspective, the key element of the match was the alleged malpractice by St Johnstone in fielding an ineligible player. This is what the Blairgowrie Advertiser had to say…

OUR BOYS V ST JOHNSTONE, PERTH

"These clubs met in the first round of the Perthshire Cup on the St Johnstone Recreation Grounds on Saturday.

The match was decided as a win for the St Johnstone by 1 to 0.

The home club were without Sorlie, and the Boys' forwards showed a lack of combination through the absence of Bisset.

Our Boys have protested against the result of the match, and also against some of the St Johnstone players.

Mr Watson, Dundee Strathmore, was referee."
Blairgowrie Advertiser,
Saturday 21st November 1885.

Amongst the things these reports don't tell us is what colours the teams wore. We can fairly safely presume that St Johnstone turned out in the maroon tops they had registered with the SFA as the club's official colours. Blairgowrie, on the other hand, probably took the field in blue and yellow quartered shirts and blue shorts. These are the colours that Peter Baxter described in the section on Blairgowrie in his book, *"Football in Perthshire,"* and he also tells that *"They (Blairgowrie) had the misfortune to be drawn from home, and had to travel to Perth to meet the newly-formed St Johnstone. The result of a hard game was a win for the Perth Saints, the deciding goal being put through from a long shot from McLean, the Saints' full-back."*

It seems that, as with the first ever game recorded above, we can also report a victory in St Johnstone's first competitive match.

Unfortunately, as the Blairgowrie Advertiser had noticed, one of the Saints' team was actually a member of another football club and therefore ineligible to play. Blairgowrie lodged a protest with the Perthshire FA and the player in question, whose surname was Bremner (he and McLean are the only two of the Saints' team whose names we know), admitted that he was indeed a member of Dundee Strathmore. He confessed that he had been playing in Dundee that season but had played for Saints against Blairgowrie because two of his cousins were members of the St Johnstone members club. We know there was an R. Bremner and a D. Bremner playing for Saints later that season, so we presume these were the cousins.

Today, such blatant chicanery would probably result in immediate expulsion from the competition, but they were more lenient back in those days and the PFA committee simply insisted on the match being replayed. This game took place, again at the Recreation Grounds, on 5th December 1885.

In between the first tie and the replay, Saints warmed up with a friendly against Dunblane. It wasn't a good move: *"the Heather"* (as Dunblane were known) won 14-0. In Saints' defence, it should be recorded that due to the terrible weather a telegram had been sent to Dunblane asking to cancel the match. Consequently, most of the Perth team didn't turn up, but the telegram arrived too late: Dunblane had already travelled and, with only four of the regular Saints' players in a 10-man side that day, the result was a foregone conclusion. Dunblane at that time had a very strong team and would go on to win not just that first Perthshire Cup but also to dominate the competition for the next few years, winning four out of the first five tournaments. Strangely, in that 1885-86 season the Perthshire FA had not actually bought, or even commissioned an actual Cup and *"the Heather"* had to celebrate without a trophy.

After the drubbing from Dunblane, it's unlikely that St Johnstone players would have been full of confidence going into their replay with Blairgowrie. They certainly didn't appear to be, for, despite the fact that they once more had home advantage, they went down 3-6 to their county opponents. In time, St Johnstone would leave Dunblane, Blairgowrie and the other local teams far behind, but that was for the future. For the newly-formed St Johnstone club, with no local league in which to test their mettle, their next goal was success in a local cup competition. Fortunately, they only had to wait a few years for that to happen…

Saints team: the only players we definitely know played were Bremner and McLean.
Attendance: 300

On the whole, the play was very rough

**The first Cup win,
St Johnstone 7, Erin Rovers 2, Reid Charity Cup,
St Catherine's Park, Perth, Saturday, 4th May 1889**

Picture of the first St Johnstone FC team to win a trophy. The players, splendidly attired in their cricket whites, pose with the Reid Cup. Photo: St Johnstone FC.

In the latter half of the 1880s, football in Perth and district had become reasonably well established, albeit it was still regarded locally as the poor relation of cricket by many. In its edition of 1st May 1889, the Perthshire Constitutional bemoaned the encroachment of friendly football matches onto the cricket season, taking aim in particular at a game between Saints and Fair City Athletic, noting that neither side fielded their strongest eleven and, as a result, Fair City won 7-1.

In the same day's paper, there is also a report of what was described as the *"abominable, contemptible and mean practice"* of *"fisting out."* This was the deliberate clearance of a goal-bound shot by a defender, using his hand for the purpose. The paper's report goes on to wish that the football authorities, *"eradicate a practice which, when wilfully committed, is beneath contempt... I regret to say it is far*

too prevalent in a certain club in Perth for the last three seasons at least." We believe the club referred to is Fair City Athletic as a match report in the Perthshire Constitutional from December 1887 records, *"One very dirty trick – not unfamiliar to the Balhousie team* (i.e. Fair City)*, as is well known – was the 'fisting out' at goal by – well, not the goalkeeper."*

In a further article in the edition of 1st May 1889, under the heading *"Port Echoes"* (i.e. gossip) on the same page it is recorded that *"the only talk is the St Johnstone addendum to Law 4 at the last meeting of the SFA as to fisting out."* This comment was made because St Johnstone had petitioned the SFA to have this practice outlawed – or at least punished by the referee awarding a goal if it happened, but their request was rebuffed as it was up to IFAB to change the laws, not the Scottish football authorities.

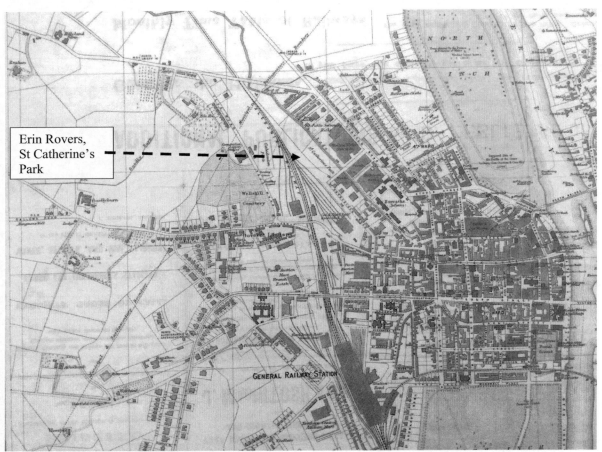

Erin Rovers, St Catherine's Park

Erin Rovers' ground, St Catherine's Park, 1895.

To say this was casting Perth in bad light is an understatement, because *"Port Echoes"* goes on to say, *"that to have the whole gaze of Scottish players turned upon your club for 'fisting out' is not appreciated by the Fair City."*

This was the background to the Reid Charity Cup final, played between Saints and Erin Rovers on St Catherine's Park only three days later – and almost a year to the day (5th May 1888) that the same teams had played out the first final of this trophy - with Erin Rovers winning on that occasion by four goals to two. It should be noted that in this game, Alex Christie, one of the St Johnstone outfield players, *"fisted out"* to prevent a fifth goal for the Rovers.

The Cup was the brainchild of Mr Dan Reid of the Hammerman Tavern in Perth. As reported in the PA, at a meeting of the local

football clubs on Friday 2nd March 1888, Mr Reid had presented his eponymous trophy, saying *"that his intention was that it should be played for annually by the leading Clubs of the city, and that the proceeds, after defraying the necessary expenses, should be given to the local charities… The Clubs selected to take part in (the first) competition are Caledonian Rangers, Fair City Athletics, St Johnstone, Erin Rovers, and Bridgend Athletics."*

Stuart Cosgrove, whose great grandfather and great uncles all played for the club, has researched Erin Rovers history extensively and tells us that their officials and players were mostly based in the older parts of the city, particularly around the Meal Vennel and South Street. Erin Rovers was founded by Irish immigrants, many of whom had come to Perth from County Galway and County Mayo, initially taking jobs in the fields and then, as more industry was introduced to Perth, in dye works and the textile mills in and around the city. Several of the team's members (specifically the Tea Family) had been expelled from their home on the Twining Estate in Connacht.

Unsurprisingly, Irish names featured in their team lines, including not just Cosgrove but also Lyden, Coyne and Coyle. Equally unsurprisingly, they played in green shirts. They, like Saints, began playing on the South Inch, but then acquired a 'home' ground at St Catherine's Park, which was situated (as shown on the map on the preceding page) by the town Lade, behind the Wallace (textile) Works and very near the old Swimming Baths on the Dunkeld Road.

As to the second Reid Cup final, we know it was a nice day, because the PA's report tells us the match was played in *"fine weather."* Similarly, we know there was a decent crowd, because the same report says the game was played *"before a large concourse of spectators,"* although an actual number is not given.

There is a match report of the game in the PA, but only a relatively brief note on it in the Perthshire Constitutional. The latter, following on from its previous edition – in which it had suggested that interest in football was waning as the summer arrived – was not especially complimentary about the game or about St Johnstone, telling its readers that, *"The Reid Charity Competition finished on Saturday without creating much excitement even in football circles. With the disqualification of the Fair City Athletics the final was robbed of much of the interest it might have had. From the newspaper accounts of the match it must have been a rough one ...*

"The St Johnstone will be proud of being able at last to put their names on a cup, and it is to be hoped its possession will help to *put more life into the Club than it has shown in the past season."*

The Perthshire Advertiser was more fulsome in their praise for the efforts of the players, but they too noted the rough and tumble of what was clearly a hard-fought match…

"On the whole, the play was very rough and especially in the second half. Feeling between the players ran high, and two of them actually got to blows indulging in a set-to. This regretable (sic) incident caused the crowd to break into the field, and play was suspended for several minutes."

The first half had seen the Rovers open the scoring, hit the bar twice and also have another goal disallowed, seemingly because it was directly from a corner-kick and no other player had touched the ball before it entered the goal (it wasn't until 1924 that, following a motion to IFAB from the Scottish Football Association, the laws were changed to allow a goal to be scored directly from a corner). Saints fought back and equalised before half-time, but in the second half, with a strong breeze at their backs, they dominated possession *("nearly all the play during the remainder of the game was at the Rovers' end")* and scored a further six times, with only one counter from the *"Greens."*

In an indication that football in Perthshire was now being noticed on a wider stage, the Scottish Referee carried a one-paragraph report of the match. Under the heading, *"Cup-Tie Game in Perth,"* they reported that, *"The final for the Reid Charity Cup took place on Saturday, the finalists being the Erin Rovers (present holders) and the St. Johnstone. The game was played on the Rovers' ground. The cup was gained by the Saints by 7 to 2. The winners played a good game all through."*

The Reid Cup win is especially important because, as a result, a photograph of the winning eleven was taken. Not only is it the first photo we have of St Johnstone with a trophy, it's the first team photo of St Johnstone in existence. This was a significant victory. Erin Rovers would not last much longer, but Fair City Athletic were generally regarded as the biggest team in Perth in the 1880s and for much of the remainder of the nineteenth century. Brian Doyle's forensic research shows that Fair City had the upper hand in the period from 1885 to 1889, but thereafter, Saints were the more successful. Between 1885 and 1901, when Fair City Athletic met their demise (due to financial difficulties as a result of moving to a new ground in 1899), the head-to-head record shows there had been 71 games played between the two teams, with Saints winning 30, Fair City 27 and 14 matches drawn. The tightness of the games between them is demonstrated by the number of goals scored, with St Johnstone just having the edge with 166, compared to Fair City's 152. It's also worth noting in passing that James Buchan, who went on to become Saints' manager after the First World War, began his playing career with Fair City in 1897, before moving to St Johnstone in 1899.

However, by winning their first cup – and going on to win more and more local cup competitions, Saints gradually became recognised as the equal of Fair City Athletic and, in time, the dominant club in Perth. And of course, after winning a cup or two the next step was to find a proper league to play in…

Saints team: from the photo, the only player we can identify with any certainty is John Robertson, on the far right of the back row. Attendance: unknown.

No. 4
The ball had been fouled immediately before

The first League match,
St Johnstone 6, Aberdeen 2, Northern League,
Recreation Grounds, Saturday, 3rd October, 1891

Although St Johnstone have had some impressive victories over Aberdeen in more recent years (a certain 5-0 score-line may well feature later in this book), it should be emphasised that it was not the current Aberdeen club that went down so heavily in this first ever league match for Saints. The present Aberdeen FC were not formed until 1903, being an amalgamation between the Aberdeen side featured here and Orion and Victoria United.

Like Saints, this Aberdeen club were one of the eight founder members of the Northern League, a competition that came into existence due to clubs' desire for more regular, competitive games.

The Scottish Referee's report was brief and to the point. At this time, their football reports were grouped by generic regions – Glasgow and District, East, South, Midland, etc. However, Perthshire, for some reason, was given its own section and there we can read, *"St Johnstone played their first Northern League match, and have started with two points. The Aberdeen side were a good deal softer than expected and the Saints had little difficulty."*

In contrast, the Perthshire Constitutional was fulsome in its praise of both sides. However, reading between the lines, we do get an idea of the very different way in which football was conducted in the late nineteenth century compared to the present day. We need to bear in mind that the formation was nearer the old-fashioned 2-3-5 but, in reality, with far more emphasis on the forwards, who tended to run in packs, working the ball along the wings and

generally shepherding it towards the opposition goal. From the press reports, it seems that some of the visitors' play was a bit wayward: for example, the Constitutional's report tells us that, *"the Aberdeen back division was the weakest point of their team, and their kicking gave indication of a strong want of judgement."*

In contrast, Saints were, as we would say nowadays, right at it and took the game to their opponents…

"The St Johnstone's back division was magnificent, and the long-kicks by Robertson, when taking the ball from the feet of the Aberdeen forwards, caused a sort of consternation in their ranks." This is the same John Robertson who had two trials for Scotland, although he was never actually selected for the national team. The rest of the side almost all performed well on the day. *"The half-backs worked with a will and put in a lot of useful work. Rodger, as centre-forward, has made a vast improvement in his play since the previous Saturday and made himself pretty conspicuous. Smith and Anderson played, probably, the best game they have done this season, and their smart runs down the field were deservedly applauded. Burnfield played a fast game, but he was not so strongly backed-up as usual by A McFarlane, who looked out of sorts and whose shooting was very erratic. Tulloch at the goal had a very easy time of it, and his powers were not put to a thorough test. On the whole, the Saints are to be congratulated…"*

Given that Andrew McFarlane scored two

of Saints' six goals, this seems a bit harsh. Burnfield, Robertson and Rodger also scored, with the sixth being an own-goal by Aberdeen's left-back. Burnfield also had a goal disallowed when, *"The Saints carried the ball east, where they had a few more shots at the strangers' goal, and shortly afterwards Burnfield rushed the sphere through; but the ball had been fouled immediately before, and the point was not allowed."*

The language used in match reports at this time is wonderfully archaic to our modern eyes and ears. The away team are frequently referred to as *"the strangers,"* with the home side being *"the ground men."* The ball becomes *"the sphere,"* or *"the leather,"* while goals are generally referred to as *"points."* Instead of the Ormond or North Stand being reference points for the direction of play, the points of the compass are used, with the PA telling us that Aberdeen kicked off the match attacking the west goal while Saints, as the quotation about David Burnfield's disallowed goal describes, *"carried the ball east."*

The view of this match from the North-East was actually not much different from what we can read in the local Perth papers. The Press and Journal found it necessary to tell its readers that St Johnstone were a team from Perth, but other than that its report is brief and factual, describing how some of the goals were scored and noting that after they had gone behind Aberdeen played slightly better. However – and this is a problem for all football historians – the P&J's summary fails to record all the goals. For example, their record says, *"at half-time the scores stood – St Johnstone 4; Aberdeen 0,"* then they continued, *"On the resumption of hostilities Aberdeen played hard and about the middle of the game scored their first point. The Saints retaliated and scored again, and the game ended, St Johnstone 6; Aberdeen 2."*

No mention is made of the other two goals scored in this half!

Perhaps one of the reasons Aberdeen succumbed so easily was because, unlike some teams from that city in more recent times, they adopted a more gentlemanly approach, with the Constitutional noting that, *"the memory of Aberdeen's clean play will live after their defeat is forgotten."*

Aberdeen had not got off to a good start in this new competition. They had already lost their opening game against East End by 5 goals to 1, so they were propping up the Northern League table with no points and a gap in goal average/difference between them and Forfar Athletic.

	Played.	Won.	Drn.	Lost.	Goals For.	Agst.	Pts.
East End.	2	2	—	—	6	1	4
St Johnstone.	1	1	—	—	6	2	2
Our Boys.	1	1	—	—	6	2	2
Harp.	1	—	1	—	4	4	1
Montrose.	1	—	1	—	4	4	1
Arbroath.	—	—	—	—			
Forfar Athletic	2	—	—	2	2	7	0
Aberdeen.	2	—	—	2	3	11	0

The following is now the score in the Northern League competition :—

More importantly from our perspective, St Johnstone were in second place and the Constitutional was getting ahead of itself, expressing their hope that they might see, *"the Saints keeping up their form, and making a bold bid for the Championship of the Northern League."* Unfortunately, and as more pessimistic fans might well have expected, St Johnstone, after this initial success, had a terrible season. In their very next game, they lost 5-2 to Montrose and, instead of *"making a bold bid for the Championship,"* had two points deducted for fielding an ineligible player and eventually finished in bottom place in the table, with only four wins and nine points from their 14 games.

Saints team: Tulloch, Robertson, Rodger, ?, Winton, ?, Smith, Anderson, D Burnfield, A McFarlane.
Attendance: unknown

Any man in the same position would have been a better choice

The first match in the Scottish Cup,
St Johnstone 4, Dundee Wanderers 3, Scottish Cup,
Recreation Grounds, Saturday, 11th January 1896

Report: Perthshire Advertiser

Although St Johnstone had played in the Scottish Qualifying Cup since their second full season (1886-87), they had never won through sufficient rounds (four) to qualify for entry to the Scottish Cup proper. However, in 1895-96, they did just that, defeating Vale of Ruthven, Dundee Hibs (who became Dundee United in 1923) and Orion (of Aberdeen) and then receiving a bye in the fourth round before departing that competition in the fifth round, at the hands of Kings Park (of Stirling). Having successfully 'won' through four rounds, Saints were now, for the first time, in the hat for the first round of the Scottish Cup itself. Drawn at home against Dundee Wanderers, the match was scheduled for the 11th of January, 1896.

In their preview, the Scottish Referee's reporter was confident of an exciting match, telling their readers that it *"promises to be a rare good tussle tomorrow."* They also recorded that White, the Saints' centre half, was unavailable (he had had an accident) and, to make matters worse, various other newspapers noted that another half-back Hill, was ineligible, so changes to the expected starting line-up were required. The Scottish Referee told us, *"Rumour has*

it that Alick Buttar is to turn out in the emergency and play half-back. The old centre once or twice played half-back for Dundee."

In the event, Buttar wasn't available (he may simply not have turned up – it's not clear from the various papers' reports) and as a result Saints had to re-arrange their team, drafting in Scott to fill the centre of defence. It was to prove an unfortunate move for the lad…

The Dundee team travelled to Perth by train, leaving their home city on the 12.45 from Dundee West Station. It would seem likely that a decent number of their supporters also travelled, for the Dundee Courier noted the *"presence of a large attendance of spectators,"* and the Scottish Referee said there was *"an immense crowd."* - The PA poured a little cold water on this, stating, *"the attendance was not so large as anticipated,"* an opinion shared by the Perthshire Courier, which recorded that there was *"a good attendance, but it was not so good as we expected."*

Not only did opinions vary as to the size of the crowd, but also as to what constituted a good playing surface. The Perthshire Advertiser records that, *"The weather was fine, and the ground, although greasy and slippery, was in fairly good condition."*

The Perthshire Courier saw the conditions as an advantage, telling its readers, *"...the frost, which had set in, had firmed up the turf, so that the going was faster than it had been for several Saturdays."* The Perthshire Constitutional went even further, claiming that *"The ground was in splendid condition, as far as appearance went from outside the ropes, and this had been brought about by the use of the roller before the frost came and put its iron stamp on the ground. There was little or no danger in playing on the ground because, although it was hard, and slippery, and greasy, there were no ruts over which the players might fall and hurt themselves."* So that was alright then…

Health and Safety not being an issue in those days, and undersoil heating being a technological innovation that lay well in the future, all this suggests the game might have been a bit of a lottery. Indeed, it was suggested in a post-match comment in the Constitutional *"that the Saints' supporters thought some of the team were afraid to run for fear of coming a 'cropper'."*

To make matters worse, in the first half Saints had to defend the end where the pitch was most slippery. This led to them conceding the first goal, with Scott, at centre half, failing to keep his footing and allowing the Dundonians in to score in the first few minutes. Then the unfortunate Scott slipped again whilst attempting to put in a tackle and from the resultant corner the Wanderers headed home to go two up. The Perthshire Courier was scathing about Scott, suggesting that *"any man in the same position would have been a better choice"* and going on to state, *"Practically the St Johnstone played the match with ten men, Scott being quite unreliable. It was not that he failed himself, but he, to a large*

extent, neutralised the movements of the whole forward line. I presume he is not likely to be asked to play again for the St Johnstone even in times of great stress."

The Perthshire Constitutional was similarly critical, noting *"Saints possibly would not have lost the first two goals had it not been for Scott's sliding propensities."*

It wasn't just Scott who got it in the neck. Poor Dakers, the St Johnstone half-back, *"was another weak man. He frequently made blunders and seemed to be easily beaten. It was just occasionally that he put in some good work."*

Somehow, we can't see the PA getting away with quite such thorough character assassinations as this nowadays - although they may occasionally be tempted. Nevertheless, from the team-lines we have, it does appear that Scott did not play for Saints again…

Despite poor Scott's travails, Saints then scored in a like manner to the Wanderers' second goal, when Anderson headed home from a corner (thus setting a precedent for men called Anderson to score with headers from corners in the Scottish Cup) and before half-time they had brought the scores level. As we've mentioned before (and will again) the language used by the 19th century versions of (the present-day) Courier's Eric Nicolson and (the PA's) Matt Gallagher is wonderfully descriptive, although this doesn't actually make it any easier to visualise what happened. For example, Saints second goal happened thus…

"Burnfield got hold of the ball and placed beautifully, and after some stubborn kicking-out by the Dundee defence, Crawford bounded in and whisked the ball into the net."

We venture to suggest that it is some time since you've heard a goal being described as *"whisked into the net."* Unfortunately, and just to prove that football journalists have always been occasionally unable to identify who actually scored a goal, the Perthshire Courier records this goal as being by McFarlane. The PA, however, concurred with the Constitutional and awarded the goal to Crawford.

At half-time, the score was 2-2. Of course, in those days there was no radio or internet for far-flung fans to find out the scores of games. However, the importance of a first round Scottish Cup match was such that, as the Dundee Courier reported, the Wanderers' second eleven had arranged to have the result at half-time wired (sent by telegraph) to Clepington Park in Dundee, where they were playing their game.

The second half saw the Wanderers having to cope with the more slippery goalmouth, but they had the best of the early exchanges. Saints, in due course, *"peppered away at the goal without avail,"* until John Robertson's free kick was flicked in by the head of one of the Perth forwards. Only a minute or so later Saints scored their fourth. Again, it's hard to work out what happened from the Constitutional's description, which tells us, *"Saints burst away again, and rushed the ball into the net."*

They could have had a fifth, when George Cairncross, Saints' right wing – who had already missed what seems to have been a sitter earlier in the second half – took off on a brilliant run which ended when he shot tamely at the Dundee Wanderers' keeper. This wasn't the end of the action though, because Saints' Robertson and Burnfield played 'after you Claude' (or, as the Perthshire Courier put it, there was a *"misunderstanding"*), allowing one of the Wanderers' wingers an open shot at goal, which he duly took. There were only five or so minutes of the game left at this point and, unsurprisingly, the Dundonians made strenuous efforts to get an equaliser, but St Johnstone held out for a 4-3 win.

All in all, based on the three match reports in the local Perth press, this seems to have been a very exciting game. The Perthshire Advertiser tells us that once the score went to 2-2, *"It was now evident that the winners would have a hard fight for their victory and the excitement among the spectators was high."* Prior to this, *"The Saints still kept pressing and was* (sic) *having most of the play. Time after time they experienced exceedingly hard lines in not scoring, shot after shot being sent in and just missing by inches."* Then, in the second half, with the scores still tied, *"Shot after shot was sent in, but the Wanderers custodian was showing some admirable saving."*

One thing that all three Perth papers did agree on was that the 'man of the match' (although that term had not yet been invented) was St Johnstone's right back, Johnny Robertson, without a doubt, the first great player in the club's history. The Constitutional said, *"Robertson really won the game with his place kicking,"* and the Perthshire Courier's summary of the match, in a column titled, *"Notes by Athleta"* said, *"he was far and away the best back on the field."*

In the same *"Athleta"* column, we can find some other comments about the performance of the various St Johnstone players, including this summary of who had turned in the best performances: *"Four men were conspicuously prominent for grand play, Cairncross, Burnfield, Anderson and Robertson. The Saints attack was mainly, almost wholly, delivered by the right wing and centre, and Cairncross was always the busiest and most determined. His fine speed and pluck were a constant trouble to the Wanderers left back, who by the way played a particularly fine game."*

The Scottish Referee headlined their report, *"St Johnstone Joyous,"* and recorded that after Wanderers' good start, *"St Johnstone gradually improved,"* although they *"eased off towards the close."* Unlike the

Perthshire Courier, the Referee's description of the Wanderers' final goal makes no mention of a Saints' defensive mix-up, but instead says it was *"a grand shot."* Then, as the Dundee side pressed for a third and equalising goal, *"St Johnstone rushed the ball to the opposite end* (there was a lot of rushing the ball in those days)*, but the parting shot went behind. Amid cheers, St Johnstone were hailed victors, and the victory was a popular one, considering the rearrangements that had to be made owing to the accident to Whyte* (sic) *and the non-appearance of Buttar. In the closing minutes of the game it looked as if the Wanderers would draw, but they never looked like winning."*

Given that this was the first time the club had played in the Scottish Cup, it's not hard to imagine that there was a huge amount of interest locally in this match. The fact that there was obviously a decent crowd, allied to the exciting nature of the game itself, suggests this was a memorable occasion. Moreover, the tension that we have all experienced as Saints try to hold out and defend a one-goal lead (especially in a cup-tie), must surely have been present in spades that afternoon. Conversely, for the Dundee side and their fans, the closing minutes will have been equally nerve-wracking as their team pursued an equaliser. The match reports do not report a huge cheer at the end of the contest, but we think it's safe to assume it was very loud indeed.

Saints team: Tulloch, Robertson, Dakers, Burnfield, Scott, Crawford; Cairncross, Waddell, Moir, McFarlane, Anderson. Attendance: unknown.

No. 6
No space for spectators on the Dundee Road

**The first match as a professional team
Arbroath 3, St Johnstone 1, Northern League,
Gayfield Park, Saturday, 18th August 1906**

Sporting Intelligence.

Football.

EASY VICTORY OVER ST JOHNSTONE.

ARBROATH began the Northern League journey promisingly enough on Saturday by defeating St Johnstone on Gayfield to the tune of three

Headline: Arbroath Herald

In the 1905-06 season, St Johnstone were playing amateur football in the Northern League. As the season came to an end, there was much debate in and around Perth about the possibility of the club becoming professional. The arguments for and against were reported in the local press and then, at the club's AGM on 23rd April 1906, a motion for this pivotal change was carried, along with wholesale changes to the club's committee.

The move to professionalism resulted in an almost immediate improvement in Saints' performances. In the previous two seasons as amateurs, they had finished 9th and 12th respectively in the 14-team Northern League. However, after turning professional they were fourth for two seasons in a row. Performances in the Scottish Cup were also better in that the margins of defeat (which had been, on occasion, substantial – especially a 10-1

hammering from Third Lanark in 1903), were much reduced.

St Johnstone's first competitive match as a professional club was away to Arbroath. Gayfield Park was built on a rubbish tip (and we'll avoid the obvious joke), but not quite in the same place as the current ground. One of the most obvious differences was that there was no space for any spectators on the Dundee Road side of the ground: a problem that was remedied in 1925, when the pitch was moved by some 60 yards, with the previous halfway line becoming one of the new goal-lines. This meant that Saints' first competitive professional game was played on a ground that only had three sides.

Under the headline, *"Easy Victory over St Johnstone,"* the Arbroath Herald's reporter struck a triumphant note, telling his readers that, *"Had the Maroons cared to apply the pressure more severely for a time after they got on the lead they would easily have added to their score."*

The match started 15 minutes late in front of crowd that was described as *"not of the largest when the game started, but it was of average size."* Both sides probed at each other's defences, with Saints having the ball in the net early on, although the goal was disallowed for offside – *"or he would not have put the ball between the posts at all."*

Despite this excitement, Arbroath - at least according to their local paper - were clearly the better side and, in the lovely language of the day, described how, *"A lively forward dash toward the east goal, with the defence crumbling like matchwood, boded ill for the Saints: and when Crockatt whipped across the ball a goal seemed certain. But the astute Turner had played Gray offside, and the clever work of the preceding minute went for nothing."*

Crockatt was not to be denied though and in the 15th minute he scored the first goal of the game. It was, according to the Herald, *"so lovely an effort that one may be pardoned for regarding it as a good omen for the coming season."*

Despite Arbroath's dominance, one St Johnstone player did catch the eye of the local press. Sergeant Turner (of the Black Watch), whose first name, memorably, was Grantley, was, in their view, the pick of the Saints' defenders, although they were not especially flattering in their (to be fair, accurate) description of his appearance, viz, *"The lengthy one with the bare cranium made the utmost use of his height and played with rare judgement throughout."*

An indication of just how dominant Arbroath were can be gleaned from the fact that Strachan, their keeper, was scarcely troubled for most of the first half (*"he could have read a chapter of Marie Corelli's new novel for all the work he had to do."*).

Against the run of play, and just before half-time, Saints scored, with Hynd netting with ease while the Lichties' defenders stopped to claim offside.

The second half was a continuation of the first. Arbroath's second came when Gray walked the ball into the Saints' net after it rebounded from the crossbar following a cross-cum-shot from Black. The third followed in due order and, according to the local paper, *"in exactly the same manner"* – that is following a shot from Black that hit the bar and was then turned in by Gray.

The PA, displaying a refreshing honesty, took a similar line to the Arbroath Herald. The Perth reporter acknowledged the key change from the previous season in his first sentence, *"Perth's new professional organisation opened their season's work at Gayfield on Saturday with Arbroath,"* before going on to note that not much else had altered… *"but the result of the game reminds one very much of the weekly occurrences last year."*

They also singled out the tall, bald Saints' left back (*"Turner's height stood him in good stead…"*) and noted that the home team's goalkeeper was not exactly troubled by the St Johnstone attack (*"The Saints rarely visited Strachan, who had a clear view of the work of his forwards."*).

Similarly, the PA agreed with the Herald's assessment of the first forty-five minutes, recording that Hynd's equaliser, *"allowed the Saints to cross over on level terms after having the worst of the play."*

They were also in agreement about proceedings in the remainder of the match, although they summed them up in one pithy paragraph, rather than the much longer descriptions of the general play and the other two goals that featured heavily in the Arbroath Herald's report. The PA made do with, *"The second half was monopolised by the home team, who scored on two* occasions. *The Maroons kept the defence on tenterhooks practically the whole time, and Saints have to thank Graham and company that the score was not largely augmented."*

The Scottish Referee's report, under the heading, *"Perth,"* consisted of only three paragraphs. It was brief and to the point and, interestingly, noted the continuing dominance of cricket in the area…

"Although cricket still holds sway in Perth, not a few thoughts were directed towards Arbroath."

"It was hoped that the new professional combination would not be overwhelmed.

"St Johnstone did well in only dropping by 3-1 in the first League match of the season, and it is just possible the score may be reversed when the teams meet at Perth."

The Evening Telegraph and the Dundee Courier, presumably having to keep their readers happy in Perth and Arbroath, both made do with a short report, although they too made no attempt to disguise the reality of the afternoon's entertainment.

The Courier's report admitted that, *"Arbroath had much the better of a rather quiet game with St Johnstone at Gayfield. The teams played almost from the start as if the result had been a foregone conclusion, that conclusion being, of course, a win for Arbroath."*

Unsurprisingly, the Courier was not overly impressed by some of the St Johnstone team, telling its readers, *"Turner was the salvation of his side. The halves were only*

moderate, and the forwards, when the halves did support them, did well enough."*

The Telegraph recorded that, *"the Maroons played so quietly that it seemed as if they felt they had the measure of their opponents, and need not unduly exert themselves… But for Turner the Saints would have lost more than one goal in the last half hour, but he gave a display worthy of his reputation."*

Like the Scottish Referee, the Evening Telegraph finished their report by noting that despite this reverse, all was not lost for this new, professional St Johnstone team, noting that, *"The Saints team has possibilities, however, and should do well after a game or two together."*

Indeed they did. Saints won their next seven matches; a mixture of Northern League, Perthshire Cup and Scottish Qualifying Cup ties. They lost the eighth match, a fourth round Qualifying Cup game at Forfar Athletic, but then didn't lose again until the 5th of January 1907.

Unfortunately, despite the Scottish Referee's prediction, they only managed a draw (1-1) in the home league match with Arbroath, although they did eventually get their revenge when they beat the Red Lichties 2-1 in the Dewar Shield semi-final later in the season. Clearly, this St Johnstone team were learning what it means to be professional…

Saints team: Graham, Harvey and Turner; McFarlane, Sampson and Fleming; Lumsden, Westwater, McDonald, McCulloch and Hynd.
Attendance: unknown.

The largest crowd ever assembled at a football match in Perth…

An introduction to the Old Firm
St Johnstone 0, Rangers 3, Scottish Cup,
Recreation Grounds, Saturday, 23rd January 1909

Like them or not (and, other than their own fans, we think it's fair to say that most don't), the Old Firm dominate Scottish football. *"The Forces of Darkness"* or *"The Ugly Sisters"* are just two of the more printable descriptions commonly used to describe these Glasgow teams and it's undoubtedly true that when your team - be it Ayr United, Kilmarnock, Dundee, Partick Thistle, St Johnstone or whoever - overcome either Rangers or Celtic it is a cause for prolonged celebration. At time of writing (summer 2023), Saints have played both members of the Old Firm 327 times, losing 241, drawing 43 and only winning the same number as we've drawn (43), of which only 14 of our wins were away from home.

Consequently, when we were considering which games we should include in our 'Milestones' section, it seemed not unreasonable to include the first time Saints came up against one of the Glasgow giants. Unfortunately, as was to become the norm, we didn't win….

There were mitigating circumstances though; principally that in 1909 Saints were not even a Scottish League side, but rather, having only just turned professional a few years earlier, they were still plying their trade in the Northern League. Moreover, in the years prior to the advent of professionalism in Perth, on the relatively few occasions when we won sufficient Qualifying Cup matches to make it to the first-round draw of the Scottish Cup itself, the results were nothing to write home about. In January 1903, Saints hosted Third Lanark, going down by a (still) record Scottish Cup defeat of 10-1. Then in

January 1905, a visit to Airdrie in the first round led to a 7-0 hammering.

After becoming professional, the losses in the Cup didn't stop, but the margin of defeat diminished. In January 1907, a trip to New Cathkin Park to meet Third Lanark only resulted in a 4-1 defeat: a year later, a visit to Edinburgh in the first round yielded the same score, this time in favour of Hearts.

Despite these defeats, it must have whetted the appetite of everyone in Perth and Perthshire when the Ibrox giants came out of the hat for Saints' first round tie in 1909. Nonetheless, we suspect there was a degree of trepidation on the part of the local authorities and, in particular the police. The previous season's Cup final had been between Celtic and Rangers and it has passed into infamy as one of the (many) times in which their fans' hatred of each other spilled over into outright, sustained violence.

The first match in the 1909 Cup final took place at Hampden and ended in a 2-2 draw. The replay finished 1-1 and the fans expected there to be extra time, but when this was not forthcoming (according to the competition rules, extra time would only take place after a *second* replay), a full-blown riot then took place, with the crowd invading the pitch, tearing down the goalposts and setting fire to the wooden pay-boxes. The mounted police who were trying to restore order were attacked, as were the fire brigade who came to attend to the burning pay-booths. Over 100 people were injured and as a result neither club wanted to risk a further replay, so the Cup was withheld, with Celtic and Rangers being fined £150 each (£19,237 today) and Queen's Park, the owners of Hampden, being given £500 (£64,123) compensation by the SFA for the destruction at their ground.

Despite their success in getting to the final the previous season, and also being the then leaders of the First Division, Rangers did not come into the match in good form. The PA, unusually, carried a brief report of Dundee's match against the Ibrox side from the week before the Cup tie. Dundee, who would finish second in the Championship that season, with Rangers five points back in fourth, had won comfortably by four goals to nil at Dens. The PA's report concluded, *"Dundee's win was a very popular one, and it will do the Rangers directorate a world of good in connection with future League games and Cup ties. Their team as presently constituted will not create any world's records, and the sooner a ship-shape eleven, one that can pull together is decided upon, the better it will be for the followers of the 'Light Blues'."*

Below their report from Dens, the PA set out what it believed St Johnstone might do to prick the deflating Rangers' bubble. Although noting that, *"the Rangers are nothing potent as far as opposition goes,"* they went on, *"It stands to reason that they are, however, the Saints superiors in all departments of the game, but the presently strong-going Saints have it within their power to put a spoke in the wheels of the unreliable Rangers, and Perthshire folks are looking forward to that surprise coming off on the 23rd."*

One pre-match concern for St Johnstone was that their indefatigable full back, Sergeant Turner, had been sent off in the New Year's Day match against Dunfermline. Having contributed *"songs and recitations"* to a military Smoking Concert (we suspect that younger readers will be amazed to find that this was a social event where smoking tobacco was

positively encouraged) at the Queen's Barracks during the last week of 1908, Turner then fell foul of the referee during the Ne'er Day game against Dunfermline at the Recreation Grounds.

As usual, the playing surface was more suitable for wellies than football boots and *"Mud-larking and sky-larking then began to creep into the game, and the large crowd enjoyed the antics of the players on the watery surface."* Then, *"just before half-time a regrettable incident occurred, Sergeant Turner and McLeod, Dunfermline inside left, being ordered pavilionwards for alleged over familiarity with each other."* It appears that the official may have over-reacted, at least in terms of the standards of the day. Bearing in mind that being sent off was a major disgrace back then – and required a heinous act to result in the referee taking such drastic action – it was unsurprising that the PA was so supportive of the Saints' player, telling its readers that *"The offence (if there was any offence at all) did not warrant their being ordered (off)..."*

In the event, the SFA's hearing took place just before the game against Rangers: fortunately, the case was adjourned until the next meeting, so Sergeant Turner's suspension did not begin until the next match after the Cup tie and he was able to bring his considerable skill and experience to the task of trying to overcome the Ibrox side. When the case was eventually heard he was suspended for a month.

While this distraction was bubbling away in the background, Saints were doing what they could to maximise the gate takings from the visit of Rangers.

As the Perthshire Constitutional recorded, *"The St Johnstone Committee had their arrangements completed by the end of last week, so energetic were they in pushing forward matters as to additional grand stand accommodation, increasing the standing accommodation for spectators at the north end of the ground, and the terracing and penning of the eastern embankment."* As you'll discover later in this chapter, there were sound financial reasons for increasing the capacity of the grandstands in particular.

However, the other major concern, noted in the report of the Dunfermline game, was the state of the pitch. At its best, the Recreation Grounds' surface was hardly conducive to good football, but the weather in the winter of 1909 made matters considerably worse. The PA lead article on Wednesday 20th January was headed, *"The Storm and Floods,"* with a sub-heading telling us, *"Tay and Tummel valleys inundated,"* before beginning the story thus... *"The flood of 1909 will be remembered long after its effects are entirely wiped out."*

In these circumstances, it is entirely understandable that the Saints' pitch would struggle to be in anything remotely approaching a playable condition. The *"Football Notes"* section of that Wednesday's edition of the PA had a headline that squarely addressed the problem, *"Will it be Polo, Skating or Football?"* – going on to say, *"The oldest member of the St Johnstone F.C. will fail to remember of the Recreation Grounds having been flooded to such an extent as has been the case since Tuesday of this week, and from then the three feet of water which has submerged the whole of the ground is making very slow egress."*

To make matters worse, it being January, the temperatures plummeted and the playing surface was in danger of being iced over. Today, it would be unthinkable for a Cup tie to be played less than a week after a pitch had first lain under three feet of water and then been subject to freezing conditions – and, worse still then had tons of ash ground into it in an effort to allow the players to keep their feet. Fortunately, in the early twentieth century, they were made

of tougher stuff. The PA described the situation thus (from the paper of 20th January) ...

"The scene at the grounds is one well worth seeing, and hundreds were at the spot yesterday. It was generally thought that St Johnstone's Park would not escape the flooding, but no one dreamt of the ground being transformed into a swimming pool or a miniature lake.

"The question that is engaging everyone's attention in the city and throughout the shire is – will the ground be playable for the Cup tie on Saturday first? It is all a question of conjecture, and the frost which has set in has only added to the troubles of the St Johnstone Executive. If the water is allowed to take its natural course the ground will certainly not be playable for Saturday first, or even if the Corporation fire engine be requisitioned for pumping operations, or a gulley made for the egress of the water, the ground even when cleared of the water most certainly will be in a very sodden and "lifting" order. The standing ground all round the pavilion side will also when the water disappears have to go in for a course of 'quick drying.' So much for the prevailing state of affairs out Edinburgh Road way."

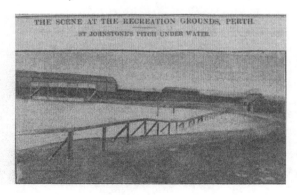

The picture here, from The Courier of 21st January, shows just how bad things were. Against this soggy background, it was suggested that the game be switched to Glasgow, but Saints were not keen to give up home advantage, even when Rangers offered them first £80, then £100 for the tie to be played at Ibrox.

In order to ensure the game went ahead at Perth rather than Glasgow, the Fire Brigade were called on to pump the water from the pitch. This they did from Thursday morning until noon on Friday. A squad of men was then assembled to scrape more water from the field, before rolling in tons of ash in an attempt to make it playable. Their efforts were sufficient that, when the game kicked off (at 2.40 pm, presumably to allow it to be concluded in daylight), the Scottish Referee reported, *"On Saturday the playing pitch was clear and the footing good, but heavy."* That is, perhaps, one of the most masterly understatements in the history of Scottish football … after the match, the PA commented, *"it was expected that the ground would cut up and be dangerous to the players, but a good footing was got on every part of the field, though the ball travelled slow on patches where the cinder coating was thickest."*

While all this pumping, scraping and rolling was going on, Rangers, despite their obvious superiority, were leaving nothing to chance. They went to Troon for what the Scottish Referee described as *"special training"* for the entire week beforehand and then travelled up to Perth by train on the Friday. Upon arrival, *"they were received with hundreds and hundreds of local football supporters ... cheered and cheered in true international style."*

Today, the arrival of a Rangers team at Perth Station might well be met with relative indifference and, perhaps, a small crowd of their own supporters (Perth, unfortunately, still having a number of misguided souls who prefer the blue of the south side of Glasgow to the west end of Perth). And it wasn't just in the reaction of the local fans to the arrival of the visitors that things were very different in those days.

Firstly, the crowd – at least those in the grandstands - seems to have been largely in place well before the kick-off. Perhaps it was the incentive of hearing the Fechney Industrial School Band (under the leadership of Bandmaster Wadsworth), who were performing from 1.15, but *"by two o'clock there was no sitting room available in either of the stands and many were disappointed."*

Secondly, it seems that there was little or no warm-up by the players. Given that, as noted above, the match kicked-off at 2.40 pm, it is remarkable to read in the PA that, *"At twenty-five minutes to three the Rangers driving directly from the Station Hotel arrived at the ground, and prompt to time the teams appeared."* Had they already stripped for the game at the hotel or did they get changed in the coach on the way?

Thirdly, unlike today, when a player leaps about and cavorts like a kangaroo on acid when he scores a goal, such behaviour would have been anathema to the footballers of the early twentieth century. The most they deemed appropriate was what happened when the Rangers' centre half, Stark, scored the first of the match, namely that he *"was heartily hand-shaken by his clubmates for his goal."*

Stark's goal came early in the second half. Prior to this, it had been a close contest, with the Scottish Referee's report, noting that, *"The first half was quite interesting, with the locals putting up stiff opposition all the way, and giving the Rangers plenty of right hard work ... the home defence was very safe, and playing a hard and dour game managed to keep their goal intact."* In the second half, with Rangers now two goals to the good, *"The Saints, despite these reverses, played with great dash, and several times looked like scoring, but Rennie and his backs were unbeatable."*

The descriptions of the course of the game are broadly similar in the local press.

The PA recorded that, *"the feature of the first half was the grand defence put up by the Saints against the eager Rangers,"* although subsequently, *"Superior training was, however, the undoing of the Saints during the second period."*

Another column in the PA noted that, *"The visitors were quite evidently relieved when, after an hour's play, they scored the first goal; more relieved when they scored the second, and highly delighted when they reached safety with their third. The last ten minutes found Saints doing all the pressing and able to do anything but score. After all, though, 3-0 was not a great beating at the hands of the present leaders of the First League."*

The Dundee Evening Telegraph said that *"3-1 would perhaps have been a better reflex of the run of the game, as the Saints were worth a point, while two of the Rangers' goals were notched in rather lucky fashion."* That said, the Telegraph did concede that, *"there were several almost certain goals averted by Cant's clever display between the uprights."*

The St Johnstone keeper seems to have had a splendid match. The Telegraph recounted that, *"Cant was a tower of strength for St Johnstone in goal, and he never gave a better display between the sticks. Time after time his valiant work averted certain disaster, and he was repeatedly cheered for clever saving."*

Cant could do nothing about Rangers' second, scored by Bennet (interestingly an ex-Celtic player), described by the Dundee Courier as *"the best seen on the Recreation Grounds for many a year."* Bennet beat three St Johnstone players before *"tipping the ball into the net out of Cant's reach."*

The Saints' custodian may have received the plaudits from the Evening Telegraph, but the Courier's reporter did point out that Rangers' third was a bit of an embarrassment (or, *"lucky,"* if you prefer the evening paper's version). Scored by R G Campbell, it was *"a lofty punt from about forty yards out catching Cant, who was out of his goal, unawares."*

Of the rest of the Saints' team, the defence, unsurprisingly, came in for honourable mentions, with *"Hannah and Turner being in great form, the former perhaps a shade in front of the tall soldier. Johnny Cameron was easily the pick of the half-back line, and he got in a tremendous amount of work during the afternoon. Bert Sampson also played pluckily against a bustling set of forwards, but Ogilvy was below par. The forwards were never allowed to settle down, Law and Craig doing great work at the back for the visitors, but they were not hotly enough pressed. Moir and Lavery were a shade better than the others, all of whom played keenly, but were unfortunate in their shooting."*

The Saints' committee's decision to do whatever it took to keep the match in Perth was rewarded with what was reported to be the biggest crowd and the most gate money ever received by the Perth club. The Evening Telegraph described the attendance as *"the largest crowd ever assembled at a football match in Perth..."*

Estimates of the number of spectators vary. The Scottish Referee said it was between 5,000 and 6,000; the Glasgow Herald said c. 7,000. The PA reported that despite its huge size, the crowd dispersed quickly after the game, helped considerably by the two large exits that had been made in the fencing leading to South Inch Terrace. The St Johnstone committee had had these specially cut for this game and consequently the record takings of £157: 16: 9d, £25 of which came from the grandstands, were most welcome. In contrast, the previous highest gate money was for a fourth round Qualifying Cup match against Raith Rovers in the preceding season, when a crowd of c. 4,000 produced receipts of £98. To put this in context, on that same day in 1909 the highest gate of the day's Scottish Cup ties came at Tynecastle, where Kilmarnock were the visitors, generating £471: 9: 6d. At the other end of the scale, West Calder vs Partick Thistle produced a gate of £20.

As was the case up until the 1980s, match receipts were reported for the stand and ground separately. Spectators who came in via the terracing could pay an extra amount to enter the grandstand(s). These people were not counted twice in the final attendance figure, but the advantage to the home club (and the reason – as noted above – that Saints were so anxious to increase their stand capacity) was that the home club retained the entire premium the spectators paid for access to the stand. The balance, after a retention for the costs of putting the match on (which must have been substantial, given all the pumping of water, etc.), was then split between the two clubs. In the event, it's probable that St Johnstone actually made a bit less than the £100 guarantee Rangers offered for taking the match to Ibrox.

Ironically, this chapter was written in 2023, just as Saints' board announced a steep, one-off increase in seat prices for another home tie against Rangers in the Scottish Cup (the board subsequently admitted this was a wrong decision). Consequently, a home crowd of only about 500 turned out for that game: very different from the contest in 1909.

After the 2023 tie, the Rangers' manager, Michael Beale, described McDiarmid Park as a *"cow-field."* He was lucky his team were not playing in the 1909 match. On that occasion, at the close of proceedings the Rangers' players were described as *"blowing* (a) *little harder than their opponents at the finish, though sores were visible as a result of falls among cinders."* More of a railway siding than a cow-field perhaps!

Saints team: Cant, Turner and Hannah; Cameron, Sampson and Ogilvie; Lavery, Bannerman, Moir, Robertson and McGregor.
Attendance: 7,000.

The first national trophy
St Johnstone 2, Dumbarton 1, Scottish Consolation Cup,
Ibrox Stadium, Glasgow, Saturday, 22nd April 1911

Football Features.

The Scottish Consolation Final—A Great Day for Perth—An Old Saint's Reflections.—Doing the Honours.—The Dewar Shield Final for Perth.—A Unique Display of Football Trophies.—Incidents of the Week.

Headline: Perthshire Courier

In the way that one's most recent lived experience is always uppermost in the human mind, it is commonly believed that the Challenge Cup win over Dunfermline in 2007 was the first time St Johnstone had won a national football competition of any kind. Not so. In the years before the First World War, Saints competed in three national finals, losing the first and winning the next two. These were the ultimate matches in the Scottish Consolation Cup, which, as its name suggests, was very much a national trophy, albeit contested by teams of also-rans by way of consolation for their inability to progress sufficiently far in the Scottish Qualifying Cup to be given entry into the Scottish Cup proper (as described in the previous chapter). Organised in the early rounds on a county/regional basis, by the time the third and fourth-round ties were drawn (at the same time), it's obvious that most parts of the country and a variety of different levels of football were represented, as evidenced by the diversity of the winners, ranging from current senior teams like Saints and Alloa to the small

Ayrshire town of Galston. The cutting here, from the Scottish Referee, also shows the reach of the Consolation Cup across the country.

FOURTH ROUND
North.
Forres Mechanics v. Aberdeen University or Aberdeen Harp or Peterhead.
Midlands.
Montrose or Dundee Hibernians or Dunfermline Athletic or Cowdenbeath v. Kirkcaldy United or East Fife or Arbroath or St. Johnstone.
Stenhousemuir v. West Lothian Albion or Broxburn Shamrock or Berwick Rangers or Peebles Rovers.
Coldstream or Armadale or Broxburn v. Alloa Athletic or Clackmannan.
South.
Beith or Girvan Athletic or Ayr United v. Dumbarton Harp or Albion Rovers or St. Cuthbert Wanderers.
Dumbarton or Dykehead or Vale of Leven or Abercorn or Arthurlie v. Hurlford or Douglas Wanderers.
To be played on ground of first-named club on February 18.

There were many similar "consolation" or "plate" trophies available across Scotland for many decades of the 20th century. For example, a week before Saints played Dumbarton at Ibrox, there was the Scottish Junior Consolation Cup final, the East of Scotland Consolation Cup final and also a match in the Lanarkshire Consolation Cup. Closer to home, there was the Perthshire Junior Consolation Cup (also known as the Constitutional Cup), which ran from 1920 to 1968 (and some readers may recall Jeanfield Swifts dominating the last few years of this competition).

The Scottish Consolation Cup itself only ran from 1907 to 1914. In the 1909-10 season, St Johnstone had reached the final, where they lost 4-2 to Arthurlie after a replay.

As noted, the competition was structured on a regional basis in the early stages, as is evident from the teams Saints beat in the first three rounds, namely, Tulloch, Vale of Atholl and Arbroath, before overcoming Cowdenbeath and then being drawn against Ayr United in the semi-final. Ayr United had only been formed in 1910, from a merger of Ayr Parkhouse and Ayr, and eventually finished second to Dumbarton in that season's (1910-11) Scottish Second Division. They were, on paper, a much stronger outfit, but Saints prevailed 1-0 in the semi-final.

A good indication of the relative merits of the Dumbarton and St Johnstone teams can be found in the Scottish Referee, published the day before the final, *"At Ibrox Park tomorrow Dumbarton and St Johnstone will battle for possession of the Consolation Cup and with both sides confident we anticipate a most interesting and keen encounter. The 'Sons of the Rock,' who have distinguished themselves by winning the Second League Championship, are keen on securing the Consolation trophy also, and on their present form will doubtless start favourites..."* This match preview reports a Perth correspondent as saying, *"little else is being talked of in Perth this week... that it is not all talk is borne out by the fact that a special train is to be run from Perth to Glasgow in connection with the event and 600 Perth supporters are expected to make the journey, as they did to*

Cowdenbeath (in the quarter-final)." It was also anticipated that many Perth people living in Glasgow would turn out to lend their support to *"The team that comes from 'the bonnie knowes o' Craigie.'"*

As well as speculating on the numbers of fans who would make the effort to attend, the Referee also noted that, *"St Johnstone have been strengthening their front rank by a Ranger in Cunningham and a Queen's Parker in Herbert Murray."*

That said, Saints were, literally, not in the same league as Dumbarton, having been plying their trade in the Central League since 1909. St Johnstone's investment in quality players at this time was part of a serious attempt to gain admission to the Scottish League: a plan that had come off the rails the previous season when Saints' application to make the step up was, unexpectedly in many people's views, thwarted by Dundee Hibernian being given the one available place. This was a surprise, because Dundee Hibs had only been in existence for one season.

To strengthen their case for admission, every member of the St Johnstone team, with the exception of Wilson, Ferguson and Mackay, had at least some First Division experience. The Scottish Referee described the Perth half-backs as *"exceptionally strong,"* noting that as well as George Bennett, the former Hearts' player, Sampson and Cameron were *"two out-and-out Perth players who have played some half dozen years together"* – the equivalent of Liam Gordon and David Wotherspoon perhaps? Saints also boasted Aitken, *"the former Junior international player of St Ninians and Kilmarnock"* as well as former Scottish international Tom Jackson, who had his best years at St Mirren but was finishing his career in Perth. The Referee concluded by saying that Saints had enjoyed a good season up to that point, having already won the Perthshire Cup, being in the yet-to-be-played

Action from the match: Photo, St Johnstone FC

Dewar Shield final, as well as finishing sixth (on goal average) in the 12-team Central League and with a firm intention of re-applying for admission to the Scottish League again in the summer.

The final itself seems to have been a great spectacle. The Scottish Referee's reporter, who noted he had seen every one of the previous Consolation Cup finals, wrote, *"I have no hesitation in saying that the last one played at Ibrox on Saturday was the best of the lot… The play of both teams was much above the average class identified with provincial teams; it was brimful of excitement all through; and last, and not the least important, there was a record attendance for the event."* The crowd was estimated at c. 6,000, of whom about 1,000 were there to support St Johnstone.

We also know that the game was around 15 minutes late in kicking-off. This was because Saints' kit (they played in white) hadn't arrived in time, but once play got underway it was clear that Dumbarton were keen to take the game to their lower-ranked opponents, doing so in an, at times, overly robust manner.

It's always instructive to compare the match reports in the local press with those in the national papers. Invariably, the latter paint a different, almost certainly more objective, picture of the proceedings. This is apparent in the report from the Scottish Referee where we can read, *"To state that the better team won the cup would hardly be correct,*

yet it is not wrong to remark that the winners deserved their victory." The local Perthshire papers were, generally, even handed. The (Dundee) Courier was the only one that really flattered the Perth club, suggesting, *"The Saints won because they were the better team, played better football than their opponents, and displayed throughout better training and stamina."*

In contrast, both the PA and the Perthshire Courier conceded that Dumbarton were the better side in the first half as was reflected in their being one up at half-time. Having said that, the Perthshire Courier seems to have employed the same journalist as the "Referee" because the language and phrases used are identical in many places. However, no matter who wrote them, almost all the reports, with the exception of the Scottish Referee's, cast doubt on the validity of the Dumbarton goal, with allegations not just of a hand being employed by Robertson, the scorer, but also a clear offside not being spotted by the match officials. Plus ça change…

All the papers made it clear that St Johnstone dominated the second half and deserved to win at the end. The Perthshire Courier's reporter was honest enough to admit that, *"St Johnstone had played a dour and plucky game up to this point, but now they opened out and showed form which at periods fairly bewildered the Dumbarton defence."* An equaliser by George MacKay was described in the same paper as *"something to enthuse over,"* while

The Saints team: back, left to right: J McVean (trainer), Sampson, Cameron, Aitken, Cunningham, front, Bennett, Wilson, Ferguson, Jackson, MacKay, Steven and Murray: photo: St Johnstone FC

Cunningham's winning goal created *"a feast the like of which I have never before enjoyed"* - which can be roughly translated for twenty-first century audiences as, *"we went mad when we got the winner."*

The trophy was presented in the Ibrox pavilion (the ground being nothing like it is today). The Perthshire Courier has a wonderful description of this ceremony, very much of its time and seeming to suggest that their correspondent had been enjoying the many toasts that were being made to the winning St Johnstone team…

"Then there was the presenting of the trophy. Bailie Henderson had that honour, in the absence of the Scottish Association President. He, of course, paid the Saints high tribute. Reference was made to the high position Dumbarton had occupied in football. The Bailie was pleased that they were still enjoying some of their old glory, being a West country man, he would have liked to have been handing over the trophy to them. He, however, had interests in Perth as well, and on his visits to the Fair City he had frequently seen St Johnstone

play. They were a gentlemanly lot. H'm! Correct Bailie! Tell you, Mr Sporting Editor, I believe I was hustled off to another duty about this stage. 'Good old Saints!' 'Here's a health' My word, it was the time of my life. Yes, the Bailie said he had presented the Scottish Cup – representing another class of football – the previous Saturday. The Consolation Cup, he thought, had done a deal for provincial football. To cut the Bailie short, he handed over the trophy to that good old Saint, Bob Campbell, the Chairman of Directors. We had a tidy speech from him. He is the right man for the job. Did not forget anything. There were opportunities for cheering. Oh, my! It was cheery. Cheers for the winners, cheers for the losers, cheers for the Bailie – nothing but cheering!"

The Saints' players each received a bonus from the directors for winning the Cup. It was 10 shillings (50p), equivalent in today's money to £63, but to put this in context, in the following season (1911-12 – the first year Saints were in the Scottish League), the cost of a ground season ticket for the Recreation Grounds was 6 shillings (30p) and a stand season ticket was 10 shillings. The players were lauded by their fans as they left Glasgow by train and on the way back to Perth there were substantial crowds at both Larbert and Stirling stations to cheer goalkeeper Aitken and goal-scorer Mackay as they alighted at their respective home stops.

The fans, both those who had travelled and those who remained at home, seem to have had a good night. Thousands were waiting at Perth Station - there being, of course, no broadcast media to let them see the players and the Cup beforehand - and speeches and cheers all round. Then there was the function at the *"Bank,"* where *"the landlord had to fill the flowing bowl."* More cheers and, as the Perthshire Courier reported, *"more 'good healths!' ... more speeches, more cheering."* Draw a line back in time, if you can, from the celebrations after the Scottish Cup win in 2014 and you should get the picture…

Saints team: Aitken, Jackson, Ferguson, Bennett, Sampson, Cameron, Wilson, Cunningham (1), Mackay (1), Steven, Murray.
Attendance: 6,000.

Goal after goal fell to the victorious Saints

The first match in the Scottish Football League
St Johnstone 4, Arthurlie 1, Scottish Football League, Second Division,
Recreation Grounds, Saturday, 19th August 1911

Headline: Dundee Courier

Having achieved their ambition of gaining a place in the pre-eminent league in Scotland, Saints went into their first match in the Scottish Football League in a high state of excitement – but also, it must be said, some disarray. It was only three weeks before this first game that the directors engaged a painter and joiner to spruce up the ground and a week beforehand when the Burgh Surveyor came to inspect the stands and grant the club a certificate attesting to their safety and stability. His report duly came in, two days before the match, noting that the stands were still covered by the certificates when they were originally erected. As we noted previously, health and safety was not quite as robust then as it is nowadays…

The painter and joiner must have been joined by a plumber, because we know that for their first Scottish League match Saints improved the accommodation in the pavilion at the Recreation Grounds, particularly for the visiting teams. Baths were provided and, as the PA described it, *"the latest arrangements as to hot and cold water for both teams."* This seems to imply that the players must have been a hardy lot in those days, with only cold water available to wash the Recreation Ground mud off after a tough match. Doubtless, the players were delighted at these *"latest arrangements."*

At their meeting on 3rd August, the board also approved the purchase of new goal-nets, because *"the repairing of the old ones would be unsatisfactory."* This was only the third set of nets the club had bought since they first used them… in 1895! That first set of nets was gifted by David Banks, a former secretary of the club. Although Mr Banks had since died, the trainer in 1895 was the same Jock McVean who was the trainer in 1911.

Reflecting the commercial reality that underpinned football clubs even back then, the board also awarded a contract for advertising in the stand in the forthcoming season to Mr W Buchan, who paid £4 for the privilege. Similarly, Mr James Guillanotti paid the club £2 to erect a refreshment stall in the ground, which in turn led to the previous provider of this service not having his contract renewed.

In addition, and as part of a tradition that has continued across the decades, a pipe-band (in this case the Cherrybank Pipe Band) was hired to entertain the spectators before the game.

At this time, Saints only had 15 players on their books and, to make matters worse, Johnny Cameron and Bert Sampson were unavailable for selection, having fallen out with the directors (there was no manager at this time) over the pay on offer for the new season. Both men had already accepted the new terms, but tried to get more money and were rebuffed (they eventually bit the bullet and re-joined the ranks on their original pay). Trainer Jock McVean had also refused the salary on offer (£8 a month) and, after the club advertised his post at a fixed salary of £10, the board then voted to re-appoint him! As the current directors and officials would probably agree, not much has changed since then…

In their preview of the match, the PA noted that *"an immense crowd"* was expected, and it's also interesting to see that the kick-off was at 4.00 pm, rather than today's normal 3.00 pm.

The actual attendance is not reported anywhere, although the Dundee Courier refers to a *"large crowd,"* but it seems likely, given that we know of crowds of up to 4,000 for other league matches that season (and 8,000 for the visit of Motherwell in the Scottish Cup), that there would have been several thousand at this particular milestone on the St Johnstone journey. We do know that the gate for the Arthurlie game was £40, which, based on the known price of six shillings (30p) for an adult ground season ticket, suggests a crowd of perhaps over 4,000. Interest in St Johnstone was clearly growing, with one spectator reported as cycling seven miles to see the match.

The game was played in brilliant conditions. Britain was in the throes of a heatwave at this time, with fine weather and very high temperatures running from early July to mid-September, and temperatures on the two days before the game of 80F (27C) and 78F (28C). As the PA noted, *"the weather* (was) *rather warm for football."*

The contest itself was not a thing of beauty. Most of Saints' team were relatively young, with the exception of former St Mirren and Scotland player, Tom Jackson. Alex Stewart scored the first, driving the ball in from a corner. In the second half, Arthurlie equalised from a free kick just outside the Saints' penalty box. The stalemate continued until 20 minutes from time, when inside left George Steven took a punt from goalkeeper Aitken, beat the full-back and, from a tight angle, squeezed the ball between the keeper and the post. Minutes later, the former Hearts' centre forward, Bail Colombo, who had been a virtual passenger for most of the game after sustaining a bad knee injury in the opening minutes, headed the third, before outside right Willie Wilson completed the rout with a fine goal, haring up the wing and unleashing a powerful shot that beat the Arthurlie goalie all-ends-up. The Perthshire Courier described it as *"undoubtedly the cleanest and best-taken goal of the match."*

On the face of it, a 4-1 win in a first ever match at this level ought to have been a cause for celebration. However, the ability of different papers' journalists to come to a common agreement on a football match is not unknown today, yet this particular game proved, if we ever doubted it, that, like love, the events of a football match are in the eye of the beholder.

The Perthshire Courier was not impressed, telling its readers that, *"(the) play, although it was fast, was very ragged and disjointed…"* For some reason, they also had it in for Saints' new centre forward. After he had been injured twice in rapid succession by kicks to the knee, he had to leave the pitch, only returning after some time *"with his knee in an elastic band."*

The reporter continued to complain, noting, *"he was obviously unfit for play…and was frequently in the way."* Furthermore, *"The Directors of the club have made a great song about the capture of Colombo* (but) *if we may safely judge from his appearance on Saturday, the Directors are not to be congratulated upon having secured his services. The ease with which his knee was knocked out at the very start of the match leads to the suspicion that it must have been in a weakly condition before he took the field."*

In Colombo's defence, it should be noted that he hadn't played at all the previous season and had only been on loan – at Leith

Athletic from Hearts - the season before that. It seems very likely that he was not match-fit.

The grudging manner in which they reported Colombo's goal - *"It is true he scored a goal off his head, by leaping in the air when the ball hung between the heads of several players and the cross-bar, and carrying it and himself into the net, but it was the only thing he did of any consequence throughout the entire game."* - makes us wonder what on earth poor Colombo had done to incur such criticism.

The Dundee Courier, in sharp contrast to its Perthshire counterpart, was much more upbeat and commiserated him on his bad luck… *"Colombo, the sturdy centre, was temporarily put out of action twice in the first period by nasty injuries to his knee and his absence accounted for a falling off in the attack. He had some measure of compensation, however, in afterwards helping to add to a Saints' victory."*

The Dundee Courier was also more generous in their summation of the match, telling us that *"St Johnstone have proved themselves worthy of inclusion in the Second Division, if only by reason of their splendid form, let alone a runaway victory against Arthurlie…*

"Well might the large crowd which filled the Recreation Grounds at Perth keep up a continuous cheer as goal after goal fell to the victorious Saints … the Saints' prospects are of a rosy character, and a continuance of Saturday's form should result in the bagging of a number of points and a corresponding measure of financial success…"

The Barrhead News, covering the match from the Arthurlie angle, seems to have been both putting lipstick on a pig while, paradoxically, also seeking excuses in their report, recording that, *"Twenty minutes from time, the score stood at one goal each,* *with Arthurlie having slightly the better of the game. The St Johnstone had two goals gifted them, the first palpably offside, and the other scored by one player while his partner in front of him bundled Malcolm out of the way."*

The Scottish Referee, which unlike the Perth and Barrhead papers, was relatively unbiased, was decidedly on Saints' side, commenting, *"St Johnstone are to be congratulated on winning their first game under Second League auspices. It was no indecisive victory, either, and no doubt all the clubs will take due note of the fact that the 'babies' of the division were able to beat Arthurlie with three goals to spare."*

The last press report comes from the curmudgeonly Perthshire Courier, who continued to moan, *"If Saturday's game may be accepted as a fair sample of Second League, then it is no better than is to be found in less ambitious combinations, and St Johnstone will find it no more attractive. On the other hand, if the tousy, rushing tactics which were so prominent on Saturday are below Second League form, then St Johnstone and Arthurlie will require to improve very considerably if they are not to be hopelessly outclassed."*

SCOTTISH LEAGUE—DIVISION II. TABLE TO DATE.							
	Plvd	Won	Lost	Drn	For	Agst	Pts
St Johnstone	1	1	0	0	4	1	2
Dumbarton	1	1	0	0	3	0	2
E. Stirlingshire	1	1	0	0	3	1	2
Ayr United	1	1	0	0	4	2	2
Vale of Leven	1	1	0	0	3	1	2
Leith	1	1	0	0	1	0	2
Albion Rovers	1	0	1	0	0	1	0
Abercorn	1	0	1	0	2	4	0
Dundee Hibern's	1	0	1	0	1	3	0
Cowdenbeath	1	0	1	0	1	3	0
St Bernards	1	0	1	0	0	3	0
Arthurlie	1	0	1	0	1	4	0
Two points for a win; one point for a draw.							

In fact, the paper was wrong. Not only (as the table here shows) were Saints sitting proudly atop of the Second Division after this first match, but they would go on to

43

prove they did have the necessary qualities to sustain a place in the second tier of the Scottish League, finishing in 5th place of the 12 teams in the Division, with 10 wins and 24 points.

However, in one area (which, it must be said, has been repeated from time to time over the intervening years) there was a cause for concern, because the team only scored 29 goals (with only four other teams scoring fewer), suggesting a lack of firepower that would need to be rectified in future seasons. Nevertheless, it was a solid start on which to build a new chapter in the St Johnstone story. The next step was promotion to the First Division and the chance to play in the top flight of Scottish football. But before that could happen, the First World War intervened…

Saints team: Aitken, Jackson, McGowan, Anderson, MacPherson, Stewart (1), Wilson (1), Page, Colombo (1), Steven (1), Brown.
Attendance: unknown, possibly c. 4,000.

The first use of a substitute by St Johnstone
St Johnstone 2, Perth Junior Select 0, Friendly match,
Recreation Grounds, Wednesday, 19th April 1922

In a Worthy Cause.

SAINTS GIVE CRAIGIE A HELPING HAND.

If the fare at the Recreation Grounds on Wednesday evening was nothing to write home about, the cause was decidedly a very worthy one, and it is to be hoped that the Craigie team and officials have reaped a tidy little reward. It was a sporting action

The first substitution in Scottish football history took place in a wartime match in 1917, when a player called Morgan took the place of the injured Morrison for Partick Thistle in a game against Rangers at Firhill.

The first record we have of any St Johnstone player being substituted comes not too long after this, in a friendly match in 1922. There was then a very long wait, until 1954, before the second Saints' substitute, and then a further longish wait until the first officially sanctioned substitution, which happened on 20th August 1966, when Drew Michie replaced Gordon Whitelaw in a 2-0 defeat to Dundee at Dens Park.

The 1922 friendly match was played against a Perth Junior Select XI; the game being played to help raise funds for the local junior side Craigie, who were struggling financially. Given that Saints' footballing roots lie in Craigie, this was an entirely appropriate and generous gesture on the part of the city's senior club.

The Junior Select was composed of players from Craigie and a variety of other local clubs – Scone, St Leonards, Violet, Celtic, Caledonian, Roselea and Kinnoull.

The PA carried a brief report - the heading and first few lines of which are shown here - which explains what happened and why the match took place. Under the heading, *"In a Worthy Cause,"* and the sub-headline, *"Saints give Craigie a helping hand,"* we can read: *"If the fare at the Recreation Grounds on Wednesday evening was nothing to write home about, the cause was decidedly a very worthy one, and it is to be hoped that the Craigie team and officials have reaped a tidy reward. It was a sporting action on the part of St Johnstone to come to the rescue of the junior club at this particular time, and if any were enticed by the attractive title – "Scottish Select" – doubtless they did not object to be 'had.' There were some dainty touches, but for the most part the exchanges were of a decidedly friendly nature. It was a rather costly match for Lamont, inasmuch as his old injury reasserted itself, and he was obliged to retire in the first half.*

"In the second period his place was taken by Pullar, the Jeanfield pivot, and he, along with Heggie, was responsible for the brace of goals by which the seniors prevailed."

The Courier also covered this match, albeit with a briefer but nonetheless more detailed report, telling us that the Saints' team was a bit thrown together, noting that, *"A somewhat scrappy team representing St Johnstone, and including several Dundee juniors* (in the team lines in both the Courier and the PA, Laahs is shown as belonging to Harp), *last night met on the Recreation Ground an eleven drawn from the junior clubs in the city in aid of the funds of the Craigie Club. Play was disappointing.*

This interesting photo from The Courier shows trainer Billy Bowman with five players from 1921-22.
Left to right they are: J Duff, P Gardiner, A Taylor, J Lamond and A Wilson.
Saints wore vertical stripes for a few seasons after the First World War.
Note the state of the Recreation Grounds terracing and pitch.

"About twenty minutes after the kick-off, Lamond, the Saints' centre forward, was unfortunately injured and had to retire. Heggie, the outside left, added to the Saints' score."

The Courier refers to this player as "Lamond," while the PA calls him "Lamont." In fact, the Courier was correct and the Perth paper wrong. However, in an adjacent column in the PA, we find a little more information about the unfortunate Lamond - and this time they got his name right: *"Lamond did not do himself any good in the friendly game on Wednesday. Let's hope that a few months' rest will make the youngster fit for 'keeps.'"*

Unfortunately, for John ('Jock') Lamond the PA's hopes for his future did not come to fruition. He had joined Saints in 1921, from local junior club Huntingtower. In the 1921-22 season, when Saints and the other Central League teams were re-admitted to the Second Division of the Scottish Football League, he was mainly played at centre-forward, but occasionally on the left wing. It was not a good season and they spent some time at the foot of the table, before gradually climbing to 13th place (in the 20-team league) at the season's end. They had only scored 41 goals in 38 games and of these Lamond had scored 10 in only 14 starts: an impressive record by any standards. Sadly, it seems this injury ended his career, because he was released at the end of the season and there is no record of where he went afterwards, suggesting he had to stop playing.

Saints team: Gardiner; McDonald and G Forbes; J Forbes, McGuire and Duff; Laahs (Harp), Paterson, Lamond (sub Pullar), Rodgerson and Heggie.
Attendance: unknown.

46

The official was subjected to some nasty outbursts of jeering

**The first promotion to the top league of Scottish football,
Forfar Athletic 1, St Johnstone 2, Scottish Football League, Second Division,
Station Park, Forfar, Saturday, 29th March 1924**

It is a measure of just how good this season was for Saints that they secured promotion almost a full month and four games before the end of the campaign. However, as the headlines above suggest, the game that produced the necessary points was controversial, to put it mildly. For St Johnstone that was a minor issue: what mattered was the result and that was a 2-1 win, which meant Saints - in first place in the table and with the top two going up - then had 51 points, two ahead of second placed Cowdenbeath but nine ahead of Bathgate in third, who now could not make up the ground to catch them. Moreover, it was the first time Saints had won at Forfar in 20 years.

There was a lot of interest in the game, both in Forfar and Perth. The Forfar Herald reported, *"There was early evidence that a big crowd was to witness the encounter between Forfar Athletic and St Johnstone on Saturday. Early in the forenoon, motor cars and motor cycles from the fair city were much in evidence."*

The other Forfar paper of that time, the Forfar Dispatch, estimated that there were around 1,500 fans from Perth in a crowd of around 4,000. The Forfar Herald had

carried an advert the previous week to promote the game. Interestingly, it gives top billing to Saints rather than their own, local team. Also, given that football was very much regarded as a male preserve, it's worth noting that there were separate prices for ladies, who were admitted for the same charge as juveniles.

In modern day prices (correct in 2023), the costs of admission for the different groups in the advert were as follows: adults - £3.60; ladies and juveniles - £2.37; boys - £1.51; with a further £3.60 for anyone who wanted entry to the grandstand.

The match reports tell us that the game was played in brilliant sunshine. Forfar won the toss and elected to play against the sun and with the wind at their backs in the first half. Jimmy Fleming then got the game underway for Saints, who proceeded to dominate the early phases of play. The Forfar Herald tells us that *"Saints at this period were certainly in the ascendancy but their finishing was bad."*

The home team came back into the match and were unlucky not to be awarded a penalty. Here's the Forfar Herald again: *"The 'Loons' are now holding their own and getting the Perth team rattled. Gay almost gave away a penalty and the foul kick was placed just on the line."* The Forfar Dispatch recorded that, *"...the Athletic appealed strongly for a penalty, but the referee awarded a free kick on the penalty line, which brought no result."* According to the laws of the game, if the foul was on the line, then it should have been a penalty. This was not the first time that the referee, a Mr W F Campbell of Dundee, proved wanting in the eyes of the home supporters.

As well as the penalty incident, the referee seems to have failed to spot an obvious handball in the build-up to Saints' first goal. Here's how the Forfar Dispatch described it...

"His first glaring and costly mistake from the home point of view occurred in the first period. During a raid on the Forfar goal, Ribchester, the St Johnstone outside right, stopped a volley by Smart with his hands before squaring into the goalmouth. The Athletic players, appealing for a foul kick, made no real attempt to clear, and Gibson, who was apparently in an offside position, had little difficulty in scoring – in the referee's opinion – a legitimate goal."

While it might be argued that the old adage of 'play to the whistle' would have been better than standing about appealing to the referee, it does seem that the home side were hard done by here. To make matters worse, the second St Johnstone goal was equally, if not more, contentious. Here's the Forfar Dispatch's version…

"In the second instance Wilson essayed a corner kick and the swerve of the ball carried it over the goal line before Bruce (the Forfar 'keeper), who was the first player to touch it, knocked it against the meshes of the net. Being in a most favourable position we are positive, as were the Athletic players and linesmen, that the ball was at least a foot over the line before Bruce handled, but once again Mr Campbell awarded a goal."

The Forfar Herald's post-match comments were, in the language of the era, highly critical of the referee…

"The referee showed a lamentable lack of common-sense in not at least listening to an official whose duty is to help the referee and assist in difficult position.

"Right from the start of the game Mr Campbell seemed desirous of carrying on under any conditions and had he adopted a firmer attitude much useless charging and tripping would have been stopped.

"To order off Alan Smart savoured of the heroic and whether justified or not was too late. No doubt the player was exasperated at a glaring injustice.

"The goal which Miller scored was a beauty and richly deserved. Why the same player did not count again will for ever remain a mystery.

"St Johnstone gained the points, but the glory of the game certainly rested with Forfar."

The Forfar Dispatch contended that, *"Throughout the game the referee failed to give satisfaction and appeared to have no control of the players. There was far too much arguing and ankle-tapping and towards the close of the game Smart got his marching orders for making what the referee considered an objectionable remark. He is reported to have said, 'Some refereeing'."*

The PA was in (almost) complete agreement with its Forfarshire counterparts, commenting, *"The two goals which were conceded the Saints were hotly disputed, and we are not surprised that they were."*

Although claiming that the first St Johnstone goal was *"richly merited,"* the PA's reporter came up with a novel way of describing what the Forfar papers regarded as Ribchester's clear handball. Instead, Perth readers were told that, *"... the ball had fouled Ribchester..."*

Forfar then equalised with what seems to have been an excellent goal, described thus by the PA: *"It was a beautifully executed movement which led to the downfall of Dempster's charge. Nicol swung a fine pass to the unmarked Herron, and judging the strength of the winger's cross to a nicety, Miller met the sphere with his head and deftly put past Dempster."*

As for the second Saints' goal, the PA's scribe seemed to equivocate, claiming not to have seen exactly what happened...

"A corner cleverly forced by Wilson led to the much-disputed winning goal. Bert (Wilson) took his right foot and swerved in a curling ball at the corner of the near post. From the grand stand it was a trifle difficult to observe what actually transpired, but Mr Campbell at once gave the goal, and it is significant that the only player who did not protest against the decision was the only man who was in a position to judge the legitimacy of the award – Jock Bruce, the goalkeeper. The 'Loons,' however, did not forget to let Mr Campbell know of their dissatisfaction, and invoked the aid of their

linesman to have the decision reversed. It was all to no purpose however. Mr Campbell refused to change his mind, and as showing the temper which was displayed at that particular moment, three-and-a-half minutes were lost ere the ball was set in motion for play."

It is worth noting that the PA report mentions *"their linesman."* The use of neutral linesmen is a relatively recent development in Scottish football: up until the Second World War, most lower Division games would have an independent referee, but each club would provide an official or surplus player to run the line.

This caused considerable debate, with the Daily Record's 'Waverley' writing, in the paper of 29th September 1927, *"For some time I have been hearing complaints against the conduct of certain linesmen at Second Division matches. From now on no player will be allowed to wave the flag, the right way or the wrong way. The job must now be done by a club official."*

Whether or not it was a Forfar player or official who was on the line that afternoon is not known. However, in either event, it does seem quite possible that, based on the laws at the time (scoring directly from a corner wasn't made legal until June 1924), this goal should not have stood.

In fairness to the officials, there is no doubt that this was a very rough game. The PA described the enthusiastic way the players set about each other as follows: *"The 'feature' of the game was the temper which was in evidence during the whole ninety minutes. One can always admire keenness, but when keenness gives place to brute force, and to deliberate brute force, then those who participate in tactics of this kind should remember in the first instance that it is discreditable to themselves and that the public do not pay to be purveyed with something which can be seen inside the ring."*

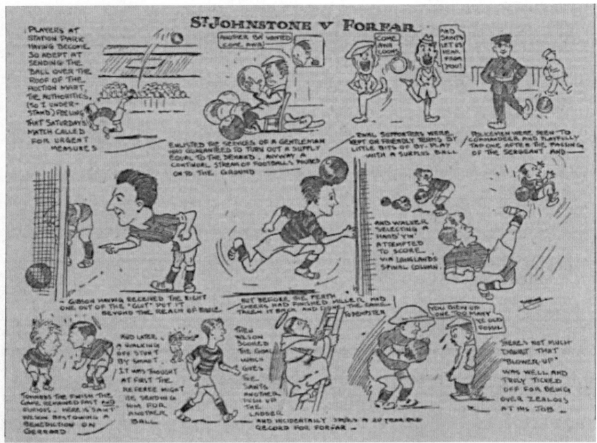

Cartoon: The Courier

It wasn't just the Forfar players who took umbrage at the referee's performance. The PA tells us, *"At the close of the game the field was invaded by the spectators and apprehension was felt as to the fate of the referee. Players and Forfar officials formed a sort of bodyguard to Mr Campbell as he made his way to the stripping quarters. Harvey, it is understood, reported to having been twice kicked and there was* (sic) *one or two miniature boxing displays in midfield which the police nipped in the bud."*

The other feature of the game, which seems to have been commonplace at matches at Station Park, was the problem caused by the ball going out of the ground. As the cartoon here, courtesy of the Courier, shows, Forfar employed the services of a man to ensure there were enough serviceable footballs to make up the shortfall. The cartoon, while hinting at the aggressive nature of some of the play, makes light of the sending off of Smart.

Despite the unfortunate nature of the proceedings, once the dust had settled the fact remained that St Johnstone had achieved promotion to the top rank of Scottish football. Over the remaining four games, all that remained was to see whether it was them or Cowdenbeath who took the title. This was not settled until the very last day of the season, when a 3-1 win at Armadale gave Saints the Second Division Championship. It was a vindication of all the hard work of the previous, near half-century and the start of the next chapter of establishing the club on the Scottish footballing map.

Saints team: Dempster; 'Newman' and Gay; Harvey, Walker and McRoberts; Ribchester, Hart, Fleming, Gibson and
Attendance: 4,000.

**The first match in the top league of Scottish football,
Hamilton 3, St Johnstone 2, Scottish Football League, First Division,
Douglas Park, Hamilton, Saturday, 16th August 1924**

St. Johnstone Open First League Programme at Hamilton.

A Costly Half-Hour's Stage Fright; Defensive Blunders.

Team Must Be Given Time to Settle.

Headline: Perthshire Advertiser

This was the first time the club had played at the top level of Scottish football, that is in the old First Division of the Scottish Football League. As the scoreline indicates, it wasn't the start they were hoping for…

Following their success in gaining promotion in 1923-24, Saints went into the new campaign full of hope. The board had spent decent money over the close season – an unspecified amount on new turnstiles, £5:13:6d on a Second Division Champions' flag, plus £2:7:6d each on silver badges to commemorate the event. Perhaps more importantly, they also spent money on a number of players in order to boost the club's chances of success, with Bob Pender coming from Middlesbrough for £150, Jock Nicholson from Rangers for £530, Tommy Glancy from Falkirk for £241 and 10 shillings, Jimmy Howieson from Airdrie for £385 and – perhaps most significantly - Bob Penman from Albion Rovers for an unknown fee.

The first game of the new season was to be away at Douglas Park, which had been home to Hamilton Academical since 1888 (and continued to be so until 1994). The Accies had been a fixture in the old First Division since the 1906-07 season, albeit generally finishing in a mid-lower league position, and as such were expected to provide a stern test for any newly promoted side.

Even though it was August, the game was played in very wet conditions. The PA noted that for a First League baptism, water would naturally be expected, but, *"water is all right in its place, but it can be overdone…*(and) *despite the somewhat treacherous surface it was quite an interesting match."* Their reporter also noted that the inclement weather had affected the crowd, which was estimated at no more than 4,000. In those days, the gate money was split between the two clubs (67% - 33% in the home team's favour), with a minimum 'guarantee' of £5 that helped meet the visiting team's costs. In fact, despite the PA's concern, the St Johnstone directors' Minute Book reveals that Saints actually made a profit of £7:0:10d on the game.

Even with their new signings, Saints struggled in this first test in the top-flight, especially in the first half. *"It could not be said that their play was quite up to First League class during the first half,"* reported 'The Pilot' in The Sunday Post. It must be said this was an understatement, to put it mildly. Hamilton opened the scoring after only three minutes, doubled their lead some 15 minutes later and soon after increased the margin to three goals.

FIGHTING SAINTS AT HAMILTON

TRANSFORMATION AFTER INTERVAL

Experience Will Tell

BY GRENADIER.

Headline: The Courier

At this point, any thoughts of St Johnstone making their mark in the top tier were doubtless waning, but the players redoubled their efforts and, as the Dundee Courier's sub-headline put it, there was a *"Transformation after the Interval,"* with Howieson and Wilson scoring within a few minutes of each other to make the match much more of a contest and, by the end of the game, *"they were within an ace of drawing, after the situation seemed to be hopeless."*

Howieson came the closest to securing a point for Saints when *"he let go a great left foot drive which found the wrong side of the post with Somerville* (the Accies' keeper) *'not at home'. The remaining play was brimful of interest, but that was all – no more goals accrued."*

Overall, the general tenor of the press reports is that Saints began poorly and were given a lesson by Hamilton for the first half an hour at least. After the Accies' third goal, the PA reported, *"for the remainder of the first half the Saints were a pretty disjointed lot. Their attacks, few and far between, were generally initiated by Howieson, and for the most part the half-backs got rid of the ball without troubling about direction."* Centre half Davie Walker

was also at fault, due to his *"tendency to balloon the ball."* Centre forward Jimmy Fleming, who had been scoring for fun in the previous, promotion season, was obviously well watched by the Hamilton defence for *"he never got a shot in."* This was something he would rectify over the course of the season and in due course, as we noted in our book, *"Hagiography, The Great Saints,"* become one of the club's best players of all time.

The PA's match report concluded that only time would tell if Saints were fit for the First Division, describing their attitude thus, *"The PA is far from being pessimistic, but prefers to steer a middle course between those who cannot see beyond the Saints and the other fellows, who are striving with might and main to keep in the limelight... The team must be given time to settle, even if there be one or two positions which seem to require strengthening straight away."*

There are a couple of other interesting things we can discover from the contemporary match reports. Firstly, given that it is normally Rangers who are referred to as the 'Light Blues," the fact that the PA's report uses this expression to describe Saints might occasion surprise amongst today's fans (the majority of whom would, we suspect, hate the thought).

Secondly, as we've noted in the pages above, there was far more willingness to make direct criticism of individual players on the part of the local press than there is nowadays. Perhaps that's why they frequently appeared under a pseudonymous bye-line, such as the aforementioned 'Pilot' in The Sunday Post, (although we believe that, in reality, people did know who were the men behind the nom-de-plumes). The Dundee Courier's correspondent hid behind the title of 'The Grenadier,' and he did not hesitate to lay the blame for St Johnstone's defeat at the hands of John Gay, the Perth left back, telling the paper's readers, *"Undoubtedly, it was the weakness of Gay* at left-back which cost the Saints both points. Whether it was the big occasion that affected him, the wideness of the ground or the general lack of understanding amongst the players cannot, of course, be definitely stated; but there's no blinking the fact that for quite a long spell in the first half he was disappointing. He failed to keep a grip of Kelly and Miller, and there was an apparent weakness in covering up between him and Pender."

To be fair, the Courier did note that, "in the second half Gay was an entirely different player." The PA concurred, noting, "he played really well in the second period."

Despite the disappointment of defeat, one Saints' player who did catch the eye was the debutant, Bob Penman. The Courier reported that, "Penman was strong at right back, and all the time he gave the opposing wing little rope." It was to be the first game of a record-breaking career at Perth – as we shall find out in a subsequent chapter ...

Saints team: Dempster, Penman, Gay:
Nicholson, Walker and Pender:
Ribchester, Glancy, Fleming, Howieson, Wilson.
Attendance: 4,000.

An entire lack of deliberate fouling

**The last game at the Recreation Grounds,
St Johnstone 4, Kilmarnock 2, Scottish Football League, First Division,
Recreation Grounds, Saturday, 13th December 1924**

Headline: *The Sunday Post*

Many of those reading this will have been at the last game at Muirton Park. For those who are too young or were simply not able to be there, it was an occasion for looking back and remembering all the great times we'd had in the years gone by. It was also a sad occasion as we surveyed the shabby state of the ground and tried not to remember some of the more recent seasons when Saints had plumbed the depths of Scottish football and, had it not been for the intervention of Geoff Brown, nearly gone out of business. At the end of the 90 minutes, the home fans were probably even more depressed, having watched Saints (as described later in this book) go down 0-1 to Ayr. However, to counter the gloom as the supporters wended their way out of the old gates for the last time, they had the prospect of a shiny, new stadium, then nearing completion off the Crieff Road on the outskirts of the city.

We can fairly safely presume that those attending the final game at the St Johnstone Recreation Grounds 12 days before Christmas 1924 will have had very similar feelings. Like those seeing the pitch, the stands and the terracing at Muirton for that last time in 1989, they must have had fond memories of standing around the perimeter fence at the Recreation Grounds or, for

those so inclined, taking a seat in the grandstand. They too were able to look forward to a shiny, new ground: in their case Muirton Park, which had been constructed amidst great fanfare on the Dunkeld Road, although it should be noted that even on the 13th of December there was still uncertainty as to whether the next match would be at Dunkeld Road or the Edinburgh Road.

As we've described earlier, the Recreation Grounds were really not fit for senior football, especially now that Saints were playing in the top flight. The principal issue was the state of the playing surface, which might best be described as boggy and sad. A pitch suitable for Eeyore perhaps, but not for the best footballers in Scotland. That said, it should be remembered that all playing fields in the country at this time tended to be somewhat agricultural by today's standards, although we must concede that the Recreation Grounds, especially when at their worst, were spectacularly bad.

Just how bad is apparent in the Ayrshire press's reporting of the game. The reporter for the Kilmarnock Herald and North Ayrshire Gazette was succinct and to the point, telling his readers in only the second sentence of his brief report, *"The ground was a quagmire, and militated against any good football."* Was he getting his retaliation in early? In its preview on the day of the match the PA had referred to the Kilmarnock ground as a *"midden heid,"* which is hardly complimentary. Alternatively, the Ayrshire scribe was simply preparing the Kilmarnock readers for what was to come next, because his first sentence read as follows: *"Kilmarnock went to Perth not too confident, but hopeful."*

In contrast, the Courier and the Sunday Post made no references to the state of the pitch, but the PA's scribe was as unimpressed as his Killie counterpart. He too described the pitch as a *"quagmire"* as a result of the heavy rain that had fallen all morning, which he further described as *"very depressing,"* before going on to blame the weather for the poor attendance. For today's fan, used to McDiarmid Park being half full for most games, it might be a surprise to learn that a crowd, estimated at between 7,000-8,000 was a disappointment. Despite the club's poor form that season, the Perth supporters had been turning out in their thousands to see their favourites perform for the first time in the top flight of Scottish football.

Up to that point in the season, the PA reckoned Saints had been averaging 10,000 at their home games (in fact, from the figures available we think it was 10,500) and the reporter suggested that if the sun had come out a bit earlier (it seems that it did shine in the afternoon) then that figure would have been met for the last hurrah at the old ground. Interestingly, the PA's report suggests there were over 5,000 present to watch the start of the game, so it seems there must have been a lot of late arrivals.

Saints went into the game with concerns over their league position. They had only been promoted to the First Division at the end of the previous season and were clearly taking time to acclimatise. They had won only five league games so far that season, the last of which was the previous week, away to St Mirren. Before that trip to Paisley, Saints had lost every game bar one in November (the other was a draw) and, as the PA's notes on the Wednesday before the Killie match sadly made clear, *"the*

situation still remains critical, and great care is to be exercised if the position is to be eased."

Fortunately, Kilmarnock's record was pretty poor up to this point too, although that didn't prevent them from taking an early lead when Bird fired home via the crossbar in the 10th minute. However, Saints were not behind for long, with Jimmy Fleming equalising two minutes later after what the PA described as *"an exciting scrimmage in front of goal."* He had another great chance almost immediately after this, but was thwarted by a superb block by Gibson, the Kilmarnock left-back. However, both teams were merely warming up, and Smith restored Kilmarnock's lead some ten minutes later, although his low shot, like that of Bird earlier, only went in off the woodwork - in this case the foot of the post - with Dempster in the Saints' goal going down a touch late.

Saints were not behind for too long, with Glancy equalising just before the half-hour. Then Sanderson fed Hart who bore down on Gould in the Killie goal before he was up-ended by centre-half Clark. Glancy stepped up to fire the penalty home and put Saints into the lead for the first time. The final goal was scored by Fleming, who tricked his way past Gibson before slotting home. Even looking back over the decades since then, Jimmy Fleming remains one of the best centre forwards ever to turn out for Saints and the PA reporter on the day recognised his talent too, commenting, *"For my part, the St Johnstone have never had a better centre than Fleming, nor a player with such a rare temperament for the game."*

All the goals came in the first half. The second forty-five was, in contrast, dire. We've all been at such games, where one or other half is jam-packed with excitement and the other is tedious in the extreme and this final match at the Recreation Ground certainly seems to have fallen into that category. It wasn't even enlivened by any robust tackling or dirty fouls: indeed, both the Sunday Post and the Courier commented about how clean a match it had been. The Sunday Post said, *"all through the play there was an entire lack of deliberate fouling,"* while the Courier reported, *"It was the cleanest game seen at the Recreation Grounds this season."* The PA even praised the referee, Mr Bell of Motherwell, noting, *"If (SFA) Secretary McAndrew has a few more of his type he might send them along to Perth now and again, where the crowd keenly appreciate an official who makes up his mind and sticks to it."*

Although Saints were struggling at the time of this match, by the time the dust settled at the end of the 1924-25 season, they were comfortable in 11th place in the First Division with 35 points (remember, there were only two points for a win in those days), with Kilmarnock only one place behind them on 33 points.

We leave the last word to the PA… *"The Recreation Grounds, with all its faults and failings, will always be a happy memory, by reason of the many stirring games that it housed. The position of Perth, however, demands an up-to-date enclosure and there will be no crocodile tears shed at the flitting. In point of fact, it has been long overdue."*

Saints team: Dempster; Penman and McClure; White, Swallow and Pender; Ellis, Glancy, Fleming, Hart and Sanderson.
Attendance: c. 7,000-8,000.

No. 14
McDonald came in for a lecture for interfering with the referee

The first game at Muirton
St Johnstone 2, Queen's Park 1, Scottish Football League, First Division,
Muirton Park, Thursday, 25th December 1924

The idea of a football match taking place on Christmas Day seems strange to us today. Yet, it ought to be remembered that Christmas Day was not an official public holiday in Scotland until 1958 and both authors are old enough to remember businesses and shops being open on that day in the early 1960s. Thus, in 1924 it was not unusual for football fans to wend their way to a match on the 25th of December. And Christmas Day 1924 was an especially auspicious day in the history of St Johnstone, for that was when Muirton Park was officially opened, with a league match against Queen's Park. The PA reported how local employers, happy to enter into the festive spirit, gave their staff the day off so they could go to the game. As a result, the crowd of around 12,000 featured many people from the towns and villages across Perthshire as well as those from the city.

While impressive, it wasn't actually the biggest home crowd of the season – that came when 15,000 watched Saints against Dundee in October 1924. In fact, 12,000 was not untypical of the attendances at Perth that season, with the lowest home crowds being only 5,000 each for the visits of Kilmarnock, Third Lanark and Hamilton Accies. It is a source of constant wonder just how many people turned out to watch football back in those days. To illustrate the point, consider this: on 3rd September 1924, some 12,000 came to the Recreation Grounds to see Saints play Cowdenbeath (then a very strong side, who finished fifth in the First Division that season). Four days before that game, 16,000 had attended Central Park in Cowdenbeath for Saints' visit and a friendly between these two clubs at Muirton on 7th February 1925 produced a crowd of 4,000. To put this in context, the population of Perth at the 1921 census was 33,208.

The tale of how Muirton came to be built is told in detail in St Johnstone's official history, but, briefly, it was clear that the Recreation Grounds were not fit for First League soccer and, in particular, the lack of a suitable grandstand was a major problem. This was important, because under League rules, although clubs split the gate money this only applied to the ground (i.e. the terracing) and not to any money from the grandstand(s) or enclosures. In addition, clubs were only allowed to retain the money from the first 1,000 season ticket holders: any surplus was shared with the visiting club, at the prevailing turnstile price - usually around one shilling (5p) in the 1920s. As always, finance was crucial and so the board sought an alternative ground where they would be able to construct a substantial grandstand.

The work was completed in only a few months. Although the pitch had already been laid, the construction of the terracing and the stand only began in late October. A debenture scheme raised £7,500 towards the £9,259 estimate for the entire works – with nearly half of this sum coming from Lords Forteviot and Mansfield, the latter being the owner of the land on which Muirton was built. As the year wound down, there was much concern that the ground would not be ready for the Queen's Park game, but in the event it was, although the dressing rooms were not finished in time and both teams had to change in the Perth Baths on the Dunkeld Road.

The local press made much of the opening of the new ground, with a famous cartoon commissioned and much congratulation given to the club's directors, especially to Mr Donald MacIntosh, described, correctly, by chairman Robert Campbell as *"the father of Muirton Park."*

Although not the force they had been in the 19th century, Queen's Park were still expected to provide stiff opposition. It was entirely fitting that they were our opponents on that historic day, because they had taken part in the first match (the official opening) at the Recreation Grounds, nearly 40 years earlier, although on that occasion Saints weren't involved in what was, in effect, an exhibition match against Our Boys of Dundee.

Muirton's first match took place in mild weather conditions, with barely a breeze ruffling the Second Division Championship flag that was proudly fluttering in the north-west corner of the ground (on the corner of the stand and what was known to later generations as 'the ice-rink end.').

Fans travelled from all over to the match. Many years later, on the occasion of the last ever game at Muirton, the PA interviewed George Wightman who, as a 13-year old, had come from the small Perthshire village of Waterloo, telling the paper, *"There was a special train ran from Bankfoot and I travelled in by myself to see the match."*

The weather was ideal for the occasion, and there was not even a breath of wind to flutter the Second Division championship flag which occupied a prominent site at the north end of the ground. Tommy Glancy won the toss, and R. Gillespie kicked off at 3.17. Queen's immediately bore down, and their attack

The kick-off time as stated in the PA's report

According to the PA, the game kicked off at 3.17 pm. We are certain this must be a typographical error as it would have been almost impossible to play – and certainly to see - football without floodlights at this time of year with a kick-off at this time. Moreover, the original, official poster for the game, which is on display in the foyer of McDiarmid Park, states clearly that the kick-off time was 2.15 pm.

Queen's Park dominated the early proceedings and Saints struggled to make much of an impression. Even Jimmy Fleming, one of the greatest centre forwards in our history, was not at his best, occasionally taking too much time on the ball – or, as the PA put it, *"when well placed ... he tried to diddle too much for even better position and T Sneddon put the finishing touch to his ideas."*

St Johnstone came more into the game, with Jimmy Sanderson showing fine skills on the wing and beating several players in one mesmerising run. Then Jimmy Fleming came close with a header which was superbly saved by Gibbs in the Queen's goal, before the visitors' centre, Bob Gillespie, missed an absolute sitter at the back post.

Four minutes from the interval, Saints went ahead. As the PA described it, *"Jock White sent a ball goalwards, Johnnie Hart just touched the leather with his head, but Sanderson was up and waiting, and he whipped the ball into the net."*

Queen's Park spent the remainder of the first half on the attack, so much so that the PA reported *"the Saints' defence had a hot time ... and Dempster saved two terrific drives in quick succession."*

Having scored his first some four minutes before half-time, Jimmy Sanderson then scored his second four minutes into the second half. He advanced towards the Queen's goal, beating two defenders before firing in a powerful shot, with the PA telling its us that, *"the custodian had no chance."*

The game seemingly became tousy after this. The language used in the press reports demonstrates how usage changes over time, with the visitors *"inclined to adopt tactics that were not in the book."* Indeed, the Spiders' J McDonald *"came in for a lecture for interfering with the referee."* Or, as the Dundee Courier put it, *"Queen's were now inclined to use their weight."*

A further indication of the rough and tumble nature of inter-war football came soon after McDonald's altercation with the referee. The PA describes how *"the same player was 'laid out' in a collision with Sanderson. He had to be assisted from the field, but resumed in a few minutes."*

Soon after this, Sanderson nearly secured his hat-trick. It's hard to tell from the match report in the PA (strangely, for some reason the Courier doesn't mention it), but it seems he flashed over a cross that rebounded from

the post. Despite Saints' pressure, Queen's pulled one back, with Gillespie and Russell carving through the home defence and the latter slotting past Dempster.

Understandably buoyed by their goal, Queen's set about Saints, throwing men forward in an attempt to secure a draw. It seems to have been an extremely exciting finale to the game, as (from the PA's report), *"Repeated shots were blocked by Saints' defenders, and when Dempster fisted the ball among a crowd of sprawling players it only added to the great excitement. Fortunately, however, Swallow was first to find his feet, and just succeeded in getting the ball away."*

After this stramash, Jock White committed what would now be regarded as a professional foul, hauling down the Spiders' J B McAlpine inside the box. In those days, that was very much par for the course and the match reports do not even report that White was cautioned (booked), far less sent off. The Queen's fans in the crowd cheered in expectation of an equaliser, but Dempster made a sensational save from Gillespie's spot kick. The Dundee Courier tells us that although Dempster had made a great save, the ball rebounded to Nicholson, the Queen's outside left, *"who narrowly kicked over."*

The game ended, appropriately enough, with the ball at Sanderson's feet. Andy Swallow had made a terrific tackle on Gillespie, the Queen's centre forward which caused the latter to spiral over the Saints' man and land full-length on the ground *("to the amusement of the spectators")*. Johnnie Hart then took control of the ball as it broke loose and promptly fired it up the field to Sanderson, at which point the referee blew the final whistle.

Given the time of the year and the fact that there were, of course, no floodlights, even if the kick-off was, as per the official poster, at 2.15 pm, it can only be guessed as to how hard it was for the players and the spectators to see what was going on in the latter stages of the match as Queen's Park laid siege to the St Johnstone defence for the final 20 minutes. Nonetheless, it is not difficult to imagine the intense excitement that this late onslaught on the Saints' goal generated in the crowd – both home and away fans. The fact that this was such a notable occasion – the hanselling of the new stadium – must have made it doubly so. Any modern-day supporters who were present at the first match at McDiarmid Park, will have had similar feelings, albeit on that occasion, the final few minutes were considerably less stressful than they had been in 1924. As the Courier's report on Queen's Park's visit noted, *"It was all very rousing and thrilling, and seldom will there be anything more exciting seen at Muirton Park."* Given it was the first ever match at the new park, that judgement was perhaps a little premature, but things had certainly got off to a good start and augured well for the future.

For the record, Saints finished 11th in the 20 team table scoring 57 goals and winning 12 matches and ending with 35 points. Queen's Park were only three points worse off, but the First Division was so tight that they were in 17th place, fourth bottom of the table.

Saints team: Dempster; Penman and McClure; White, Swallow and McBoyle; Ellis, Glancy, Fleming, Hart and Sanderson.
Attendance: 12,000.

No. 15
Mere pigmies of the League

A first win at Ibrox
**Rangers 0, St Johnstone 1, Scottish Football League, First Division,
Ibrox Stadium, Saturday, 26th December 1925**

ST JOHNSTONE'S GREAT TRIUMPH AT IBROX PARK.
BY THE WATCHMAN.

Headline: The Sunday Post

In case anyone is wondering which clubs were the *"mere pigmies of the League,"* in 1925 (at least according to the Dundee Courier), one of them was Dundee United. St Johnstone was the other one. And while we might, naturally, take umbrage at St Johnstone being thus described, it has to be admitted that, at this particular time, the Courier's reporter did have a point…

After gaining promotion in 1924, Saints had finished their first season back in the top flight of Scottish football in 11th place in the 20-team league. Consequently, they went into the 1925-26 campaign in good spirits. The first match was at home to Rangers, which they lost 3-0, but the second, away to Dundee produced a much more pleasing 1-0 win. Over the remaining months of 1925, performances and results were generally poor though.

The week prior to the Boxing Day game at Ibrox had seen Dundee come to Perth and eke out a no-score draw in conditions that might have been more suitable for the Inuit rather than professional footballers. The Courier described how "…the full effects of the frost were felt at Muirton Park (and) *goalscoring was indeed a problem on a ground in some bits of which wreaths of snow held the ball as in a vice, while in others it travelled so fast as to be completely beyond control. Both sides*

found the handicaps too great." As we have mentioned before, they were much hardier in the days before health and safety was invented. Perhaps the most significant thing that happened that day was the debut of a new, young centre forward for St Johnstone. The Courier described him thus, *"Munro, the reserve centre, made a creditable first appearance. Although not just a Gallacher in polish* (a reference to Patsy Gallacher, Celtic's free-scoring forward of the period), *this youngster has any amount of pluck, and was a continual source of worry to the Dundee defence."*

After that scoreless match in the snow and ice, Saints were second bottom of the table on goal average, with only 13 points from 19 games. Consequently, going to Ibrox on Boxing Day was not a match that any rational Saints' fan would relish.

Rangers, by their standards, were not having a great season, being only 7th in the table with 23 points from 20 games. Nonetheless, they were the current League champions and expected to beat the pigmies from Perth.

A crowd of 8,000 braved some rather inclement Boxing Day weather. The Courier described the pitch as *"…not perfect. There was no frost on it, however, and it was rather soft on top than otherwise,* and the players had quite a good grip," before going on to add, *"For a spell it looked as if the game would not be started, and after it started it looked as if it would not finish. The fog was thick, and at times during the game the players from the lofty press-box looked like so many marionettes running after something invisible, for often no ball could be seen. However, the mist periodically cleared away, and only in those brighter times could it be clearly seen that the game was being keenly fought."*

After the match, the Courier tells us, *"The defeat of the Glasgow club was keenly discussed by followers of football in that city in view of the presence of discarded Rangers players amongst the Perth men and Fleming, the ex-Saint, at centre forward for the ground team. On Saturday's exhibition St Johnstone came out well in the deal of a few months ago."*

The ex-Rangers' men in question were John Jamieson and Andrew and Dan Kirkwood (the latter was on loan rather than signed), with Fleming going to Ibrox. This happened at the end of October 1925 and the newcomers joined another former Ranger, Alex Dick, whom Saints had signed a few weeks before. All four played in the Boxing Day match at Ibrox, as did the young man who had made his debut against Dundee the previous Saturday, having just been signed by Saints from Ardrossan Winton Rovers for the princely sum of £10 at the end of November 1925. It would prove to be one of the best tenners spent by the Perth club.

Saints took the game to Rangers. The Courier tells us, *"The new combination of the forwards appeared to work satisfactorily, and, indeed, the Rangers defence was kept well employed. On the other hand, the Rangers attacks were never long sustained, and from the point of view of the home supporters the exhibition must have been very disappointing. Rangers looked an entirely different lot from the*

Rangers who beat Saints at Muirton Park. At no time were they convincing, and seldom were they even dangerous."*

St Johnstone, on the other hand, had a good day at the office. The Courier again…

"This was a big day for the Saints. They have done nothing better since they became First Leaguers. In the first half they so persistently attacked that a goal to them was anticipated, and when it came fifteen minutes after the interval it was thoroughly deserved.

"There was nothing spectacular about the score. It came during a scrambling mix-up practically under the bar. In the darkness, Munro appeared to be the player who gave the finishing touch."

The PA tells us a similar story…

"For the first fifteen minutes the Saints were easily 'top dogs.' The half-backs, as the game went on, got a good grip of the Rangers forwards, some of whom made the mistake of attempting to get the ball under complete control before passing. This was a fatal policy, because, while they were trying it the St Johnstone half-backs nipped in and took it from them…

"The contrast between the teams could be described by saying that while Robb had a dozen shots to save, Page had scarcely one."

The PA's description of the game's only goal is far more detailed than that of the Courier…

"Twice in quick succession Dixon conceded a corner, and from the second of these St Johnstone scored. Wilson put the ball nicely across and an exciting minute occurred in front of Robb. Black sent the ball in and Robb jumped to it and punched outwards. It struck the inside of the bar and went out again to Munro, who promptly

headed into the net. This goal was well deserved."

The Sunday Post's summary records how Rangers grew more desperate as time marched on, with their reporter telling us, *"Andy Cunningham, Cairns, Morton and the other Ibrox forwards tried all their wiles to beat a defence whose keenness and first-time clearances revealed the determination of the Perth team to prevail at all hazards. The Rangers had more of the play in the second half. Nearing the end their desperate anxiety to draw level proved their undoing. All too late in the contest they recognised that their early scheme of attack had gone all wrong...Determination and zeal, coupled with impetuous dash and confidence, carried St Johnstone through to make more merry the Christmas feeling shared by them all."*

The Edinburgh Evening News carried a brief report, which mainly focused on the travails of Rangers, but also noted that Saints had *"a very plucky and go-ahead attack in which D Kirkwood and Munro, a hefty centre, were outstanding."*

Jimmy Munro would also go on to become one of St Johnstone's greatest players. He had three separate spells at Perth, scoring 67 times in 98 games, including an unlikely-to-be-equalled three, four-goal-haul, against Queen's Park (twice) and Hibs. He was also included, with team-mate Andy Swallow, in the SFA's trip to Canada, playing in 15 of the 20 tour games and scoring 26 goals. However, as none of these matches was against a Canadian international side, no caps were awarded, otherwise Jimmy would have been our first Scottish international.

Despite their relatively lowly league position, this was no mean Rangers' team. As well as Jimmy Fleming, it contained the legendary winger Allan Morton and also other Scottish internationalists including Davie Meiklejohn, Andy Cunningham and Tommy Muirhead: the latter, of course, would go on to become one of St Johnstone's greatest managers. However, when all was said and done, this first win at Ibrox was only the proverbial two points. Over the remainder of the 1925-26 season, Saints continued to struggle, eventually finishing 18th in the 20 team First Division thus avoiding relegation and laying a platform for several more (successful) seasons in the top flight of Scottish football.

Saints team: Page; Penman and Jamieson; White, A Kirkwood and Swallow; Dick, D Kirkwood, Munro, Black and Wilson. Attendance: 8,000.

Celebrating his hundredth consecutive game by revealing perfect form

The first player to reach 100 consecutive appearances
Celtic 4, St Johnstone 0, Scottish Football, League First Division,
Celtic Park, Saturday, 11th December 1926

Saints' Shooting Shocks Supporters.

Celtic Opportunists Win Great Game at Parkhead; St. Johnstone Play Good Football, but Forwards Fail to Finish.

Is Shooting a Lost Art with Muirton Pack? A Centre Without a Shot.

Celtic, 4—(By "Muirton.")—St. Johnstone, 0.

Headline: Perthshire Advertiser

In its edition of June 17th, 1924, the Evening Telegraph reported that St Johnstone had signed Robert Penman of Albion Rovers. One of the more interesting facts (from a historical perspective) is that Penman was only 5 ft 8 inches tall (173 cm) and weighed 12 stone (76 kg). In team photographs, he looks very much about average in terms of weight and height. The increase in the size and weight of footballers in the intervening period is substantial, with the average weight of the Saints' squad in 2022-23 season being 13 stone, four pounds and five ounces (81.5 kg), while the average height was six-foot one inch (186 cm).

Born in 1891 in Holytown, in Lanarkshire, Bob Penman began his football career with Ashfield Juniors before being signed by Motherwell in 1914. He made 83 appearances for the Steelmen before joining Albion Rovers during the 1917-18 season. Looking back from the perspective of 2023, this might seem a retrograde move, but in fact Bob was joining one of the Wee Rovers greatest sides. In the 1920 Scottish Cup they had what was arguably the club's finest hour, when, having beaten Rangers

2-0 in a replay at Celtic Park, they reached the club's only ever Scottish Cup final. Sadly, with Bob at right back, they went on to lose 3-2 to Kilmarnock in the final at Hampden on 17th April 1920, in front of 95,000 spectators. This was reportedly a record attendance for a club match in Scotland at that date.

IN THE WORLD OF SPORT.

Albion Rovers' Back For St Johnstone.

Dundee's Trip Shortened.

Robert Penman, of Albion Rovers, has been secured by St. Johnstone. Penman is a right back and has been with the Rovers for several seasons, forming, along with M'Colgan, now in England, one of the best defences in the League. He was a junior with Glasgow Ashfield. He belongs to Bellshill, is 5 ft. 8 ins. in height and weighs about 12 stone.

Evening Telegraph

At Perth, his wage was initially £3 a week (£193 in current money) from 12th June 1924 to the 14th of August, then £8 a week

64

(£515) from 15th August 1924 until 7th February 1925, then £5 a week (£322) from 8th February until 30th April 1925 (effectively the end of the season). In addition to his wages, he received a £20 signing-on fee (£1,288).

When Penman joined Saints, the club was, for the first time, embarking on life in the top flight of Scottish football. Having been promoted in 1924, the board's first move was to secure a proper manager (the directors had been picking the team since 1922), with Burnley's Davie Taylor joining in May 1924.

Thereafter, several signings were made with a view to strengthening the defence and attack. As well as Penman, half-backs Bob Pender from Middlesbrough and Jock Nicholson from Rangers also joined, along with inside forwards Tommy Glancy from Falkirk and Jimmy Howieson from Airdrie. After the previous season's promotion, the players had been agitating for improved terms, which the directors eventually granted, promising a bonus of £1 per point in the new season. Everything was in place: it only remained to see how St Johnstone would adapt to their new surroundings and whether they could rise to meet the challenge of coming up for the first time against the giants of Scottish football on a regular basis.

Bob Penman made his St Johnstone debut on 16th August 1924, in a 3-2 defeat away at Hamilton Accies. On the 11th December, 1926, he made his 100th consecutive appearance for Saints, again in an away defeat, this time 2-0 at Celtic Park. In the interval between his first appearance and that 100th match milestone, Penman proved his worth time and time again, turning in consistent performances that must have made him amongst the first names on the team-sheet every week. In that first, First Division, season, he helped the team finish comfortably in a very commendable 11th place.

That said, Saints did take some real hammerings, in those days, although on the other hand they also administered some similar drubbings to several big teams. The more open nature of Scottish football back then is revealed in the wide variations in scores that not infrequently occurred from one game to the next. For example, in three consecutive league matches in September 1924, Saints lost 6-0 away to Airdrie, then beat Third Lanark 4-0 at Perth before succumbing 5-3 away to Ayr United.

Bob Penman played in all these matches, and, more notably, also in the last game at the Recreation Grounds and the first game at Muirton, before eventually retiring from playing after his last match with Saints. Given that his first was away to Hamilton, there was a neat symmetry in that his last appearance for (as Saints were then often called) the "Light Blues" was also against the Accies. This time, the game was at Perth and, unlike his debut, Saints didn't lose, instead drawing 2-2.

The final match of his record sequence was, as stated, away to Celtic. It must be said it wasn't a happy occasion. Celtic, who would go on to finish third in the League that season saw off the Perth men by four goals to nil.

Despite this, the PA was not convinced Celtic were particularly good, instead preferring to place the blame on the Saints' forwards who, their reporter said, *"experienced perhaps their worst spell of shooting this season. It was certainly not the Celtic opposition that beat them."*

While the final scoreline might refute that last statement, the match report in the PA does make a reasonable attempt at making the case for Saints. By all accounts it was a very open and (unexpectedly) clean game. The PA's scribe wrote, *"It was one of the best League games it has been my pleasure to see in the First Division. Throughout, it was fought on the most clean and sportsmanlike lines, and the first infringement I can recall took place in the second half when McInally was penalised for hands."*

The difference between the sides was summed up thus: *"only the Celts could cap their outfield play by securing goals, something that St Johnstone completely failed to do. As a matter of fact, I don't think it's any exaggeration to say that Peter Shevlin had more to do than Peter Gardiner, but those shots with which the Celtic custodian had to deal lacked sting, and were not of the same calibre as those that came from the Celtic batteries."*

There were only a few references to Bob Penman in the PA's report, both of which stressed how well he had played. The first was as follows: *"The second half was nine minutes old. Soon afterwards, Penman robbed the Celtic Centre (McGrory) of increasing his goal average."*

Perhaps surprisingly, given that there had been considerable comment in the local paper in the week beforehand about Penman's forthcoming 100th consecutive match, there was only a brief mention of it towards the end of the report when, in a paragraph that is more about John Jamieson than Bob Penman, we can read, *"It was a long time before Jamieson found his feet, and perhaps it was fortunate for 'Saints' that 'Bob' Penman was celebrating his hundredth consecutive game by revealing perfect form."*

In its pre-match report, on 11th December, the Dundee Courier suggested that not only was this a club record but also that his appearance *"will set up what is generally accepted as a record for Scottish football."* In passing, we should note that it was not a record as (unsurprisingly) several goalkeepers had already played 100 consecutive matches. In addition, leading Scottish football historian John Litster has identified nine outfield players who probably beat Penman to this feat, notably Robert Russell of East Fife, who played 114 consecutive league and cup matches in seasons 1923-24 and 1924-25.

Nevertheless, the Courier went on, *"Bob is one of the best club players in Scottish football, and a wide circle of admirers will join in wishing him a long continuance in his number of consecutive games."*

However, the Courier was slightly less effusive in its match report, commenting that, *"Bob Penman, playing his hundredth consecutive game for his club, put in some good work, but he was never brilliant."*

The Courier also noted that Penman had also played every match for Albion Rovers for the two seasons prior to joining Saints, giving him a mammoth 180 (or thereby) number of consecutive games.

After Bob retired from Scottish football, he went to live in Canada, where he continued playing until 1935, before returning to Perth in 1938 (PA cutting below).

Ex-Saint Returns From Canada

" Bob " Penman's Long Innings In Football

Perth Folks Out West

Mr " Bob " Penman, one of the most popular members of the St. Johnstone team during the Perth club's initial spell in the First Division, has returned to the Fair City after almost ten years in Canada.

There are two further things about Bob Penman which we think are worth noting. Firstly, apart from his then record-making run of consecutive appearances, he only played a further 33 times for Saints, but in not one of those 133 games did he score a goal for the club.

Secondly, after he sustained an injury in this game against Celtic, his replacement in the Saints' team was a young right back, signed from Bridgeton Waverley, who - like Penman - didn't score for Saints and in fact, and as we shall see in the next chapter, never scored a goal in his entire professional career. Despite this, he went on to eclipse Bob's record and set a new one that, given the demands of modern football, is unlikely to be broken by any other St Johnstone footballer in the near future – if at all…

Saints team: Gardiner; Penman and Jamieson; Swallow, McBain and Lochhead; Kirby, McLean, Munro, Black and Toner.
Attendance: 6,000.

No. 17

Had it not been for the inches of mud, at least two of the goals would never have entered the net

The all-time record number of consecutive appearances (Willie Steel, 162)
Armadale 3, St Johnstone 0, Scottish Football League, Second Division,
Volunteer Park, Armadale, Saturday, 25th April 1931

St. Johnstone's Wind-Up.

Same Old Tale from Armadale—No Results.

Cowper and Fairbairn Show Up Well.

(By " BARBARIAN.")

ARMADALE, 3 - - - - - - - - - - - ST. JOHNSTONE, 0

Headline: Perthshire Advertiser

Football reporters (and indeed football historians) have a distinct disadvantage over most of us in that their/our musings are readily available in print and if, indeed when, they/we make a right Horlicks of a prediction it's there for all to see for posterity.

This applies in spades to an unfortunate PA reporter who, writing under the pseudonym, 'The Rover' prior to a St Johnstone match against Airdrie in December 1926, noted that with Bob Penman having sustained an injury against Celtic (see previous chapter), his replacement would be a young lad from the west called Willie Steel.

To-day's Football.

BOB PENMAN CRIES OFF: A BIG TEST FOR STEEL.

The PA was generally enthusiastic, but, on the other hand also seemed to be hedging their bets as to how Steel would fare against an Airdrie forward line that included the

celebrated Bob McPhail, who went on to play for Rangers and Scotland. 'The Rover' was hedging his bets about the young lad's chances...

"Pitchforked into the first eleven all of a sudden, Steel is set a big job to tackle ... and the Bridgeton Waverley recruit has a rare opportunity to do himself proud. His first real test synchronises with Airdrie on the crest of a wave ... my only fear is that Steel is not quite ripe for First League fray, although it will be pleasing to be mistaken in this viewpoint."

The Dundee Courier was a bit less concerned, focusing more on Penman's absence and blithely noting that *"Steel will be drafted from the reserves into the breach."*

In the short term, it might seem that 'The Rover' was correct. Airdrie proved, as they have at other times, to be a bogey team for Saints and Steel and his fellow defenders endured a torrid afternoon at Broomfield, eventually running out losers by six goals to one.

The Courier didn't beat about the bush, commenting *"Their defeat by Airdrieonians can only be described as humiliating. Never has the Perth defence undergone a more severe gruelling, and at times they were made to look almost foolish by the clever play of the smart home forwards."* The real blame was placed on the half-backs (*"In the pivotal berth, McBain has never played a poorer game for St Johnstone"*), but the debutant right-back got off lightly, with the Courier telling its readers that, *"Steel, in place of Bob Penman, played a whole-hearted game, and did not let his team down."*

Bob Penman returned to his accustomed berth but age was catching up with him and he had serious competition from Steel for much of the rest of the 1926-27 season, with the older man increasingly moved to left back, thus allowing Willie to become firmly established on the right.

Indeed, he became so firmly established that from the 13th August 1927 until the 25th April 1931, Steel played every League and Cup match for Saints. This meant that he played every league and major Cup match for four seasons in a row, a total of 162 consecutive games.

His last match for St Johnstone came at the end of Saints' first season back in the Second Division. Having been relegated in 1930, it was thought that Willie would be snapped up by a bigger club and although that did eventually happen, Saints did benefit from his presence for the entire campaign. He was clearly playing at a level below his ability though and at the end of the season Liverpool came in for him and he went to the English First Division, where he demonstrated his quality by only missing a handful of games in the next four seasons.

Before all that, there was the small question of whether Saints would be able to regain their top flight status at the first time of asking. Sadly, that proved beyond them

and, as they approached the final match of the season, they were several places below Third Lanark and Dundee United, the eventual champions and runners-up respectively.

Armadale, on the other hand, were in the doldrums. By the end of the 1920s, the West Lothian club was in dire financial straits, employing mainly local lads on expenses and striving to avoid finishing bottom of the Second Division and having to apply for re-election to the Scottish League. Although a cup tie with Rangers in 1931 helped swell their coffers, the poverty of the area conspired with the unhelpfulness of the SFA (who refused to allow Armadale to organise dog racing at their ground to try to raise money) and the club eventually folded in November 1932.

Unsurprisingly, Armadale were in amongst the clubs at the foot of the table when Willie Steel and his team-mates came to visit for the final league match of the season. But when they arrived at Volunteer Park, the St Johnstone players must have realised that it was going to be a strenuous afternoon. Today's younger fans will find it hard to believe, but in days gone by, the quality of the pitches often had more in common with cow pasture than with the pristine sward that we are used to nowadays. This is how the PA described the conditions at Armadale…

"The pitch was a perfect quagmire with pools of water spread over it, and at the goalmouths the mud was inches deep."

This was not a day for fancy football: something that the home side realised but was seemingly lost on the Saints' team as they *"played the short-passing game to perfection but due to the appalling ground conditions it did not pay. When it came to the critical point the ball either stuck fast in the mud or came to rest in a pool of water and by playing a waiting game the defenders had an easy job in stepping in and punting clear. In comparison, the homesters swung the ball hard from wing to wing, keeping it in the air, and as a result they spread-eagled the Saints' defence."*

One other difference from today's football was in the conduct of the linesmen. The PA's reporter was unimpressed, noting that *"on numerous occasions the half-backs, of both teams, sauntered up and threw in the ball at a point yards away from the actual spot."* Perish the thought that players in the 21st century would never take a throw-in from where the ball went out, but back then this was regarded as a disgrace, or, as the PA's scribe wrote, *"This would not be tolerated in the premier Division and it should not be allowed in the Second."*

The reason for this is not hard to find. Unlike today, when there are official SFA linesmen for all senior matches (and other grades), up until the Second World War the linesmen in both Cup and League matches were officials (or players) from the competing clubs for games outside the First Division. For Saints, relegation had brought not only a decline in the quality of football but also in the quality of officiating.

With a dreadful pitch, dodgy officials and opponents on their uppers, the inevitable happened and Saints lost 3-0. However, it should be recorded that, at least as far as the Perth press was concerned, the score did not reflect the game. The PA reported that Saints *"gave every whit as much as they received and a draw would have been a fair result to both sides."*

Whilst not so upbeat, the Dundee Courier put the blame squarely on the Saints' half-backs (although they gave Bain an honourable mention, stating he *"deserved a word of praise"*), but over the piece their reporter concluded that, *"in all other departments they were quite equal to Armadale. Their forwards, however, were not so deadly when near goal."*

To be fair to Saints, their team that day included Cowper at right back, who was a juvenile trialist from Craigie, while other youngsters in the team included Fairbairn, an ex-YMCA player, at left half and Caul on the right wing. According to the PA, Cowper, *"did not let the side down,"* although, *"he was to blame for the loss of the first goal."* In contrast, *"the play of Fairbairn was a revelation,"* but unfortunately *"Caul's showing was as disappointing as Fairbairn's was successful,"* and *"in the end (Caul) was the weakling of the team."*

The conditions undoubtedly played a major part in the final score. Even Sandy McLaren, the best and most famous of all St Johnstone's goalkeepers, struggled, with the PA recording that, *"(he) had a trying time. He was unlucky to be beaten three times, and it is perfectly safe to say that had it not been for the inches of mud, at least two of the goals would never have entered the net."*

The Courier took a similar line, telling its readers that *"It was thanks to particularly fine goalkeeping by McLaren and steady work by the backs that kept scoring against the visitors within reasonable limits."* It's worth noting that when papers of this era refer to *"the backs"* they generally mean the full-backs rather than the entire defence as we would today. And of course, one of those full-backs was Willie Steel.

Like his first match for Saints, it was not an occasion, to remember. However, as on his debut, Willie was one of the few Saints' players to emerge with pass-marks. The PA noted, *"Steele (sic) put in a power of work at left back and helped to retrieve some of the mistakes of his partner. He kicked the ball from all angles, with both feet, with perfect freedom and accuracy and was easily the best of the backs."*

The end of this game meant the end of the season. St Johnstone, hoping to get straight back into the First Division, finished fifth in the Table with 44 points, (Armadale finished third bottom). Of the 38 matches Saints played, half of them had been won, 13 had been lost and there were six draws. That would be a reasonable performance in today's Scottish Premiership, but there was a substantial difference between then and now. In the 2020-21 season, when Saints also finished fifth in the table, we had more or less the same number of points (45 - although remember that in 1931 there were only two points for a win) but had scored 36 goals and conceded 46.

In contrast, in 1931, the PA was very disappointed with the goals for and against tallies, commenting, *"Their goal average makes poor reading. The team have scored seventy-six goals while sixty-one have been scored against them."*

We suspect that many of today's fans would be delighted for such *"poor reading..."*

Saints team: McLaren, Cowper and Steel; Bain, Pryde and Fairbairn; Caul, Ferguson, Cameron, Miller and Cargill. Attendance: 500.

Egged on by the vocal exhortations of 8,000 frenzied spectators

St Johnstone are top of the First Division for the first time
Queen of the South 0, St Johnstone 2, Scottish Football League, First Division,
Palmerston Park, Wednesday, 12th September 1934

Headline: Perthshire Advertiser

In Scotland, our football is dominated by two teams, both of which have so much more money than all the others that it's very hard for any other club to win the top Division. Indeed, other than for brief periods, such as Aberdeen's dominance in the 1980s, or perhaps some freak results in the first few games of a new campaign, the names of either Celtic or Rangers have invariably been first (or second) in the table for most weeks of every season. During the inter-war period, only one club other than Celtic or Rangers won the First Division, and that was Motherwell, in season 1931-32.

In the 1934-35 season, Saints had made a good start and after six games were jostling amidst a pack of other clubs for the top spot. Moreover, at this point they were unbeaten in the League and had only conceded four goals. For good measure, they had also won all their Dewar Shield matches, including the final against Aberdeen. A round of midweek fixtures, played on 12th September, offered St Johnstone the opportunity to top the First Division for the first time in their history. To do so required the team to travel to Dumfries and beat a solid Queen of the South team on their home patch.

As the press made clear, this is just what they did. The Courier, under a headline that proclaimed, *"Saints still winning,"* began its report by stating, *"St Johnstone were in first rate fettle at Dumfries and won well."* The Evening Telegraph, under their headline of *"Saints Sitting Pretty at the Top,"* went on to say, *"Great stuff this by the Muirton boys ... It is Queen of the South's first home defeat this season and their first defeat at Palmerston in a league game since January 2."* The Scotsman recorded, *"St Johnstone played brilliant football to beat Queen of the South by two goals to nothing at Dumfries last night."*

The PA had a much more comprehensive report, in their case under a gleeful headline that announced, *"St Johnstone Lead Footballing Scotland"*- before going on to say, *"Saints had to play for their victory, let there be no mistake about that. There was one period in the game in fact when there was grave danger that Saints might surrender their undefeated record. For about fifteen minutes of the second half* the homesters, egged on by the vocal exhortations of 8000 frenzied spectators, launched a desperate attack upon Wylie and there was a suggestion of panic in Saints' efforts to meet the onslaught." And, in a situation which will seem familiar to many modern-day fans who are regularly subjected to ultra-cautious and defensively-inclined football, "The inside men fell back so far that when the ball was cleared there was no one to carry it upfield."

That said, the visitors did start much the better and opened the scoring in only three minutes with what seems to have been a slightly fortuitous goal involving two Saints' forwards, one of whom, Alec Stewart, had been playing principally at outside left for the previous few seasons but had been converted into a centre-forward early in the season. He rewarded his manager with two more goals in this match, taking his tally for the season to six, although it must be said that his first in the game in Dumfries seems to have been a trifle lucky. Here's the Courier's reporter again with his description of how Stewart's first counter came about: "Fotheringham only partially cleared a Tennant corner, and Davidson paved the way for the goal with a snapshot. The ball rebounded off Stewart into the net."

The Scotsman's account is very similar to the Courier's, stating: "St Johnstone had an early success, and three minutes from the start Davidson sent in a short range shot after Fotheringham made a partial clearance of a corner kick by Tennant. The ball rebounded off Stewart's body and went into the net."

Still, they all count, and any quality Stewart's first goal lacked was more than made up for by his second. It was, by all accounts, well deserved, with Saints dominating the first third of the contest, as observed by the PA, although it was also noted that Stewart could, perhaps should, have had even more goals to his name…

"During the first half hour Saints bewildered the homesters and their supporters by the regularity with which they found their men, by the speed at which they carried out perfect forward moves, and but for brilliant defending by Allan, and to a lesser degree Culbert and Savage, Saints would have had the game won during that spell when they played football several degrees higher than anything they had produced in the opening games. Their lead should have been greater than it was at the interval for Stewart missed two excellent chances and the level of marksmanship was not very high."

It wasn't only Saints whose standards of marksmanship were lacking on occasion. The PA described how it took Queen of the South nearly half an hour to force their first corner of the match, but when their outside left, Tulip, went to take it, "he was so surprised that he almost had a 'fresh air' from the triangle."

To be fair to Queens, they took the game to St Johnstone in the second half, but they were considerably hampered by an injury to Allan, their centre half. This happened in the 52nd minute when a clash with Bobby Davidson resulted in Allan having to leave the field. With no substitutes in those days, Allan did what was expected of him, namely to return to the field and limp along by the touchline or, as the PA put it, "He returned to cripple on the right wing." Queens reshuffled their team, with right half Gordon going to centre half and inside right McGinley dropping back to right half. For whatever reason, this acted to the home side's advantage and it was after this enforced, tactical change that they rallied and put St Johnstone under considerable pressure.

However, Saints weathered the Dumfries storm, with the half-backs and full backs performing admirably in repelling the home forwards. Particular mention was made in the PA of Littlejohn, who was reported as playing *"the game of his life,"* and Welsh, who *"was the most polished player afield."* The game had only some 20 minutes left on the clock when St Johnstone scored a decisive second goal: *"From a throw in, Tennant caught the home defence by surprise, cut in, and transferred to Stewart who took on the turn a ball which came awkwardly and drove it into the corner of the net away from Fotheringham."*

With 15 minutes remaining, Allan's injury was causing him such discomfort that he had to leave the field again, leaving Saints able to play out the remaining time without much pressure, as the PA related: *"From then until the close Saints were the masters of a leg-weary Queen's."*

The crowd was largely composed of locals from in and around Dumfries, but it was noted that there were also *"a few enthusiastic supporters who had made the long journey from Perth to Dumfries by road."* Bearing in mind there were no dual carriageways or motorways in those days and cars were nothing like as reliable as they are today, that was a lengthy trip for anyone to make.

One fan who made a slightly shorter journey was Robert Campbell, the Saints chairman. He had been on holiday at Turnberry, but travelled south to watch his beloved team outperform Queen of the South and *"lead footballing Scotland."*

Mr Campbell, and the other enthusiastic supporters who travelled from Perth, must have had an enjoyable journey home. Over the next few days, as they looked at their newspapers, they will have seen the happy sight - shown here – of St Johnstone at the top of the First Division table. This was something they got used to over the next few weeks and indeed months as Saints continued to outperform their rivals and be regularly mentioned in the press as genuine title challengers.

SCOTTISH LEAGUE—DIVISION I.

Airdrie	0	Dundee	3
Dunfermline	1	Ayr United	2
Hamilton	6	Aberdeen	1
Hearts	4	Albion Rovers	0
Partick Thistle	1	Motherwell	1
Queen of the S.	0	St Johnstone	2

The Positions.

	P.	W.	L.	D.	F.	A.	Pts.
St Johnstone	7	5	0	2	13	4	12
Clyde	7	5	0	2	14	7	12
Rangers	7	5	1	1	20	7	11
Hamilton Ac.	7	4	1	2	20	10	10
Motherwell	7	4	1	2	12	4	10
Dundee	7	3	1	3	11	7	9
Aberdeen	7	4	2	1	10	10	9
Hearts	7	3	2	2	10	5	8
Airdrie	7	4	3	0	15	18	8
Celtic	7	2	2	3	9	4	7
Hibs	7	3	3	1	7	10	7
Queen's Park	7	2	3	2	8	10	6
Partick Thistle	7	2	3	2	7	12	6
Queen of South	7	2	4	1	5	10	5
Albion Rovers	7	2	4	1	7	13	5
Ayr United	7	2	4	1	13	17	5
Kilmarnock	7	2	5	0	13	16	4
St Mirren	7	1	4	2	5	12	4
Falkirk	7	0	6	1	5	15	1
Dunfermline	7	0	6	1	6	19	1

SCOTTISH ALLIANCE.

Kilmarnock	2	Galston	2

Sadly, it was not to be. They remained top for a few weeks before slipping up against Falkirk, but then regained the initiative with a number of good wins which took them back to the summit in mid-October, where they remained until the 10th of November. They were still in contention at the end of the year, being only one point (although in fifth place) from the top at Christmas, but by mid-January a slump in form meant the leeway became too great and they eventually finished fifth. Nonetheless, this was the first of St Johnstone's great sides and, in many respects, arguably the second best of all time, after Willie Ormond's Saints.

These were, of course, different eras, but the fact that this St Johnstone team was considered to be genuine championship contenders for almost half a season – something it's almost impossible to conceive of nowadays – shows how good they were and, equally importantly, how highly they should be regarded today.

Saints team: Wylie: Welsh and Clark; Mason, Littlejohn and Campbell; A. Ferguson, Davidson, Stewart, Dickie and Tennant.
Attendance: 8,000.

The type of soccer we associate with Continental sides

The first game against European opposition
St Johnstone 1, Admira Wien 2, Friendly match,
Muirton Park, Wednesday, 21st April 1954

Headline: Perthshire Advertiser

Unlike St Johnstone, Admira Wien no longer exists today: having merged with several other clubs in the post-war period they currently ply their trade as FC Flyeralarm Admira Wacker Mödling (the first part of their name being their major sponsor) in the Second Division of the Austrian Bundesliga. Despite their most recent ups and downs, Admira Wien (as they were then) were one of the more successful Austrian clubs during the inter-war period, winning the national championship eight times and the Austrian Cup three times.

In April 1954, Admira embarked on a tour of Scotland, playing matches against Kilmarnock, Hearts, Aberdeen Reserves, a Rothes/Elgin XI, Stirling Albion, an Inverness Select XI – and St Johnstone.

The first inkling we have of their match at Perth comes in the Directors' Minutes dated 16th March 1954, where there is a note to say that a letter had been received from Admira FC, Vienna, requesting a game against St Johnstone. The directors sent a response with the terms they wanted for such a match. Clearly, Admira were casting around for games, for Saints received a speedy reply and at the board meeting of 6th April the game was set for the 21st of that month.

This meant that the friendly against Admira would be the third last match of the season, sandwiched between the last two B Division games and another friendly, against Blairgowrie. Saints knew they weren't going to get promoted that season (they eventually finished 6th), so there was presumably not the same pressure as there would have been if they had been in with a chance of going up to the First Division (and in those circumstances it's hard to imagine the directors agreeing to the Admira match).

The game itself was a revelation for the fans who came along to see Saints play a European team for the first time. It's clear from the match reports that this wasn't football as it was then known in Scotland. The PA made their feelings clear in the first few paragraphs of their report, telling readers, *"In deservedly winning at Muirton Park on Monday night the Austrian tourists played the type of soccer we associate with Continental sides. Masters of the close-passing technique, they were backward perhaps in shooting. But the 4,500 spectators came to see an exhibition match, and in that respect they were not disappointed. Dominating the first half, Admira impressed with the accuracy of their short passing and their ability to keep themselves and the ball constantly moving. The spectators also enjoyed the experience of seeing a typically Continental defence formation in action. Their attacking centre half adopted a roving commission in midfield. The duties of a stopper pivot were taken over by the right back, whose own role was the special assignment of the right-half. On the evening's showing, the system worked effectively, although the guileless St Johnstone forwards did not provide a difficult test."*

Another unusual feature of the visitors' play was that their goalkeeper invariably threw the ball rather than kicking it. Here's the PA again, *"The safe showmanship of 'keeper Gilly was a further diversion, but there was nothing showy about his prodigious throws. Seldom kicking the ball, he found a colleague with 100 per cent accuracy by hurling it, sometimes as far as the mid-way line. In his hands it was a quick and reliable way of turning defence into attack."*

Faced with this – for them – novel approach to the game, it was perhaps no wonder that the Saints were a bit overwhelmed. This was despite the manager, Johnny Pattillo, taking the field. Pattillo had joined Saints as player-manager in February 1953, but had only played a handful of games in the last few months of that season. Presumably (and, let's be honest, who can blame him), he probably couldn't resist the opportunity

to test himself against a different type and calibre of opponent.

Led by Habitzi, their captain and inside right - what we'd today call a midfield general - Admira seemingly bemused the home players, but by half time only had one goal to show for their dominance. This came in the 25th minute, when centre forward Weissenboek touched home a cross from Soldattisch.

This game was also notable as being only the second time that Saints used a substitute (see Chapter 10 above for the first time). We can only presume this had been agreed beforehand, because Admira also made a substitution during the match; in their case during the first half when Weissenboek sustained a cut to his leg and was replaced by Ceyka. In Saints' case, left back Montgomery had also injured his leg and left the field some eight minutes before the interval, with Ernie Ewen dropping back into defence. In the second half, Saints put on Landles to replace Montgomery. Interestingly, given they had no experience of describing the business of substitutions, the PA's team-lines - as shown in the cutting here – suggest Landles replaced Ewen, but what they meant was that he went into Ewen's left half position, rather than replacing him on the field.

ST JOHNSTONE—Maclaren; Fraser and Montgomery; Pattillo, Woodcock and Ewen (Landles); Tobit, Steel, Rodger, Young, and Newlands.
ADMIRA WIEN — Gilly; Line and Hansy; Schuller, Fichtl, and Ganger; Soldattisch, Habitzl, Weissenboek (Ceyka), Tapy, and Pingerra.
Referee—E. Yacamini, Perth.

Whether this substitution made any difference is not mentioned, but Saints came more into the game after the resumption and scored an equaliser in the 51st minute when, as the PA described it, *"a smart Rodger pass gave Steel a chance to snatch the equaliser with a shot from almost the penalty spot."* The Austrians were not going to be denied though and in 71 minutes substitute Ceyka fired home a 20-yard drive that left Roy McLaren in the home goal with no chance.

The Courier only carried a very short report which, despite its brevity, encapsulated everything that the PA had said. The Courier's acknowledgement that *"St Johnstone were a bit behind in the arts,"* was supported by one of the Saints' fans who was at the game. Donald Paton, was 13 years old at the time…

"I remember particularly that Saints wore a different strip from our normal one: instead, we had white tops with a broad, blue band, in the style of Motherwell's kit. As for the game itself, I recall that it wasn't the best match I've seen, but the excitement came from the fact that we were playing a continental team for the first time.

"Admira's style of play was certainly different from Saints' – we were used to the old 2-3-5 formation, getting the ball forward, whereas Admira attacked out of defence in a way we hadn't seen before."

Donald's recollection is particularly useful because we, in common, we suspect, with the vast majority of Saints' fans, will have seen the only photo of this game (which is, of course, in black and white) and thought that it was Admira Wien in the strip with the broad band.

The results of Admira's tour were mixed, including a heavy defeat (0-5) at Kilmarnock, a win at Hearts (2-0), a win (2-1) over Aberdeen's reserves, another big loss at Stirling (1-5) and a defeat by both the Inverness Select (1-2) and the combined Rothes/Elgin side (2-3).

Whether this puts Saints' loss in any kind of perspective is very hard to tell. We might presume that Admira's players found it difficult to maintain any level of consistency, given they played seven games in 15 days. Nonetheless, for St Johnstone and their fans, this was an enjoyable first taste of foreign football. It would be some 11 years before the next one, when Slovan Bratislava played a friendly at Muirton in November 1965, and then a further six years after that before Saints played their first competitive match in Europe.

Saints team: McLaren; Fraser and Montgomery (Landles); Pattillo, Woodcock and Ewen; Tobit, Steel, Rodger, Young and Newlands.
Attendance: 4,600.

A great cheer rose from the crowd as the new floodlighting system was brought into operation for the first time

The first match under our own floodlights
St Johnstone 0, Hearts 3, Scottish Football League, First Division
Muirton Park, Saturday, 28th November 1964

Sport

Hearts Will Be First to Play Under Lights

THE St Johnstone match against the English Cup winners, West Ham United, to hansel the new Muirton flood-lights has been arranged for Wednesday, December 16.

Both clubs agreed on the date, but West Ham may have to call off if a third game is necessary to decide their European Cup-tie. Such a match would have to be played in Germany on the 14th, and it would be out of the question for them to rush to Perth for a "friendly" two days later, and then be expected to play on the following Saturday.

Saints hope to play their first competitive match under the new lights a week on Saturday, with a 3 o'clock kick-off, against Hearts. Manager Bobby Brown has been assured the lights will be in action by that time.

There are still some fans alive today who remember matches having to start early in the winter months because otherwise they would have finished in almost total darkness. Clearly, as lighting technology improved (think of wartime searchlights for example), it made sense to consider how artificial lighting might allow football matches to be played at night

Although there were experiments in the nineteenth century with lighting, the first Scottish club to make any kind of effective use of floodlights is reckoned to be Inverness Caledonian in the 1930s, although even then these were just powerful light bulbs mounted on poles. They were used for a testimonial match against Clachnacuddin on 22nd March 1933 and bizarrely they were then taken away to be used to help in the search for the Loch Ness Monster.

Stenhousemuir then became the next club to try to use floodlights, introducing them in 1945 for training. At the same time, they introduced a sound system. The latter was used for what is believed to be the first time in Scotland to play music and announce the team for a match. This newsworthy event took place on 22nd December 1945, against, believe it or not, St Johnstone.

When floodlights were properly introduced in the 1950s, St Johnstone were in the Second Division and not exactly flush with cash. Although there were 'training lights' alongside the pitch, the board had discussed the possibility of erecting proper floodlights for some years, but these discussions grew more earnest in the early 1960s. In the summer of 1961, the directors sought tenders for the supply of floodlights and for the construction of an enclosure roof at Muirton. The latter went ahead, while the lighting project was put on hold and then relegation in 1962 put a further damper on any aspirations in this regard. The manager, Bobby Brown, was keen that the board move ahead quickly on the issue and his cause was aided by the team regaining their top flight status at the first time of asking, in season 1962-63.

As a result, the directors asked the electrical contractors James Scott and Co to revise their previous tender bid with a view to the project going ahead at the end of 1963. However, this didn't happen and it wasn't until February 1964, when Saints sold Jim Townsend to Middlesbrough for £20,000 that the club eventually had the money for the floodlights to be erected. The final decision to install the lights wasn't made until July 1964, but once James Scott were given the go-ahead the work proceeded quickly.

The game that most people, erroneously, regard as Saints' first floodlit match is the official 'switch-on' against West Ham on the 16th of December. This featured some of England's most famous footballers, including two, Geoff Hurst and Martin Peters who would go on to win the World Cup in 1966. The Hammers' - and England - captain, Bobby Moore, was injured and had to watch the game from the grandstand.

The West Ham match was played in dreadful conditions, which probably accounts for the fact that only 4,800 turned up to see it. This match was significant for another reason, namely that, to the best of our knowledge, it was the first time Saints produced a programme that had more than two colours: in this instance blue white and red, rather than the usual blue and white. For the real anorak programme collectors out there, the first time Saints had a proper, full-colour programme was for a Drybrough Cup match against Partick Thistle on 31st July 1971. The programmes were predominantly blue and white throughout the 1940's, 50's and 60's, although in 1955-56 and 1956-57 they very occasionally black and white and in 1957-58 there were two red editions for the League Cup. There was also a further black and white production for a game on 1st January 1958.

However, although this is the match everyone remembers, the first use of the new lights actually came a few weeks earlier, at the end of November, when, as the cutting from the PA shows, Hearts were the visitors and thus the first club to play against St Johnstone under the Muirton Park floodlights.

Hearts were very much a team in form, being unbeaten to this point in the season. They would eventually go on to finish equal on points with Kilmarnock, but lost the title on goal average by the incredibly slim margin of 0.042. However, on this historic occasion they had to weather a promising opening flurry from the Saints, who forced a corner in the opening seconds and another soon after, but failed to score. At this stage in the proceedings, the PA tells us that, *"Hearts really had their backs to the wall during this relentless opening spell by the Muirton boys ... A clever Kerray-Duffy-Flanagan move had Cruickshank looking lively to prevent a score. Minutes later, Cruickshank made a great save from a close-range Kerray rocket."*

Hearts then had a purple patch towards the end of the first half but, like Saints earlier, were unable to turn their pressure into a goal. As the next day's Sunday Mail described it, Hearts' centre forward, Tommy White, *"could do absolutely nothing right and it looked like being one of those days."* In particular, there was a concentrated period of pressure from the Jam Tarts from around the half hour mark when, *"in ten fantastic minutes Hearts had an amazing series of misses. In the 32nd minute White shot high over from barely six yards and shortly afterwards the centre had a header pushed out by McVittie. Wallace hit the 'keeper's foot with a fierce shot, and White missed from close range. Gordon finished it off by hitting the post."*

It's not hard to get a good impression of how this game had gone up to this point, with Saints having opened well but then being forced on the back foot as the half wore on. Then, just before half-time, Saints put together another spell of pressure *"and for a while completely unsettled the Tynecastle defence, which had previously looked so confident. But the homesters were unable to find the net."*

During the half-time interval the new floodlights were switched on. The PA tells us that, *"A great cheer rose from the crowd as the new floodlighting system was brought into operation for the first time. The most up-to-date in the country at present, the lights looked impressive and were extremely effective."*

Perhaps they shouldn't have flicked the 'on' switch, because, although guilty of those bad misses in the first forty-five, White and Hearts did most things right in the second half. As the PA described it, *"Superior teamwork and striking power were what really told in the end... If determination alone could win games, then Saints would have been in with a real chance, but though their spirit didn't fade*

under the second half floodlights, the incisiveness of the attack, particularly the inside trio, was not sustained at the pre-interval level. Once they had snatched the lead, Hearts never looked back."

The Jam Tarts' first goal came on the hour mark, when White headed home a cross from Willie Wallace. The latter also made the second Hearts' goal with a cross from the right, which White headed down to Hamilton who had an open goal in front of him and didn't miss. Then, three minutes before the end, White got his second after Ron McKinven misjudged the flight of the ball and his header was wayward, straight to the Hearts' centre forward's feet. White hammered it past McVittie in the Saints goal to seal the victory.

Saints team: McVittie; McFadyen, W. Coburn; McCarry, McKinven, Renton; Flanagan, Duffy, J. Coburn, Kerray and McGrogan.
Attendance: 10,000.

No. 21
Beaten, but certainly not disgraced

The first major national final
St Johnstone 0, Celtic 1, Scottish League Cup Final,
Hampden Park, Saturday, 25th October 1969

EARLY GOAL PUTS CELTS ON VICTORY PATH

Saints Go Down Fighting in Scottish League Cup Final

CELTIC 1, ST JOHNSTONE 0.
(Half-time: 1-0.)

Scorer—Celtic—Auld (2 minutes).

Headline: Perthshire Advertiser

For those who are old enough, perhaps their abiding memory of the Ormond team that contested the League Cup final of 1969 was of a team that ought to have won *something*. That was certainly the view of Jim Craig, one of the Lisbon Lions who played against St Johnstone that day.

This was arguably the season when the masterly mix of youth and experience that was Willie Ormond's Saints' team really began to gel, as amply demonstrated in the first competitive games of the season in the Scottish League Cup…

In those days, as is the case today, the League Cup began with groups of teams playing each other in a mini-league to see who would earn the right to go through to the next stage of the competition. For Saints, this round-robin of matches saw them drawn in a group with Kilmarnock, Partick Thistle and the old enemy from down the Tay.

They breezed through the qualifying, beating Dundee 3-1 in the first match of the competition at Muirton and then 2-1 in front

of a 13,500 crowd at Dens in the second last group match. In between those games, Killie were defeated 3-2 at Rugby Park and 2-1 at Muirton, but the really impressive performances came against the hapless Partick Thistle, where there was an aggregate score over the two games of 12-1 in favour of Saints. Eight of these goals against Thistle came in the famous 8-1 win at Firhill (of which more below).

The quarter final was played over two legs, home and away, against Falkirk. The Bairns were greeting at the end of the first match, after Saints came away with a 5-1 victory. The margin of victory at Brockville was exactly the same, except this time Saints won 6-2.

Motherwell were our semi-final opponents, this time in a winner-takes-all contest on the neutral turf of Hampden. Goals from McCarry and Aitken were sufficient to see a classy Saints' side through to the final. Lifelong fan Ian Slater recalled that, in his opinion, *"this was one of the best performances I've seen. Jim Argue at left back played a stormer and the interplay and balance between the forwards and defence was excellent. As a result, we went off to the final full of anticipation, mixed, naturally, with trepidation."*

The final, also at Hampden, was against Celtic. Seven of the Celtic 12-man squad (only one substitute was allowed then) had been in the Celtic squad for the European Cup final in 1967. Fallon, the goalkeeper against Saints was the unused sub for that match, while Jimmy Johnstone was on the bench for Celtic in the League Cup final. There was some speculation at the time – in the PA at least - that the reason wee Jinky was left out of the starting line-up was because Jock Stein *"felt that Johnstone never really turns in a good display against Willie Coburn."* It had been expected that another Lisbon Lion would be on show, but, in a surprise move, Tommy Gemmell was left out of the side, possibly because he had been sent off playing for Scotland against Germany the previous week.

At this time, Celtic were already past the midway point in winning their first 'nine-in-a-row' League Championships (from 1965-66 to 1973-74) and Jock Stein's side were, unarguably, the finest in Scottish football history. That said, Saints had drawn 2-2 with them at Parkhead, just over a month previously (see Part III below) and, on their day, were a match for anyone. The PA carried an article that gave pen portraits of each St Johnstone player. What's really interesting about this is that it shows that the physical differences between players then and today. In 2023, it's normal to have several six-foot-plus defenders and the occasional big striker - and it's not unexpected for a goalkeeper to be six foot five. In contrast, it is remarkable to see the heights and weights of this 1969 team.

Saints' fans of this era will remember we all talked about 'big' Freddie Aitken. Here, he's listed as being only 5 foot 9 inches tall. Kenny Aird was the archetypal 'wee' Scottish winger, and at 5 foot 6 inches that

sounds about right. There are only three players recorded at six foot or over – Buck McCarry and Ian McPhee, who were both six foot exactly, and the biggest man in the squad, Jim Donaldson, who was 6 foot 2 inches. Amazingly, the two central defenders, Benny Rooney and Alex Gordon, were only 5 foot 9 inches and 5 foot 10 inches respectively. The full backs, John Lambie and Willie Coburn, were only 5 foot 7 and 5 foot 8 inches. The average weight was c. 11 stones 5 lbs, compared to 13 stone today (see chapter 16 above), with only one man (Buck McCarry) being over the current squad's average weight.

John Connolly remembers that as a result of Saints' epic results in the earlier rounds, the press hyped up the team. However, as John says, *"this was entirely deserved. In particular, I remember Jock Stein was quoted as telling his Celtic players that this was going to be anything but an easy match."*

Nonetheless, before the game, the Saints' players were, understandably, somewhat nervous. Jimmy Donaldson told us, *"We were staying in a hotel and got to the park quite early. We went out to kick the ball about – there was nothing like the warm-ups they do nowadays – and there was this huge roar from the Saints' fans. Then the Celtic team came out. The roar from their fans was deafening, eclipsing the noise of our supporters."*

Henry Hall has similar memories to Jim, telling us, *"It was a big occasion, our first cup final and we were really up for it. That was the biggest crowd I played in front of in my career. We did enjoy it, even though the result wasn't there. Both sides were built on attacking football but their defence was very solid. John Clark and Billy McNeill made a formidable pair of centre halves who just played hard and fair. They were surrounded by decent players and there wasn't really a weakness anywhere in their team. That made it very difficult for* us to create many chances. They were just slightly better than us."

As Henry noted, it was not to be St Johnstone's day. The Sporting Post, in its rolling record of the proceedings, commented in its half-time *"Reflections"* that *"Celtic deserve their interval lead which could have been greater. Harder in the tackle, they have been stronger off the ball and quicker to it. Saints have tried hard, but so far have been well below their best. The occasion and the loss of that early goal have definitely affected them."*

That *"early goal"* came in the second minute, but only after Fallon had saved from Henry Hall in the opening seconds of the game. Jimmy Donaldson recalled the Celtic goal for us, as follows…

"We were under pretty much constant pressure in the first part of the game. Their goal came when I tipped Chalmers' header on to the bar. It simply bounced back and Auld was there to knock it in."

The second half saw St Johnstone come back into things, with the PA telling us, *"Saints turned on a great display after the interval, and in fact had the bulk of the play, but the equalising goal eluded them."*

They might have lost, but it should be emphasised that this was an excellent, entertaining match. The PA reported, *"The opinion of the crowd was that it was one of the best finals for many a long year, and the excitement was at fever pitch throughout. Both sides played excellent, attacking football, and it was a 90-minute thriller that will be hard to better."*

Other than the single goal, both sides had opportunities to score throughout the 90 minutes. Hughes missed what looked like an open goal for Celtic, while on another occasion, Chalmers failed to convert when clean through. For St Johnstone, the PA reported that, *"Rooney – who played his*

heart out – had probably Saints' best effort with a tremendous right-foot shot that deserved a goal, but somehow Fallon managed to turn the ball round the post."* In addition, *"Saints were also denied a penalty when Connolly was brought down in the box by Billy McNeill, when clean though, but the referee ruled that he was outside the box."*

This wasn't the only time Connolly was kicked to the floor by McNeill. It should be borne in mind that in those days, fouls that would today result in an instant yellow, or even red, card were ten a penny. The PA's reporter summed up the contemporary ethos thus, *"Although this was never really a dirty game, tackling was hard. I was very disappointed in the tactics of Celtic's internationalist centre-half Billy McNeill, who seemed more intent in going for the man rather than the ball, and Saints' inside forwards Hall and Connolly suffered many crude tackles."* At one stage, the PA tells us, *"Three times in the space of a minute the Saints' inside forward was sent tumbling by the Celtic centre-half."*

Ian Slater believes this was a key part of Celtic's match plan – to nullify Saints' danger men. He was still at school and, to his surprise, his dad, who normally took him to the terracing at Muirton, bought tickets for the stand.

"We – me, my dad and grandfather - were in the main grandstand, right in the middle, just below the press box. My memories of the game are a bit sketchy, but I do remember the huge Saints' following in the 'Rangers' end' of the ground. Obviously, I remember Auld scoring in the first couple of minutes. They couldn't do much about the goal. However, one thing that did stick out was the way McNeill went for Connolly straight from the kick-off. The Celtic skipper knew he wouldn't get booked. As a result, Connolly had a quiet game which was an injustice I still feel aggrieved about today. Saints had quite a few breaks and

chances, Hall in particular, but it wasn't our day. I was very sad for my father and grandfather, neither of whom saw Saints lift a trophy. But 45 years later, I did!"

The aggression wasn't only in one direction, however, with Jimmy Donaldson receiving a booking *"after a clash with Harry Hood."* What happened was Celtic had a goal disallowed for offside but Hood didn't move ten yards back from the resulting free-kick, so *"The Saints' keeper took exception to this..."* For all those who remember seeing big Jim Donaldson in action, this will come as little surprise...

More seriously, in the 33rd minute, Buck McCarry was badly hurt in a tackle with Jim Craig and had to have four stitches put in a gash caused by the Celtic right back's studs. While Saints' fans and players tend to remember this and believe that it was a deliberate ploy to take out one of Saints' most durable performers, it ought to be remembered that Stevie Chalmers was also forced to leave the field after a tussle with John Lambie in the 50th minute. This St Johnstone side could dish it out as well as take it.

Well as Saints played, at the end of the day though, the Sporting Post's final summary is, it has to be admitted, both fair and accurate...

"Summing-Up – Gallant Saints put up a brave show in their first Hampden final. They had more of the second-half play, but just not the decisive finishing punch. They were beaten, but certainly not disgraced in this very hard-fought, but always interesting match. The Perth men were naturally very disappointed and showed it as they left the pitch. At the end of the day there was only one goal in it. On chances, Celtic just deserved their win.

John Connolly told us that after the game, as the players sat dejectedly in their dressing room, it was hard to take: *"It has*

always struck me that Jock Stein came into our dressing room to congratulate us on how well we'd play. Jock had that respect for our team. But that early goal was a killer, especially after we could have gone ahead in the first minute. Henry, bless him, is always reminded of his chance by the lads, but later that evening, after we'd had a few drinks, we sat back and thought we'd not done badly and the game could have gone either way. I still have my runners-up medal, somewhere..."*

There were 73,067 fans in Hampden that afternoon. It's reckoned that around 15,000 of these were St Johnstone supporters. Here are a few of their stories...

Like Ian Slater, Andrew Tulloch was also in the main stand. He told us, *"My dad bought stand tickets; it wasn't like him. I was only eight so perhaps he wanted to make sure I could see. I do remember feeling very small, even though I was sitting down. Our seats were towards the 'Rangers' end' where the Saints fans were and before the match started one of our fans ran on the pitch and got arrested. I remember my dad saying, 'that was a waste of a ticket.' Of course, Celtic scored very early in the game and the whole stand erupted, but despite losing that early goal my memory is that Saints were dominant in much of the match. At the end of the game, I wanted to see the Cup being lifted but my dad said, 'no, let's go.' I'd been to see Saints at Celtic Park before and I'd been at Hampden for the semi against Motherwell, but this was the biggest crowd I'd been in to that date. Just a pity about the result."*

Another Saints' fan who didn't get to see the game was a friend of Jim Masson, who told us that his mate had come through on a well-refreshed bus and discovered an urgent need to relieve himself. He found a close off Somerville Drive only to discover that the Glasgow polis, understandably, took a dim view of that sort of thing. Consequently, he spent the afternoon in a cell on the southside of the city and didn't get to see any of the game. Unfortunately, as explained later in this book, this wasn't the first time he'd missed an entire Saints' match due to errant behaviour.

Ian McLaren was only nine when he attended the final. He recalled...

"I used to go to Muirton from an early age. My dad and his dad used to stand at the top of the terracing at the Florence Place end, but I was trusted to go down to the barrier and watch the games from there. For the next few years, I was always down there, behind the advertising hoardings. Standing there, you got a different perspective to what we have at McDiarmid today. You felt very close to the players, which somehow made the match seem more real. As an 11-year-old, I remember that adults could bring cans of lager and export into the ground and the aroma of beer – and cigarettes – was all round, especially when the cans were thrown onto the pitch-side track. Also, by then I was allowed to walk home by myself – something I suspect that not many parents would allow an 11-year-old to do nowadays."

For the final, we went to Glasgow on a supporters' bus and my sister came with us. She didn't often go to games, so it was a measure of how much of a milestone my dad thought this was that she was encouraged to be there.

Unfortunately, we were slightly late in getting to the ground and had to queue to get in. We were in the old North Stand and I distinctly remember how tired my nine-year old legs were as we climbed up the steps. It was just past three o'clock as we made our weary way up the flight of stairs. Then we heard an enormous roar. Of course, we didn't know who had scored and I was downhearted to get to this stupendously high-up seat with an amazing view to find out that Bertie Auld had put Celtic one up."

Bill Powrie was a student at Edinburgh University in 1969. He hired a bus to take all the Perth boys from Edinburgh to Glasgow for the final. Like others, he recalls that, *"there was no segregation, so we were mixed in with the Celtic fans, who considerably outnumbered us. Their presence had a not-unexpected inhibiting influence on our conversation and our ability to be free in our match observations.*

"After Auld scored a tap-in in the second minute, my recollection is that Saints controlled the game. John Connolly came very close and Henry Hall missed an absolute sitter as Saints outplayed the 'home' team.

Being surrounded by green and white scarves it was difficult to feel totally relaxed, and I remember feeling quite threatened by the proximity of the opposing fans. However, when the final whistle blew and we all turned to leave the ground, one of them turned to speak to me. I wasn't sure what kind of threat he was about to make, but, to my astonishment ... and relief, he simply said "No a bad wee team ye hiv there."

Not every Saints' fan had such a happy experience of the Celtic supporters. Alistair Forbes, who was on the bus from Edinburgh University with Bill, told us that *"I was fortunate to make it back to Edinburgh, as upon leaving Hampden I was accosted by a very large Celtic fan who took umbrage at all of the blue attire I was wearing. He picked me up by the lapels, and threatened to make it an unhappy day for me. Luckily, he then just put me down - I was glad, at that point, that Saints hadn't won."*

Among the many other fans who we spoke to about this game, one, Alastair Mitchell, emailed with a fascinating story about the plans that were made in advance in case Saints did win the Cup. Unlike in more recent years, bespoke 'Cup-Winners'

T-shirts were not in vogue (or easily printed), but in the week before that match someone wondered, *"what do we do if Saints win?"* The answer was for the team to be met at the station by an open-top bus, and taken down South Street, then along Tay Street to the City Chambers for a reception. This was a very exciting prospect in 1969.

Sadly, there was no open-top bus available locally but one was fortunately found - in Aberdeen. The bus set out in the morning - not a simple journey on the route or roads in 1969 and in a vehicle with a top speed of 50mph at best. It duly arrived and waited for its moment at the Tay Street bus shelters. As we know, the team and the city were denied their parade and the poor bus had to make its lonely way back up the road to the Granite City.

St Johnstone team: Donaldson; Lambie, Coburn; Gordon, Rooney, McPhee; Aird, Hall, McCarry, Connolly, Aitken.
Substitute: Whitelaw (for McCarry)
Attendance: 73,067.

The first competitive European match
SV Hamburg 2, St Johnstone 1, UEFA Cup, First Round,
Volksparkstadion, Hamburg, Wednesday, 15th September 1971

SAINTS' HARD FIGHT

HAMBURG 2,
ST JOHNSTONE 1

ST JOHNSTONE must be happy about their first foray into European competition, for their display in Germany last night means that they have a great chance of going forward in the UEFA Cup.

Headline: Press and Journal

When the draw was made for the first round of the new UEFA Cup tournament in 1971, St Johnstone found themselves paired with SV Hamburg, or to give them their proper name, Hamburger Sport-Verein. The German club had much success in the 1960s, winning the DFB-Pokal (the German equivalent of the Scottish Cup) in 1963, then reaching the final again in 1967, where although they lost, they were still admitted to the European Cup-Winners' Cup because Bayern, who won the DFB-Pokal, were also Bundesliga champions and therefore played in the European Cup.

Subsequently, Hamburg reached the final of the Cup-Winners' Cup, where they lost to AC Milan. Their star player throughout this period was Uwe Seeler, who was named German Footballer of the Year three times, the last in 1970. Seeler spent virtually his entire career with Hamburg, scoring 507 goals from 587 appearances in all competitions. Along with another Hamburg colleague, defender Willi Schulz, he played for West Germany in the 1966 World Cup final against England and was captain for that match. These were the two big names, but the Hamburg side was filled with other very talented footballers and there was no doubt that Saints were the underdogs. Perhaps fortunately for the visitors, two hours before the game kicked-off, Schulz, along with two other Hamburg players, called off with flu.

Going to Europe was a much bigger thing then than it is today. John Connolly told us that he had never been abroad until he joined Saints – and that this was true of some of the other players, both old and young. In contrast, Henry Hall told us that when he was at Stirling Albion he had actually been on a tour of Greece, Iran and Japan, playing in a number of friendly matches. The Binos' goalkeeper on that tour was former Saints' great Billy Taylor, while another former Saint, Jim Kerray, scored a brace in a first match against an all-star Japanese eleven - with Henry also scoring a double in the second game against this same Japanese select side.

It should also be noted that foreign travel wasn't quite so easy in those days as it is today, but quite a lot of Saints' fans made the effort to see their team in European competition for the first time. Consequently, when the players left their Hamburg hotel for the match, some 30 or 40 fans were there to cheer them as they set off with a police escort to the ground.

Amongst those who travelled were Stewart Duff, who would go on to become St Johnstone's Managing Director under chairman Geoff Brown, and Donald Paton.

Stewart told us how he was one of a group of fans who met at the St Johnstone Aid Club on North Methven Street, who then travelled to Edinburgh for the flight to Hamburg. As they flew into Germany and began their descent, Stewart noticed that there were, in effect, two Hamburgs, the one that was heavily damaged during the war and the new city, rising from the ashes of the old one. Donald remembered this too, reminding us, *"we are talking about 1971, only 25 years after the end of the war, so there was still a lot of bomb damage. I particularly remember an old church spire, twisted incongruously amongst the modern buildings."*

When they got to the stadium, Stewart recalled that, *"It was like the old Ibrox, steep and high. We were on one of the higher bits of terracing, so we got a good view, including their first goal, which we all thought was offside."*

The players themselves had no time to take in the sights before the match. Henry Hall told us, *"Even in Scotland, we didn't see much of a town when we travelled. We were in a coach and there to play the game rather than admire the scenery.*

That said, the players did have time for some social activities. Jimmy Donaldson recalled how, *"We went to a bar where there was a German 'Oompah' band, with all their big brass instruments playing away. The trombone player wasn't taking part, so John Lambie marched up and took the conductor's baton, rapped the trombonist on the knuckles and told him to start playing!"*

After the match, many of the Saints' fans descended on Hamburg's infamous tourist attractions and, as Stewart Duff and Donald

Paton both told us, were slightly surprised to see some of the players out on the town as well. Having been a star player, Willie Ormond was not daft and he knew how footballers behaved, but even so he was happy to let them off the leash. Gordon Whitelaw recounted how Ormond told the players that night, *"Just make sure you're back in time to catch the plane"* Donald Paton recalled how he and his pals helped some of them do just that when they met *"Jim Argue and a very drunk Derek Robertson. Jim didn't know how to get Derek back to the hotel so we all carried him back!"*

For those younger fans who have been fortunate enough to see St Johnstone's greatest era during the last decade, games against European opposition have become relatively commonplace. Back in 1971, because this was all new, the excitement was off-the-scale. Although there was a lot of experience in that Saints' team, there was also some younger talent, with Jim Pearson being only 18 while John Connolly was 21.

It's fair to say that the style of play in those days was very different from today. At that time, Scottish teams were all set up to play in more or less the same way, namely in a 4-2-4 formation with an emphasis on attacking. However, some aspects of the 'continental' style that Saints encountered on that trip to Germany were different. John Connolly told us that he found that there was more of an emphasis on man-marking from the Germans, something he encountered again later in his career when he moved to Everton and played a number of pre-season friendlies against German sides, noting how, *"Bertie Vogts, who subsequently became the Scottish national team manager, was one of the best at this: he'd literally follow the left-winger around the pitch and ignore the other players."*

Whereas modern teams will invariably set out 'not to lose' the away leg of a European tie, Willie Ormond's Saints simply couldn't play that way. It's noticeable in the Courier's report of the game in Hamburg how many chances Saints made and also how, *"Willie Ormond's boys did what they promised – they attacked throughout the match."*

John Connolly confirms this, telling us, *"We were going to Hamburg to have a go. In those days, you didn't have video analysis and mountains of research and statistics and there was no real tactical stuff. We never changed our system, no matter who we were playing."*

Another feature of football in the 1970s was just how tough and uncompromising it was, or, as the Courier put it, *"It was a hard, bruising tie, with many players taking knocks."* Once more, John Connolly corroborated this, noting, *"that's one of the things we did find about all the European teams we played that season. Those guys knew how to throw tackles in and they didn't take any prisoners."*

Gordon Whitelaw recalled that, although he wasn't playing, one 'continental' feature of the game, which was anathema to the Saints' players, was the behaviour of some of the German fans, who spat on the players as they came down the tunnel at the start of the match.

The Germans opened brightly, although John Connolly tested their keeper with an early shot. Then Bjornmose brought out a great save from Jimmy Donaldson before Hamburg took a controversial lead. The Courier describes what happened…

"A dreadful decision by the referee cost Saints a goal in 10 minutes. Seeler tried to go through on his own, but was stopped by Rennie. The ball broke into the Saints' penalty area and it seemed at least three German players were offside. But the referee allowed Zaczyk to go through and net. The St Johnstone defence waited for an offside decision, and Donaldson just stood

and watched the German put the ball past him into the net."

Donald Paton remembers this well, telling us, *"It was a blatantly offside goal. Jim Donaldson let him walk round him and the ref gave it so we were one down. Then Pearson equalised, it was a bit of a sclaffy goal to be honest. Towards the end Hamburg got their second, but everyone I was with thought we'd do them at home. That Ormond team had old-fashioned wingers in Aird and Aitken, playing in the old Scottish style. It was a far better game to watch in those days."*

Jimmy himself confirmed that both the Courier and Donald Paton's descriptions were spot-on, telling us, *"It was so far offside that I didn't go for it!"*

In contrast to the first Hamburg goal, when Hall netted for Saints on the half-hour mark, the referee (correctly) had no hesitation in disallowing the goal for offside. In the same move, Jim Pearson collided with the German goalkeeper, Kargus, who was then carried off on a stretcher and replaced by Oscan.

Henry Hall had another great chance when clean through in the 37th minute, but Oscan managed to deflect his shot over the bar. Both sides were causing each other problems, with Seeler pulling the strings for Hamburg and Ian McPhee coming close with a couple of shots for Saints before the half-time whistle sounded. The Courier's verdict at that point was, *"They (St Johnstone) suffered the loss of a highly controversial goal … but came back fighting off the ropes and were unlucky to be trailing by the only goal at the interval."*

There was nothing controversial about Saints' equaliser. John Lambie crossed from the right and when the ball was deflected off a defender, keeper Oscan was caught on his heels, allowing Jim Pearson to steer the ball into the corner of the net.

Jim Pearson was only 18 at this time. The prospect of an 18-year-old being selected to play in European competition for Saints today is remote, but as Jim told us, *"At that age, as far as I was concerned, it was just another game. You don't think too deeply about it at the time, but I do remember it was a nice stadium and we were aware of just how good a team Hamburg were, but Willie Ormond sent us out to take them on.*

"Even today, I can remember Willie before the match, telling us, 'Right, we're going to have a go, we're playing 4-2-4 and at that point I could see some of the older lads thinking, 'is this right?' but we went out and did what the manager asked.

"John Lambie made my goal. John was a great lad who made me laugh – in fact, talking to you about him I'm starting to laugh now. He laid it on a plate really and all I had to do was tap it in. Then he ran across and said words to the effect of, 'I've made you a star again son'..."

After Jim's goal, Seeler then had another terrific shot well saved by Jim Donaldson, while at the other end, the Courier tells us, *"Oscan remained the busier keeper, although shots from Pearson, Connolly and Hall all went wide of the mark."*

Inevitably, and against the run of play, Hamburg went back in front. Naturally, it was Seeler who instigated the move, passing out to the previous scorer, Zaczyk, who closed in on the goal before firing a low shot which deceived Jimmy Donaldson and went in at the far corner.

Their tails up, Hamburg pressed for a third, but Saints held firm. Four minutes from the end, Aitken came on for Hall, to become the first substitute used by St Johnstone in European competition, and then it was game - but not the tie - over. Defeated, yes, however, as the Courier noted, *"they will have a second chance on September 29."*

Henry Hall summed up for us how the players felt after this match: *"I think we surprised ourselves a wee bit in Hamburg. After all, they were a great team, but Willie Ormond was a master at making us feel positive. He never had any doubt in his mind that we could get a result by playing our normal, attacking game. Even at 2-1 down, having seen Hamburg, we felt we could turn the tie around when they came to Perth..."*

And as we shall see later, turn it round they most certainly did...

Saints team: Donaldson; Lambie, Coburn; Rooney, Gordon, Rennie, Aird, Hall, Pearson, McPhee, Connolly.
Substitutes: Robertson, Aitken (for Hall), Whitelaw.
Attendance: 14,000.

The first ever game on a Sunday
Forfar Athletic 1, St Johnstone 6, Scottish Cup, Third Round,
Station Park, Forfar, Sunday, 27th January 1974

Headline: The Courier

When organised football began in the late nineteenth century, the idea of playing on the Sabbath was anathema to everyone involved in the game. Sunday was a day of rest, not recreation, reinforced for centuries by the presbyterian ethic that permeated most of society and culture in Scotland. In 1424, even before John Knox arrived on the scene (in the 16th century), King James I approved a law which meant that anyone caught *"playing the futball"* was punished by a fine of four pence.

It wasn't just football: golf was also banned. The intention was that men should, instead, practise archery to prepare for battle when required. The 1424 Act decreed that *"...football and golf should be utterly condemned and stopped. And that a pair of targets should be made up at all parish churches and shooting should be practised each Sunday ... And concerning football and golf, we ordain that [those found playing these games] be punished by the local barons and, failing them, by the King's officers."*

In 1491, James IV continued with this ban on both sports, despite it being known that he actually enjoyed them. There are Treasury accounts that show several footballs were bought for the King and also that handcrafted golf clubs were made for him in Perth in 1502.

However, the Scottish Parliament generally disapproved of ordinary people playing golf when they should have been at church. In Perth in 1604, six boys were caught playing on the Sabbath on the North Inch. The ringleader was fined and he and all the others were ordered to repent publicly before the congregation.

Things had changed a bit by 1974. Morals and ethics tend to move with the prevailing winds. For better or worse, depending on your age and point of view, it was from that year that football in the United Kingdom began to be played on every day of the week.

The first professional match played on a Sunday was an FA Cup tie at 11.30 am on 6th January 1974, at Cambridge United's Abbey Stadium, with Oldham Athletic the visitors. A record crowd for that season attended, and there were high attendances at the other FA Cup matches later that day.

Other games in England, especially in the lower Divisions, were played on a Sunday that season, although there was then a hiatus, with relatively few Sunday matches until 1983, when the first-ever televised league match on a Sunday took place between Tottenham Hotspur and Nottingham Forest. Money talks, and Sunday football has been a regular feature of every season since then, both north and south of the border.

Scotland, like England, had introduced Sunday football in January 1974. One of the reasons for this (as was the case in England) was the OPEC crisis of 1973, exacerbated by the national miners' strike and continuing industrial unrest, all of which led to power cuts and consequently clubs wanted to alter kick-off times so they wouldn't need to pay for floodlighting. Earlier kick-off times were not popular, so an alternative was to play on Sundays. The PA of Wednesday 30th January explained that the SFA had held a special executive meeting to allow clubs *"to play on a Sunday during the present crisis."* The previous Sunday, St Johnstone had taken part in the club's first ever match on the Sabbath, a Scottish Cup tie at Forfar.

With Saints the First Division club and Forfar in the Second, an away win might have been expected. Certainly, manager Jackie Stewart was disarmingly honest in a programme interview a few weeks before this cup tie. He wrote, *"I must admit the thought of facing Second Division opposition in a cup competition concerns me in view of Saints track record of late in games of this nature. Raith Rovers, Stranraer and Kilmarnock dismissed us in second games and I can assure you these experiences have not been at all forgotten. At Station Park we will be extremely alert and all out to end the Second Division hoodoo in decisive fashion."*

In the event, Mr Stewart was proved right, but it must also be said that what wasn't expected, at least according to the PA, *"was the poor show put up by the Second Division side."*

The Courier agreed with the PA, commenting that while Saints *"were expected to win, of course ... most onlookers thought Forfar would put up a much better show."*

The Dundee paper also noted that Saints' first penalty was *"a soft award but technically a penalty."* This brings to mind the famous referee Willie Young's exasperated response to a manager (Sandy Clark, when he was at Hamilton) when he was berated for giving a 'soft' penalty. *"It's like boiled eggs,"* Willie said to Sandy, *"They can be hard boiled or soft boiled, but they are still boiled eggs."*

Once Saints had opened the scoring, they settled into the game and – as the Courier recorded, *"It was really all over by half-time. The only question was how many would Saints' score."*

The final score was a reflection of almost total domination by St Johnstone. Brian Doyle, who was one of the 3,635 attending that day, recalled, *"The winter of 1973-74 was really a tough time for the whole of the UK, with the miners' industrial dispute resulting in a three-day working week. Shops, factories, and offices were all affected. Football was not exempt and games had to kick off early in order to finish in daylight, as floodlights could not be used. As was usual at that time, I travelled to Forfar with my father, father-in-law, and brother-in-law to watch the game. It was a cold day and there were no programmes issued. The game itself was very much a one-sided affair, reflecting the difference in the quality of players, with Jim Pearson's hat trick being the highlight of a match made memorable only for being played on a Sunday."*

Although the first five years of the 1970s saw the gradual break-up of Willie Ormond's great Saints' side, it's easy to forget just how much talent there was in this team. Jim Donaldson was still between the sticks, Jim Argue at left-back, Alex Rennie in midfield alongside the two Gordons - Smith and Cramond - the latter being accurately described by the PA as the *"wee general (whose) passing was inch-perfect and his positional sense uncanny."*

Gordon Smith, *"topped a fine performance with the best goal of the match, crashing home an Argue cut-back from the edge of the penalty box."* and was then described as *"one of the best young midfield players in the country."*

Henry Hall, still playing his heart out for the blue jersey, could have scored a hat-trick, but was defied time after time by Milne in the Forfar goal. And, of course in those days most sides, Saints included, had two wingers to add entertainment and goals. At Forfar, these were John Muir on the right and John Hotson on the left. To show how good they were, Fred Aitken was only on the bench, along with John McQuade, another mercurial talent.

Despite Henry Hall's bad luck, Saints did run amok; however, although the final tally was six, only three players actually scored the goals - Pearson, Muir and Smith - and the one who made the biggest contribution to the outcome was Jim Pearson, who notched his first competitive hat-trick in senior football. The PA recounted how the young, blond striker had *"one of his best displays of the season* (and) *must be happy to see his return to the goal standard."*

Jim himself recalled that although two of his goals were penalties, he had a tough struggle against the Loons' centre-half, Bob Hopcroft: *"In those days, centre-halves liked to get stuck into you, especially if they were from a lower league side. There was a different attitude towards violent play back then. When I played in England, if one of the notorious hard men, Norman Hunter of Leeds or Chopper Harris of Chelsea, put on you, you just got on with it and pretended not to be hurt. Nowadays, forwards would be rolling around in agony if someone like Bob Hopcroft 'tackled' them.*

"I remember when I went to take the first penalty, Hopcroft said, 'if you're taking it the ball will never reach the goal' – well,

something like that – then after I scored, I ran past him, saying, 'It just made it, eh?'

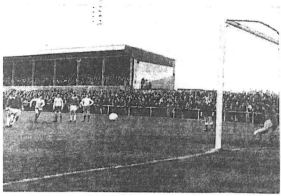

Forfar keeper Jim Milne goes the wrong way as Jim Pearson converts from the penalty spot for the Saints' first goal.

Photo: The Courier

"The third goal was actually something we'd worked on in training. The idea was that when we got a corner, someone would block the defender at the front post and then I'd flick the ball on for someone to score at the back. The block worked well, but I obviously got it wrong, because instead of flicking it on I headed it into the goal."

Forfar scored their only goal of the game in the 66th minute. Jimmy Donaldson recalled how he was at fault: *"It was such a one-sided game I can't remember too much about it, other than I was so untested that I spent some time speaking to the fans in the crowd. Then, all of a sudden, Forfar attacked, I was out of position and they scored. I got some stick for that, I can tell you."*

Despite Forfar getting that consolation goal, the reality was, as the Courier called it, *"a slaughter on the Sabbath ... Saints coasted near the end and could afford to be careless. They could easily have grabbed more goals."*

Saints team: Donaldson; Ritchie and Argue; Rennie, Kinnell and Cramond; Muir, Smith, Pearson, Hall, Hotson. Substitutes: Aitken (for Hotson) and McQuade (unused). Attendance: 3,635.

"Opportunist" could have been John Brogan's middle name

John Brogan becomes Saints' top scorer
Alloa Athletic 0, St Johnstone 2, Scottish Football League, First Division,
Recreation Park, Alloa, Saturday, 20th November, 1982

Champagne Brogie

Graham Fulton

ALLOA ATHLETIC 0, ST JOHNSTONE 2
(Half-time 0-1)

Scorers: John Brogan (44 mins.), Stuart Beedie (53 mins.)

Saints had rolled into Alloa as proud table-toppers with a good volume of support and helped to make up the home club's best league gate of the season. Alloa, on the other hand, showed they had no fear of reputations and

half-time advantage. As a contest, the game looked over in 53 minutes when a great Pelosi shot was punched away by Hunter and in the resultant scrimmage a free kick was awarded to Saints on the edge of the box.

dit, however, they played their hearts out, with Brannigan in particular, giving 101 per cent. endeavour. It showed the superb physical fitness that has been achieved with the Perth squad and at the end of the day it

Headline: Perthshire Advertiser

Just in case, a box of Moet & Chandon champagne had been brought on the bus through to Alloa. The reason why was simple: John Brogan, having equalled Ian Rodger's club record number of 116 goals the previous week, when he got one of the two goals Saints scored against Raith Rovers, was hoped – nay, expected – to become St Johnstone's all-time leading goalscorer. Naturally, Brogie didn't disappoint…

St Johnstone, under manager Alex Rennie, were trying to get back into the Premier Division. They had been trying since 1976, with no success up to that point. Having lost the young star that was Ally McCoist the previous year, Saints were actually looking like they might, at last, restore themselves in the top flight, although they were facing stiff competition from Hearts, who were not enjoying one of their periodic spells outside the Premier League. Going into the game, St Johnstone were top of the table and consequently took a healthy away support through to Clackmannanshire, helping produce the best league gate of the season at Recreation Park.

Alloa, in contrast, had only been promoted to the First Division that season, having finished second behind Clyde in the Second Division in 1981-82. On paper, which is

always a dangerous place to play football, Saints would have been expected to win.

The home side, who eventually finished comfortably in mid-table, actually started the match pretty well, forcing a number of corners and also having a claim for a penalty turned down by the referee. The Sporting Post recorded that, *"In the 20th minute they were unlucky not to open the scoring. Smith sprang Grant clear and his sweeping cross was sliced past the post by Campbell."*

The PA agreed that Alloa had begun the match well, telling their readers, *"Alloa … showed they had no fear of reputations and stormed down the considerable slope towards Mike McDonald's goal.*

"It must be said that in territorial terms, Alloa had the bulk of that first half." However, *"While big striker Ian Campbell, recently signed from Montrose, caused a considerable amount of trouble, his shooting was inaccurate and it was the Perth side that retained all the composure that was going."*

Saints settled into the match and Andy Brannigan hooked a Tam McNeil cross wide before they took the lead late on in the first half. And, of course, the goal that put

St Johnstone ahead was scored by that man. Here's the PA's Graham Fulton describing the record strike…

"'Opportunist' could have been John Brogan's middle name and he showed why in that history-making minute. A few seconds earlier he had what looked a reasonably good goal chalked off for offside when he got a touch to a John Pelosi corner kick.

"That merely delayed the celebration. Pelosi came right back with a strong run and a shot which Alloa keeper Donald Hunter could not hold. Brogan was lying in the right place to collect the loose ball and hit it home."

The Sporting Post, recording in real time as always, was much more succinct…

"Brogan had the ball in the net following a couple of corners but offside nullified the score.

"In the 44th minute, Brogan netted easily after Pelosi's shot had been parried.

"His 117 goals for Saints is a team record.

"Half-time – Alloa 0, St Johnstone 1"

And here's John on the goal…

"I had had a goal disallowed, a bit harshly in my opinion, but to be honest I really wasn't too concerned about whether I scored or not. What mattered was winning promotion: achieving the record didn't enter my mind. In the event, the goal was a bit scrambled - nothing spectacular. It's just the striker's instinct: being in the right place at the right time. They all count, whether they are long-range spectaculars or tap-ins. I remember a game against Arbroath at Muirton when I was up against big Joe Carson. It was a miserable game, going nowhere, then in the last minute Micky Lawson chased a ball to the bye-line,

got it and crossed for me to tap in from about a yard. I remember Joe saying, 'you are so jammy, you've done nothing all game,' and I just turned to him and said, 'in tomorrow's Sunday Mail the score will be 1-0 to St Johnstone and I'll be down as the goalscorer'."

The second half saw Saints continue to press, although their task was made harder by the pitch, which was cutting up badly. While there was delight at Brogan's feat in becoming the record goal-scorer, the objective was to win the game and, eventually, to gain promotion. To that end, a second goal was required and it was duly delivered in the 53rd minute. Here's the PA's description:

"… a great Pelosi shot was punched away by Hunter and in the resultant scrimmage a free kick was awarded to Saints on the edge of the box.

"Jim Morton tapped the ball to Stuart Beedie who blasted it right-foot into the corner of the net for a well-struck goal."

Once again, The Sporting Post was a bit more sparing in their description…

"In 53 minutes Saints went two up when Beedie shot home from a set piece from 20 yards out."

Jim Morton then blotted his copybook by taking a swing at Alloa's Grant. He landed his punch right on the winger's beezer and Grant, who was also booked, was taken off with a suspected broken nose. Morton also left the field, although in his case it was at the request of the referee who reckoned that punching someone in the face deserved a red card.

The PA was a little more reserved in its description of Jim's faux pas, merely recording that, "Morton had been having an on-going niggle with winger Arthur Grant and this flared up three minutes after the goal. The Dundee man took a poke at Grant and the referee Willie McLeish had no option but to show him the red card. Grant was booked for his part in the incident."

It's worth noting that the man himself doesn't agree with this. When we spoke to Jim in 2023, he remembered it well and told us, "It was a niggly game. In those days you had to keep an eye on everything, what happened, and learn to look after yourself as some players would deliberately leave a foot in.

"What happened with Grant, who was just a wee guy, is that I had tackled him and the ref blew for a foul. I then saw someone running at me at speed so I put my hand out to fend them off and hit him in the face, right in front of the ref. It wasn't a punch."

Unfortunately, the referee didn't agree with Jim and sent him packing anyway.

When we asked John Brogan if he agreed with Jim's version of events, he said, "That's as good an excuse as you'll get! Willie McLeish was an old school ref, who wasn't up for any nonsense."

A few weeks after the Alloa game, Ian Rodger, the former record holder, graciously agreed to hand a specially made commemorative trophy, in the shape of a golden boot, to the man who had taken his crown.

The picture here shows Brogie receiving the award from Ian at Muirton. Sensibly, the number of goals was not added to the trophy as he went on to score another 23 before his career at Perth came to an end. The golden boot now has pride of place in John's Hamilton home. While records are definitely made to be broken, given the paucity of goals in the modern game and the relatively short tenure most players have at

any one club, it's unlikely that we'll see a Saints' player presented with a similar trophy by John Brogan in the near future.

John Brogan receives a golden boot from Ian Rodger to mark his record goalscoring feat: Photo: St Johnstone FC.

It's fairly obvious from the various match reports that the contest at Alloa wasn't the best of games ("Not the greatest victory of the season," said the PA), but it was nonetheless another significant step on the way to promotion back to the Premier league. The battle for the championship went to the wire, with Saints having to defeat Dunfermline on the last day of the season to secure the title. They won 1-0 and the man who scored the goal was, of course, John Brogan. On that occasion, it was a spectacular effort, but it was a very difficult game, as John recalled: "I remember that goal very clearly. I picked the ball up from a throw-in, turned inside and hit it from about 25 yards into the bottom corner. However, Dunfermline really hammered us that day; I seem to recall we had the ball cleared off our line, but we hung on, rode our luck and got our reward of promotion to the top flight."

Saints team: McDonald, McVicar, McNeil, Beedie, Caldwell, Rutherford, Addison, Brogan, Pelosi, Morton, Brannigan. Substitutes: Fleming, Barron (neither was used). Attendance: 1,772.

No. 25
My pal took a large piece of turf home with him...

The last game at Muirton
St Johnstone 0, Ayr United 1, Scottish Football League, First Division,
Muirton Park, Saturday, 29th April, 1989

GUESTS SPOIL SAINTS' PARTY

Headline: Perthshire Advertiser

Muirton Park, the theatre of dreams for several generations of Saints' fans, was at the end of the road. The plans for the new Asda supermarket had been drawn up and the bulldozers and demolition crews organised. The old Dunkeld Road ground - where thousands had thronged over the years, hoping (often in vain) for a St Johnstone victory, and where epic, bravura performances were but a few seasons (sometimes only a few games) away from dismal defeats – was about to host its last ever match.

The visitors for that match, Ayr United, had not had a good season and were in the lower reaches of the table, just two points above second-bottom Clyde and in danger of relegation. Saints, in contrast, had been on a fine run of form since the start of the new year and had made the semi-final of the Scottish Cup, where the then part-time side had held Rangers to a scoreless draw at Celtic Park before being overwhelmed 4-0 in the replay. On the day of the first semi-final, fans leaving the ground had heard the news of the tragic events at Hillsborough. If ever anyone questioned whether leaving an old, decaying stadium was a good idea,

the rising death toll from Yorkshire put an end to any argument.

Although, perhaps understandably, St Johnstone's form had fallen off after the defeat by Rangers, they were still comfortably in mid-table, with 40 points and a goal difference of +13. Ayr were on 31 points with a goal difference of -13.

It's worth remembering that this was still the era of two points for a win (three points for a win didn't start until 1994-95) and also a rather bonkers format in which the clubs outside the top Division played each other three times each season, thus giving one team the advantage of two home games over a potential rival for promotion or relegation. For some reason, doubtless kept a closely-guarded secret by the football authorities, this was never proposed for the Premier Division...

Home crowds had been rising steadily over the previous months, with over 8,000 at the Scottish Cup quarter-final replay against Morton and over 4,000 for the visit of promotion-seeking Falkirk only two weeks before the Ayr United game.

Consequently, another large attendance was hoped for Muirton's last hurrah and, while not matching the Morton game, a very satisfactory 6,728 wended their way along the Dunkeld Road for one last time.

The club made strenuous efforts to mark the occasion in grand style. The Perth and District Pipe Band were engaged to perform – the first time they had done so for many years – and a special, 40-page souvenir programme, on sale for £1, was produced, as were 4,000 commemorative lapel badges with 13 of these having a numbered card attached that could be exchanged for the respective player's shirt. A 'last game' poster was created and first day cover Royal Mail envelopes carrying a history of Muirton Park were on sale. In addition, the club held an Open Day so that fans would be able to tour Muirton from 11 am to 1 pm on the day of the game, letting supporters see the dressing rooms and other facilities for a last time. The fans were also let onto the pitch, as Ian McLaren remembers…

"I was there with my good friend, Dave Amos, the well-known Perth soul singer. After the game, he posed for a photo on the pitch, pretending to take a corner. I bought a poster and a badge and then we made our way to the Florence Place end, where my dad had stood for many years. The other memory I have is that one of my friends used to travel out by the Crieff Road regularly and he told me how the new ground was developing. I have to admit I was more excited at the prospect of going to our new home and had no major regrets about going from the fading glory of Muirton to this brand-new, all-seated stadium."

Alongside the sale of souvenirs and other paraphernalia, another pre-match highlight occurred in the Saints' Social Club when, at 1.30 pm, Doug Barron received his testimonial cheque for £18,000. Equally importantly, and with an eye to the future, the club announced a four-year, six-figure sponsorship with Low and Bonar, the Dundee-based floorcoverings and plastics group.

In their Friday edition before the game, the PA paid its respects to the lady they described as *"St Johnstone's Greatest Fan,"* the 83-year-old Mary Gibson. Mrs Gibson's association with the club is perhaps less well known nowadays than that of her famous successor, Aggie Moffat, but, in fairness, it should be noted that Mrs Gibson has a far greater claim to be the most important 'tea-lady' in St Johnstone's history. Here's what the PA said…

"No question, St Johnstone's greatest fan is 83 year old Mary Gibson. She remembers watching the club in the old Edinburgh Road Recreation Grounds and was present when Queen's Park opened Muirton in 1924.

"'Bowler hats were all the fashion at that time and I was at the game with my mother.'

"Little did she think that one day she would work for the club and become the friend of some of the top names in football.

"It was in 1947 that she took up duty as a backroom assistant, washing jerseys and making sandwiches and tea for the players on training nights. She went on to work with eight St Johnstone managers starting with Jimmy Crapnell and finally calling it a day in 1983 when she retired at the age of 77, with Alex Rennie the man in charge.

"She is still remembered by the many players connected with Saints over the years. Ally McCoist is one of her favourites ('An awfu' nice laddie') and he made a special trip last month from the Scottish international team HQ at Gleneagles Hotel to dash to Mary's Inchaffray Street home for a chat.

"Manchester United's Alex Ferguson never fails to ask for her when he is in the Perth

area as does Hearts' Alex MacDonald. The pair met last month at Doug Barron's testimonial game. John Lambie sought her out when he was back at Muirton with Partick Thistle three weeks ago.

"She hopes to be there tomorrow for what will be a rather sad goodbye to Muirton."

Another long-term Saints' fan who was present at this last match was Tom Gorham, aged 85. Tom had helped construct the Muirton Park grandstand back in 1924 and his family connection continued into the 1990s, when his grandsons, Tom and John, produced the fanzine, 'True Faith.'

Lifelong fan Derek Mitchell recalled that before the match fans had a chance to see around Muirton, *"I had a season ticket in the centre stand and I just remember the long queues to get in. John Sludden, who scored the Ayr goal but had also played for us, was a great player, very skilful. At the end, I wasn't one of those jumping on the pitch but I do remember my sister and her husband took my nephews down to see the dressing rooms before the match. It was a sad day in many ways, but with McDiarmid getting ready it was also an exciting time."*

The game was six minutes late in kicking-off, largely because of the long queues of Saints' fans wanting to get in. The Ayr fans were segregated at the Ice Rink end and they had no such problems. Once the supporters walked through the turnstiles, they immediately saw that four major things were missing. There were no floodlighting pylons as these had been already dismantled, prior to their move to the new ground.

Before the match kicked-off, a largish group of former players and managers took a final stroll round the pitch they had graced in years gone by, receiving an understandably warm reception from the fans. The ex-managers were Bobby Brown and Johnny Pattillo and the former players included Willie Clark who had played in the 1930s, Johnnie Mathers, Charlie Robbie, Willie Peat, Joe Carr, Charlie McFadyen, Paddy Buckley, Jimmy Donaldson, Willie Coburn, John MacKay and Drew Rutherford. After the players had done their lap of honour, some 500 blue and white balloons were released to trouble air traffic over Scone aerodrome. At this point, as Gordon Bannerman recounted in the PA, one wag in the crowd was reported as saying, *"that's 478 more than most Saturdays."*

Unfortunately, when the ball actually started rolling, the game itself was, for Saints' fans at least, not quite as memorable as the occasion.

St Johnstone had gone into the match with many of their likely starting line-up missing due to suspension (Messrs Grant, Treanor and McVicar) or injury (Maskrey and Coyle). Despite a decent opening period, with Sammy Johnston hitting a powerful shot that was brilliantly tipped over by Ayr keeper Watson, the visitors created the more dangerous opportunities, hitting the woodwork (and it was wood in those days) twice. Then, two minutes from half-time, the PA tells us that, *"McCann's long kick out of defence found Sludden on the right. Showing strength and composure, he shook off the opposition and drove the ball low into the right-hand corner of John Balavage's net."*

Ayr went into their dressing room with a lead, while the home fans hoped for a second half resurgence from Saints. Unfortunately, the second half was not especially riveting. The PA suggested that *"a full-strength St Johnstone would have won comfortably,"* and although *"Saints rang the changes in the second half by introducing the talented Gary Maher for John Irvine and striker Billy Spence for Sorbie ... it made no great difference. The nearest the Muirton men came was in 65 minutes when a Cherry shot beat Watson but McAllister popped up to clear off the line."*

The Ayrshire Post, not unnaturally, took a different line from the PA, telling their readers that, *"United rolled up their sleeves and served up a gritty display that was worthy of both points."* The Post's description of the goal adds some more detail: *"McCann's push forward was rewarded when Sludden cleverly held off a challenge inside the penalty area and slotted the ball away from Balavage."*

In a mark of how little the principal Scottish tabloids seemed to care about lower league football at this time, the report in the Monday edition of the Daily Record on this last match at Muirton was as follows: *"St Johnstone hopes of a winning finale at Muirton Park were dashed when John Sludden got the only goal for visitors Ayr."* That was it: one sentence.

To be fair to the Record, they did cover the fact of it being the last game at Muirton in their Saturday edition … in two sentences. In contrast, in their Monday edition, they carried an entire report with a proper heading and several paragraphs on a Scottish Junior Cup semi-final. Clearly, Lesmahagow and Ormiston Primrose were more important than Saints to the Record.

For those St Johnstone fans who had been traipsing up to Muirton for years and, in many cases, decades, it was a strange occasion, tinged with sadness (which was not helped by the result) and also happiness at memories of days gone by.

The great Saints' fanzine, 'Wendy Who?', produced a special issue that included a free plastic fork for fans to dig up some of the hallowed turf after the game. Some supporters took more robust measures to ensure they would be able to remove some of what had been one of the best, and biggest, playing surfaces in Scotland in previous years. Long-standing fan Dave Anderson told us, *"I went with my pal and his young son. There was a huge crowd as I recall and the weather was really sunny.*

We had all turned up for a party, but sadly Ayr burst our bubble. We were terrorised by Henry Templeton, the tricky Ayr winger who always seemed to play well against us.

"Like most of the crowd we were on the pitch at the end and my pal had brought a Tupperware box and trowel and duly took a large piece of Muirton turf home with him, which has now grown into a lawn."

For Alistair Lowe, this last game provoked all sorts of nostalgic feelings… *"I was on my own at Muirton and found it quite an emotional game, standing behind the goal at the Florence Place end as I traditionally did. It was always an amazing feeling being on that particular stretch of terracing, especially in the dark as the floodlights came on, with Saints shooting towards the town.*

"My dad was a dyed-in-the-wool football man. Born in 1922, he played junior football locally and began to take me and my brother to the football in the late 1960s. When I was 11, I became a regular attender at home matches. Saturdays meant football, parking at the Barracks car park, walking up the Dunkeld Road and then standing on the terracing at Muirton. In those days, kids were given a lift-over the turnstiles for free and I remember when I became 17 and could drive, I parked in Florence Place and walked across the road to the ground where a wee boy called out to me, "Lift me over mister." I helped him over the turnstile and I recall thinking, 'I'm an adult, now.'

"At the end of the game, we were allowed on to the pitch. It was the first time for me and I remember thinking how big it was and how pronounced the camber on the playing surface.

"There were balls on the pitch and I 'scored' into the net at the Ice Rink end. Then we were allowed inside, to be amazed at the terrible condition of the facilities. However, I do remember that I

met Alex Totten and thanked him for all he was doing for Saints at that time."

Sadly, it also has to be recorded that, despite the horrendous scenes from Hillsborough only a few weeks before, a small knot of Saints 'fans' thought that the afternoon would be improved by a fight, or, as Graham Fulton in the PA described it, *"a brief flurry of the disgraceful behaviour that had made segregation necessary ... The moronic Perth fans who were involved only served to underline the reasons for a new, all-seated stadium where they will have no place."*

Of course, where there are warring fans there are (usually) the police. Amongst the officers in attendance that day was Jim Mackintosh, St Johnstone poet emeritus, who was then a young constable. Jim recalls that in the pre-match muster for the game, *"We were told that we had to watch out for a pitch invasion and in particular try to prevent people removing any souvenirs from the ground, including digging up the pitch – with the famous plastic fork that was issued with Wendy Who? being mentioned.*

"At that point, there was a tumbleweed moment as a wave of silence swept over the assembled polis. I didn't have the Wendy Who? fork, but I did have a teaspoon and a plastic bag in my pocket, specifically for the very purpose of removing some of the hallowed Muirton turf. From a glance around the room, it was obvious I wasn't the only one.

"I don't know about my colleagues from that day, but I think my hat may have accidentally fallen off and in stooping to retrieve it I may have inadvertently dislodged some earth and grass. I still have, somewhere in my attic, a Bluebell matchbox, wrapped in clingfilm, with a centimetre of very dry soil in it."

As for the players, Ian Heddle recalled that the mood in the dressing room afterwards was sombre. They had, after all, just lost

the last ever match at the stadium that had been their club's home for almost 65 years. He told us, *"We knew we weren't getting promoted, and that we had been up against a really good team, with one of the best finishers in the lower Divisions in John Sludden, but we'd lost. It wasn't a good way to finish at Muirton. However, we also knew that we'd come on massively under Alex Totten. We were not the finished article, but we were a decent side. We proved that the next season ..."*

The press box had been fuller than usual that afternoon, with many old familiar faces saying their farewells to the cramped surroundings. Graham Fulton and the rest of the PA crew posed for a final photo - reproduced here (courtesy of Gordon Bannerman) - showing the gentlemen of the press in their element and not a laptop in sight! For younger readers, those things the reporters are holding are telephones!

After the match was over, and with the BBC cameras on hand to film it all, the champagne flowed and the chairman, manager and the Beeb's celebrity reporter, ex-Ranger Derek Johnstone, found themselves afloat in the small, sunken players' bath. Overflowing bath water mixed with overflowing champagne made for a somewhat sticky situation, but it's not every day that St Johnstone relinquish their home to a major supermarket chain.

With that last thought in mind, and to finish this chapter and put this final game at Muirton into context, it's worth reminding ourselves just how low Saints had sunk in the previous few seasons. Relegation to the lowest tier of Scottish football in 1985 was followed by three seasons at that level. The week Geoff Brown took over, the team was statistically speaking, the second worst in the country and the following week saw St Johnstone hit rock bottom at the foot of the lowest senior league in Scotland. Things did pick up, but the fact was that in only 13 home (of 22) games in the 1986-87 season was there a crowd of more than 1,000 in Muirton Park.

The following season, under Alex Totten's astute guidance, the process of rebuilding St Johnstone continued on and off the pitch and the club gained promotion back to the First Division (then the second tier). After this last ever match at Muirton (and buoyed by finishing in what was regarded at the time as a reasonable sixth place in the league) the mood music was much better than it had been for many years and Saints' fans could now look forward to watching our team play in what was then regarded as one of the best, most modern, stadiums in Britain. Which, you'll perhaps not be surprised to learn, is the subject of our next chapter...

Saints team: Balavage, K. Thomson, Heddle, Barron, Nicolson, G. Thompson, Sorbie, Cherry, Jenkins, Johnston, Irvine. Substitutes: Maher (for Irvine), Spence (for Sorbie).
Attendance: 6,728.

Thankfully, it all came right in the end

The first game at McDiarmid Park
St Johnstone 2, Clydebank 1, Scottish Football League, First Division,
McDiarmid Park, Saturday, 19th August 1989

Headline: Perthshire Advertiser

McDiarmid Park is, at the time of writing, more or less as old as Muirton Park was when the authors first started going to watch St Johnstone. This means there is an entire generation who have no experience of seeing Saints play at Muirton and can't remember just what a major event the opening of McDiarmid Park was back in 1989.

As noted in the previous chapter, the stands, terracing and facilities at Muirton were clearly wearing out by the 1980s. Money, needed to be spent, but it simply wasn't available. The takeover of the club by Geoff Brown and the creation of McDiarmid Park were seminal events in our history, but as always it is what happens on the playing park that determines the immediate happiness, or otherwise, of the supporters.

In August 1989, that park was brand new, as were the stands and facilities that enclosed it. Crucially, the playing area was spacious, allowing Alex Totten's new flying winger - Allan Moore, an £85,000 (then a club record) buy from Hearts - the room to make his lightning forays and

create the chances that could turn a game. The other new boy was also the result of a big (for Saints) transfer fee: the £50,000 that brought Harry Curran from Dundee United.

The kick-off was delayed, partly due to traffic problems as the fans tried to work out their routes to the new ground. The Crieff Road in particular was solid before and after the match. However, at eight minutes past three, and in front of a large crowd of 7,267 the match eventually got underway.

Graham Fulton in the PA recorded that *"McDiarmid Park came brilliantly to life on Saturday and proved itself a great arena for football,"* adding, *"...it has generated its own atmosphere with splendid viewing and civilised comfort."*

The big crowd that day was one of many that season – and for a few years afterwards. The excitement and interest generated by the new ground (and the promotion at the end of this season) meant that there was a real buzz about the place and a pride in Perth that permeated the club and its

103

supporters. In more recent years, McDiarmid Park has developed a reputation for not having a great atmosphere. However, as fan Ian McLaren pointed out to us – and we agree – this wasn't the case for the first few seasons at the new ground. Matches such as the famous win over Airdrie and the 5-0 defeat of Aberdeen (both of which are covered below) were played in front of huge crowds and in a phenomenal atmosphere of partisan fervour, underpinned by joyful, boisterous camaraderie between players and fans.

Unfortunately, for this opening fixture, Clydebank clearly had not read the script. The visitors had the effrontery to take an early lead in the seventh minute, when Jim Hughes took advantage of the home defence's inability to clear the ball and hammered home from some 20 yards.

However, Saints' new signings started to take a grip on the game, as the PA described it: *"The equaliser came in 19 minutes and it was the other big cash buy, Harry Curran, who finished off in style ...hammering high into the net after an Ian Heddle cross had been headed against the post by Grant Jenkins."*

Of course, the major difference between this goal and the last one scored at Muirton was that against Clydebank, everyone had to rise from their seat to acclaim Curran, whereas previously, the majority would already have been standing. However, with Hillsborough and the Bradford fire still fresh in people's minds, this was not regarded as any hardship, and neither were the clean toilets with hot and cold water and paper towels – a substantial improvement from the brick urinal at the back of the enclosure at Muirton.

Like the first half, the second forty-five was late in starting; this time because one of the linesmen had pulled a muscle when he ran out after the break. Local referee, Graeme Cowper, took over on the line and the game restarted. The actual ref that day was Joe Timmons, who would go on to become the first referee to officiate at the top level in both Scotland and England.

As in the first half, Clydebank continued to pester the Saints' defence, with one of their danger-men, Ken Eadie, hitting a post. Thereafter though, Saints took charge. However, despite their dominance, it looked as if time was slowly ebbing away, until 11 minutes from time, when, as the PA tells us, *"Curran, Jenkins and substitute Sorbie all lined up for pot-shots at goal which were blocked with the final attempt being handled by Sean Sweeney."*

Sweeney was booked. Don McVicar, the St Johnstone captain, stepped up and lashed the ball high into the net. Once again, the home fans rose to their feet – *"a happy conclusion to a day that will not be forgotten."* It was indeed a happy conclusion, or as the PA put it, with perhaps just a slight sigh of relief, *"Thankfully it all came right in the end."*

Ian Heddle told us that the players hadn't really had many opportunities to train on the pitch beforehand, because *"it was very new and not as good as it became later on. In those days, you used to crave a decent playing surface: a few of the pitches at some of the lower Division grounds were rutted and really poor. But there was a feeling that we were part of a football revolution, with the best new stadium in Britain, which, after the events of Hillsborough was very important.*

"The fact that there was a big crowd there helped the players that day. We could sense the club was going up another notch in the football world - which we were. Alex Totten had brought in more attacking players and these were magical days for me during my career – and for St Johnstone."

Dave Anderson, who you'll recall fondly remembering Muirton in our last chapter, told us how, *"We approached this game with a lot of excitement and anticipation and were just totally amazed at our new ground and the comparison to Muirton, where we normally stood in all weathers. It seemed to have everything and being seated seemed strange and a bit of a luxury.*

"In my mind's eye the crowd seemed really big and our team that day featured Allan Moore in his first home game for Saints. We instantly took to Moorie and saw the beginning of what was to become a great partnership with Roddy Grant. Other fans' favourites who played included Harry Curran and Don McVicar.

"As a lifelong Saintee and season ticket holder, my lasting memory is leaving our wonderful new stadium and hearing two older Saints fans have an interesting conversation, which went something like this: "What do you think of the new stadium Willie?" "Oct it's aw right, but it's a shame we didnae get the undersoil heating too..."

Which just goes to show, even when you give them the most up-to-date stadium in Britain (with running hot water in the Gents and Ladies loos - a real novelty back then!), you can't please all of the people – and certainly not all of the Saints' fans - all of the time...

St Johnstone team: Balavage, Cherry, McVicar, K. Thomson, Nicolson, Johnston, Moore, Curran, Grant, Jenkins, Heddle
Subs: Sorbie (for Grant), G. Thompson (for Heddle).
Attendance: 7,267.

No. 27
The first major national trophy
St Johnstone 2, Dundee United 0, Scottish Cup Final,
Celtic Park, Saturday, 17th May 2014

No. 28
The first League Cup
St Johnstone 1, Livingston 0, Scottish League Cup Final,
Hampden Park, Sunday, Saturday, 28th February 2021

No. 29
Only the fourth team in Scotland to do the Cup double
St Johnstone 1, Hibernian 0, Scottish Cup Final,
Hampden Park, 22nd May 2021

These three matches follow on from each other as key milestones in the club's history, however, they also fall, for obvious reasons, into the category of 'Great Games' and so are covered in Part III of this book.

It should also be recorded at this point that, without a shadow of doubt, winning these three major Scottish trophies is, individually and collectively, the greatest achievement in St Johnstone's history. If they are being honest, for most fans the excitement of Tommy Wright's team winning the first Scottish Cup was not something they expected to be replicated in a hurry, yet within a decade, Callum Davidson's side had achieved immortality by winning the double of the Scottish Cup and the Scottish League Cup in the same season: a feat that will, almost certainly, not be repeated by any club outside the Old Firm for many years to come.

No. 30
Take a bow, Liam Craig

The all-time appearance record
St Johnstone 3, Dundee 1, Scottish Premiership,
McDiarmid Park, Saturday, 2nd October 2021

This one is all for you legend Liam

Saints produce best performance of the season to mark special day

Headline: The Courier

If you're going to break the all-time appearance record for St Johnstone you want to do it in style. Preferably with a win over some team that the fans will really, really appreciate you beating. Like Dundee for instance...

There was a time when it looked as if Liam Craig wouldn't be in a position to overtake Steven Anderson's impressive tally of 441 games for St Johnstone. That was when he decided to move to Hibernian in the summer of 2013. If he hadn't done that, his career total at Perth would have been off-the-scale, almost certainly considerably over 500. However, move he did, and he subsequently enjoyed, at times endured, two seasons at Easter Road, including a stint down a league after Hibs were relegated at the end of his first season. Loyalty has always been a strong suit for Liam and although he was told he could leave Edinburgh, he stayed for a second season, only departing when Hibs failed to gain promotion and his contract was not renewed. Having kept in touch with Tommy Wright, it was perhaps no surprise when he re-signed at McDiarmid.

Liam had trained with Saints – and a number of other clubs - as a boy. He was then on an S form with Hearts but had an opportunity to go to Ipswich Town, where he captained their youth team that won the 2005 FA Youth Cup final.

His first team opportunities at Portman Road were limited, so in January 2006 he decided to come back north, to Falkirk. He was only 19. In December 2007, he came to Perth, initially on loan before Saints paid £25,000 to the Bairns for his services. It was to prove money well spent.

If it wasn't for the coronavirus pandemic, it is highly likely that Liam would have passed 400 appearances before the end of the 2019-20 season. The last game he played that season was a fairly dire, scoreless draw against St Mirren. He was sent off about ten minutes before the end and with the Covid crisis no-one was sure when - or if - football would resume. That game against St Mirren could have been his last match for the club. Liam joked that he would have been in good company, because of the answer to the following question...

"What's the similarity between Liam Craig and Zinedine Zidane?" – to which the answer is "they both got sent off in their last football match!"

Fortunately, for both Liam and Saints, this wasn't to be his footballing epitaph. At the time of that game in Paisley, Craig had played 398 times for St Johnstone. When football returned to something like its normal state, he still had much to offer the first team; not just his innate ability but a vast treasury of experience and knowledge of game management, offset, as throughout his career, by the occasional outburst of excitement that led to disagreements with the match officials about what precisely had, or had not, happened in the previous passage of play.

In the course of his entire Saints career, he started 374 games and came on as a sub in 79, giving him the record total of 453 appearances. He scored 61 goals, was booked 92 times (roughly once every five games), and sent off four times. That disciplinary record is not bad for a combative midfielder, but for a different perspective we turned to former Grade 1 referee David Somers, who remembers refereeing Liam both at Falkirk and Saints. David described him to us as, *"a wholly committed player who gave as good as he got and it was always a pleasure refereeing him. I also bumped into him one Saturday night at City nightclub in Falkirk and we bought each other a drink and had a good chat about football."*

As for the actual record-breaking match itself, Liam had played fairly regularly throughout the earlier months of that 2021-22 season, including in the 2-0 win at Dens in the League Cup just a few weeks before. There was obviously something about Dundee that appealed to Liam, because it was against them that he passed Alan Main's 361 appearances, scoring in his 362nd match in a 2-0 victory.

Going into his record-breaking 442nd match, Saints were without Murray Davidson, Jamie McCart, Liam Gordon and James Brown, but the men who came in blended seamlessly and put on what the PA

said was *"their best performance of the season."*

One unusual feature of this game, at least in the modern era, was that both sides wore their first-choice strips - Dundee in navy blue and Saints in their normal mid/royal blue shirts – and both wore white shorts. Whether this caused any confusion is highly debatable, but what is not is that Saints were comfortable winners, courtesy of two goals from Chris Kane and one, the third, from Stevie May.

On the day, Liam was, naturally, made captain and as he and his team-mates ran out, they were greeted by a large banner in the East Stand that simply said, *"Liam Craig, History Maker, 442 and counting, Legend."* Fans around the stadium then sat back and enjoyed themselves as Liam and his team-mates put Dundee to the sword once more.

Michael O'Halloran threatened down the flank early on, then repeated the feat to play a key part in the first goal. This came when, as The Sunday Post described it: *"Shaun Rooney played a great pass down the right and O'Halloran timed his run to perfection before pulling the ball back. Kane then produced a thumping shot for his first league goal of the season.*

"His second wasn't far away – May came up with the cross and the 27-year-old was first to the ball as he stabbed it home."

Dundee were largely conspicuous by their absence in the first half. Kane's first goal was in 31 minutes, his second in 39 minutes. The Dens Park side were at the foot of the table on only three points before and after the game and posed little threat in the early stages of the second half, conceding a third within 30 seconds of the re-start when, the PA tells us, *"May swept the ball into the bottom corner."* The Sunday Post added a little more information, telling us that it was Michael

O'Halloran who had crossed the ball for May. Given his role in two of the goals, O'Halloran was named as the Sunday Post's 'Star Man.' A small consolation came for the visitors when Ryan Sweeney headed their only goal in the 74th minute but although the Dark Blues raised the tempo of the match the Saints' defence held firm.

Other than the top and tail of the match reports, where they loudly praise Liam Craig's St Johnstone career, the press don't make much, if any, reference to how he actually played in the game. Having played in a variety of positions from left back to almost every place across the middle of the park since he first joined Saints, by this stage in his career he was very much operating as a sitting midfielder, monitoring and controlling the play in front of the back-four and providing forays up the field where and when appropriate.

Celebrations carried on in the home dressing room, with a huge round of applause from the rest of the players and a string of compliments from the manager to the media. Callum Davidson was quoted in almost all the press as saying, *"It's unbelievable for Liam. It's a fantastic achievement and something he has to be really proud of. He got a big ovation in the dressing room and rightly so. We talked about it before the game. It was difficult for Liam not to get too emotional."*

The match over, Liam and a few other players could just have gone home as normal. This being a special occasion, they wanted to share it with the people who support them every time they pull on a St Johnstone shirt: they went to the Cherrybank Inn and then the Caledonian Bar, where several beers were sunk and Liam was feted as the man who now held the all-time appearance record.

After this, their eighth League match of the season, St Johnstone were in eighth place in the Premiership. As we know, they fell from grace fairly quickly thereafter and only kept their place in the top flight after defeating Inverness Caledonian Thistle in the play-off. Over the remaining 34 games, Liam Craig only started four and made substitute appearances in a further seven. Although age was catching up on him, it is interesting to speculate what might have happened should he have been able to add his vast experience and game-knowledge to more games that season. We'll never know, but it's possible we might not have been quite so nervous come the end of the season than we actually were.

Of course, for one man, Liam's record meant the end of his. Steven Anderson is philosophical about it though, telling us, *"Records are there to be broken. Liam has been a fantastic player for St Johnstone, but one day someone will overtake his number of appearances. Then he will be the same as me - as I was for Alan Main and Alan was for Drew Rutherford. The record is your legacy and part of your history with the club. I was proud to hold the record for a while and now I'm happy that Liam has done it."*

One thing about Liam that some fans may not have noticed, but which didn't escape the eagle-eyed Maggie Anderson, was his habit of always pulling his socks up every time he took a corner. As Maggie related to us, *"Every time he stood over the ball, we all waited for him to pull up his socks - and he always did it!"* You can watch the YouTube video of the last-minute goal against Rangers in the 2021 Scottish Cup semi-final and you'll see that Maggie is right (on that occasion at least!)

Other than his two-year sojourn to Hibernian, Liam spent 13 seasons playing for Saints. He averaged 35 games each season, so if he had not gone to Easter Road he would have created the all-time appearance record much sooner and would have ultimately ended up with around 520 games for St Johnstone.

Almost the last words go to the PA's Matt Gallagher, whose second paragraph finished with these sentences: *"Take a bow, Liam Craig. Saturday was always going to be his afternoon."*

As for the man himself, he was typically modest when we spoke to him, pointing out that he was lucky to be playing in a series of exceptional St Johnstone teams, where lots of other good players also had extended careers with hundreds of appearances.

"I was lucky enough to have played with both previous record-holders – Alan Main and Steven Anderson," he told us, and having been to a lot of the club's Hall of Fame dinners and spoken to a lot of supporters, *I know that the great thing about Saints is the family feel around the club. By being here for so many years, you get to know the impact that players have on the club and the supporters, so for me to break the record it was huge personally, but the fact that it happened during St Johnstone's most successful period makes it even more special. What I've seen during my time is that so many players just loved playing for the club and the fans. I've also heard the same from many of the players from bygone days, which tells you so much about how well organised St Johnstone are compared to some others. One of the key things is that we've always had a great dressing room with no big-time Charlies – we all got on and wanted to do our very best for each other.*

"In that game against Dundee when I broke Ando's record, I found that there was an interesting symmetry about the whole thing. It was my 442nd game, and 4-4-2 was the formation that, until recently, almost every Saints' team I'd played in had favoured. Going out onto the pitch, seeing the banner, then beating Dundee of all teams – these things all made it such a special day. For me, it wasn't so much about how I played, but the fact that we won. It's not easy to win games in the Premier, but we were pretty comfortable that afternoon.

"On the day, it's perhaps difficult to take it all in, but when you retire and look back then there is a degree of pride, not just for me but for everyone who is involved in St Johnstone, that we've had so many great moments during the years I've been here."

Time waits for no man, and Liam hung up his boots in 2022 after coming on as a sub in a game at Easter Road on Sunday 15th May 2022. Subsequently, he moved into a coaching role at McDiarmid, where his influence on the youth team was both obvious and encouraging as he helped guide them to a tremendously successful season in 2022-23. Until recently, he had been working as Steven MacLean's assistant. At the time when we first talked, Liam was helping to source new players for the 2023-24 season. If any of them are as good for St Johnstone as Liam Craig has been then the future of the club is in safe hands.

Saints team: Clark; Rooney, Ambrose, Dendoncker, Booth, O'Halloran, Craig, Wotherspoon, Crawford, May and Kane. Substitutes: Muller (for O'Halloran), MacPherson (for Crawford), Middleton (for May). Unused subs: Parish, Devine, Bryson and Vertainen.
Attendance: 5,097.

PART II

SIGNIFICANT GAMES

This section describes games which we consider amongst the most significant in St Johnstone's history. The field of possible candidates for inclusion here is, of course, extremely wide and fans will have similarly wide-ranging opinions as to what constitutes a *"significant"* match. Although some of the *"milestones"* in Part I undoubtedly qualify for inclusion here, we have left them where they are, simply because, in our view, they fit better into that particular timeline of the club's history. Other than those matches, for a game to be included here, our criteria were straightforward. These matches are those that commanded attention at the time they were played for a multiplicity of reasons, from the alleged transfer shenanigans around the 'Reid Case' of 1923, which led to Saints failing to gain promotion to the top flight of Scottish football for the first time, to key relegation and promotion deciders, as well as matches which, in our view, were turning points in crucial seasons and also one oddity which is included for reasons to do with the illegal footwear worn by the Saints' players. As a result, there are a couple of boring no-score draws, alongside some notable and important victories (and one historic defeat).

The games are:

1. (Glasgow) Thistle, 1st January 1886
2. Tulloch, 17th September 1887
3. Our Boys Blairgowrie, 21st December 1889
4. Arbroath Wanderers, 23rd December 1893
5. Clydebank, 14th April 1923
6. Dundee United, 17th April 1926
7. Arsenal, 26th September 1932
8. Berwick Rangers, 27th April, 1960
9. Rangers, 21st December 1963
10. Hibernian, 24th December 1966
11. Clyde, 10th April 1971
12. Celtic, 26th April 1975
13. Ayr United, 28th April 1990
14. Rangers, 29th November 1998
15. Dunfermline Athletic, 25th October 2007
16. Aberdeen, 13th April 2014
17. Kilmarnock, 5th December 2019
18. Inverness Caledonian Thistle, 23rd May 2022

No. 1
The St Johnstone defence was never seen so bad - there was no defence worth the name.

The record defeat in any match
Friendly, St Johnstone 1, Glasgow Thistle 18
Recreation Grounds, Friday, 1st January 1886

There is no disguising the fact that, however much we might not like it, St Johnstone do occasionally lose games. Consequently, and with a view to getting it out of the way at the start of this section of the book, we thought it only fair to record not just this match, the worst score in the club's history, but also, briefly, the other scores in the games played before and after it, which cumulatively rack up the most appalling series of heavy defeats the club has *ever* experienced.

This run of disaster began on New Year's Day 1886, when, the *"Famous Glasgow Thistle"* (not Partick Thistle) were the visitors to Perth. Also known simply as The Thistle, or Bridgeton Thistle, they were one of the oldest football clubs founded in Scotland and famously the first ever opponents of Queen's Park, in 1868. That particular incarnation of this Thistle team folded in 1873 however, before resuming life in 1875. At the time they played Saints, their home ground was in Dalmarnock, Glasgow, where they were early rivals to Clyde, but it was really the emergence of Celtic nearby that eventually saw Thistle off, although not before they had established a decent reputation locally and further afield. They played in one inch wide blue and white hoops (which were called stripes in those days), with blue shorts – a bit like a blue version of the famous Queen's Park hooped kit.

Thus, when the Dundee Courier announced on 1st January 1886 that there were three big clubs from the west coming to play St Johnstone over a four-day period, starting on the 2nd of January, it was hailed as exciting news in Perth.

PERTH NOTES.
The St Johnstone have been successful in providing a trio for the holidays which cannot be surpassed. To-day the famous Glasgow Thistle tackle the ground men. To-morrow (Saturday) the 3d L.R.V., who have been creating such a stir in the west of late, are on the card. This team is presently credited with possessing the best set of forwards in Scotland, and may surprise not a few in the closing ties for the Scottish Cup. On Monday the Clyde, who thrashed the great Hibs, last Saturday, have been secured. Such an array of talent in Perth will doubtless turn out large crowds at the Recreation Grounds, sufficient, we trust, to warrant a return in the future of such crack teams.

The Evening Telegraph too was eagerly looking forward to these matches, telling its readers, *"The Perth St Johnstone have shown commendable enterprise for so young an organisation. After a game with the Glasgow Thistle to-day, the athletic portion of the inhabitants of the Fair City are promised a visit from the well-known exponents of the scientific style of play, the 3d Lanark. On Monday, the Clyde on their homeward journey will have a parting game with the Saints. Although the Perth team can hardly yet hope to score a victory over either* (sic) *the strong elevens which will oppose them, excellent exhibitions of the code should reward those who find their way to the matches; and I hope that the enterprise of the Saints will be amply rewarded."*

This was the first time Saints had played any team from outside Perthshire or Dundee. In the event, each of these games proved a bridge too far for the fledgling footballers of Craigie. The Dundee Courier tells us what happened when the Thistle turned up…

"This was a walk over for the Glasgow men. The Saints' defence was weak in the extreme. In fact there was no defence

worth the name. *From start to finish the ground men were pressed, and certainly they had a first-rate set of forwards to contend against. The play of the Glasgow men was a treat to see. We need only mention the record to indicate the one-sided nature of the game - Thistle 18; St Johnstone 1.*"

The Dundee Advertiser had a more detailed report, which also tells us the name of one of the St Johnstone players…

"*The Thistle (Glasgow) played the St Johnstone at Perth, in presence of a large crowd of spectators, yesterday afternoon. The weather, though dull, was dry, but the ground was not in very good condition. The St Johnstone kicked off against the wind, and the ball was got hold of by one of the Thistle's backs and returned to the St Johnstone territory, where operations began. About three minutes from the start the strangers scored their first goal. The passing of their front rank was excellent, and completely puzzled the efforts of the St Johnston's (sic) to keep the ball out of their ground. The Glasgow men had the game well in hand all through, and at half time had 11 goals – the St Johnstone having failed to score. With the wind in their favour, it was expected that the Saints would do a little better; but the Thistle showed themselves in good form, and soon registered four other goals. McKenzie, in the centre of the St Johnstone forwards, got hold of the ball, and ran it down the field, and sent it through amid loud cheering. When time was called the game stood – Thistle 18; St Johnstone 1. The St Johnstone's defence was never seen so bad. The Thistle team was a good one, and their forwards gave a very fine exhibition of short passing. The game was of the most friendly nature, and satisfaction was expressed at the gentlemanly way in which the players conducted themselves on the field. After the match dinner was served in the Victoria Hotel. To-day the St Johnstone meet the 3d L.R.V.*"

The next day's match, against Third Lanark (or to give them their original name, the Third Lanarkshire Rifle Volunteers), produced a slightly less embarrassing result, with the visitors departing with a 5-3 victory. Two days later, Clyde put nine past Saints, with only one in reply.

The Perthshire Constitutional was bullish about these matches, telling its readers that, "*Although outdoor sports are discounted by reason of weather considerations at this season of the year, yet the first attempt by our leading local Club in bringing forward three of our leading Scotch Football Clubs has been crowned with success. The weather on Friday and Saturday was good, and though Monday turned out stormy, the large and increased turn-out of spectators at the Recreation Grounds showed the increasing interest of the public in the popular game. The St Johnstone have shown no small enterprise in securing such crack teams as the 'Thistle,' '3rd L.R.V,.' and the 'Clyde,' and they will doubtless profit by the exhibitions given. The first-named team appeared on Friday, when the ground men were fairly non-plussed by the smartest display of the short-passing game yet seen in this quarter: it was quite a treat to watch the clever manipulation of the ball by the 'forwards' and some idea of what the famous 'Battlefield' will show in their approaching visit has thus been gained.*"

The reference to Battlefield was because that team were to be the next Glaswegian visitors to Perth, albeit not until the 8th of April 1886. However, despite the Constitutional's hope that St Johnstone might have learned from their initial contact with teams from the west, it seems clear that clubs from that part of Scotland were simply far more advanced and skilful than those from Perth at this time. Certainly, the score in the Battlefield match, which was 13-0 to the visitors, showed that there was not so much a gulf as a chasm still to be crossed before St Johnstone could take a place at the top table of Scottish football.

It wasn't just teams from the west who were capable of giving Saints a serious pasting. Twelve days after the Clyde match, they played Forfar Athletic in a friendly in Forfar and went down 10-3. That meant that in four successive games St Johnstone had scored eight goals but shipped 42 – an average of over 10 per game. In mitigation, it must be said that this was a St Johnstone team that was learning as it went along, as indeed the other local teams were, and gratifyingly, by the end of the 1885-86 season (the first full season in the club's history) Saints had scored a highly impressive total of 77 goals in 31 games (chance would be a fine thing today…). The only problem was that in those same games they had conceded 150 goals in return!

You might have forgiven them if they had decided this football lark was a bit too much and thrown in the towel. Fortunately for us, they were made of stern stuff in the 1880s and carried on…

Saints team: we only know of one player, the centre forward, McKenzie.
Attendance: unknown.

No. 2
The first twenty minutes were spent shooting for goal without result

The record score in a competitive match
Perthshire Cup, First Round, Tulloch 0, St Johnstone 13
Tulloch, Saturday, 17th September 1887

In the late 19th century, Tulloch was frequently described as a suburb of Perth. Peter Baxter in his 1898 book, *"Football in Perthshire,"* gives us a little information about *"the Tulloch club,"* specifically that it was formed in 1885-86 (Baxter's dates are not always reliable – especially for the formation of St Johnstone) and *"for four or five years kept close upon the heels of the Perth clubs. So much so that the latter found the simplest way to keep the suburban team under subjection was to 'lift' the most promising of the Club's players ... Fair City, especially, benefited ... and so did Caledonian Rangers and St Johnstone to a lesser extent."*

Such pilfering of the suburban club's best players may help explain the rather large number of goals racked up by St Johnstone in this Perthshire Cup match. It is, at time of writing, the biggest winning margin for Saints in any competitive game, and sadly, given modern-day football's excessive defensive emphasis, likely to remain so for the foreseeable future.

That said, before the game was played there were some who believed that Tulloch might spring a surprise on their bigger neighbours. The Crieff Journal, published the day before the match, had a column on the forthcoming Perthshire Cup ties in which their correspondent observed that the Erin Rovers vs Comrie match, *"will be the hardest contest, unless the Tulloch come up to the expectations I hear they have of throwing out the St Johnstone. The Tulloch lads recently drew a combination of Perth players, and think they may just have luck enough to put the Saints on the wrong side of the account."*

While researching this game, we noted that the same issue of the Crieff Journal also contains an account of the Pitlochry Sports, in which the St Johnstone captain, right back John Robertson, displayed his athletic prowess in a number of disciplines, with *"a place in no less than five of the events,"* including winning *"the running long leap"* (long jump), the *"hop, step and leap"* (triple jump) and the hurdle race – *"On the whole, a day's performance seldom equalled."* Bearing in mind that he also had trials for the Scottish national team, Johnny Robertson was, without doubt, the first great St Johnstone player.

In a similar vein, that same paper included a brief article on the injuries that footballers were apt to sustain in those long-gone days. Played in tackety boots on rough pitches, football was potentially a more dangerous sport than it is today. It should be remembered that the law as regards fouls or dangerous play was not the same as today, as this quotation vividly illustrates: *"Two accidents to football players in our own immediate vicinity have been recorded within the past fortnight. The first of these occurred a week past at the St Johnstone Recreation Grounds, when one of the St Johnstone Wanderers (the second team) named Gardiner was heavily thrown, and had one of his arms dislocated at the shoulder. The other occurred last Saturday at Stanley during a match between Stanley and Methven, when a player belonging to the former club, named Chalmers, was so severely injured that he had to be conveyed to a neighbouring farm, and afterwards taken home. That many accidents occur which one scarcely ever hears of is unfortunately too common.*

All votaries of the game of football will admit that the game from its very nature is especially liable to cause occasionally serious accidents ... The rules that govern the Association game are as yet not stringent enough against violent charging, tripping, and the like. Instead of the game being played scientifically, it too often degenerates into a mere scramble, in which there is so much of kicking and shoving about of one's opponents that were the same to take place in the public streets ... the majority on both sides would soon find themselves in 'durance vile' on a charge of assault and breach of the peace!"

Any notions the Tulloch lads had of *"throwing out the St Johnstone,"* were soon, although not swiftly, disabused. There is only one actual report of the match, which appeared verbatim in two publications, the Perthshire Constitutional and the Crieff Journal. Unfortunately, it contains a word that, while in common use at that time, is strictly verboten in the 21st century. With the caveat that this is simply a record of what was written, this is what purchasers of these two papers were able to read the following week...

"The St Johnstone did not turn out in full strength to tackle the Tulloch, Robertson and Christie being absent, but as the result proved it was strong enough, 13 goals to nil being a one-sided record. Curiously enough, the first twenty minutes were spent shooting for goal without result, so that the rest of the game was mainly occupied in centering (sic) the ball and target practice. Allan at half-back, and Elliot, Dewar and Bremner forwards, were conspicuous for the winners. The Tulloch wrought like n****** for some time after the start, but they were out of the running, and might have acted more wisely by taking a share of a 'gate' in town."

This wasn't the only tie of the first round to feature a lot of goals. As the cutting here (from the Dundee Advertiser) shows, Erin Rovers hammered Comrie 15-0, while Dunblane emulated Saints in scoring 13 times; their luckless opponents being Scone. It's also worth noting that the Advertiser's brief note describes Tulloch as being *"near Perth,"* rather than in the city as it is nowadays.

These early days of Perthshire football saw far more high scoring games than we would get nowadays. As well as the huge wins noted above, Saints had hammered Erin Rovers 9-3 in the first round of matches for the Scottish Qualifying Cup the week before the Tulloch game, thus making a total of 22 goals in two games; the highest number of goals in consecutive matches in the club's history.

The Dundee Advertiser

This 13-0 score still stands as St Johnstone's record in a competitive match. However, it's not the highest ever score for the club in any match and, perhaps unsurprisingly, that particular record also comes from the late nineteenth century, as we shall see in the next two chapters...

Saints team: the match report in the Perthshire Constitutional only records the names of four players: Allan at half-back and three forwards, Elliot, Dewar and Bremner.
Attendance: unknown.

No. 3
The game throughout was uninteresting and one-sided

The record score in any match (1)
Friendly match, St Johnstone 15, Our Boys (Blairgowrie) 0
Recreation Grounds, Saturday, 21st December 1889

Having described in a previous chapter the heaviest defeat in Saints' history (and many other terrible drubbings) we thought it only fair to redress the balance a bit with an account - in this and the next chapter - of the two games in which St Johnstone scored their record number of goals.

Once again this was in the nineteenth century, when big scores were - as we have noted previously - fairly common. Both these matches were played at the Recreation Grounds in the days before Christmas, but four years apart, in 1889 and 1893 respectively.

The Evening Telegraph, in its preview of the first match, noted that, *"Tomorrow the St Johnstone and Our Boys (Blairgowrie) meet at the Recreation Grounds, Perth. In former games victory favoured the Saints, and on the present occasion it is probable they will add another victory to their list."*

The Dundee Courier took a similar line, commenting, under the heading, *"Blairgowrie,"* that, *"Our local team journey to Perth to-morrow to play the St Johnstone. The Boys eleven is a pretty fair one, and perhaps although not victorious to-morrow, will undoubtedly give a good account of itself ere the season is finished. Being aware of the fact that the Boys have no fewer than eight matches to play in a processional order, and all at home too, after the New Year, it is about time the Committee had a regular team put together."*

The actual match itself was described by the same paper, with considerable understatement, as *"a very one-side game."*

The Dundee Advertiser did not disagree, commenting, *"The game throughout was uninteresting and one-sided, and ended in a decisive victory for the St Johnstone by 15 goals to 0."*

This was the entirety of their report and it seems that it was written by the same correspondent who wrote the Perthshire Constitutional's report, because his account also contains this same phrase. It also contains the suggestion that the Our Boys side did not have a full complement of players, which might go some way to explaining the final score.

Paper cuttings from this period can be (very) hard to read. The Constitutional's report above tells us...

"These teams met at St Johnstone's Recreation Ground. The Boys not being fully represented. In the first half the Saints had the game well in hand, and scored 7 goals, while their opponents failed to notch a point. During the second period the St Johnstone played with much dash, and maintained their supremacy up to the close. The game throughout was uninteresting and one-sided, and ended in a decisive victory for the St Johnstone."

The Saints team and attendance are both unknown.

The goal-keeper was the best man on the strangers' side and kept the score from approaching the half-century

The record score in any match (2)
Friendly match, St Johnstone 15, Arbroath Wanderers 0
Recreation Grounds, Saturday, 23rd December 1893

We noted in the last chapter that there were a lot of high scoring games in Perthshire football in the nineteenth century. After Saints hammering of Arbroath Wanderers two days before Christmas 1893, the Perthshire Constitutional emphasised that point, recording in the following table just a few of the huge wins/heavy defeats some clubs had enjoyed/suffered. Gratifyingly, the name of St Johnstone features more than any other local club, although the strength of Fair City Athletic and Dunblane also shines through.

are among the heaviest scores ever put on in Perth football :—

Dunblane, ...	13	Fair City Athletics,	1
St Johnstone,	13	Tulloch, ...	0
" ...	15	Our Boys (Blair),	0
Dunblane, ...	13	Scone, ...	0
Fair City, ...	9	Erichtside, ...	2
" ...	9	Vale of Athole, ...	1
" ...	10	Black Watch, ...	2
Erin Rovers ...	15	Comrie, ...	0
Dunblane, ...	15	Breadalbane, ...	0
St Johnstone,	11	Black Watch, ...	2
" ...	10	Glasgow-Perthshire,	0
" ...	13	Auchterarder, ...	1
Fair City, ...	12	Bridge of Allan,	3
St Johnstone,	15	Arbroath W'derers,	0

The Constitutional's match report of the Arbroath Wanderers game, while noting that Saints had played well, rather poured cold water on their parade by its disparaging remarks about their opponents, whilst also revealing one of the principal reasons why the Forfarshire visitors were so badly beaten, namely that it seems to have been the second game they had played that day.

"St Johnstone do some very unexpected things, and Saturday was another instance. The Arbroath Wanderers are not considered of outstanding merit at any time, and when they attempt to play two matches in one day it is only to be expected that they will come out on the wrong side. The players which met the St Johnstone were of very moderate ability. Had they been any combination all might have been well, but in that they too were deficient. The St Johnstone from first to last ran through the strangers. Goals were got in the easiest possible manner, and after the forwards had tired of the goal-taking, the back division wandered forward to try their luck. The strangers' goal-keeper, notwithstanding the large score against him, was the best man on the strangers' side, and kept the score from approaching the half-century."

Today's Red-Top newspapers' tendency towards journalistic hyperbole is clearly nothing new, but in the event that Saints had scored a half-century, they would, by a huge margin, be the record-holders in world football.

The west coast papers also ran reports on this match. The Glasgow Herald felt it necessary to explain to its readers that St Johnstone hailed from the Fair City. Its report was as follows:

"St Johnstone (Perth) v. Arbroath Wanderers –

From the very commencement the home team showed superiority, and before half time had arrived had put on 9 points, while their opponents failed to score. In the second period of the game play was somewhat similar, and the St Johnstone left the field with 15 goals to their credit and Arbroath Wanderers 0."

The Glasgow Evening Post took a similarly disparaging line towards the visitors as the Perthshire Constitutional, noting:

"The Perthshire Cup holders were fairly on the dot on Saturday, and in view of the near approach of the Perthshire semi-finals, will cause a few folks to rub their eyes. Arbroath Wanderers on a recent visit to Perth showed they were no great 'shakes,' and Saturday's total does not at all enhance their reputation. Arbroath never settled down in the first half, St Johnstone scoring no fewer than nine points. Matters in the second half were scarcely so bad, but the Wanderers very seldom had a look in. St Johnstone added other (sic) six goals, which ended a very one-sided victory. St Johnstone excelled the strangers at every point"

The Saints team and attendance are both unknown.

No. 5

The decision is not only radically wrong, but it is unjust and illegal

The SFL case against Alex Scott Reid
Scottish Football League Division 2, St Johnstone 1, Clydebank 0
Recreation Grounds, Saturday, 14th April 1923

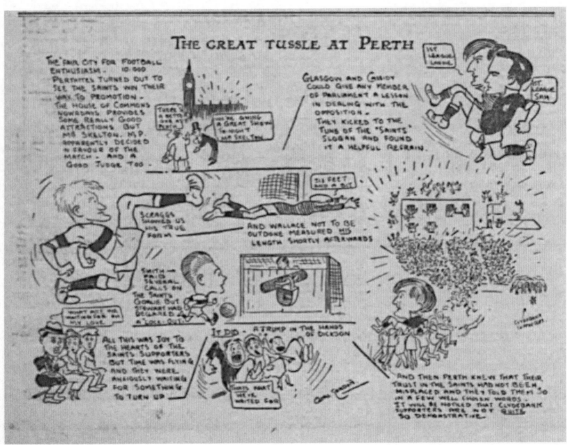

Cartoon: The Courier

Having been granted a place in the Scottish Football League in 1911, Saints had plied their trade in Division 2 for three seasons until the outbreak of the First World War. During the war and in the first, full, post-war season (1919-20), the Second Division was suspended and its clubs split into East and West regional leagues. Previously, there had been no automatic promotion and relegation between the First and Second Divisions of the Scottish Football League and the clubs who were now competing in these new regional leagues demanded this should change. To help force this through, a new Central League, distinct from the Scottish League was formed.

For a time, there were serious concerns that Saints would not be given a place in this competition and there was even a danger that, if they were not admitted, the club would have no-one to play and might go out of business. Fortunately, due to the sterling work of Robert Campbell and Alex Latto, Saints were able to join the Central League for the 1920-21 season and then, at the end of that campaign, the Scottish League decided to reinstate the Second Division, with automatic promotion and relegation - and St Johnstone were invited to join. Robert Campbell's leadership was vital at this time and, as was the case with Geoff Brown over 60 years later, he was instrumental in keeping St Johnstone in the business of playing football.

The board were naturally keen to try to gain First Division status. In 1921-22, Saints, disappointingly, finished 13th in the 20 team Second Division, but the following season they were going well and looking a good bet for promotion as the final furlongs of the season came into sight. There were several rivals for the two promotion places available, including Dumbarton, Queen's Park and Clydebank…

In an effort to strengthen the side, in March 1923 Saints paid Airdrie £50 for centre-forward Alex Reid, known as 'A S' (his middle name was 'Scott'). On 24th March, the PA told its readers, *"The latest acquisition, A. S. Reid of Airdrie, will make his initial appearance as a Saints' player. Standing near six foot high, and weighing twelve stone… he has made numerous appearances for the First League team, and is highly recommended as a clever distributor of play and a deadly shot."*

A S Reid, Picture, The Courier

In that same issue, the PA were talking up the forthcoming trip to Boghead to play Dumbarton, stressing the importance of a win. In the event, the match finished goalless and Reid does not seem to have made a huge impression. This left Saints third in the table, on 43 points, with Clydebank just above them on 45 points. Both clubs had played 33 matches. Top of the table was Queen's Park, on 47 points but with only 32 games played.

The next weekend saw Saints at home to Bathgate. Although they eventually won 3-1, it was a close-run thing and, with the score at 2-1, Bathgate had pressed hard for an equaliser, until Ribchester scored Saints' third right at the end of the match.

The Dundee Courier was not taken by Reid, commenting, *"Reid, the new centre-forward, was closely watched, and the spectators must have been disappointed with him. On the day's play he failed to combine his wings, and did nothing special individually, although responsible for two of the goals."*

To make matters worse, Saints' most prolific goal-scorer, Davie Anderson, had been out of form, so the directors sold him to St Bernard's (according to the PA, much against the player's wishes – or, as they put it in 1920s' language, *"not altogether a very willing consenter"*). The Saints' Minute Book reveals that the Edinburgh club had telephoned at the end of March to ask that Anderson be loaned to them. The Minute for 24th March records that, *"The meeting instructed the Secretary to point out that according to League Rule no player could be granted on loan after 16th March but that we were prepared to transfer Anderson to them at a fee of £20, the St Bernard's of course to pay Anderson's wages of £3 a week."*

The Minute for 4th April confirms Anderson's transfer, adding, *"The Secretary read letters from the St Bernard's with regard to Anderson suggesting that in the event of the Scottish League not approving of his transfer that the fee of £20 would be returned. The Secretary was instructed to reply that in view of their having played Anderson that we could not agree to the suggestion."*

What's interesting about this Minute is that it suggests that the St Johnstone board ought to have realised what they were doing when they signed Reid *at the end of March.* This Minute regarding Anderson's move to St Bernard's makes it clear that the board knew that the transfer deadline was the 16th of that month. As we shall see, this came back to haunt them...

The departure of Anderson put a lot more pressure on the newcomer Reid. The PA also noted this after the win at Bathgate, telling its readers that, *"The fact of the matter is that the Saints have transferred their most prolific goal-scorer – never mind the number he has missed – and at a time when they should have had their house on a sure foundation they have in a measure to start rebuilding by introducing a stranger into the pivotal position in the side.*

"Reid's position is no bed of roses. We do not envy him in his new found quarters. So far, the Airdrie player has not set the heather on fire."

After beating Bathgate, Saints then won against Lochgelly. Over the same period, Clydebank dropped two points, meaning that the forthcoming game between the two sides, scheduled for Perth on 14th April, was vital for both teams. Queen's Park were clear and obviously going to win the league, but second place – and promotion – was still up for grabs. Clydebank were three points ahead of Saints, but with only one more game to play after their visit to Perth, while Saints had two more games, against Forfar and Broxburn; two teams they would expect to beat.

It would be fair to say that this match was the most important in St Johnstone's history

to that date. The prospect of playing in the top flight of Scottish football for the first time was both real and tantalisingly close.

Today's fans, used in recent years to the fervour that grips Perth when Saints have a big match, will not be surprised to learn that it was little different in the early 1920s (other than there being no internet, social media or television). There was huge interest in the game, reflected enthusiastically in the local press, and an enormous crowd flooded to the ground. Bearing in mind that Perth's population was smaller back then (as noted previously, it was 33,208 in 1921), the PA noted that, *"A quarter of the population was there supported by several thousands from different parts of the Big County ...*

The attendance was estimated at over 12,000, but the actual number paying at the gate was only 11,154. The difference is because the lower figure did not include season ticket holders or the many women and children who attended. The implication is that both these groups were allowed in free. The youngsters were almost certainly lifted over the turnstiles, but it was unusual then for women to have been given free entry (as they were in Victorian times).

As well as the main railway station there was, until 1966, Perth Princes Street Station – situated just behind where the Fergusson Art Gallery is today and obviously nearer the ground for those fans travelling from far afield. Presumably, they would have joined up with their fellow supporters in the city centre, finding lunch or a bar before walking across the South Inch and along the Edinburgh Road. Doubtless, there were also many who made the journey from the west and together they must have presented a very colourful spectacle as they progressed to Craigie Haugh. The PA recorded that, *"Half an hour before the game started the ground seemed packed but still the crowd flocked in and found positions for viewing the encounter."*

Before the days of modern health and safety, it must have been very busy indeed. If you've never looked at the site where the Recreation Ground was, it's worth doing the next time you are anywhere near the Edinburgh Road, just so you can imagine what it was like back in those days. The land is now occupied by the offices and yard of A J Stephen, the builders, situated just across the road from the prison and overlooked by the houses on South Inch Terrace (see the map in Part I, Chapter One, the photo in Chapter Seven and the cartoon above). There was no substantial terracing as there was at Muirton; just a shallow bank of earth and the grandstands.

Once the match got underway, it was clear Saints were the better side. The Courier's headline was, *"St Johnstone's Bid for Promotion, All-Round Brilliance in Thrilling Match,"* while the PA declared triumphantly that the result was, *"Changing the History of Football in Perth."*

Despite Saints good play, unfortunately A S Reid continued to fall short of expectations. In the first half, the Courier tells us he had *"a great opportunity"* only to waste it, then, *"Reid got a gilt-edged opportunity early in the second-half when, with only the goalkeeper to beat, he placed the ball in Wallace's arms."*

The PA was slightly kinder to the new striker regarding Reid's first-half chance, telling us it was actually a *"terrific drive blocked by Murphy,"* but they were scathing about the miss in the second half and give us a far better mental image of just how bad it was, describing the play thus, *"Reid failed miserably when only a yard or two from Wallace. Hart sent forward a beautiful low pass, but the centre hesitated, and although he had only the custodian to beat he sent the ball softly into Wallace's arms."* This was such a sitter, the PA also noted, *"The shout of 'goal' from the excited spectators was of no avail."* Even before

VAR ripped all the joy from celebrating a goal, we've all been there, rising excitedly to our feet only to have our hopes dashed…

Fortunately, the fans did not have to wait too long before they could celebrate in earnest. The PA tells how, some 15 minutes after Reid had passed up his big chance, *"Wilson (Saints' outside left) bore down on his own, and at the crucial moment he sent back to Dickson who was waiting in a rare position, and without hesitation the little inside left crashed the ball through many players into the net."*

Picture: The Courier

To say the crowd went wild is a gross understatement. Dickson's strike resulted in one of the loudest cheers ever to greet a St Johnstone goal. The PA's reporter seems to have shared in their enthusiasm, demonstrating that it's not just today's tabloids that can overdo the hyperbole: *"What cheers rent the air when the point was secured, and the echo by this time will only be reaching Chicago. No one was more jubilant than Wilson, the player who had engineered the move. He immediately ran to Dickson and about smothered him. The scene generally, however, was one of the most memorable in the annals of Perth football history. As a matter of fact, if there were really any Clydebank supporters in the crowd at all, they too must have been dancing – but not with glee. The cheers were deafening, and they could be heard as far away as High Craigie, where many people thought it was a railway smash, but with the prolonged noise of cheering they at last came to the conclusion that it was a goal for the Saints. No one in the park could control themselves, and it was a case of throwing up a hat and catching a bonnet. Blue and white balloons were sent flying into the air, and the referee's whistle could not be heard for some time later."*

It was agreed that the entire St Johnstone team played well, with particular plaudits going to full-back Glasgow in defence, McRoberts at half-back and Ribchester and Hart on the right flank of the forward line. Despite his goal, Dickson *"aggravated the crowd with his slowness on occasion,"* while Reid *"was curiously uneven…Two pinches he missed, and of course it's goals that count, but at the same time he cannot be said to have failed."*

Flushed with success – and with money, for the match had realised a record gate of £515 from the turnstiles, with a further £52 taken for admission to the stands, leaving the club with a profit of £105: 8: 4d – everyone connected with Saints now believed that promotion was in sight. The PA, in a precursor of the commentator's curse, had even begun to discuss how they would fare in the First Division. However, a storm was brewing in the west…

On Friday, 20th April, the Daily Record ran a story under the headline, *"A S Reid and St Johnstone – have Perth put their foot in it?"* The gist of the story was that the League Management Committee, which was meeting that same afternoon, was to consider the case that Saints had signed the player after the deadline.

One of the possible reasons why this had occurred was revealed in the Edinburgh Evening News of Saturday 21st April. After pointing out that St Johnstone, by way of *"a very serviceable side, a splendid spirit* (and) *the capacity of the enclosure and drawing powers of the district,"* would be a welcome addition to the First Division, it was noted that prior to the introduction that season of automatic promotion and relegation, *"a player was eligible for a match if his registration form was in the hands of the League secretary 'prior to the advertised time of kick-off of such match.' This rule altered with the formation of a Second Division, and the Perth club, breaking the new rule, have had enforced upon them a tremendously heavy penalty."*

The same day's PA ran a huge story, over several columns, headlined, *"Fatal Damper to St Johnstone's Promotion Aspirations,"* and detailing what had happened in great detail. In addition, the PA reported that for signing Reid after the deadline of 16th March, Saints were to be fined £5 for each of the four games in which he had played and, more importantly, the League deducted them two points, putting the prospect of promotion in serious jeopardy.

Then, as Saints were preparing for the next match, away to Forfar, a telegram came from Mr McAndrew, the Secretary of the Scottish League. Brief and to the point, the telegram read, *"Reid ineligible, must not be played, McAndrew."*

Amazingly, this was actually the first official contact Saints had had with the League about the issue. But even before this communique landed, the reaction of the directors and supporters was unanimous: namely, that Saints were being unfairly treated and although the term *"west-coast bias"* wasn't in common use in those days, that was clearly the underlying sentiment in and around Perth.

The fact that Reid had played in four games before any problem was raised was a particular source of concern. Had the League just been slow in noticing, or was there some skulduggery afoot? The suggestion at the Perth end was that the latter was very much the case, with many people believing that Clydebank, having lost the crucial game at the Recreation Grounds, then 'shopped' Saints to the League once they realised that Reid was ineligible. Conspiracy theories were seemingly rife, with an anonymous letter writer to the PA claiming, *"It was current talk at the finish of this game that a Clydebanker declared the defeat to be of no consequence because they had a trump card to play later."*

Nevertheless, the Edinburgh Evening News believed that there were no behind-the-scenes shenanigans. On 23rd April, they reported, *"We learn today that the Clydebank had made no move in the matter, but that the League, on their own initiative, took the business in hand, solicitous of their constitution and rules. It was a pity, however, that they had left it over till the settlement, as to which club was to join Queen's Park as qualifiers, became so imminent."*

Others were not so sanguine. A Mr James Milne, from Glasgow, wrote to the Saints' board with information about Clydebank. Two of the Saints' directors went to Glasgow to meet him, where they learned that Clydebank had also fielded an ineligible player, called John Swan, earlier that season. In this instance, the crime was even greater, for as well as playing Swan, he appeared under the name James Stafford, who was properly registered by Clydebank. Once this was made known to the League, they deducted two points from Clydebank and fined them the larger sum of £100, on the grounds that the deception was clearly deliberate. However, all this took place in late April, after the end of the season.

It should be noted that, doubtless dispirited by what had occurred, Saints only took one point from their last two games, so even if they had been successful in their appeal, Clydebank would still have been promoted on goal average. Having failed to set the heather on fire, A S Reid was given a free transfer at the start of the next season. By the end of that season, St Johnstone, doubtless still smarting from the perceived injustice, went on to win promotion to the First Division for the first time in their history.

Saints team: Stewart, Glasgow, Cassidy; Roberts, Walker, McRoberts; Ribchester, Hart, Reid, Dickson, Wilson.
Attendance: 12,000.

A dour, desperate encounter was anticipated and the anticipation realised

Scottish League Division One
Dundee United 0, St Johnstone 0
Tannadice Park, Saturday, 17th April 1926

Will It Be "Death Or Glory" For St. Johnstone At Tannadice?

Result Fraught With Momentous Issue To Both Teams: A Final Word On The Prospects.

Headline: Perthshire Advertiser

After gaining promotion to the First Division in 1924, Saints then finished in 11th place in their first season in the 20-team top league. The following season (1925-26) was less successful and with only two games left for most teams the only thing up for debate was whether relegation was probably or definitely going to happen.

By the start of April, it was clear that St Johnstone were in trouble. With only a few games left, Clydebank were almost certainly destined for the drop, but the identity of the club that would join them was still to be decided.

Three clubs - Dundee United, Saints and Raith Rovers - were all in serious danger and as the season drew to its conclusion it was a question of which of them would succumb. To make things even more nail-biting, the fixture list compiler had decided that Saints' last league match of the campaign would be at Tannadice. Although this was our final match, both United and Raith Rovers had one further game in which to secure their status, although as United's was away to Celtic this might not have seemed a big advantage. Raith, in contrast, were to finish their season at home to Queen's Park.

Before the match at Tannadice, Saints and United were level on 27 points, while the Rovers had 25 (Clydebank were already doomed, on 21 points). In the event of two of the three relegation contenders ending up tied on the same points, both United and the Rovers had a superior goal average to Saints, so, from a Perth perspective, a win in Dundee was essential. Depending on the result of Raith's game at Aberdeen, Saints knew that in the event of the Rovers (unexpectedly) pulling off a win at Pittodrie, they had to win to have any chance of staying up. For United, with a superior goal difference to Saints, a draw was sufficient. If Raith, as expected, were to lose at Aberdeen, then a draw for St Johnstone would have been enough to guarantee safety.

Doubtless, across the city and county of Perthshire, bars and workplaces saw little groups of men clustered together to work out the permutations and, as we all do in these circumstances, fear the worst. Just as in the last game of the 1961-62 season, when there were strong (and possibly accurate) rumours of the result between Saints and Dundee being fixed, with a draw meaning Dundee being crowned First Division champions and St Johnstone avoiding relegation (the rumours never materialised for, as we know, Saints were relegated after a 3-0 defeat), in 1926 there were some who believed that the final result of the game at Tannadice was also pre-arranged. The PA's scribe was not amongst them, however, telling his readers, *"Some go to the length of suggesting that the game with Dundee United on Saturday was 'cooked.' I mean for a draw. Take it from me this allegation, as Winston Churchill might say, is absolutely devoid of the slightest shade of a shadow of the shred of the foundation. Both teams were out to win, and had Bob Penman not been crocked early in the second half, I believe Saints would have beaten their keen rivals. The excitement of the occasion caused the game to be a scrappy one, but nevertheless some 20,000 spectators got plenty to enthuse over."*

With Tannadice bathed in sun and the ground conditions seemingly hard and dry, The PA reported that, *"from the word 'go' ... both sides were out to fight a tooth-and-nail battle ...(and)... Saints' policy appeared to be to get the ball to goal at any cost."* Their match report certainly substantiates this, with its account of two teams who knew that victory was vital and thus were going hammer-and-tongs to achieve it.

The Courier was somewhat less fulsome in its report, describing proceedings as, *"A dour, desperate encounter was anticipated and the anticipation realised. To search for real exciting incidents is to follow the futile process usually associated with the needle in the haystack. There were mighty few."* The Sunday Post was even more disparaging, claiming that St Johnstone *"were just as inept as the Dundee boys, and a goalless draw was a fair result for the poor exhibition of football."*

Both United and Saints were seemingly lucky to avoid at least one penalty being given against them. The first was when United's Davie Walker brought down Alex Dick in the penalty area, but the referee ignored Saints' pleas. The second occurred when Saints' Andy Kirkwood knocked the ball downwards with his hand. The United players were so convinced of the merit of their appeals that they *"stood as if it were a sure thing, but again the referee saw nothing."* In their next attack, United again appealed for a penalty when *"the ball was handled by Jamieson, although on this occasion it was accidental."* This, of course, was before VAR and IFAB started interfering with the previous, eminently sensible law that decreed that handball for a penalty had to be deliberate and not simply have rebounded from millimetres away onto a defender's arm.

If, despite the match reports of constant attacks at each end of the park, anyone seriously doubted the players' commitment, they would only need to look at the constant stream of injuries that disrupted the match. Indeed, the seeming lack of concern about incidents that today would be treated in a totally different way is almost shocking. According to the PA, the injuries began in the very first minute, when, *"Andrew Kirkwood came into collision with Welsh. The United inside left sustained a nasty cut over the right eye, but fortunately, he was able to resume in about ten minutes."*

Still in the first half, the PA reported another serious injury... *"Then came a time when it looked as if Saints' citadel could not but meet with disaster. Jock Macdonald it was who got the chance, but just as the winger's lightning drive was going home all the way, Penman nipped in and met the ball with his body. He was temporarily laid out. The sphere went for a fruitless corner."*

Today, Bob Penman would almost certainly have been taken off, but they were made of sterner stuff in the 1920s. He might have been better if he had been though, for in the second half he, *"met with an unfortunate injury which crippled him for the remainder of the game. It was Welsh who shot the ball, which Penman stopped with his foot, and Bob was laid out."* As the Sunday Post noted, *"he carried on, but it was obvious he was far from well."*

And the PA recorded that despite this, *"The Saints' skipper took up the right wing berth, while Munro went to right half, and Jock Whyte partnered Jamieson. Penman's injury tended to disorganise the team, but still the Saints fought bravely."*

This wasn't the end of players suffering for their respective causes. Towards the end, Jimmy Sanderson brought out a great save from Paterson in the United goal. The ball rebounded to Dick, who fired it goal-wards, only to see that Paterson, *"raised his head and the sphere struck him in the neck. The custodian was knocked out, but soon came round."*

Next, it was another Saints' player's turn to suffer, with *"Bauld making a hefty clearance, Dan Kirkwood received the full force of the ball on the head and went down like a log. It was some time before he really came to himself, and although obviously in pain he pluckily stuck on to play the game."*

Although these injuries were just the normal accidents that can occur in football, it does seem to have been what we'd now call a really dirty game. Both sides were culpable. The PA's match report was honest enough to admit, *"The game was moving at a fast pace, and the eagerness tended to fouling, and in this respect Saints appeared to be the greater sinners."*

At the end of play, the Courier concluded that Saints *"are really a bunch of boys who deserve something better than a Second Division gate. With all due sympathy to Raith Rovers in the plight in which they find themselves, Dundee enthusiasts have a* sneaking regard for the Saints of Perth. That, at least, was the Tannadice sentiment on Saturday."*

That same afternoon, to the surprise of many, Raith Rovers drew 1-1 with Aberdeen at Pittodrie, where, the Sunday Post tells us, *"9,000 spectators saw an uninspiring game."* This meant that, going into the final day of the season, Dundee United were safe, although they would go on to lose their last game 6-2 at Celtic. Raith, in contrast, simply had to win to get the two points that, along with their superior goal difference, would guarantee their continuation in the First Division and Saints' demotion from it.

To illustrate just how close it all was, on that final Saturday of the season, the Courier published the League table and the goal-averages for the respective clubs to show what they needed to do to avoid relegation. According to their reporter, St Johnstone's prospects were dire.

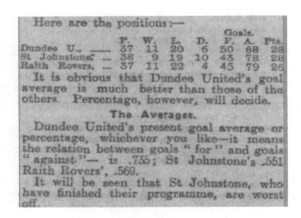

The PA, most unusually, carried a report from Stark's Park of the Rovers' final match of the season – and not just a brief note but (as shown below) the same full coverage that they normally gave to St Johnstone. Queen's Park, who were the visitors at Kirkcaldy, were safe on 32 points before the ball was kicked-off and had nothing to play for but their famous amateur spirit.

Headline: Perthshire Advertiser

In similar circumstances, most Saints' fans would be dreading the result, knowing that there was seemingly nothing they could do about it. However, in these particular circumstances, quite a few did do something: they headed to Kirkcaldy to support the Spiders. Not only the fans, but the directors too made their way to Fife, where, the PA tells us, they and the Raith board *"foregathered before the game in a very anxious frame of mind."*

As for those who made the journey from Perth, some of their behaviour was, by the standards of the day, beyond the pale. A letter, signed *"Fifer"* (but apparently from a Saints' fan) below the PA's match report, commented, *"There were many Saints' supporters present, the Queen's victory, naturally, causing the keened delight. There was only one thing, I think, out of place, and that was the numbers from Perth who were 'Sporting the Queen's Park colours.' That, to me, was not in keeping with the fair-minded criticism of the 'P.A.' each week and was hardly fair to a neighbouring club."*

The first paragraph of the PA consisted of one word – *"Saved!"* They could probably have stopped there and saved the ink and newsprint, but in order to set the scene the second paragraph continued, *"Raith Rovers and St Johnstone stood, as it were, between two fires, with Queen's Park acting the role of extinguishers. The piquant situation, abounding with all manner of interesting possibilities, had caught the popular fancy, and the result of the match was waited with breathless interest."* This proves yet again that it's not just the newspapers of today that make use of entertaining metaphors and flamboyant language.

The PA's sports editor (who wrote the piece) also took the opportunity to have a less than veiled swipe at William Maley, the Celtic manager, who, *"went out of his way a few months ago to broadcast to the soccer world that the Saints and Dundee United would descend to the Second League. It was a piece of gratuitous advice for which Mr Maley is notorious."*

Again, we can perhaps note the contrast with the modern world, where it would be very rash for any manager to pass judgement publicly on which club (or clubs) he expected to be relegated. In a similar vein, while it's easy to be magnanimous in victory, we really can't see today's local press coming up with something like the following: *"In the hour of the Saints' success – thanks to the Queen's – my sympathy goes out to Raith Rovers. And the St Johnstone directors and supporters will join hands with me on that issue. Self-preservation is, of course, the*

129

first law of nature, but for the bottom dogs there is always an unbounded admiration, and I doff my hat to the 'Lang Toun' representatives. They went down fighting – like veritable tigers."

The PA's match report itself did not actually mention the goal-scorers, although it does tell us that, unsurprisingly, *"the Rovers' play became decidedly windy. Small wonder. Anxiety was written large on their faces."* That said, the PA's scribe, while commenting that *"The Rovers struck me as a very ordinary side,"* also recorded that they did not have any of the luck that a team in their predicament needed and, more importantly, the Queen's goalkeeper, Jack Harkness, *"played a wonderful game in goal. It is no exaggeration to say that he stood between the Rovers and victory. Time and time again he saved when all seemed lost."* Harkness went on to play in the famous Wembley Wizards of 1928, when Scotland beat the auld enemy 5-1, and latterly became a celebrated sports journalist with the Sunday Post.

In Kirkcaldy, the Fife Free Press adopted a more sanguine approach, telling their readers, *"It became apparent as the season neared its close that Raith, hard workers as they were, lacked a something which is present in most First League clubs, that indefinable touch of class which shows itself in head work rather than footwork – the little discomfiting tricks which gall opponents and blind them to the real move on the board. Raith simply played straight football."*

And just to prove that it's a near universal sentiment, the Free Press also reported on 'west coast bias,' noting, *"It is curious that the West of Scotland folks should appear to have a dislike to Raith. Several who attended the match were jubilant at Rovers' defeat, but why they should have a preference for Perth is difficult to imagine."* They went on, *"There was a keen Perth contingent at the match, not*

surprising when the stakes are considered, and they no doubt moved a hearty vote of thanks to the victors for their entry among the great in football circles."

The Scotsman also noted the Rovers' failure to take the chances they created, and like the PA also credited Harkness in the Queen's goal with an outstanding display. But despite their praise for the goalkeeper, they damned the rest of the Spiders' defence with faint praise, noting, *"it is impossible to withhold sympathy from the Rovers, as numerous good shots were* <u>*accidentally*</u> (our emphasis) *blocked by the Queen's Park defence…".*

So that was that: Saints were saved. But in the summer of 1926, the problems besetting the team were all-too-evident, at least according to the press. The PA didn't pull its punches, insisting *"There will require to be a good deal of hard thinking in a team sense. It is impossible that so much dead weight can be carried next season… Sentiment must be discarded."*

At the AGM in May 1926, the directors, listened to complaints about a lack of fight, disunity amongst the playing squad and a forward line that simply didn't score a sufficient number of goals often enough to win matches. With a commendable degree of honesty, the club Minutes record that the board simply had not recognised quickly enough the lack of harmony amongst the players.

Despite this, St Johnstone had fortuitously had an important reprieve and they used it well, bringing in better players and developing a team that gradually improved its league position every season until 1929-30 - when it all went pear-shaped and they were, on that occasion, relegated.

Saints team: Page, Penman, Jamieson; Whyte, A. Kirkwood, and Swallow; Munro, D. Kirkwood, Dick, Black, and Sanderson. Attendance: 20,000.

One of the finest football spectacles Perth fans have been privileged to see

Friendly match
St Johnstone 0, Arsenal 0
Muirton Park, Monday, 26th September 1932

There are many reasons why clubs play friendly matches. Usually, they are pre-season looseners, designed to help the players get up to match-fitness and see who will be struggling for a first-team place and who will be the first name on the manager's team-lines. Sometimes, they are played as part of a transfer deal – as for example when Saints sold Ally McCoist to Sunderland in August 1981 and the Wearsiders came north to play a friendly at the start of the 1982-83 season. Often, they are testimonial games, but sometimes they are played simply because a director or manager has a good contact with another club and wants to give their team a change of scenery and a chance to play against a different opposition from those they normally face.

That last one was the situation which pertained to the match between St Johnstone and Arsenal in 1932. Although Saints had played against a big English club before, that was on the 27th August 1886, only a year or so after our club had been formed. Their opponents that day were Aston Villa, who themselves had been founded only 12 years earlier. Two years later, in 1888, Villa would become one of the founders of the English Football League. It's fair to say they were recognised as a power in the land well before they came north to play St Johnstone and unsurprisingly the game finished 11-1 to the visitors.

By 1932 things had changed considerably for Saints. Now a rising power in Scottish football and with a famous and well-respected manager in Tommy Muirhead, they were able to attract high quality players to the club. Also, courtesy of Muirhead's contacts (he was a personal friend of Herbert Chapman, the Arsenal manager), they were able to play a friendly in the autumn of 1932 with the Highbury club, then starting their ascent to dominate the English football landscape of the 1930s and become, in many people's eyes, the best team in the world at that time. The arrangements for the game were made earlier in 1932, with the St Johnstone Board Minutes of the 19th of April recording that the club had received a letter from Arsenal about the game.

In August, the PA ran a brief story, saying, *"The famous London combination will travel north to Gleneagles on the night of Saturday, 24th September, and they will stay at the Gleneagles Hotel until Monday evening, when their full League side - unless injuries supervene – will meet Saints in what should be one of the finest football spectacles Perth fans have been privileged to see."*

This would be like Saints arranging a friendly with Liverpool, Manchester United or Manchester City today, but with the added difference that no-one was able to see these teams on television back then, so if you wanted to see the stars you had to get to the match. Moreover, the other big difference in 1932 was that, as the PA noted, Arsenal brought their entire first team and played the strongest side available to them; something that is unlikely to happen today.

When the news of the match became public, there was huge interest, not just in Perth but for miles around. The cost of admission to the game was, as shown in the advert here from the Courier, much cheaper than today, with the most expensive stand seat of three shillings being equivalent to £12.13 in 2023. However, in relative terms, this was a far larger percentage of the average wage at the time. To put this in context, Davie Rutherford, the Saints' trainer (and future manager) was on £5 a week, while the players were on about £3-£4 a week during the playing season and £2 a week during the close season. In other words, entry to the stand was equivalent to 7.5% of a player's close-season wage. It's also worth noting that the time of the kick-off was 6.00 pm. Bearing in mind that this was late September and there were no floodlights, it is likely that the spectators would be peering through the gloom ere the end of the match.

This was a very good St Johnstone side. The previous (1931-32) season they had secured promotion back to the First Division, scoring 102 goals in the process. Spearheading the attack was Jimmy Benson, who had made his debut at 16 and was still only 17 when he scored 44 League and Cup goals in that promotion season, a record that still stands today. Although he found it harder in the top flight, he ended his Saints' career with 53 goals from 50 matches, thus making his Saints' most prolific goalscorer of all-time.

At the back was Sandy McLaren, the (joint, with Willie Imrie) first Saints' player to be capped for Scotland and described by many contemporaries as the best goalkeeper in Scotland at that time. Other stalwarts of the side were full backs Johnny Welsh and Willie Clark, veteran centre-half Bob Ireland, inside forwards Lawrie McBain, Harry Ferguson (although he didn't play against Arsenal) and Willie Benzie, and outside left Harry Nicolson.

The biggest attraction for the fans that night was undoubtedly Alex James. He was Arsenal's star player; what we would now call a deep-lying or sitting midfielder, regarded at that time as one of the very best in his position in the country (and therefore the world) and justly famous across Scotland for his brace of goals in the celebrated Wembley Wizards' defeat of England in 1928.

The match was played in front of a crowd of around 16,000. This was the figure given in the PA: the Courier agreed while the Scotsman reported 18,000. The London paper, the Daily Herald (the precursor to The Sun), said 15,000. No matter, those who remember Muirton will know that even at the lowest figure this meant the terracing and stands were packed. They had come from all over to see some of the greatest players in the world. Possibly the best modern(ish) day analogy would be if Liverpool team of the 1980s came to Perth and Kenny Dalglish, at the peak of his powers, was playing alongside the rest of the team that won the 1981 European Cup.

The first paragraph in the PA's match report made it clear just how good the Arsenal stars were…

"The matchless wizardy of Alec James … the phenomenal speed of Joe Hulme. These are the two most vivid impressions which the St Johnstone-Arsenal match at Muirton Park on Monday evening has left on my mind. At James the wonderful crowd of 16,000 just marvelled - Hulme simply made them gasp."

The Arsenal team that played against Saints in 1932. Picture, The Courier
These strips were all red: the famous white sleeves were introduced in 1933.

Later, the correspondent wrote, *"When I come to say a word or two about the players I simply come back to James. But what more can one say about James. He was just James, obviously enjoying the opportunity of playing before his own folk."*

The match reports in the PA and the Dundee Courier make it clear that Arsenal had turned up to entertain, but that they didn't expect to be extended.

Saints quickly dispelled that idea, as the PA described: *"No one would suggest, of course, that Arsenal went all out. I received the impression that, to begin with, vigorously as they played in the outfield, they palpably slackened near goal under the supposition – which proved to be a delusion – that they would score as many goals as were necessary in good time. When they went to within shooting distance they over-elaborated and made it easier for*

the home defence. And when they set themselves seriously to get results they discovered that it was not such an easy matter after all. Indeed, after the interval, against a strong breeze, they found themselves hard put to it to repulse sustained St Johnstone attacks and at the finish a draw was a fair reflex of the run of play."

That said, there was no doubt that Arsenal had the better players. Here's the PA again…

"This was an experience which should be valuable for the Muirton players. Arsenal illustrated, particularly, the value of the first-time pass and of quick positional moves. The London forwards, in everything except shooting, taught Saints' attack a lesson. They did things in less than half the time some of our best Scottish forwards require, and they did it just as accurately

133

despite the speed with which they worked. Arsenal did everything more quickly than Scottish teams are in the habit of doing, and made the other fellows look sluggish in comparison. No time was wasted, even in throwing the ball in...

"St Johnstone, without being wholly out of the picture as an attacking force, were struggling for most of the first half. Against the wind they found it difficult to make headway...

"By way of interlude to repeated Arsenal offensives, in which the moving spirit was generally the amazing James, St Johnstone made periodical raids through Nicholson and Sherlaw. Ballantyne had one good shot charged down by Compton, but it could not be said that Moss's charge was ever in real jeopardy. The Perth attack was never able to keep the ball for long and the home rear lines had good reason to feel satisfied when the interval arrived and they still retained a clean sheet."

The Courier's reporter was of much the same opinion, writing of Arsenal that, "At any rate they did not display any undignified keenness to press home their scientific advantage. Of that advantage there was no doubt.

"They were much ahead of the Saints, whose main claim to distinction was their determination... Right at the start the game gave promise of big thrills. That first quarter of an hour of dash and dazzle, positional interchange and rapid first-time passing had the Saints flummoxed."

The second half, however, was a different kettle of fish. The PA said that, "It was at once seen that Arsenal were not to have matters all their own way... Benson rattled into Roberts and his backs with a will, and while Hulme suddenly flashed into the game with a series of terrific bursts, it was now no one-side affair. McLaren effected a clever save when Bastin's head turned in a Hulme cross. Immediately afterwards Priestley narrowly missed with a fine hook shot; Benzie middled a fine ball which swung just over; and Sherlaw was only inches high with a fast drive after he had worked inside which showed that Saints were giving rather more than they got. If Roberts had not impeded Benson the latter might very well had gone clean through on more than one occasion. But Mr Craigmyle (the referee) did not see things that way."

The Scotsman recorded that towards the end of the game, Moss, the Arsenal 'keeper, "saved magnificently from Benzie when a goal seemed certain," before finishing their report by saying, "For the Saints, Clark, Ireland, Priestley and Ballantyne shone in a sound side. A draw was a good result."

The PA described Saints' final chance as follows: "From Benson's pass Benzie shot hard and true, to find Moss saving brilliantly... In the gathering darkness Saints produced some of their best work and the finish found them giving tit for tat."

For a London-centric view of the game, we were able to find a match report from the Daily Herald. They too exulted in the performance of James, noting that, "the home goal had several extremely narrow escapes during the game and McLaren the Scottish international 'keeper, was forced to make some wonderful saves," but also paying a serious complement to St Johnstone in recording: "There was no question of Arsenal not attacking their hardest. In the second half, especially, they exerted all their wiles, shooting hard and often in an endeavour to score the winning goal but before the finish matters had reached a point where the London club were fighting desperately to save themselves from defeat."

That might have been an overly-generous summation, but there seems to be no doubt that Saints deserved the draw.

It must have been an enjoyable break for their normal routine for the Arsenal party. With St Johnstone picking up the entire tab for their visit, the PA reported that Alex James and his companions were *"put up at the Gleneagles Hotel, enjoyed golf there on Sunday, were entertained to lunch in the Station Hotel by the Town Council in addition to receiving a civic welcome, and before journeying south on Monday night enjoyed dinner in the Royal George Hotel."*

That last event in the Royal George Hotel saw some 70 people sit down to dine and watch the Arsenal director Sir Samuel Hill-Wood present Tommy Muirhead with a silver casket and praise his work for football in general and St Johnstone in particular. These remarks were endorsed by the Arsenal chairman, Mr J J Edwards, and manager, Herbert Chapman. For St Johnstone, Robert Campbell then gave the Arsenal players and their trainer, *"souvenirs of their visit in the shape of a wallet and fountain pen,"* adding that the wallet was for their bonuses and the pen was to be used when they re-signed for Arsenal.

Saints team: McLaren; Welsh and Clark; Priestley, Ireland and McBain; Sherlaw, Benzie, Benson, Ballantyne and Nicholson. Attendance: 16,000.

Rangers' centre-forward Purvis was inclined to give the 'keeper a rough passage

Scottish League Second Division,
Berwick Rangers 0, St Johnstone 2
Shielfield Park, Berwick, Wednesday, 27th April, 1960

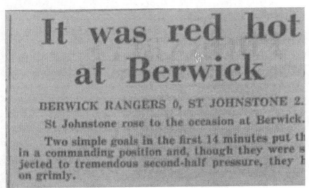

It was red hot at Berwick

BERWICK RANGERS 0, ST JOHNSTONE 2.

St Johnstone rose to the occasion at Berwick.

Two simple goals in the first 14 minutes put th[em] in a commanding position and, though they were s[ub]jected to tremendous second-half pressure, they h[eld] on grimly.

Headline, The Courier

After the Second World War, Saints were, in the view of many, somewhat shabbily treated by the Scottish football authorities. Despite having been a fixture in the First Division before 1939 and recognised as one of the better teams, when football was re-organised after the war, St Johnstone were put in the lower tier of the senior game, referred to as the B Division.

This set-up continued for over a decade, until in 1956-57 the B Division became Division 2 once more. Over all this time, Saints struggled to climb back to the top tier, but as the years - and the managers - went by, and despite the occasional near-miss, the fans could have been forgiven for wondering if they ever would achieve their former heights.

In 1958, the board decided to appoint Bobby Brown as manager. It was to prove an astute move. Popular with the fans (although not always with the players) and a great PR man for the club, Brown transformed the team's fortunes in a relatively short space of time. In his first season in charge, Saints finished 6th in the table. In his second (1959-60), came the breakthrough everyone in Perthshire wanted to see.

A combination of judicious, often highly experienced, signings, allied to free-scoring forwards and a solid defence in front of Billy Taylor in goal, meant that as the season's end approached Saints only required one point from their last two games, not just to secure promotion but also to become Second Division Champions.

The penultimate game was a midweek one: away to Berwick Rangers. Being a Wednesday, hardly any fans travelled from Perth and the match seems to have kicked off at around 6.00 pm, because the PA's report states that *"Half-a-dozen blue-scarved fans danced and hugged each other delightedly at Shielfield Park, Berwick at 8.40 pm..."*.

The game started brightly for Saints. Within the first 14 minutes, they were two goals to the good; the first from Joe Carr in only six minutes, firing home a cross by Ian Gardiner. Some eight minutes later, the margin was doubled, when Berwick's full-back, Eddie Docherty, made a hash of an attempted clearance and blasted the ball past his own goalkeeper.

Although there were no more goals, that fact alone does not tell the story of the rest of the game. The PA records that St Johnstone had been impressive, largely dominating proceedings during the first half, so much so that, *"After half-an-hour Billy Taylor had not had a direct save to make."* In the second forty-five, it was a different story and the nerves crept in as the likelihood of promotion came ever nearer and this, coupled with a change in formation from the home team, caused Saints several scary moments before the final whistle.

We tend to think that football in those days was just a question of two teams going out and giving their all, without any real thought going into tactics, but the Berwick manager, Jim McIntosh, clearly made changes to the way in which his team was set out in the second half, pressing them on to attack Saints and not sit back. In particular, as the PA tells us, *"Berwick pivot Rugg discarded his traditional defensive role guarding the centre spearhead and moved upfield, commanding the ground and the air between the two penalty areas. (Berwick) Wing halves Carr and Campbell got a grip on Innes and Haughey. Rugg improved his value immensely as a builder of offensives rather than a destroyer only."*

This strategy worked, in that Berwick put the Perth rearguard under such pressure that the PA described how the Perth forwards had to fall back to help out their defence, with only John Liddell remaining up front, *"but without support he could do little."*

Fortunately for St Johnstone, one man did keep his head while others were losing theirs. The Courier reported how Billy Taylor, *"remained calm at a vital stage when his colleagues were slicing their clearances in all directions."* Of course, in those days, roughing up the keeper was par for the course and the PA noted that *"Rangers' centre-forward Purvis was inclined to give the 'keeper a rough passage, but Taylor remained unperturbed."*

Purvis did not let up and with the tension building he *"was twice warned for his rough treatment of the 'keeper and in an isolated raid to the other end Haughey and Rugg were involved in a mix-up which ended with the pivot being penalised."*

Ultimately, all ended well and *"Saints' poise returned in the closing stages and if*

the pressure was never completely thrown off the attacks were contained in a fast, exciting finale to what was one of the best games of the season at Berwick."

The players, of course, all received championship medals: something that some of them would do again within a few years as Saints were relegated from the First Division in 1962 and then promoted again in 1963. Stephen McFadyen, son of the legendary right back Charlie, kindly sent us his dad's two Second Division Champions medals, noting that he was born in the same season as the first promotion and his brother was born in the second promotion season.

Charlie McFadyen's Division Two Champions' medals: photo, Stephen McFadyen

By achieving promotion, this Saints' team set in motion a return to the top flight and (eventually) cemented the notion that our club's place is in the foremost arena of Scottish football. That's why this game was so important: had they not succeeded, Saints might have become marooned in the Second Division, bumbling along and becoming a permanent fixture in the lower reaches of the game.

Saints team: Taylor, McFadyen and Hawthorne; Walker, Brown and Docherty; Gardiner, Innes, Liddell, Haughey and Carr.
Attendance: unknown.

No. 9
Yahoo – that was a very Merry Christmas!

Scottish League Division One
Rangers 2, St Johnstone 3
Ibrox Stadium, Saturday 21st December 1963

SHOOTING FIREWORKS BY ALEX. FERGUSON

"Hat-Trick" Feat in St Johnstone's Ibrox Triumph

Hearts Willing to Transfer Paton, But –

ST JOHNSTONE manager Bobby Brown confirmed yesterday that Hearts were willing to transfer their inside-forward Danny Paton to the Perth club. But he added: " Any deal is conditional on our seeing the player in action."

Headline, Perthshire Advertiser

Rangers 2, St. Johnstone 3.

(Half-time — 1-0)

Scorers:—Rangers — Brand (38), Provan (pen., 72). St. Johnstone — Ferguson (54, 59, 78).

ST. Johnstone provided the shock of the season and gave themselves and their fans the best possible New Year tonic, by earning a well-deserved victory over Rangers, at Ibrox on Saturday. And the man who scored all three visitors' goals was inside-left Alex Ferguson — the "forgotten man" of Muirton who was up for offer earlier in the season.

Even if he hadn't gone on to become the greatest football manager in the world, Alex Ferguson would still be recognised for his exploits on an extraordinary afternoon in Glasgow, just a few days before Christmas 1963. The circumstances surrounding his appearance at Ibrox that day were also rather extraordinary, for until he was picked for that game it seemed as if his time with the club was drawing to a close as he had been put on the 'open-to-transfer' list earlier in the (1963-64) season and nearly signed for Raith Rovers in November.

Having been promoted the previous season, Saints spent the remainder of 1963 trying to consolidate their position in the First Division. It was proving to be a tough slog and, just prior to the Rangers match, we were in the bottom six, only a few points from the foot of the table. No-one really expected anything from a trip to play the current League champions, who were also top of the table going into the match. In the event, it was one of the most memorable games in Saints' history.

Those Perth fans who made the trip to Glasgow might have been surprised to see Jimmy Harrower dropped from the team. In his stead came 23-year-old Alex Ferguson, who took the inside left berth while Bobby Craig (who was normally in that position) switched to inside right.

As is the case nowadays, there were relatively few Saints' fans in attendance at Ibrox that afternoon. One who was there was an 11-year-old boy called Charlie Smith, although as he admitted when we spoke to him in 2023, he can't actually remember who he was with or how he got there, although he thinks he must have travelled by the Glasgow Subway to the ground … *"I was very interested in football as a schoolboy and was sort-of a half-*

138

Rangers/half-Saints fan I suppose. Rangers were the champions back then and had a team full of internationalists so lots of youngsters followed them, although that day I went there supporting Saints and, I should stress, I'm now 100% a Saints' supporter.

"What I most remember was the size of the crowd, the huge terracing and the fact that everyone there seemed to be supporting Rangers. It wasn't very cultured though: the bad language was off-the-scale compared to Muirton – and it got much worse as the game went on!"

In fact, the crowd wasn't that big, although the ground certainly was. The capacity of Ibrox back then was 80,000 (it had seen crowds of well over 100,000 before the war), but there were only 14,000 at this match, although, as Charlie said, the vast majority were there to support the home team rather than Saints.

Another young lad who went to the match from Perth was former Saints' Managing Director Stewart Duff. He told us that he had no problem getting to Glasgow because, "My dad worked on the railway, so he got free tickets. My sister and my mum went shopping and my dad and I went to the football. I must have been about 12 or 13 at that time. My abiding memories are of the vastness of the old Ibrox stadium and terracing with the crush barriers dotted about, plus the fact that it was a cold, miserable and foggy day.

"We were behind the goal, where the Broomloan Stand is nowadays (i.e. where the wee knot of dedicated Saints' fans gets corralled into the corner in Ibrox today) and I remember vividly when you went in you had to climb up those steep steps. Of course, in those days, you could stand wherever you wanted. I remember the goals – a welcome antidote to the cold weather - and then the final whistle and yahoo – that was a very Merry Christmas!"

The story of the match is that Rangers started on the front foot and were the better team in the first half, going in at the break one goal up on Saints after Ralph Brand scored in the 38th minute. The Sporting Post's report (which was, as always in those days, a sort-of running match commentary dictated down a telephone wire, with summaries at 45 and 90 minutes), said that after the first half, "No doubt about it, Rangers deserve their lead, but once again Saints' rear lines had been tops. The Perth attack was still sadly devoid of punch."

They may have been devoid of punch in the first forty-five minutes, but in the second half it was a different story. Here's The Sporting Post again…

"In 54 minutes St Johnstone put the cat among the pigeons by equalising. And what a peach of a goal it was!

"McIntyre clipped a Kemp centre to Craig, who tried to force the ball through, but it broke to Ferguson. Without hesitation, the inside-left blasted the ball well beyond Ritchie's reach."

As if that wasn't enough, some six minutes later the young striker did it again, when "Kemp collected a Craig slip and put such force behind a vicious 25-yarder that Ritchie could not hold the ball. It broke to Ferguson, who slammed it home. The inside-left was swamped by his delighted mates."

Charlie Smith remembers that when Saints scored their first, "the place went silent." Then, when Alex Ferguson put St Johnstone ahead, "the Rangers' fans started on their own team: the mumping and moaning - and swearing - were incredible."

It wasn't just the home fans: The Sporting Post recounted how "Rangers were simply stunned and Millar (their centre forward) was booked following a clash with Townsend."

However, this Rangers team were not champions by accident and they came back strongly. Inevitably, they got a penalty – a highly disputed one. Buck McCarry had chested the ball out for a corner, but referee Bill Mullan adjudged that he had handled the ball. The Saints players surrounded the ref and Mr Mullan went to confer with his linesman, before returning to point again to the dreaded spot. Then, as the PA tells us, *"Provan came up, to give Fallon no chance."*

The penalty was in the 72nd minute. Normally in these circumstances, Rangers go on to win, but not that day. Six minutes after Fallon had picked Provan's penalty out of his net, Alex Ferguson was on the score sheet again, as described by the PA…

"Shearer was short with a pass-back, McIntyre beat 'keeper Ritchie to it and cut the ball back to Ferguson, who shot into the empty net from close in."

Not only had the young Rangers' supporter from Govan scored a hat-trick against his boyhood heroes, he nearly went one better in the last ten minutes when, as the Sporting Post tells us, *"Ferguson almost grabbed a fourth with a sudden shot on the turn that flew inches past."*

For Charlie Smith, or rather for those around him in the crowd, things had turned surreal, or, as he put it, *"Then Fergie got the third and the people around me couldn't believe that Rangers might lose the match."*

Sir Alex's own story of his hat-trick was briefly recounted by him to us in one of our earlier books: *'Hagiography: The 60 Greatest Saints.'* At that time, he told us, *"I'd called off with flu on the Friday – I'd previously had a broken cheek bone and played in three reserve games which we lost by big scores. The manager sent my mum a telegram to say I was in the team, so I went and scored the hat-trick. As a Rangers fan, it was interesting to see the reaction I got from my mates back home when I returned to Govan after the game!"*

This was St Johnstone's first win at Ibrox since 1925 (see Part I, Chapter 15 above) and it (still) is the only time a Saints' player has scored a hat-trick against either half of the Old Firm.

For much of the 20th century, before the days of Official Club Poets such as Jim Mackintosh, such feats were recorded in verse in the local papers. In this instance, a splendid piece of doggerel was published in the PA the week after the game…

Requiem for Rangers

Sadly they tolled each bell in the steeple,
Proud banners lay crumpled and mute were 'The People,'
Stilled was their laughter and graven their mirth,
For Rangers had fallen to the wee Saints of Perth.

The 'Gers v Saints – 'twas a foregone conclusion,
They'll rattle them in – at least half a dozen,
And when at half time one-nil was the score,
They smugly sat back and waited for more.

Alas and Alack – 'twas vain wishful thinking,
Saints equalised in less than a twinkling,
Then salted the wound by taking the lead,
While bold Jimmy Millar was 'losing the heid.'

Till sharp as a lance the ref's whistle blew,
From the penalty spot the score was two-two,
The faithful relaxed and chanted eas-eee,
And that's when young Fergie scored goal No. 3.

Three-two was the score, young Alex scored all,
The mighty have fallen how great was their fall,
And when the super leagues come to encircle the earth,
Remember Great Rangers and the Wee Saints from Perth!

The author of this, surely award-winning, poetry, appeared under the pseudonym, *"Cryptic."* Nom-de-plumes were very popular in the Scottish media, especially in the inter-war and post-war years (the most famous being the Daily Record's *"Waverley"* –Willie Gallagher). The PA has employed one or two Rangers' fans on its sports desk over the years, most notably, Gordon Bannerman, but it's hard to see them coming up with something as memorable as this.

Ironically, after the game, manager Bobby Brown was quoted by the PA as saying that Ferguson was *"very happy"* at Muirton. As regards his future, Brown noted, *"with only 23 of a playing staff at present, St Johnstone simply can't afford to transfer a player like Ferguson."*

As an object lesson in being aware that managers often say one thing and mean another, this was hard to beat, because within six months Alex was on his way out of Perth, transferred to Dunfermline in the summer of 1964. And after that, the rest, as they say, is history…

Saints team: Fallon; McFadyen, Richmond; Townsend, McKinven, McCarry; Flanagan, Craig, McIntyre, Ferguson, Kemp.
Attendance: 14,000.

It is true that the playing conditions were somewhat difficult

Scottish League Division One
Hibernian 2, St Johnstone 5
Easter Road, Saturday 24ᵗʰ December 1966

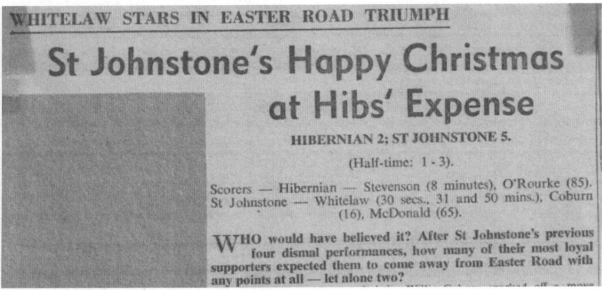

WHITELAW STARS IN EASTER ROAD TRIUMPH

St Johnstone's Happy Christmas at Hibs' Expense

HIBERNIAN 2; ST JOHNSTONE 5.

(Half-time: 1 - 3).

Scorers — Hibernian — Stevenson (8 minutes), O'Rourke (85). St Johnstone — Whitelaw (30 secs., 31 and 50 mins.), Coburn (16), McDonald (65).

WHO would have believed it? After St Johnstone's previous four dismal performances, how many of their most loyal supporters expected them to come away from Easter Road with any points at all — let alone two?

Headline: Perthshire Advertiser

We have noted in some of the earlier chapters how games that today would be cancelled in the blink of an eye were played to a successful conclusion, despite frozen and snowy conditions. This match, against Hibs, was notable not just for such difficulties, but also for a superb, all-round performance and a remarkable hat-trick (that could have been four or five) from Gordon Whitelaw. What made it more impressive was the fact that Gordon and some of the rest of the Saints' team were wearing highly illegal footwear.

Gordon recalled how he was admonished by the manager when he was at Partick Thistle in the early 1960s, *"The club paid for our boots so I went out to a local sportswear shop and got my first pair of moulded sole boots. Willie Thornton, the Thistle manager, buttonholed me and said, 'we don't normally allow players to spend that much money.'*

"Although rubber-soled boots had been introduced, the 'normal' boots still had studs that were nailed in. Unlike today, there were two big manufacturers – Puma and Adidas. I preferred Adidas because I liked a tight boot and after I'd bought a new pair, I'd soak them in the bath and the next day I'd wear them to training. They would then stretch tightly around my feet but wouldn't stretch any further, unlike Pumas, which continued to expand and didn't feel so tight. A number of players also wore quite tight boots, believing, as I did, that having tight boots helped them control shots better.

"What happened at Easter Road was that after the referee had been in to our dressing room to inspect our boots, we stripped a layer off the sole, leaving a bit of the nails showing so we could get the grip we needed when the grass was as hard and frosty as it was that day."

That it was hard, frosty and indeed snowy is beyond doubt. The PA noted that, *"It is true that the playing conditions were somewhat difficult and that the referee and linesmen delayed the start of the second half to inspect the lines and the field, but it would have been farcical if they even considered abandoning the game."*

Saints had gone into this game on the back of a dire run of form. Gordon Whitelaw, looking back on the match, recalled this as *"we'd had a hard time."* Of the previous six games, all, bar one - and that was a draw - had been lost. It was indeed a *"hard time,"* which made the final score even more surprising. As the PA said in its introductory paragraph, *"Who would have believed it?"*

Certainly not the fans, who were probably rubbing their eyes in disbelief after only 30 seconds. That's how long it took for Whitelaw to open the scoring. Here's how the PA described it: *"The second hand had only moved halfway round the watch face, when Whitelaw got hold of the ball in the box. He pushed it forward and let loose with a fierce shot which crashed into the roof of the net with Allan helpless."*

Saints could, perhaps should, have gone further ahead, when Gordon turned provider, heading the ball down for O'Donnell, but the right winger mistimed his shot and it headed skywards, to the relief of the home defenders.

Hibs then equalised in the eighth minute, when Jimmy Donaldson misjudged a cross-shot from Stevenson, pushing it on to the post and into his goal. However, while the home supporters might have imagined that they had turned the tide, Willie Coburn stepped up to hammer in another goal after the ball broke to him from a muffed cross by O'Donnell. This was only 16 minutes into the game and it took virtually the same amount of time again before Saints went further ahead.

Just past the half hour mark, there was what can best be described as a proper, old-fashioned stramash in the Hibs penalty box. The PA describes it thus: *"Whitelaw burst out of a melee in the home area and fired home past the diving keeper."*

He nearly got his hat-trick before half-time, with another strong shot that was pushed over the bar by Allan, but on this day and in this form Gordon was not to be denied.

After the interval, during which the groundsman cleared some of the lines around the pitch, the PA records: *"Five minutes after the restart, he ran on to a splendid pass by O'Donnell and carried on casually to shoot low past Allan."*

The game then threatened to flare up, with Hibs' Scott booked for *"a stupid foul on the man who proved his master, Bobby Smith."*

Alex McDonald then got in on the act, with a goal in the 65th minute that, according to the PA *"somehow got through the net."*

At this point, the Hibs' fans became somewhat disgruntled. Their displeasure manifest itself and, *"the slow handclap started about this stage and all they could muster were a few sarcastic cheers when O'Rourke scored an anticlimactical consolation goal five minutes from the end."*

Things could have got even worse for Hibernian, and even better for Whitelaw as he skated over the hard ground in his illegal boots. In the final minute, McDonald played him in but Gordon's shot hit the upright and bounced out.

The PA summed up the hat-trick hero's performance enthusiastically, claiming, probably correctly: *"He has never played better in a St Johnstone jersey, neither as a carrier nor as a finisher, and would have had a fourth goal in the last minute if the post had not thwarted him."*

Perhaps he should have worn those boots even more often, but in fairness Gordon's record in that St Johnstone jersey (and legal boots) was very impressive, with 70 goals from his 225 appearances.

While Gordon remembers scoring the hat-trick, he couldn't remember the details of the goals, but did recall hitting the post at the end of the match and also that after the game he met George Smith, with whom he had played at Partick Thistle. Smith was a very good footballer who had played for the Scottish Football League team in 1958, but by this time, he had retired from the game and was working in the media. He had waited to see Gordon and greeted him with the words, *"I didn't realise you were as good as that."* For Gordon, this was a real compliment from someone whom he really respected and admired.

Gordon also noted that he wasn't the only Saint who played well on the day. In particular, he singled out centre-forward John Kilgannon. *"John had real twinkle-toes and terrific balance. I can still see him in my mind – a great footballer."*

It's always a pleasure to see Saints score a lot of goals and with that in mind it's worth looking again at the different levels of excitement that prevailed in that era of football. If goals are what make games (and, let's be honest, they are the reason we all go), then it is fascinating to note that after this match Saints had played 15 times in the League, scoring 30 goals and conceding 40. In contrast, at the time of writing this (February 2023), the current team had played 26 League games, scoring 31 goals and conceding 43 in the process. The change in emphasis from trying to score goals to trying not to concede them is starkly evident and one of the reasons why several of the older fans we spoke to for this book told us they preferred watching football in the 50s, 60s and 70s than today.

One final footnote: although the story about the boots may seem far-fetched, when we spoke to Jim Pearson about his part in a number of the games in this book, we told him about this game. Jim, as many people know, played a key part in making Nike one of the major brands in football boots and he does know a thing or two about them. He told us, *"I came into the game a few years after this and never saw it myself, but I had heard a few stories about players leaving projecting nails in their boots to help with hard or semi-frozen pitches, so it did not surprise me one bit to hear Gordon's story."*

Saints team: Donaldson; Coburn and Smith; Townsend, Rooney and McPhee; O'Donnell, Whitelaw, Kilgannon, McDonald and Johnston.
Substitute: McCarry (unused).
Attendance: 5,688.

No. 11

Some amazing decisions from referee Henderson of Dundee

St Johnstone 2, Clyde 1,
Scottish Football League, First Division,
Muirton Park, Saturday, 10th April 1971

Connolly "heads" Saints into European football

ST JOHNSTONE 2, CLYDE 1,

(Half-time: 1-0),

Scorers—St Johnstone—Connolly (38 and 75 mins.); Clyde—Hay (71).

IT'S EUROPEAN football for Perth next season. That was the outcome of Saturday's win over Clyde at Muirton Park. Two

A Hasting effort went just over the bar and within a minute Hall saw a first-time shot skim the woodwork with McCulloch beaten.

Clyde were beginning to come more into the game as the second half wore on and first Burns and then Hay came close with good shots that Donaldson did well to save.

In the 67th minute the injured Hastings was replaced by Millar

Headline: Perthshire Advertiser

Under Willie Ormond, Saints had become, for the first time since the 1930s, a force to be reckoned with in Scottish football. Their tilt at the Scottish League Cup in 1969 was a close-run thing, but, overall, the quality of player at the club at this time was, without doubt, the highest it has ever been and consequently all other First Division sides feared meeting St Johnstone when we were on our 'A' game.

As season 1970-71 progressed, it became obvious that Saints were in with a very good chance of qualifying for European competition for the first time. With only a handful of games left, Clyde came to Muirton for what would prove to be the decisive match of the campaign.

The game was notable, not just because Saints qualified for Europe, but because by winning they were guaranteed their highest ever league place. For younger fans, accustomed to seeing the team consistently finish in the top six of the Premiership and qualify for European football, it may seem slightly strange to make such a fuss over the

first time the club actually did this, but the older supporters who remember those days will tell their younger counterparts that the excitement generated when this happened for the first time was extraordinary. St Johnstone in the UEFA Cup - that was something to behold, especially when Scottish football's stock in European competition was so high at that time.

That's another element that made the 1970-71 season so memorable. This Saints team was playing against teams that could justifiably claim to be some of the best in Europe, with Celtic having won the European Cup in 1967 and then reaching the final again in 1970; and Rangers losing the European Cup Winners' Cup final in 1967 before going on to win the same trophy in 1972.

Although we all know that it was the UEFA Cup in which Saints competed the following season, the expectation was that the competition which we were trying to get into was the Inter-Cities Fairs Cup. The PA's report even referred to the *"Fairs*

Cup." This tournament began life in 1958, but was abolished at the end of the 1970-71 season and replaced by the UEFA Cup, partly because one of the rules of the earlier competition was that only one team from any city could take part. This had resulted in a number of teams that were much lower placed at the end of a season gaining entry to the Fairs Cup. One of the worst examples of this came in 1969-70, when Liverpool (2nd), Arsenal (4th), Southampton (7th) and Newcastle United (9th) got the English places, at the expense of Everton (3rd), Spurs (6th) and West Ham (8th).

Against Clyde, there was no doubt that St Johnstone were the better team. As the PA described it, *"Saints should have had the game sewn up a lot earlier than they finally did. It was a nail-biting finish in the end, however, and the 'Bully Wee' came close to equalising in the closing minutes. A draw would have been an injustice to the Perth side for, despite the narrow margin, they were streets ahead in the skills of the game."*

As the headline in the press cutting above indicates, the star of the show was John Connolly. On the other hand, the pantomime villain of the piece was the referee, Mr Henderson (who unfortunately hailed from a city down the Tay). Although the PA acknowledged that Saints were culpable in keeping the game tighter than it should have been, their reporter also lambasted the official for his performance – *"Poor finishing was Saints' biggest fault, with Hall and Aitken both missing good chances. This was coupled with some amazing decisions from referee Henderson of Dundee, who chalked off a Hall goal – he surprised even the Clyde players – and spoiled the game with frequent stoppages when the advantage rule should have been played."*

Some of the details of the match will come as no surprise to those who remember that Saints' team. Ian McPhee did have a reputation amongst the fans - reflected in their nickname of *"Mary"* - for seemingly avoiding any situation where he might get hurt. Ironically, any fan who was stupid enough to call him that to his face would have instantly regretted it, for Ian was the hardest man in the team, but on this occasion, the PA seemed to take the supporters' side, noting, *"Skipper Rooney and McPhee played competently, although the latter often put pressure on left-back Coburn with his reluctance to tackle."*

More to the fans' liking were the performances of the forwards. Connolly, who had been linked with a near £100,000 move to Spurs earlier that season, *"was a menace to the Clyde defence and capped a great display with two first-class goals. He was ably supported by Gordon Whitelaw, who, after weeks in the obscurity of reserve football, has returned to the fore with a bang. Whitelaw, playing a fetch-and-carry role, almost got his name on the scoresheet, but his first-time shot from the edge of the penalty box was stopped on its path into the net by Hall. Schoolteacher Hall* (he had previously been a PE teacher) *was another who impressed. He got through a power of work, setting up some neat moves, but found he had left his shooting boots behind. Pearson and Aitken did all that was asked of them, although big Freddie was a little out of touch at times."*

As for the two-goal hero, John Connolly, when we reminded him of the game, expressed surprise that both his goals came from headers (*"I didn't score that many with my head"*), but he was happy to be told that the PA described them both as *"brilliantly headed goals."*

He may not have remembered the goals, but John told us he did remember the interest from Spurs. *"Willie Ormond used to keep me informed of any enquiries from other clubs and I went down to London with him to watch a match. We sat in the stand at White Hart Lane and I noticed that the game was half a yard quicker in England than it was in Scotland."*

Fortunately, any interest from Tottenham never came to anything, although with his talent it was only a matter of time before Connolly went 'down south' for a big transfer fee. But that move – to Everton – was in the future, and on this particular afternoon John was more concerned with winning this game and securing a first European spot for St Johnstone.

His first goal came in the 38th minute and put St Johnstone into the lead. In the second half, as Clyde strove to get back to parity, Alec Rennie handled the ball outside the box and *"from the resultant free kick Hay's shot was deflected past the bewildered Donaldson"* in the home goal. However, the visitors' joy did not last long and within four minutes the lead was restored when, *"Rooney sent in a neatly flighted cross and Connolly was on the spot to head the ball home from close range."*

That goal was in the 75th minute and with 15 minutes or so left, as the PA described in the last sentence of their report, *"Clyde went all out for another score to square matters once more but Saints held on for their historic win."*

It was indeed an historic win, on more than one level. Not only did it mean St Johnstone were going to compete for the first time in European football, it also secured a highest ever final position for our club in the top Division in Scottish football. As such, it was highly appropriate that the man whom we have rated as the greatest player in Saints' history should have scored both goals that afternoon.

Saints team: Donaldson; Lambie and Coburn; Rooney, Rennie and McPhee; Hall, Pearson, Whitelaw, Connolly and Aitken.
Substitute: Gordon (not used).
Attendance: 4,200.

No. 12
It was a beauty, wasn't it

Scottish League Division One
St Johnstone 2, Celtic 1
Muirton Park, Saturday, 26ᵗʰ April 1975

SAINTS SIN—THEN ALL IS FORGIVEN!

By Bill McFarlane

ST JOHNSTONE 2, CELTIC 1. (Half-time—1-1.)
Scorers:—St Johnstone—O'Rourke (41 min.), G. Smith (pen. 68); Celtic—Glavin (32).

it came as no surprise when McNeill and McGrain collided to let O'Rourke clear. Latchford whipped the pins from

Headline: The Sunday Post

The announcement of a radical shake-up to Scottish football in 1974 meant that all the 18 teams in the old First Division went into the 1974-75 season knowing that they needed to finish in the top ten to secure admittance to the new Scottish Football Premier League. In the previous two seasons, Saints had finished in 11ᵗʰ and 12ᵗʰ places respectively but it was obvious that they were a team in transition. Willie Ormond had left for the Scotland manager's job in January 1973 and his successor, Jackie Stewart, while undoubtedly steadying the ship as some of the big names left or reached the end of their careers, was striving to bring in men who would, hopefully, replicate the success of the Ormond era.

The additional pressure of having to finish in the top ten in the top Division – a ranking that St Johnstone had only achieved three times since 1939 – increasingly had an impact on all those clubs vying for the chance to be part of the new Premier League. Unfortunately, behind the scenes, some key players were in dispute and/or wanted to leave Perth. Fred Aitken and, especially, Gordon Smith were at loggerheads with the club and poor performances in the League Cup didn't help matters. The signing of Jim O'Rourke did,

however, make a difference and once the round robin of the League Cup group was out of the way (a 6-1 defeat to Dundee was a particular low for the fans), the team did pick up form and went through till the end of October with only two defeats and a number of impressive victories.

A disastrous run of four consecutive defeats in November, including another pasting (this time 4-0) from Dundee, took the gloss of the earlier gains and, apart from a scoreless draw with Arbroath on the 7ᵗʰ, the run of defeats continued throughout December and the picture on the field looked increasingly bleak.

Behind the scenes, it wasn't much better, with the club's finances causing mounting concern. A £36,000 loss, announced at the AGM in February, meant pressure on the manager to sell players. Along with Gordon Smith and Henry Hall, the big Highlander Ian Macdonald was the most valuable asset. In a measure of the relative merits of Scottish and English football, then as opposed to now, Tottenham Hotspur made several bids for Macdonald, but none were deemed to be sufficiently high for any business to result. Given that the highest was £80,000, equivalent to over £1M today, this might seem extraordinary, as indeed does the idea that a club like Spurs would nowadays be interested in a player from a mid-ranking team in the top Division in Scotland.

In the event, the team was kept together and with a 1-1 draw in the Ne'er Day game on the 2nd January at Tannadice the rot was stopped. From there on, Saints didn't lose a league match until Rangers beat them on the 8th of March.

Then nerves kicked in and the next six games saw the team draw 0-0 at home to Ayr, beat Dundee 3-1, again at home, lose 3-0 away to Motherwell, draw 0-0 away to Dumbarton, beat Arbroath 3-2 at Perth and then draw 0-0 once again, this time away to Partick Thistle. All of which meant that Saints' fate was in their own hands. They only had to win their last game to ensure a place in the new Premier Division. There was only problem: the last match was against Celtic, albeit it was at home.

Going into the game, Celtic were on 45 points (two points for a win in those days), had won 20 games and scored 80 goals, conceding only 39. St Johnstone, on the other hand, were on 32 points and had won 10 times, scoring 39 and conceding 43. Although Celtic were to finish a poor third in the final table, 11 points behind champions Rangers and four points behind second-placed Hibs, they were still a formidable outfit. Just consider some of the players who took the field at Muirton on 26th April 1975 – Danny McGrain, Billy McNeill, Jimmy Johnstone (who was substituted by Bobby Lennox), Dixie Deans (who was substituted by Harry Hood) and last but by no means least, a rather talented young footballer called Kenny Dalglish.

Both the authors of this book remember the game and the feelings of trepidation that bubbled to the surface as the teams walked out on to the park in fine, sunny weather. In theory, a draw might well have been enough, but to be on the safe side a win was required to guarantee a place in the new top Division.

Estimates of the crowd vary. The Sunday Post said 11,000, the PA only 9,000. From our own personal recollections, we think that the latter seems more likely. There were few reliable crowd statistics in those days, with the press being reliant on the estimates the clubs provided, despite the fact that the latter would, of course, know how many people had actually passed through the turnstiles.

Once the match kicked-off, Saints, being Saints, started well but passed up a couple of great chances and then Duncan Lambie missed a penalty after Jim O'Rourke had been brought down. Of course, this meant that Celtic's Ronnie Glavin then scored, with what the PA described as *"one of the best seen at Muirton this season."* The Sunday Post described how, *"He collected a Murray clearance, played a 1-2 with Deans, then from the halfway line outsprinted the home defence to crack a beauty beyond Robertson."*

The PA's version of this was that Glavin *"accepted a Deans' flick on the halfway then produced an electric turn of speed to get clear of the chasing home defence. His parting shot gave Robertson no chance."*

So, having been dominant, Saints found themselves one down. However, we were still playing well, possibly no-one more than Gordon Smith, who, according to the PA, *"sent a slide-rule 50-yard pass inside the Celtic full-back and O'Rourke homed in on goal to blast an unsaveable drive through Latchford."* The Sunday Post mirrored this description, but gives a little more detail, telling us, *"Gordon Smith sent him away with a superb 50-yard touchline pass and Jimmy exploded his angled shot high past Latchford."*

O'Rourke's goal was in the 41st minute and when the ref blew for half-time, the home fans settled down contently over their pies and Bovril, hoping that Celtic would continue to display the lethargy they had (mainly) shown up to that point, while Saints might go on to bag another goal, another two points and a place in the new League.

Which is precisely what they went on to do, with the press – or The Sunday Post at least – saying, *"Saints went from strength to strength after that shocking first half hour. They fully deserved victory and all it meant."*

It is easy to be relatively dispassionate from the press-box: for those of us in the crowd, there was always that nagging thought that, *"this is Celtic, they could wake up at any minute and score…"*

With the teams tied at half-time, the same scoreline at the end of the game would mean that Saints had gained the point they needed. Consequently, Smith dropped back to a sort-of-sweeper role while Ritchie moved from his normal attacking beat to a midfield position. However, we were always threatening on the break and it was from just such an up-field foray that O'Rourke capitalised on an error by Messrs McNeill and McGrain to race clear, only to be brought down by the Celts' keeper Latchford.

This was, of course, the second time that O'Rourke had taken a tumble for a penalty in this match. Speaking to us in the mid 1990s, when we were researching the first edition of the official club history, Jimmy confessed he'd dived for one of them, although he professed not to remember which it was. It's just as well that the passion-killer that is VAR wasn't around in 1975. With Lambie having missed from the

spot in the first-half, a hasty, on-field conference resulted in Gordon Smith taking responsibility and, as The Sunday Post described it, *"he calmly side-footed the ball home to ensure top-grade football for Perth next season."* After the match, the PA asked Gordon if he was nervous about taking the penalty, to which he replied, *"I volunteered to take the kick and the other players agreed and gave me a lot of encouragement. And it was a beauty, wasn't it – even managed to send the keeper the wrong way."*

One feature of the match that would certainly not occur today was that neither of the St Johnstone substitutes was used. Celtic, as described above, did bring on both of their subs, but as they were chasing the match that was unsurprising. Saints, in contrast, kept theirs on the bench, whereas today it is impossible not to imagine them being used, even if only to soak up time as the game reached its conclusion.

Subs or not, the game was won and 'promotion' secured. It is interesting though to speculate what might have happened if Saints had *lost* the match. Rather than a horrendous season of almost constant defeats, consigning them to a meagre total of 11 points (an unwanted record for the various incarnations of the Premier Division that still persists to this day), perhaps a season of consolidation in the new First Division would have created a platform for a more sustained stint in the top flight. We'll never know.

Saints team: Robertson; G Smith, S Smith, Kinnell, MacDonald, Cramond, Muir, O'Rourke, Thomson, Ritchie, Lambie.
Substitutes: McGregor, Hall (both unused).
Attendance: 9,000.

No. 13
Saints unleash a fruit cocktail

Scottish League Division One,
Ayr United 0, St Johnstone 2
Somerset Park, Ayr, Saturday, 28ᵗʰ April 1990

It is often said, usually disparagingly by fans of other clubs and the media, that St Johnstone has a small fan-base. Strictly speaking, that's untrue: the fan-base is actually quite substantial, but what is true is that generally the loyal fans who follow Saints to away matches the length and breadth of Scotland are not usually numbered in the thousands. Nonetheless, given that there is no other senior team in the city and, when you add in the county, there is a potential support to be drawn from over 150,000 people, it's no surprise that, when the time is right, the people of Perth and district will turn out in decent numbers to support their local team. This trip to Ayr for a potential championship decider was just such a time.

For the preceding few weeks, massive crowds had flocked into McDiarmid and to away games as Saints defeated Airdrie (a crowd of 10,170 - see Part III below), Partick Thistle (away - 5,300), Clydebank (7,328) and Clyde (5,323). The 1-1 draw in that last game opened the door to promotion: all Saints had to do was win at Ayr United and we were up…

Thousands headed for Ayrshire. As cars and buses drove westwards, the A77 backed up from the Dutch Mill roundabout and the queues down the long road leading to Ayr town centre crawled along at a speed at which the average snail would have sneered. The old ground, a proper, trim, traditional Scottish arena, filled up with

151

5,114 people, with clearly many more away fans (the Sunday Mail estimated 4,000) than home ones, and St Johnstone's final assault on the gates of the Premier Division began.

Jim Masson remembers this day well, and especially the very unusual sight that greeted him when he arrived in Ayr…

"I was doing the game for the Evening Telegraph, not the Sporting Post, which meant that I'd not spend the whole 90 minutes with my head down relaying the details over the phone. I got down very early, got parked and was walking to ground when I met a frightful sight. It was a friend of mine who is a merchant banker. Despite his respectable job and face painted blue and white, he got into the ground."

Jack Findlay remembers the pre-match excitement caused by a group of young fans who had travelled on a double-decker bus: *"we saw this bus swaying from side to side because the young lads on the top deck were rushing from side to side. The ground where the cars and buses were parked was very uneven and I'm glad I wasn't on it. Fortunately, it stayed upright."*

The game itself was actually far better than many such contests tend to be: Saints would have been excused a degree of nervousness, but Ayr, with former Scotland goalie Alan Rough being drafted as an emergency stand-in, were soon on the defensive, with Roughie making a good save from Allan Moore.

Play went from end to end, with Balavage saving from Henry Templeton (one of those players opposition fans love to hate) and then Heddle and Cherry testing Rough. Some 20 minutes into the game, Stevie Maskrey 'scored' but was clearly offside. However, the opener was merely delayed, for, as the Sporting Post records, *"there was no dispute four minutes later. Maskrey*

reaches the bye-line on the right and with Rough covering the near post his cross is headed home by Cherry."

The Sunday Post's report, by Doug Baillie, described this first goal in rather bizarre terms which were then used to construct the even more strange headline for the entire article. The headline read, *"Saints unleash a fruit cocktail,"* while the description of the goal seems painfully contrived to use the goal-scorer's name to produce a string of bad puns, to wit: *"Stevie Maskrey sent over a peach of a banana-bender from the right and Paul Cherry was the apple of the Perth punters' eyes when he rose and sent a header into the roof of the net."*

Ian Heddle remembers that goal well. *"I was right behind Cher,"* he told us, *"and I thought for a second I might score, but he got in front of me. If he hadn't got it, I would have!"*

At this point, it seemed as if Saints were going to win relatively easily, but of course this is St Johnstone we're talking about and so in the 37th minute Dougie Barron brought down Ayr's McCracken in the box and Bryce stepped up to take the resulting penalty. At this point, as the late Queen Elizabeth might have said, *"recollections varied."* On the one hand, we have the Sporting Post, which tells us, *"Bryce hits the post with the kick."* The Sunday Post agreed, telling his readers, *"Tom Bryce struck the post with a penalty just before half-time."*

However, the Sunday Mail took a different tack, with their reporter querying whether the penalty should actually have been awarded or not: *"The tackle looked good but ref George Smith ruled a penalty … Balavage refused to allow the script to be spoiled. The keeper became Saints' hero. He turned Tommy Bryce's spot kick on to the post and although it crashed back into play, Evans' follow-up was blocked. Justice was done."*

The PA was equally clear about what had happened, commenting, *"it was the big man who brilliantly touched a Tommy Bryce penalty kick against the post and helped keep the clean sheet he has completed 16 times this season."*

Every Saints' fan in the ground will have concurred with the Mail and the PA on this occasion. It was indeed a splendid save and, as well as being instrumental in helping his team win, it also earned John Balavage a man-of-the-match award – but not at Ayr. The next game was the final match of the season, at home to Forfar Athletic, and Perth Leisure Pool, the match sponsors that day, struggling to know who to award the Man of the Match to in what was a decidedly dull game, decided to reward Balavage for his heroics the previous week instead. John was somewhat bemused, as he'd not really had much to do in the Forfar game, but when it was explained to him, he was more than happy to accept the compliment.

Both sides had more chances and both keepers made good saves, but the contest was put almost beyond doubt in the 58th minute, when, as the Sunday Mail tells us, *"The pacy Moore set it up with a cross from the right. Maskrey slid in but Rough blocked his effort. But razor-sharp Stevie was quickest to his feet and bounced up to whip the ball home and that settled it."*

The Sunday Post's writer hedged his bets, seemingly not sure if it was a great goal or not: *"Number Two wasn't all that pleasing on the eye, but it was striking of the highest order by Steve Maskrey. His first effort was brilliantly blocked by Alan Rough, who didn't have an earthly when speedy Stevie pounced on the rebound and rammed the ball into the net."*

The Sporting Post, reporting in real time down a telephone wire, was even more succinct: *"Saints get the vital second goal in 58 minutes. Maskrey finds himself on the*

end of a dangerous Moore cross. Rough makes a brilliant point-blank save, but Maskrey recovers quickly to knock in the rebound."

When the referee blew for full-time, the Saints' players rushed to the fans, who responded by singing, *"You'll never walk alone"* and throwing scarves, tammies and those strange-looking jester's hats to the players and the management team.

After the game, Saints had scored 80 goals and conceded 39. They'd add one further goal, with none more conceded, in the final match of the season, a 1-0 win against Forfar at McDiarmid.

This victory brought to an end a championship-winning season based on a vast amount of hard work behind the scenes by the players, the manager and the men at the top of the club. Ian Heddle recounted how Saints' playing style had changed under Alex Totten as better players were brought into the mix…

"Alex built a really strong spine up the centre of the team, with Bal(avage) in goals, centre halves Dougie Barron - a great player - and Alan McKillop, Sammy (Johnston) and Cher – who would run all day - in midfield and Roddy up front, two great wingers in Moorie and Maskrey, not to mention two great full backs in Don McVicar and Mark Treanor. Then, when promotion to the Premier seemed a realistic goal, he had to bring in more experience in the shape of Heggie (Paul Hegarty) and Gary McGinnis. When you added their top flight experience to what we already had, it carried us through. But the one thing we had above all was a great camaraderie – a fabulous team spirit… that was what made the difference…"

This win was the culmination of a dream, born only four years previously, when, with the club at the very nadir of its fortunes, Geoff Brown had brought his considerable business acumen (and a team of like-minded directors) to turn around the fortunes of a team that he believed could make a mark at the top of Scottish football. Promotion from the lowest tier in 1988, followed by a successful consolidation in 6th place in the First Division (the Championship today), meant that St Johnstone began the 1989-90 season with not unrealistic hopes of being there or thereabout come the last few matches. The sensational rout of Airdrie a few weeks before the trip to Ayr (up to that point, the Diamonds were expected to be the First Division champions), followed by favourable results throughout April, ending in this win at Somerset Park, meant the chairman's and the fans' dreams had been realised, probably far sooner than expected when Geoff took over the club. And all this, remember, with a part-time team…

Saints team: Balavage; Treanor, McGinnis, Barron, Hegarty, Johnston, Moore, Cherry, Maskrey, Grant, Heddle. Subs: Curran (for Johnston), Ward (for Maskrey). Attendance: 5,114.

Scottish League Cup Final
Rangers 2, St Johnstone 1
Celtic Park, Sunday 29th November 1998

Rangers wreck brave Saints' cup dream

Headline: The Courier

It was just St Johnstone's luck that, having been paired with one half of the Old Firm in the 1969 League Cup final, they would come up against the other half nearly thirty years later. Although managers and players will always strike a confident note about the chances of beating the Glasgow giants, the fans tend to take a more realistic approach, based on the fact that the stats don't lie and we tend to lose to Celtic and Rangers more often than we win (although that only makes the wins even sweeter when they do come).

The path to this particular final had been impressive. After beating Stranraer and Falkirk in the early rounds, the quarter final saw Saints paired with Hibernian, but at home in Perth. In Sandy Clark's first game in charge as manager, the Hibees were routed 4-0. The semi-final (as described in Part III below) saw Saints travel to the neutral venue of Easter Road for a tussle with the team from the other side of Edinburgh. A stunning 3-0 win over Hearts meant that we were in a major final for only the second time. Unfortunately, three weeks before the final, Saints went down 7-0 to Rangers in a league match at Perth, although they redeemed themselves in the very next game by beating Celtic 2-1 and then won 1-0 at Pittodrie the week before the final. Nonetheless, that hammering by Rangers at McDiarmid must have weighed on the players' minds.

Irrespective of whether it did or not, on the day, Saints put up a very creditable performance against a very high-quality Rangers team, featuring the likes of Amoruso, Hendry, Numan, Kanchelskis, Van Bronckhorst and Albertz. Backed by a sizeable contingent – around 11,500 – of Perth fans, the team that Sandy Clark selected were, on paper at least, capable of beating anyone in the Premier Division on their day. They also had a number of players who were capable of changing a match on their own.

One of those was Philip Scott, but Fizzy had fallen out with the manager over contract

155

renegotiations. As a result, he was consigned to training on his own at 8.00 am each morning to keep fit. He remembers that, *"the only people around at that time, were Aggie and Jimmy the Groundsman. I'd come in from Monday to Friday and do 45 mins running, keeping as fit as possible as I knew I'd be required at some time. Sure enough, someone was injured in the Rangers' debacle and Sandy had to ask me to return. We arranged a bounce game – I think it was against Dundee or Hearts. This was good for me, but the rest of the players weren't exactly happy because it was the same day as one of our nights out!"*

The final itself was a strange game in some ways. It was certainly a good enough match, with Rangers scoring after only six minutes and then Nick Dasovic equalising only few minutes later. Then, about eight minutes before half-time, Albertz scored what proved to be the winner.

Rangers' opener, fired in from 10 yards by Stephane Guivarc'h, was a well-crafted goal, but not a patch on Dasovic's equaliser. Here's the Courier's description of the latter…

"John McQuillan's free-kick from deep was nodded back towards Nick Dasovic by Alan Kernaghan. The Canadian internationalist, who was to receive the man-of-the-match award, was at full stretch but managed to knock the ball forward to get him clear of the attentions of Barry Ferguson before crashing a glorious left foot shot into the top corner of the Rangers' net."

And here's the PA, whose reporter (Gordon Bannerman) identified a different player as having taken the free kick…

"A stunning retort was delivered by Dasovic, courtesy of his left foot and Colin Hendry's fringe, within the minute. Kane's searching free kick from midfield was nodded back by Kernaghan and the

Canadian outmuscled van Bronckhorst for possession before mirroring the 18-yard strike which sunk Celtic on the same turf earlier this season. If anything, this was even more spectacular and jubilant Perth fans celebrated their first ever cup final goal. One for the video collection."

It was indeed one for the video collection and if you go to YouTube you can not only relive Nick's stunning strike, you can also confirm that Gordon Bannerman was more alert than the Courier's reporter, because it's clear that the man who took the free-kick was actually Paul Kane and not John McQuillan.

One of the jubilant Perth fans was Stewart McKinnon, whose celebration of Dasovic's goal was, even by his standards, pretty intense. To be fair, he had had a rather stressful time in the hours leading up to the match, as he told us…

"We'd organised a bus from Dunfermline, where we live. There were about 30 on the bus, me, my wife Jackie, my dad and lots of friends. I'd arranged for us to go into the Celtic Supporters' Club for a pint before the game. All the buses were parked down by the waste ground by Celtic Park and we headed off to the bar. I'd barely got the head off my first pint when someone said, 'Stewart, have you got the tickets?' Now I knew I did, because someone else had asked the same question on the bus and I'd showed them to him. Unfortunately though, I'd left them on the bus, so I nipped out and walked over to get them ... only to find that the bus wasn't there. The driver had gone to visit relatives in Glasgow!

"Perhaps surprisingly, when I broke the bad news back in the Supporters' Club, most people were OK about it. Some had their own tickets, so they were alright, but I now had to try and find everyone else's briefs if we wanted to get into the game. I found a Celtic security guard, who was really decent but explained that it was

nothing to do with Celtic as the ground was being rented to the League for the match. He said, 'I can tell you are genuine, so come back about 2.00 pm once the officials are here.' At the appointed hour, I made my way to the reception at Parkhead, only to be stopped by a Steward, who said (unsurprisingly), 'You can't come in here.' I was standing there, trying to think how to explain our situation, when Saints' Helen Harcus came into view. 'Stewart, what are you doing here?' she asked, so I told her the story. Helen said, wait here – and then she returned with a pile of tickets for the old main stand so we all got in after all. Having been somewhat stressed by all this, I just remember the total release when Dasovic scored. Saints were wearing white strips that day, but even after the game Jackie said, 'your face is still the same colour as our shirts.' Mind you, Dasovic's goal was a cracker...."

It was perhaps a small consolation to Dasovic that he was named 'Man of the Match.' Asked by the Courier in the immediate aftermath of the game what that meant to him, he replied, *"That doesn't mean much at this moment in time. To leave here without the trophy is gut-wrenching."*

The PA was in no doubt that this was a fitting award, stating that, *"In midfield anchorman Nick Dasovic Saints had the most accomplished performer on the park,"* before going on to add, *"while central defenders Alan Kernaghan and Darren Dods shielded Alan Main to such a degree that the keeper's only chance to advance his international credentials ... was an extraordinary leap to touch an explosive drive detonated 20 yards out by Andrei Kanchelskis."*

Speaking to us in 2023 about the match, when asked, *"Could we have won?"* Nick said, *"Yes, why couldn't we have? We always caused the Old Firm grief. We worked hard, were decent on the ball and we had some real quality. During my*

time there, we beat Celtic three times in the one season: that was a good Celtic team and it cost them the championship that year. The Celtic striker, Mark Viduka, who I know from my time in Croatia, said he hated playing against Saints because we always gave them a really hard game.

"In the final, the difference between us and Rangers was that we didn't have that little bit extra and at the end of the day, they had slightly more quality than we did.

"Sandy (Clark, the Saints' manager) *said after the game, he wished we had a bit more belief. He was invariably positive himself, with a different demeanour from Paul Sturrock, but he had come into a well-drilled group. There was perhaps more freedom, more relaxation and more banter under Sandy, but at the same time he knew he had a quality group of players.*

"When I scored, I ran to our fans –it was great to see there were a lot of St Johnstone supporters there that day. It would have been really nice to have won and given them all something to celebrate and then look back on.

"After the game, we were in our bus, feeling down, and I saw the Rangers guys in their bus with the Cup. I caught Van Bronckhorst's eye; he looked apologetic and shrugged his shoulders as if to say 'that's football'."

Philip Scott also thinks that Saints might have done better. He told us, *"I've watched it so many times since: we played OK - we didn't allow Rangers to play, but on the other hand we didn't have too many chances ourselves. Normally we'd create five or six chances per game. We just didn't get into their box enough. That Saints side played pretty football - at times better than Rangers – and we had not only really good technical players but people who wanted to battle for each other. I had a specific role - don't let Arthur Numan forward, but if you* get the chance go forward yourself. Nick's goal was unbelievable and I wonder what might have happened if we had managed to score a second. I had a powder puff shot when I could have driven through and taken on Colin Hendry, but when you watch the game over the 90 minutes, we played well. We were able to beat Rangers and Celtic in those days and for most of the final we were in the game. It was a good experience, but you don't ever want to lose a final."

Saints team: Main; McQuillan, Dods, Kernaghan, Bollan; O'Neil, Scott, Dasovic, Kane, Simao, O'Boyle. Substitutes: Preston (for O'Neil), Lowndes (for O'Boyle), Grant (for Simao). Attendance: 45,553.

No. 15
Thankfully, it all came right in the end

The SFL Challenge Cup Final,
St Johnstone 3, Dunfermline Athletic 2
Dens Park, Dundee, Sunday, 25th November 2007

Saints and Pars in cup thriller

Headline: The Courier

This was not the first time St Johnstone had contested the Challenge Cup final. Back on the 3rd November 1996, Paul Sturrock's team had come up against Stranraer, then in the Second Division and ranked well below Saints, in a David vs Goliath final which, as we know, ranks alongside some other eminently forgettable performances (Kelty Hearts comes to mind far too quickly) in the pantheon of Great St Johnstone Disasters. Alan Main's fumble leading to Danny Griffin's own goal – the only goal of the match - were the two least memorable aspects of a game which Saints dominated without ever looking likely to score.

However, in 2007 a St Johnstone team had a chance to make up for the Stranraer debacle. This time, their opponents, Dunfermline Athletic, were at least in the same Division and on paper would provide a stiff test. Based on the two previous league matches between the teams, there was nothing to choose between them. The first of these, at Dunfermline in September, ended scoreless, as did the second, which - some 15 days beforehand - was actually the last game either club played before they met in the final. That said, there is no doubt that Saints were the favourites. The Pars went into the final in second bottom place in the table, having not won in the previous five matches.

To make matters worse, for St Johnstone at least, this game took place in the week in which manager Owen Coyle had just been headhunted and announced that he was leaving Perth for Burnley. Sandy Stewart, his assistant, stepped in as caretaker manager for this one match, supported by Derek McInnes, with Coyle watching from the stands.

One of the more obscure yet noteworthy facts about the game was that it featured a female match official. Morag Pirie, who is undoubtedly the most celebrated, ground-breaking woman in the Scottish refereeing world, ran the line that day. Up to that date, no female had officiated in any national Cup final. Like most women pioneers in sport in general and refereeing in particular, Morag had to put up with a lot of sexist comments during her career. She was involved in a penalty decision which went in favour of Dunfermline, but we suspect that most Saints' fans won't even remember that she was on the line that day. This indicates that - thankfully - women officials are now accepted as part and parcel of the game by the vast majority of supporters.

The game was played at Dens Park: the first time that venue had hosted a Cup final since 1980. Saints were allocated 4,200 tickets and given the Bob Shankly Stand and the eastern end of the Main Stand, while Dunfermline were given an allocation for the Bobby Cox Stand at the other end of the ground, as well as the rest of the Main Stand and also the East Enclosure. However, the Pars failed to sell all their tickets and the East Enclosure remained closed for the game. On the day, nearly 6,500 fans attended, with both clubs having roughly equal numbers of supporters.

Saints' first goal came early in the game. Here's how The Courier described it…

"Dunfermline had opened up brightly enough but then they pressed self-destruct and looked to be staring down the barrel of a hammering.

"Saints 11th minute opener was gifted them by Pars midfielder Stephen Simmons who needlessly barged Steven Anderson as they contested a high ball inside the area."

Ando's recollection is a bit more prosaic – *"The guy just pushed me over…."*

However it was described, it gave Paul Sheerin the opportunity to put St Johnstone into an early lead - which he gleefully took.

Peter MacDonald then scored the second in the 18th minute, with what The Courier described as *"a cracking goal, poking in a half-volley beyond the despairing dive of Paul Gallacher from 12 yards after Kenny Deuchar had flicked on a Goran Stanic throw."*

Things could only get better, and they did. With almost 30 minutes on the clock, Andy Jackson, *"cut in from the wing and found Derek McInnes. Deuchar still had it all to do when McInnes fizzed the ball into his feet, but he effortlessly turned Sol Bamba before drilling home his finish."*

An added benefit for the Saints' fans was that all three goals were scored at 'our' end, making it a very happy afternoon, up to that point…

Although the fans were delighted with the 3-0 lead, for the players, there was the ever-present awareness that Dunfermline were no mugs. Steven Anderson rightly pointed out to us that although the Pars weren't on a good run, Sol Bamba, Mark Burchill, Stevie Crawford and Steven Glass had all played at international level, which meant that Saints' defence couldn't relax for a second.

Just to prove the point, in the 37th minute Dunfermline captain Scott Wilson got his side back in the game with a header from a Stephen Glass free-kick. It could have been worse: with only seconds to go till the interval, Darren Young saw a shot come off the inside of Alan Main's post, with the Saints' keeper rooted to the spot.

As if to make up for this, Saints' midfielder Rocco Quinn hit the same post within a minute of the restart. However, Dunfermline were throwing the kitchen sink at Saints and their efforts were eventually rewarded in the 70th minute when Ando pulled down Jim Hamilton at the edge of the box. Referee Eddie Smith gave a free-kick, but then changed his mind on the advice of the lineswoman and awarded a penalty.

Stephen Glass fired the ball into Alan Main's top corner and the Saints' fans worst nightmares resurfaced. To make matters worse, as the clock ran down, first Goran Stanic nearly gifted the Pars an equaliser and then Burchill missed a great opportunity. Here's The Courier's description again…

"During those nerve-jangling latter stages Stanic very nearly scored at the wrong end when, in attempting to clear a Hamilton cross, he only got the ball to safety via his

own crossbar, and Burchill should have done better when getting on the end of a Glass cross as the Pars came up just short."

Then it was over and we had won. There was an outburst of emotion from all the Perth fans present. It might have been a relatively unimportant competition but it was (wrongly) believed to be the first time Saints had won a national trophy. The fans and players celebrated, the former perhaps more than the latter, as Ando recalled - "The players just went back to the stadium for a couple of drinks. It was good to win a Cup, but we knew it was not the most prestigious trophy around and our real focus was to win the League."

Irrespective of what the players may have thought, the importance of the game and the result was not lost on the St Johnstone support. But for Gordon Muir, it was a roller-coaster of emotions…

"Finally, we had won something…but as it was Saints, it was never gonna be as easy as it seemed. A big day out down the Tay, in the home of our fiercest rivals, a big crowd, a great atmosphere and frankly we were cruising 3-0 up in nae time at all and the cup was ours, wasn't it? Well, the 'Saints Way' that I used to refer to constantly, meant it was in no way certain - but surely we couldnae throw a three goal lead away? Well, I will tell you what, we tried our best to…

"The old feelings of doom were never far away. Don't offer them a way back was the thought in my and many others' minds. Then in 37 minutes that's exactly what we did. And lo it was 3-1 at half time.

"We got to 70 minutes at that score and then conceded a penalty and were pegged back to 3-2. It seemed like the usual disaster was gonna happen. They were all over us and we - the players and fans - were very, very nervous…

"Then, during another Dunfermline attack, our left back, Goran Stanic, a top player back in the day with a peach of a strike on him, had that proverbial peach of a strike but could only watch on as it came rattling back off the bar. The only problem was it was our bar.

"Finally, the whistle went and at last I had seen my team win a Cup. Was the hoodoo over? Well not quite, but it would be eventually. We partied into the night. Perth St Johnstone, Challenge Cup Winners 2007. A Diddy Cup? I could not have cared less - a Cup's a Cup!"

Kevin Heller has a number of reasons to remember this game…

"My wife was heavily pregnant with our first child. Nonetheless, we both went to Dens, making sure we arrived fairly late so she wasn't standing about too long outside the ground. For obvious reasons, we took it easy while we were watching the game. My memory, like, I suspect, that of most fans who were there, is of the way we raced to a three goal lead and then nearly threw it away.

"It was good doing it at Dens though, despite the massive panic towards the end. That night, the celebrations were good, but I did think it was an odd feeling, perhaps 'cos it was a minor cup which didn't mean much to other clubs' fans. We went out to the Loft, where we bumped into Alan Main.

"My wife was so excited about meeting him that she rushed to tell him she was pregnant (although it was rather obvious). We didn't know what sex the baby was, but Alan said that he could tell by feeling her bump, so she let him do this. He confidently predicted the baby would be a boy. We went out of the Loft that evening secure in the knowledge that we were having a boy. The great Saints goalkeeper had said so…

"Naturally, it was a girl…"

161

Colin McCredie had a more personal connection with the final than most…

"It was good that our opponents that day were Dunfermline. Unlike some others, we have no grudges against the Pars and, moreover, my dad came from Rosyth, which was a nice family link.

"The day itself was brilliant. Fortunately, I'd missed the previous Challenge Cup final, but I'd been at the League Cup final when we lost to Rangers.

"Of course, it had been made more difficult because Owen Coyle had just resigned as manager a few days before the final. With Sandy Stewart in charge, I didn't know whether that was going to be a positive or a negative, but it was still a chance to win a Cup, so we all went through to Dundee, had a few pints in the Clepington Bar and headed for Dens. There was a big Saints' support, but the game wasn't like us – we were three up and coasting and I felt it was as good as won, but, typical Saints, we almost let it slip and the last twenty minutes were desperate, but then came the final whistle and – a dream come true - for the first time I saw Saints' ribbons on a Cup. As we were in the First Division at the time, I saw the Challenge Cup as potentially our only opportunity in my lifetime to win something. I felt it was a real achievement and, in retrospect, provided the platform for everything that came after it."

Andrew Tulloch was also at the final with his wife - and nephew, who was only about four or five. He recalled, *"It was just a fantastic game - you felt before that Saints could win, you knew we had good players and then when it was 3-0 you thought we were safe. Even towards the end, as Dunfermline were throwing the kitchen sink*

at us, I still felt they were going to hold out. However, the ball just seemed to keep coming back towards our goal and although I thought Dunfermline wouldn't score, they did of course. But I was right and we did hold out – just! Of course, I hoped it wasn't going to be the only time I'd see Saints win a Cup and I'm glad to say we've gone on to bigger and better things since then. The irony of that Challenge Cup win is my dad thought we weren't very good that season…"

Andrew's dad wasn't entirely wrong, because although the 1994 Challenge Cup debacle had led to promotion at the end of that season, this wasn't replicated after the team's success in the same competition in 2007-08. As Ando noted, the focus was on the league campaign. He also told us that with Coyle departing for Burnley, he had an inkling of who the next manager might be…

"Del was our captain and there were good reasons why he had played at a higher level. He was a very good player who led by example rather than shouting and you could see he was going to be a manager." As indeed he soon became…

With new manager Derek McInnes taking the helm from Owen Coyle, Saints finished third that season, but the following year the team that Del built did achieve promotion as First Division Champions.

Saints team: Main, Irvine, Stanic, McInnes, McManus, Anderson, Quinn, Sheerin, Deuchar, Jackson, MacDonald Substitutes: Cuthbert, Rutkiewicz (for Anderson), Hardie (for MacDonald), McLaren, Milne (for Jackson). Attendance: 6,446.

No. 16
I don't want to be sitting on a beach…

Scottish Cup Semi-Final
Aberdeen 1, St Johnstone 2
Ibrox Stadium, Sunday 13th April 2014

Headline: Perthshire Advertiser

The powers-that-be who run Scottish football sometimes come up with decisions that are baffling to the average fan. One such was their choice of a 12.45 pm kick-off for a Scottish Cup semi-final in Glasgow between two teams that are, respectively, at least one hour and three hours' travel away. Despite this, substantial numbers made the effort, with 19,057 – the vast majority from Aberdeen – getting up early and setting out for a game that would come to define the Tommy Wright era at St Johnstone.

Prior to this stage of the tournament, Saints had not met any other Premier club. Their first Scottish Cup match that season was against Livingston, then in the Championship, followed by Forfar Athletic from Division One and then, in the quarter finals, Raith Rovers, also from the Championship.

Aberdeen were, unsurprisingly, the favourites to progress to the final. They had already thrashed Saints 4-0 in the League Cup semi-final in February that year and would go on to finish 15 points ahead of us in the Premier table. Moreover, in the four previous games between the clubs that season, St Johnstone had failed to score. To make matters worse, the Saints' players heard rumours that the Dons had already booked their bus for the final. As Alan Mannus recollected, *"it was yet another game where no-one outside our changing room and our fans thought we had a chance."*

Tommy Wright said that before the game, *"I told the players we had the experience to win the match. I looked around the dressing room and said how many Cup semi-finals some of them had come so close to winning. Do it for Midgey Millar, Cup-tie Mackay and Ando I said, and, most importantly, win it for the fans.*

"I didn't say this at the time, and people will disagree with me, but if you look at the

League Cup semi-final, we gifted the first and then got caught with three counter attack goals. Also, we hadn't done well against them in the league that year, but in the Scottish Cup semi-final we had learned from what went before. I knew they wouldn't beat us."

On paper, there is no doubt that Aberdeen had better players. But on that day, they didn't have Tommy Wright's team's heart and ruthless desire to win. One of the things that motivated the manager was the way he felt when he had gone into the press conference after the League Cup semi. There, as he told us, *"Three of the media people present had Aberdeen scarves in their pockets and I could feel my temperature rising as it seemed to me they were rubbing the result in more than they should have. I felt there was an arrogance about Aberdeen - not from Del (McInnes) but from their fans - they thought they were going to beat us again. I always thought it would be great to beat them and then get my own back at the after-match press conference..."*

Some 3,000 blue-and-white clad fans filled most of the lower tier of the Broomloan Road end of Ibrox Stadium. Along with the Saints' team, they were almost the only people in the ground hoping to go home after seeing St Johnstone victorious and looking forward a Cup final.

Steven Anderson was perhaps not quite as confident as some of the fans. He told us, *"Part of me expected to lose as my record in semi-finals was terrible. I had only won one of the seven I played in up to that point. Once you have that sort of record you get doubts. But when you go on the field, these all go and you just play the game in front of you. I should also say that after that first semi-final, when they pumped us 4-0, it was revenge time for the lads."*

The afternoon was grey and damp, but once the game got underway, it seemed that the expected result would swiftly materialise. The Dons attacked and came close early on, then scored when, the PA records, *"...the Perth defence was dissected by a slick three-man move which saw Rooney lay-off to Pawlett who played in Niall McGinn to roll a calm 15th minute finish beyond the advancing keeper."*

Most people who were at the game, or who recall the highlights on the TV, will remember Alan Mannus's crucial save with his legs from Adam Rooney when the striker was clean through on goal. But how many recall that Jamie Langfield in the Aberdeen goal also made a vital save within a minute of Rooney's miss?

This happened when Stevie May, who had, of course, been on Aberdeen's books for a couple of seasons and consequently was getting pelters from the Dons' supporters, came very close in the 23rd minute. May managed to poke a shot goalwards, only to be thwarted by Langfield throwing himself in front of the ball.

Having got to half-time without any further scoring, Saints then had to find two goals from somewhere to turn the match around. Tommy Wright told us, at half time, he sat the players down and told them, *"We're still in it - we can play better, this is what we need to do - get the ball wide, move it quicker. It was just instilling belief into the team."* Then, as the players were going back out at the end of half-time, came the famous comment by Steven MacLean which has passed into legend and song. Essentially it was a harangue to the effect of *"I don't want to be sitting on a beach on the 17th of May while they are playing in the Cup final."* There may have been some other words involved too...

Although it's Macca's extempore, half-time speech that people talk about, David Wotherspoon remembers that some of the other older players, such as Ando, also pitched in, making the same sort of points, namely that they team didn't want to miss this opportunity to make history. *"During that half-time session, with the manager and some of the older, more experienced lads all helping to raise our confidence, the boys went out believing we could turn the game around."*

But before that could happen, as the second half continued there was another scare for Saints when, on the hour mark, McGinn played in Peter Pawlett. It looked as if we were sunk, but he made a hash of it and we were still in the game.

Then in the 61st minute, a St Johnstone corner. Here's the PA: *"May slammed Saints level with a sublime touch, turn and angled close range finish after the Dons failed to clear a Wotherspoon corner and James Dunne's feed."*

And here's Tommy Wright on the same subject: *"Dunne did well, the referee Collum did well not to give a free kick, then it was down to Steve's footwork - touch, touch, back of net."*

As the second half wore on, with Saints having drawn level, the Dons, naturally, tried to gain the advantage again. Tommy Wright told us that Saints had identified Shay Logan, the Aberdeen right back, as a potential weakness due to his lack of height, so the plan was to target him with diagonal balls and for the strikers to work him hard and win their headers. This tactic was to prove decisive. The ball was played from within the centre circle up to the (Saints') left by Dave Mackay. May got in front of Logan and won the header, then, as Tommy Wright described it, *"Stevie peeled off, Macca played him in and then there was a great finish"* – and the Saints' fans went absolutely berserk.

Alan Mannus recalled, *"It was a typical St Johnstone performance. We had a great defensive unit, the back four and me, and we all had the mentality that we'd do anything to keep the ball out of the net. I remember Niall McGinn's effort late on, when he headed the ball down at the back post and it bounced just past. Apart from that, one of the things I most remember is that in injury time Dave Mackay got the ball and everyone was screaming at him to kick it down to their corner..."*

Derek McInnes told us that although he was naturally disappointed to lose, *"once we'd gone out, there was only one team I wanted to win the Cup."*

For the St Johnstone manager, who was still recovering from an operation to remove his gall-bladder, there was no opportunity to join the rest of the club officials in the celebrations. As Tommy told the PA, *"I'm still not allowed to take any alcohol so I just headed up the road. I think the doctor has said I can have some drink in May, so I'll just hang off till then...Sunday was the best day of my career, without a doubt. It was easily the best experience I've had either as a player or a manager. The way we won the game made it even better, coming from behind to beat a good team like Aberdeen."*

Graeme Buchan drove to the game rather than going in the supporters' bus...

"We drove because of the early kick-off. My brother and his family, with our youngest nephew who was only about 13, came across from Dublin, plus there was Hamish from the Highlands too, so it was quite crowded. I remember thinking at half time, that we never got going in the first half, but then there was Steve MacLean's famous, 'I don't want to watch the final from the beach,' harangue to the rest of the team in the interval and when Tommy changed things in the second we were a yard further onto Aberdeen and Midgey, Spoony, James Dunne and O'Halloran were much better. MacLean was brilliant; I think it was probably his best display in a Saints' shirt."

After the debacle in the League Cup semi-final, many fans were travelling in trepidation. Certainly, Kevin Heller was: *"For that game, I think, like many fans, I was going through to Glasgow, because it's what we do, travelling in hope rather than expectation. I certainly wasn't very hopeful after the 4-0 defeat in the League Cup, where our seats were in the front row and we got drenched. As I drove through with my father-in-law, I had a feeling it was going to be the same again.*

"Then they got the first goal and I'm thinking, what is it about Saints and semi-finals? At half-time, I went for a stroll to the pie stall. Chatting to other fans I found that virtually everyone agreed there was a lack of straws to be clutched. Then the unbelievable happened: we equalised, then, even more unbelievable, the second goal came. I've never had a better feeling watching football, ever. When Stevie May stripped his top off and rushed along the front of the Broomloan Stand, I found myself running along the rows of seats trying to keep up with him. In contrast to Stevie's ripped muscles, my middle-aged male gut was not a pretty sight. I also wondered why on earth May kept pointing to the number on the back of his shirt...

"After the game, I spent a lot of time shell-shocked, hugging mates who kept asking, 'are you sure you don't want to stay in Glasgow?' Then, as we drove north-eastwards, I finally realised why Stevie May had been making such a fuss about his shirt number. The 17th of May – the date of the Cup final.

"Back in Perth, strangely, it was a quiet night, largely because most of my friends were out in Glasgow. I just soaked it up on social media and luxuriated in the fact that we were playing Dundee United and there was a decent chance we might win..."

For Gordon Muir, the Scottish Cup semi-final against Aberdeen, was *the* game changer. However, as he confessed, *"It didn't look like it to start with though. Another cup semi, another loss? We had lost loads, including a 4-0 hosing by the same Aberdeen side only a short time before. I had seen us so close so often but had never seen us win a major semi. I missed the league cup semi win in '97 as I was working in England, although I did come home for the final, where we lost to Rangers.*

"I remember the big crowd and the great atmosphere, as well as loads of chants enquiring about Stevie May. Frances, my long time and long-suffering partner, a season-ticket holder and attendee at most games with me, was unable to be there, her son having been married the day before. She was still at the hotel in Dunfermline so I went to the game with her daughter, Alexis. We had managed to book seats on Stewart McKinnon's bus from Dunfermline as we had been staying there on the Saturday night.

"The game kicked off. I felt sick - I knew we would lose. All pretty standard Cup semi feelings. Then in 15 minutes, they scored. Of course they did. Here we go again... All I could think was 'do not lose a second before half time.' And for once we didn't. At half time, I went into the concourse for a drink and chatted to lots of my fellow Saintees. One in particular, Roy McEwen, was like me; distressed, depressed and almost at the end of hope. We both agreed that if we lost this one we might never attend another, feeling we had had enough of seeing Saints lose in semis. We parted agreeing that there was actually still plenty of hope and time for us to get back into it...

"I was seated close behind the Aberdeen goal in the second half, close enough for a bit of sledging of Jamie Langfield (or Clangers as he was sometimes known). We started the half quite brightly. I started shouting at Clangers: I felt we were gonna

score. I roared, 'Can you feel it Jamie, can you feel it? - a goal is coming' Langfield reacted; he looked over his shoulder at us and laughed. A few others joined in and we continued... 'It's coming Jamie, it's coming!' And then BOOM it came... Stevie May, whose existence had been questioned so persistently at the start, was in and hit a quick shot before the keeper could get set. It was 1-1; we went daft...

"We continued baiting Langfield, but now he wasnae quite so chirpy, not quite so cocky. More joined in – 'the winner's coming Jamie, it's coming son.' But Aberdeen had chances, really, really good chances. I recall McGinn missing a sitter. With 10 minutes to go it came, Mayso delivered after a sort of 1-2 with Macca, yet again hitting a quick shot and before the keeper could react the ball was in the net and Saints were 2-1 up.

"It was bedlam, sheer bedlam. But sitting there, in the back of my mind the doubts remained. The 'Saints Way' was never far from my thoughts. You want to enjoy it but I was wondering if it was a mistake not to have packed a spare pair of underpants.

"Time stood still. 'For pity's sake ref blow the whistle, blow it NOW! Come on Willie, that's got to be it, time's up.' Imagine - Willie Collum, a man I did not like one bit, a man who had regularly given decisions against us, a man who for once had actually had a great game - had our destiny in his hands, then in his mouth and them a sharp blow of his whistle and... oh my, we've won, we've won a semi, we're in the final of the Scottish Cup. People around me were crying, some were dancing, some just looked in deep shock. Before we left, we had a final, wonderful rendition of the Stevie May song. As I was going out, I met Roy. We hugged, no words were exchanged, I think possibly because we may have started bubbling. The Hoodoo was done, the 'Saints Way' no more. It was the greatest day in my Saints' supporting life... for a month or so..."

One fan who missed the game was Eric Nicolson, the Courier's football correspondent. Unfortunately, he was sick, and afterwards, speaking to Tommy Wright as he regularly did, the manager jokingly suggested that because Saints had won in his absence, he would now ban Eric from the press-box for the final (he didn't).

In the other semi-final, played the day before, lower league Rangers, who required a replay to beat Albion Rovers in the quarter final, had been convincingly beaten 3-1 by Dundee United. Thus, the stage was set for only St Johnstone's third tilt at a major national honour. Would it be third time lucky?

Saints team: Mannus; Mackay, Wright, Anderson, Easton, Dunne, Millar, Wotherspoon, MacLean, May and O'Halloran.
Substitutes: Cregg (for O'Halloran), Hasselbaink, Miller, Brown, Clancy, Iwelumo.
Attendance: 19,057.

Desperately turgid - battling Saints move off the bottom

Scottish Premiership,
Kilmarnock 0, St Johnstone 0
Rugby Park, Wednesday, 4th December 2019

Headline, Perthshire Advertiser

There were fewer than 90 St Johnstone fans at Rugby Park that night (Matthew Gallagher in the PA stated that the actual figure was 89). This was hardly surprising: Kilmarnock is quite a hike from Perth, it was a miserable, cold December evening and Saints, having lost far too often, were at the foot of the Scottish Premiership. The previous match had seen Motherwell hammer the Perth men 4-0 at Fir Park and, after Scottish Cup win of 2014 and the years of success under Tommy Wright, it appeared that the stardust was fading.

Consequently, that tiny knot of away fans travelled more in expectation than hope: a reverse of the normal sentiment but borne out by the fact that Saints went into the match having not won an away game in the entire calendar year of 2019.

The expectation was therefore of another beating and a further step along the path that would lead us out of the Premiership. Sitting in the cold concrete, metal and plastic surroundings of Rugby Park's Chadwick stand, the chatter was of the five changes Tommy had made to the team. Callum Booth's introduction at left-back was a particular source of debate: he had been signed seemingly as an experienced back-up to Scott Tanser, but was not seen by many fans as a likely first-team regular. In addition to Booth making his first starting appearance for the club, we also saw Wallace Duffy making way for Liam Gordon and Matty Kennedy for Liam Craig.

Looking back, Tommy Wright told us that he had always liked Callum Booth and his arrival was part of a longer-term strategy, begun a year before, to rebuild the team. In particular, there was a desire to get the average age down considerably (even though Booth was in his late 20s), but the start of the season was very difficult and, as Tommy admitted, *"we didn't get the results or performances we were looking for. A lot of games were lost as a result of individual errors. We'd have lots of possession but then lose goals on the counter attack.*

"We were not gelling and going into that game at Kilmarnock we'd come off a defeat away to Motherwell that was simply not acceptable. In those circumstances, your hand is forced; you have to make changes. Killie is never an easy place to go and they were going well. In any away game after a heavy defeat the important thing is to get something. The plan is always to win, but

this was one game we couldn't afford to lose."

Kilmarnock were sitting comfortably in fifth place in the league table at the time of the game, with 22 points compared to Saints' 11. Having enjoyed previously unimaginable success under Steve Clarke, who had left to take over the Scotland managerial role, the Ayrshire side had taken a gamble with an Italian manager, Angelo Allessio, whose tenure began at the start of the 2019-20 season but came to an end only a few weeks after this match against St Johnstone, following a run of poor results.

The Courier's reporter was probably being kind when she described the first half as *"a desperately turgid opening period, permeated by repeated fouls and both sides wasteful in possession."*

However, the view from the Chadwick stand was that, while we didn't look like scoring, at least we hadn't conceded, with Callum Booth showing all his experience and putting in a strong performance against Killie danger man Chris Burke. The Courier noted that his debut had gone well, writing that, *"The shutout certainly put a smile on the face of Booth, whose debut in Saints' colours probably went smoother than he could've hoped. He does, however, expect to be nursing some tight muscles in the days to come."* The fact that Saints had managed to get through an entire game without losing a goal really was noteworthy: the last time they had a shut-out was about 11 months earlier, on 16th February 2019, at Ibrox.

In the centre of defence, Liam Gordon, who had played 45 minutes for the reserve team only two days beforehand, demonstrated the tenacity and attitude that helped Saints get a very necessary point that took them off the foot of the table. His performance typified the local lad made good who will run through a brick wall for his club because it *is* his club. As the Courier said, Gordon *"was certainly not holding back*

and his full-blooded approach was a welcome boost."

At the other end of the park, Chris Kane ran his socks off, admittedly to no avail, but by defending from the front and showing a depth of determination and organisation that had been sadly lacking for some weeks, the team eventually made it to half-time without conceding.

Given that Saints had not kept a clean sheet in an away match since February that year, this was an improvement. It might have been desperately turgid, but there were signs in the second half of Saints slowly regaining some confidence. Chances, as they say, were at a premium and what few there were tended to be passed up – or, more truthfully, made a hash of, with both sides being guilty of not creating many opportunities and, on the few occasions they did, failing to take advantage. The BBC's match stats bear this out, with Kilmarnock only testing Zander Clark once in the entire match (it was their only shot on target) and that was not until after a full hour had passed. For Saints, Liam Gordon failed to take advantage of the best chance of the first half when his close-range shot was blocked on the line by Alan Power.

At this point, you may be wondering why a *"desperately turgid"* game like this is included in a book on what are supposed to be the greatest games in St Johnstone's history. The answer is simple: this was the turning point in the season, lifting Saints off bottom place (as shown below) and providing the stepping stone from which they gradually ascended the league table.

From being at the foot of the table in December 2019, the team gradually clawed their way to mid-table respectability before the Covid pandemic brought football to a premature close. By that time, however, St Johnstone had amassed sufficient points per game to be placed sixth in the final table.

Premiership

	P	W	D	L	F	A	Pts
Celtic	15	13	1	1	46	9	40
Rangers	15	12	2	1	45	10	38
Aberdeen	16	8	5	3	25	19	29
Motherwell	16	9	1	6	28	22	28
Kilmarnock	16	6	5	5	17	17	23
Hibs	16	4	7	5	24	29	19
Ross County	16	4	5	7	19	35	17
Livingston	16	3	6	7	17	24	15
Hearts	15	2	6	7	16	26	12
Hamilton	16	2	6	8	18	29	12
St Johnstone	**15**	**2**	**6**	**7**	**13**	**33**	**12**
St Mirren	16	3	2	11	11	24	11

This would have been the fifth time that a Tommy Wright St Johnstone team finished in the top six in the seven seasons since he had taken over as manager, but by the time the final call was made on the league positions, Tommy had gone and Callum Davidson had taken his place.

We all know what happened in the next season, but it's fair to say that if Tommy had not been able to turn the good ship St Johnstone around then the Cup Double might never have happened. In our view, this match, boringly turgid as it was for the fans, was the catalyst that made the 2020-21 success possible. And for that reason alone, it's as important as any of the other games described here...

Tommy Wright concluded his remarks about this match by agreeing with the media reports about what a poor game it was, but also with our analysis of the importance of this match in St Johnstone's history...

"Until you asked me about it, I have to admit it's a game I'd more or less forgotten about. However, even though it wasn't a great game and there were very few chances, what the team gave me was a spirit and a togetherness which we really needed at that point. It was vital to come off the pitch with at least something, which is what they did. Boothy put in a great performance, as did the others, and it was

a great result given the circumstances. If we hadn't picked up in December, maybe the chairman would have had to 'make a decision.' I think we had had one conversation at that time along the lines of 'results have to pick up,' but I wasn't stupid. More importantly, if results hadn't picked up, I couldn't have persevered with younger players. But they did, and we went on a really good run after this. And, as history will show, that point at Kilmarnock was vital in that it took us off the bottom of the table and, I believe, set the foundation for what followed."

Ali McCann told us, *"I remember that Callum Booth came in and played well, but that apart it was a terrible game."* He did add that, *"looking back it was a turning point, although I think that at the time it didn't feel like it because we didn't win the game. However, given the way our results had been going, it stopped the rot and we then went on a great run and climbed the table in the new year."*

Liam Craig, who was drafted into the side after the debacle against Motherwell, had much the same memories of the game as Ali and Tommy (in other words, not very many!) but he too agreed that it was a turning point...

"I don't think the Kilmarnock game really stood out as a classic, that season. To be honest, I can barely remember it, but I do know that after the turn of the year we went on that incredible run that took us racing up the table."

One player who did remember the game fairly well was Zander Clark. He told us, *"It was horrific, blowing a gale and terrible conditions to play in. I didn't have much to do, however, it was a big result that stopped the rot and put us back on track."*

For the few fans who made the journey, this was a game that didn't linger in the memory. Kevin Heller told us, *"I got a* supporters' bus and it wasn't very busy. I'd been at the Motherwell game where we got hammered and it was almost Christmas and I needed to save my money, but I asked my youngest, 'do you want to go?' She said yes, so off we went. It must have been the prospect of a Killie pie that swayed us...

"We were in the big stand behind the goal and there were hardly any of us. There was a bit of 'what are we doing here, we're all mad!' chat. It was an eminently forgettable game and I really can't remember much. I recall that there were photos on social media afterwards, ridiculing us for the number of away fans, but looking back, it was the start of something as we eventually crept into the top six. In retrospect, this was the catalyst for much of the success that followed."

Dave McPhee was another of the small band who made the trip from Perth and his sentiments chime nicely with Kevin's: "I remember there were very few people on the supporters' bus. The time of year, the fact it was a midweek game in winter and the moderately long journey involved, to say nothing of our poor form at the time, all conspired to reduce the numbers. As if to make up for it, the wonderful Bev Mayer,

Saints' Supporters' Liaison Officer, was handing out comps so we all got in free.

"The match itself was, it's fair to say, not a classic. However, there was a grit and resilience and that made all the difference. The old spirit that some had been questioning in the run-up to the game was definitely back and it laid a foundation for what was to follow."

It certainly did. Having been bottom of the table going into the Killie game, in the 14 remaining league matches after it, St Johnstone went on a fabulous run and only lost twice, winning six and drawing the remainder, leaving them in sixth place, (based on results to that date) after the Premiership was abandoned due to the Covid pandemic.

Saints team: Clark, Ralston, Gordon, Kerr, Booth, McCann, Craig, Holt, Wright, Kane, O'Halloran. Substitutes: Parish, Wotherspoon (for Wright), Kennedy (for O'Halloran), Duffy, Tanser, Swanson, May.
Attendance: 4,083.

Scottish Premiership Play-off. Second Leg
St Johnstone 4, Inverness Caledonian Thistle 0
McDiarmid Park, Monday, 23rd May 2022

Headline: Perthshire Advertiser

To say that the 2021-22 season was one of the most disappointing in St Johnstone's history is possibly an understatement to end all understatements. Having won the League Cup and Scottish Cup the previous season, St Johnstone were, unarguably, at the highest peak in the club's history. A succession of poor signings, coupled with the sale of the team's two best players, long runs of defeats and ebbing confidence all added up to an annus horribilis, with the nadir being a humiliating defeat away to Second Division Kelty Hearts in the Scottish Cup. Fortunately, Saints were not quite the worst team in the league, that dismal honour belonging to our friends from Dens, but come the end of the season the plain fact was that St Johnstone were in second bottom place in the table and facing

a two-legged contest with Inverness Caledonian Thistle to retain their Premiership status.

The first game, away in Inverness, saw Saints totally dominate the first half, score twice (and ought to have scored more), before the home side rallied, levelled the scores and, in the end, were pressing hard for a winner. Consequently, there were a lot of frayed nerves amongst the Perth fans when the teams ran out at McDiarmid for the return leg in front of a large crowd, given as 7,355 and including a large contingent from the Highlands.

Fortunately, as we know, fortune favoured the brave, although after the first forty-five minutes there was no obvious sign that a breakthrough was coming. Quite the opposite in fact...

Inverness started much the brighter of the two teams. The Courier recorded the early stages thus, *"Billy Dodds (the Inverness manager) made four changes to his starting line-up. And it was a bold selection. The two wide forwards who made a telling impact in the first leg comeback, Austin Samuels and Logan Chalmers, joined the duo returning from suspension, Danny Devine and (former Saint) Wallace Duffy. And it was Chalmers who had the first shot of the game with only seconds on the clock – thankfully straight at Zander Clark. The visitors made a much better start to this contest than the last – not that it would be hard – and Devine got his head to a Sean Welsh free-kick. Again though, Clark was not tested. He shouldn't have been tested by a Dan Cleary back-pass on nine minutes either but his left foot attempt at a first-time clearance came off the top of the Scotland keeper's boot and nearly ended in the back of his net."*

Saints came back into things a bit, but the most dangerous moment came some 30 minutes into the game, when Clark pulled off a terrific save to thwart Samuels.

A half-time change saw Stevie May replace Glenn Middleton and, within a minute the deadlock was broken. In fact, it was May's first touch that breached the Caley Thistle dam, when he reacted quickest to a fine save by Inverness' keeper Mark Ridgers from a seemingly net-bound header from Melker Hallberg.

A second followed just seven minutes later, when a fierce drive by Cammy MacPherson took a big deflection off a defender and away from the hapless Ridgers. There was an even bigger explosion of noise at this goal, coupled with an almost tangible sense of relief amongst the thousands of home fans. Of course, being Saints' fans, there was always the nagging doubt that, *"Well,*

we threw away a two goal advantage in Inverness, so don't be surprised if that happens again here..."

It didn't, although Caley Thistle did make strenuous efforts to get back into the match and just after the hour mark Zander Clark had to make an impressive save from Samuels. However, the Saints' defence held firm, with John Mahon, who had been drafted in for only his second start of the season as a replacement for the injured Jamie McCart, performing heroics in blocking a Wallace Duffy shot that looked destined to trouble Clark.

With time running out, Inverness seemed to know that their goose was cooked, although they fought to the end. Any slight chance they had of scratching a draw and extra time vanished however, in a frantic finale that featured two virtually identical goals. Indeed, they were so similar that the BBC produced a video that tracked each player's movement and the final trajectory of the ball as each chipped the goalkeeper and sent it into the net.

The first of these was by Callum Hendry. Having seemingly been disregarded by the Perth management and sent on a number of loans, possibly with a view to seeing one of these result in a transfer, Callum had been recalled from Kilmarnock in December and then proceeded to score regularly and - from his perspective - demonstrate what Saints were missing. Put simply, as Eric Nicolson wrote in the Courier, the answer to the question, *"Where would St Johnstone have been without Callum Hendry?"* was *"The Championship."*

Hendry's goal came when Melker Hallberg picked up a defensive headed clearance from Dan Clearly inside the centre circle, looked up and released Callum midway inside the Inverness half and in acres of space. The striker had an unimpeded run-in on goal, arguably even too much time to think, but his composure was magnificent as he skilfully dinked the ball over Ridgers in the Caley Thistle goal.

The final goal, by the shy and retiring-personality that is Shaun Rooney, was a carbon copy of Hendry's chip over the keeper. Dan Cleary collected the ball as an Inverness attack was broken up and raced from the edge of his own box to halfway into the Inverness half before slipping the ball to Rooney in an almost identical position to that in which Hendry had received the ball just a few minutes earlier.

Zander Clark, who had made some important saves earlier in the game, had a clear view of Rooney's goal. He told us, *"As Roons went through I was thinking, 'this could go anywhere,' but fair play, the finish was incredible. Mark Ridgers in the Caley goal was probably, subconsciously, thinking 'a right back isn't going to dink me, he'll probably put his laces through it' but it was a carbon copy of Callum's goal."*

Zander also made another important point that was perhaps missed by many of the fans, or rather not thought about at the time. This was that, *"It was a high-pressure game and one we were confident we could win, but the result was still a big relief. Not just for ourselves, but we were aware of what relegation might have meant for those behind the scenes at the club. Winning made all the difference: losing would have meant people losing their jobs. And because Saints is such a family-run club, we knew all these people and they meant a lot to us."*

Although not one Saints' fan was complaining, it is arguable that the final score was slightly unfair on Inverness.

Andrew Tulloch, who lives in the Borders, had not gone to the first leg in Inverness, but when he went to the match at Perth, *"I felt we were going to do it, simply because we were a better team than them. That said, the final score flattered us a bit. When the score went to 2-0, I was confident*

we were going to win. The second goal put Inverness under a lot of pressure and they had to come at us, which left them open at the back. If it had finished 2-0 then it would have been a fair result."

Kevin Heller had been at the first leg in Inverness: *"We played well in the first half and then really poorly in the second. The fans turned on the team. I've never been the sort of person who criticises – I prefer to support them as much as possible, but it was hard to defend them that night. A lot were booing, calling for Callum Davidson's head, saying 'this guy's going to get us relegated.'*

"As a result, a lot of us were fearing the worst for the return leg. To be honest, it was such a miserable time that for most of the season there were people wishing it could be finished and we might be put out of our misery. I have a feeling that is one of the reasons there was a big crowd at McDiarmid. There are a lot of Saints' fans who don't, or can't, go to many games, but they make a special effort when it's a big game.

"On the night, we watched this free-flowing football – well, in the second half mainly – and it was a really entertaining game. The two dinks, from Hendry and Rooney, were brilliant, as was Rooney cheering the ref when he got booked, as he knew he would be, for removing his shirt after his goal. I left the ground wishing we didn't have to end the season now. For those 90-plus minutes, everything that happened made everything that had gone before - all the dire performances and scores - seem worthwhile. The result gave us lots of hope for the next season, only to be dashed again this year..."

Danny Griffin told us that even before the first match he was worried: *"I was nervous, for the first time ever. When I played, I never got nervous but I had watched the first leg on Saints' TV. We had started like a house on fire, then it was 2-2 and we were going into the second leg level.*

"At McDiarmid, they started better than us and I suspect quite a few Saints fans ended up with no nails at half-time. We scored against the run of play and that knocked the stuffing out of Inverness. To come through that game and stay in the Premiership was almost a bigger achievement for Callum than winning the Cup double. Being at the club for as long as I have, I know that staying in the top flight is the first requirement and then anything you achieve afterwards is a bonus."

David Wotherspoon was another who watched from the stand. He recalled, *"It was a nightmare. I was injured so I could do nothing but watch on. We really had to dig out the result, but once we got the first goal, it was a good performance."*

In contrast, Liam Craig told us, *"I was quite relaxed about the whole situation. I remember coming back on the bus from Inverness. I had been through it with Hibs: we were 2-0 up against Hamilton but they beat us at Easter Road on penalties. So, I was thinking, 'do Inverness go for it - if we were 2-0 up and had been hauled back to 2-2 what would we have done?*

"What with the big crowd at McDiarmid that night getting behind us, especially the FCU, there was a great atmosphere. Everyone came together and it showed how close everyone is at the club – players, fans, backroom staff and the board. Shaun Rooney tends to get the headlines, but it was a real team effort."

A real team effort it may have been, but it was a team that needed major surgery before the next season's campaign. And as we know, the following season was only marginally better. However, by winning over the two legs of the play-off against Inverness and thus avoiding relegation, St Johnstone gave themselves a chance to regroup. Relegation – with all that implies for the club's finances and the players' own futures, would have been unthinkable just one season after the famous Cup Double.

Saints team: Clark, Brown, Rooney, Mahon, Cleary, Gordon, Hallberg, Davidson, Hendry, Middleton, MacPherson.
Substitutes: Parish, May (for Middleton), O'Halloran, Craig, Sang, Ciftci, Gilmour.
Attendance: 7,355.

Part III - The Greatest Games (in reverse order)

How on earth do you decide which are the greatest games in St Johnstone's history?
For many, the Cup wins will be top of their list, for others, there will be some match or other that sparks ancient memories of an afternoon of pure entertainment under a blazing sun or in the depths of winter. Then there are the European matches, defeats of the Old Firm – and beating Dundee of course.

Our final decisions are based around such key factors as the excitement and enjoyment of the game, the importance of the fixture, the strength and/or league position of each side, prodigious goalscoring or goalkeeping and, of course, the quality of the St Johnstone team's performance relative to the opposition. Bearing all that in mind, here are our choices…

30. St Johnstone 7, Leith Athletic 3, 28th January 1950
29. St Johnstone 1, Dundee 0, 23rd May 1999
28. Partick Thistle 1, St Johnstone 8, 16th August 1969
27. St Johnstone 2, Airdrie 2, 4th December 1954
26. Fair City Athletic 4, St Johnstone 9, 16th November 1895
25. Rangers 0, St Johnstone 2, 8th November 2006
24. Dundee 3, St Johnstone 4, 2nd January 1978
23. St Johnstone, 3 Rangers 3, 14th February 1981
22. Hamilton 3, St Johnstone 4, 28th April 2007
21. Rangers 1, St Johnstone 1, (2-4 on penalties), 25th April 2021
20. Celtic 0, St Johnstone 1, 16th August 1961
19. St Johnstone 2, Celtic 0, 30th August 1961
18. St Johnstone 2, Celtic 0, 12th August 1981
17. St Johnstone 10, Brechin City 1, 6th December 1919
16. Rosenborg 0, St Johnstone 1, 18th July 2013
15. St Johnstone 3, Celtic 2, 22nd December 1990
14. St Johnstone 4, Partick Thistle 3, 2nd September 1961
13. St Johnstone 9, Albion Rovers 0, 9th March 1946
12. St Johnstone 3, Hearts 0, 27th October 1998
11. St Johnstone 3, Monaco 3, 30th September 1999
10. St Johnstone 1, Livingston 0, 28th February 2021
9. Galatasaray 1, St Johnstone 1, 5th August 2021
8. St Johnstone 1, Hibernian 0, 22nd May 2021
7. Celtic 2, St Johnstone 2, 30th August 1969
6. St Johnstone 7, Dundee 2, 1st January 1997
5. St Johnstone 5, Aberdeen 0, 29th September 1990
4. St Johnstone 2, Dundee United 0, 17th May 2014
3. Stenhousemuir 5, St Johnstone 5, 22nd September 1962
2. St Johnstone 3, Airdrie 1, 31st March 1990
1. St Johnstone 3, Hamburg 0, 29th September 1971

No. 30
Leith's hopes melted away like snow

Scottish Cup, First Round
St Johnstone 7, Leith Athletic 3
Muirton Park, Saturday 28th January 1950

JANUARY 28, 1950.   5

SAINTS RUN RIOT IN SECOND HALF

A searing wind from the east brought about a lunch-time transformation at Muirton Park. In a twinkling, as it were, the pitch changed from white to green.

When both teams ran out, they found the ground hard, but otherwise in good fettle.

Headline: The Sporting Post

Paddy Buckley was one of the greatest centre-forwards in St Johnstone's history. During his four seasons at Perth, between 1948 and 1952, he scored 105 goals in only 142 games and, in addition, he scored more hat-tricks (six) than any player before or since. Saints' fan Bert McIntosh, who recalls seeing Buckley play, told us, *"Paddy was a great player. There was no messing about with him. All he wanted to do was get a shot on goal. If he got the ball in the box, he wasn't looking to pass to a team-mate; he was looking to get the ball in the net."*

To prove Bert's point, Buckley is one of only 13 Saints' players to score four times during a match and, unsurprisingly, it's that game that we're covering here, although, as you'll discover, this game was memorable for all sorts of other reasons.

In the 1949-50 season, Saints were in the B Division of the Scottish League, eventually finishing fourth. Leith Athletic, having been briefly a First Division side in the early 1930s, were now in the North and East

section of Division C, a league that was largely made up of bigger clubs' reserve sides. On the face of it, this ought to have been a relatively straight-forward passage through to the next round of the Cup.

The PA was published on Saturdays and Wednesdays back in 1950 and in their preview of the game they were bullish about St Johnstone's chances of progressing, commenting, *"Taking it for granted that St Johnstone will not treat the opposition too lightly, there should be only one outcome to the Scottish Cup first round tie at Muirton Park this afternoon. Leith Athletic, a 'C' Division club, will create something of a sensation if they prevent Saints from having a tilt in round two."*

However, as we all know, Saints don't do straight-forward passages to the next round, so as you might expect, when half-time came, Leith were leading 3-1.

The conditions probably helped the visitors. The Sunday Post records that Leith, having won the toss, had the wind behind them in

177

the first half and then they *"skated over an icebound surface to a half-time lead."* This sounds an improvement on what had been expected 24 hours earlier, when the Evening Telegraph reported that Saints' manager, Jimmy Crapnell, was confident the game would go ahead, *"despite the half-inch layer of snow on Muirton Park."*

The weather didn't seem to put the fans off, with some 6,000 in attendance. They didn't enjoy the best of starts though, and neither did Jimmy Canavan, starting for the first time at centre half, having previously played mainly at half-back for the reserves. The PA tells us what happened in the third minute: *"There were no Leith players in the vicinity when Broadley swept over a long, high cross from the right, but the ball dropped at such an awkward angle that it was clear McLaren was worried about the outcome when the pivot lunged at it with his head. His fears were confirmed when the ball flashed past him into the net."*

As the game developed, *"Leith were so far out in front of floundering Saints that their second counter, from Dalziel, on the 20-minute mark, came almost as a matter of course."* Further on we can read, *"It's doubtful if the experiment of playing Canavan at centre-half will be repeated."*

The Sunday Post was equally unimpressed by the new centre half, pithily noting, *"It's doubtful if Canavan solves Perth's centre-half problem."* Both papers were probably right, given that the unfortunate stopper only played another three competitive games for the first team.

Jock Smeaton pulled a goal back for Saints in 29 minutes with what the PA described as *"a full-blooded 30-yarder,"* but this was only a temporary reprieve for Leith soon restored their two goal advantage when Dalziel got his second in the 37th minute. Saints were clearly all over the place and only a few minutes after Leith's first goal Blyth had to clear off the line from another

Athletic attack and *"only a spectacular back-spring by McLaren prevented Broadley scoring on another occasion."*

The Sporting Post's blow-by-blow account describes this last moment in far greater detail: *"Leith supporters cheer when Anderson lets Broadley away with a crafty through pass. The winger cuts in with a hard shot, McLaren punches up in the air, and as the ball swirls back into goal he executes a hand-spring that succeeds spectacularly."*

With Leith comfortably ahead at the interval, the shock was on, but the second half saw a turnaround in the respective fortunes of each side. Ironically, it wasn't until Saints were down to 10 men that they started to make an impression. Having just had a header saved at the post by Wallace in the Athletic goal, Clarke had to leave the field for attention to a cut on his head. While he was off the park, Paddy Buckley scored when he flicked in a shot from Smeaton and Saints' fight-back was on.

However, Leith were not giving up lightly and just after Buckley's goal they hit the post, but thereafter it was a procession towards the visitors' goal. Having saved impressively from Clarke, Wallace then spilled a shot from Buckley in 62 minutes and the score was equal. Three minutes later and Saints were in front, this time after Peat and Buckley created a chance for Irving to score. Two minutes after his goal, Irving returned the compliment, crossing for Buckley to net his hat-trick and put the game well beyond the visitors' reach. Paddy then hit the post before, the Sporting Post tells us, *"Buckley rounds off with a perfect goal – a swerving shot that gives Wallace no chance. Time, 82 minutes."*

The scoring wasn't over yet, and Clarke, who had been absent while Saints scored four goals, returned to the fray with three stitches in his head-wound and scored St Johnstone's seventh.

178

GRAND-SLAM SAINTS

ST JOHNSTONE, 7; LEITH ATHLETIC, 3.
(Half-time—1-3.)

Scorers:—St Johnstone—Buckley (58, 62, 69, 82 min.), Smeaton (29 min.), Irving (65 min.), Clarke (88 min.); Leith Ath.—Canavan (o.g. 2 min.), Dalziel (18, 37 min.).

This match featured one of the most intensive bursts of goalscoring in St Johnstone's history. As the cutting here from the Sunday Post shows, the team scored four goals in 11 minutes – that's a goal every 2 minutes 45 seconds on average. Very few other matches can equal this and only a few can beat it, as we'll describe later...

Despite their heroics against Leith, Saints interest in the Cup didn't last much longer that season. Paired against Stenhousemuir, they drew 2-2 at Ochilview, before losing the replay 4-2 at Perth.

Saints team: McLaren; Goldie and Blyth; Lindsay, Canavan and Smeaton; Clarke, Irving, Buckley, Peebles and Peat. Attendance: 6,000.

Scottish Premier League
St Johnstone 1, Dundee 0
McDiarmid Park, Sunday, 23rd May 1999

Gordon Bannerman reporting . . .

Euro-bound Saints first among equals

Headline: Perthshire Advertiser

"Twenty-eight years after the last venture into Europe, someone, somewhere on the continent will be perplexed trying to locate this place St Johnstone on a map of Scotland..."

Thus began the second paragraph of Gordon Bannerman's report on this pivotal match in the club's history, based, no doubt, on the story that the driver of the coach that, in 1972, was taking the Vasas Budapest team to play against Saints drove to Johnstone in Renfrewshire rather than Perth. The reason for this potential cartographical confusion was simple: Saints had, for the first time in nearly three decades, qualified for European football. That we did it against our favourite enemy made it even more sweet, as did the fact that Alan Main made what many people regard as the greatest save in not just his career but possibly the entire history of St Johnstone FC.

This was the last match of the 1998-99 season. The week before, Saints had come from behind at Kilmarnock to earn a vital draw: a point which meant that they knew if they could win the final match of the season, at home against Dundee, they would be guaranteed third place in the Premier League and entry into the UEFA Cup, albeit in the qualifying rounds.

The season was already judged to be a success. Not only had Saints made it to

their second, major national final – the League Cup, where they lost by the odd goal in three to Rangers – but they had also reached the semi-final of the Scottish Cup, where, once again, it was the Ibrox side who ended their interest in the trophy. Despite all this, it had been a trying few weeks prior to the Kilmarnock game. A superb 1-0 win at home against Celtic, courtesy of a bullet header from Irishman Keith O'Halloran, was followed by a defeat away at Pittodrie and a scoreless draw with Motherwell at Perth. The next match was the 1-1 draw at Rugby Park. That result meant Kilmarnock were still in pole position: one point ahead of Saints but with the serious disadvantage of a trip to Ibrox on the last day of the season.

Saints' visitors, Dundee, were in good form, having won all of their four previous matches. And of course, some of the older supporters of both clubs could remember the last time an end-of-season contest was imbued with such great meaning, namely the 1962 clash at Muirton when Dundee won the (old) First Division and relegated Saints in the process. In the second last year of the twentieth century though, things had changed and off the pitch Dundee were in trouble; threatened with expulsion from the Premier League due to the run-down state of Dens Park.

The stage was set for an epic battle. With new manager Sandy Clark replacing Paul

Sturrock very early in the season, the St Johnstone team was still very much built on the defensive rock that Paul and John Blackley had assiduously constructed. At the other end of the park, there was no out-and-out goalscorer, but instead goals were shared around the team.

The crowd that flocked to McDiarmid that day is still a record for the ground. It was not all-ticket and consequently hundreds were locked out. The sun shone and 10,595 people watched on as the two teams lined up to do battle.

Not many of the players in the home dressing room had any real experience of the pressure they now felt. The same applied to many of the fans in the ground. Yet for many, there was a feeling that this was indeed a day to make history.

Nick Dasovic remembers that the mood in the dressing room beforehand was that Rangers would beat Kilmarnock. Having been at Perth for a few seasons, he was also well aware of the demand for a Saints' victory. He told us, *"I had absorbed the Perth mentality by that time and knew that Dundee was our big derby – one we had to win. The squad knew what was at stake: if we won, we qualified for Europe. We also knew that Dundee had nothing to play for, but that didn't mean it would be easy.*

"I remember walking out onto the pitch. It was a beautiful, sunny day. I knew it was a big day for the city. In the first half I had a chance when a rebound came to me: I hit it but it was blocked. Then, when it was still scoreless at half-time, I think we got a bit nervous, but we knew all we had to do was win: we didn't care how, we just had to get over the line."

Given what was at stake, it was perhaps inevitable that the game would fail to live up to its billing. The PA described it as a *"tension-ridden, nerve-jangling derby* (that) *wouldn't have lingered long in the*

memory." The Courier said it *"was nothing to write home about."* Yet for those (Saints') fans who were there, it was everything to write home about. Especially when they saw the final Premier League table…

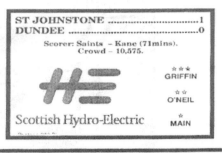

| ST JOHNSTONE | 1 |
| DUNDEE | 0 |

Scorer: Saints – Kane (71mins).
Crowd – 10,575.

★ ★ ★ GRIFFIN
★ ★ O'NEIL
★ MAIN

Scottish Hydro-Electric

SCOTTISH PREMIER LEAGUE FINAL STANDINGS						
	P	W	D	L	F	A	Pts
Rangers	36	23	8	5	78	31	77
Celtic	36	21	8	7	84	35	71
ST JOHNSTONE	36	15	12	9	39	38	57
Kilmarnock	36	14	14	8	47	29	56

Unmemorable the game may have been for some in the press-box, but for the St Johnstone fans it was indeed *"tension-ridden"* and *"nerve-jangling."* The vastly superior goal difference enjoyed by Kilmarnock meant that we had to win – and hope that Rangers did likewise against the men from Ayrshire. Fortunately, that latter part of the deal was secured, but it took a very long time for Saints to solve their side of the equation.

Throughout the match there was the ever-present fear that Dundee might just go and score, thus making it much harder for Saints to win. And with 68 minutes on the clock, that was what nearly happened…

In the PA, Gordon Bannerman described the incident as only he could: *"The reflexes of a test-pilot and the agility of an acrobat were required to flick over the bar a net-bound close-range header delivered by James Grady. It was a breath-taking stop which got Saints out of jail."*

Everyone who was there can recall that save. However, Nick Dasovic made the point that, while it was undoubtedly outstanding, Main's contribution had been immense all season, noting, *"People perphaps forget that in some games we got pummelled and Alan made saves that got us victories. We all felt that if the opposition got past our defenders Alan would deal with it. That said, our defenders were pretty good and I always had confidence in those behind me – Kerny (Alan Kernaghan), Darren Dods and, of course, Jim Weir.*

"I keep in touch with Jim. He exemplified grit, determination and playing for the badge. I realised what he meant to the club after I left. Although he was from the west of Scotland, he made sure that while anyone was playing for Saints, they supported them and left other allegiances behind. As the captain, he refused to wear a captain's armband, but by his demeanour and commitment on the pitch he demonstrated that he was the leader. Strangely, off the field and in the locker room, he could be quiet, like a church mouse, but when we went on the pitch..."

Having got out of jail, Saints still needed to score (and not concede) to guarantee European football. Fortunately, as the Courier tells us, only two minutes after Main's heroics, *"Kane fed John McQuillan who, in turn, fed John O'Neil. Kane nodded his cross downwards past Douglas, who was slow to react, and into the far corner."*

The PA doesn't provide quite such a detailed description, merely recording *"... an unattended Kane stooped to guide home a precision 12-yard header from John O'Neil's skilfully crafted right flank cross."*

No matter how it was described, the ball was in the net and, as the fans (and, famously, club doctor Alistair McCracken) went wild, St Johnstone had about 20 minutes to hold out for the win. In the event, the Courier reminded us that *"the nearest thing to another goal came when Simao amazingly failed to convert a McQuillan cut-back, then (Dundee's) Miller, in*

attempting to clear the ball, almost directed it into his own net."

Nick Dasovic told us that once Saints went ahead, he and his team-mates did what was required. *"I remember grabbing Dundee players when we were defending corners,"* he told us, *"I was telling them, 'We're taking this victory.' It wasn't pretty, but it's what you do. Then at the end, seeing grown men and women crying I realised just what this meant to the fans, the club and the city."*

Danny Griffin also remembers it wasn't the greatest example of the beautiful game, telling us, *"It wasn't pretty, but we knew we had to get two results: first Killie at Ibrox, where it was out of our hands but we were just hoping someone would do us a favour; and then our own game. Once Rangers scored, I remember I was trying to block out the shouts of 'they are getting beat' – and concentrate on grinding out the result. I can still picture the ball being played out wide, then going bananas when Kano's header went in. It was a massive, brilliant achievement, made even better by knowing that it meant the fans could have a special holiday abroad somewhere watching the team compete in European football for the first time since the 1970s."*

While it may not have been the most entertaining spectacle for the neutral (not that there were many of them in the record crowd), for the home fans, it was nonetheless a day to be celebrated, and celebrated well into the night where possible. Jack Findlay remembers that he was in the hospitality for the game and afterwards, *"we ended up in my brother's back garden, having a barbeque. It wasn't a great game, but it was a great result, and that's what mattered. (Un)fortunately, one of my brother's neighbours was a Dundee fan and it must be said we may have reminded him of the score more than once during the evening..."*

Allan Preston wasn't in the team that day. At that time, both he and Roddy Grant required hernia operations and they had been to Leeds to get this done. Biscuits also told us that when they were in hospital, Roddy set the fire alarm off by having a fly cigarette in one of the toilets. It appears that contrary to hospital rules, the two of them had also managed to acquire some beer on that occasion and Roddy told us that a few days later, when they had lunch, *"it included a nice bottle of wine, and I put it all on Biscuits' bill, so Stewart Duff wasn't very pleased with him when he got the expenses claim."* Despite all these shenanigans, as a result of their surgery the pair ended up watching the game alongside the directors.

Here's Biscuits on what happened next: *"Of course, having had a hernia op, I had stitches in my groin. It's not a good idea to jump about too much when you have stitches, especially in your groin, but we were both on our feet when Alan Main made that save and then, soon afterwards, when Kano scored. After the final whistle, Kano came into the directors' box and it was madness. I particularly remember Doc McCracken on his knees on the turf and it was brilliant for all the people behind the scenes – Aggie, Jocky Peebles and the rest. It was brilliant.*

"Then we headed out into Perth city centre and made for That Bar, all dressed up in our club suits. I remember I gave my tie away, bought it back, then gave it away again. Someone brought a ball out and we had players and fans kicking it about in Perth High Street. The police came and we were asked to get into a police van, which then took us to the Ice Factory. The rest of the team were in the back, but I was in the front with Roddy, who asked the driver if he could put the siren on, except that Roddy couldn't remember the proper name for it and asked him to switch on the 'nee-naw'- which he did!"

This was a sensational season for St Johnstone. Not only had they finished third in the top flight for only the second time in their history, thus qualifying for Europe for only the second time, they also reached the final of the League Cup and the semi-final of the Scottish Cup. The last game might not have been the best, but there was no doubt that this was one of St Johnstone's best ever sides…

Saints team: Main, McQuillan, Bollan, Dasovic, McCluskey, Griffin, O'Halloran, O'Neil, Kane, Simao, Lowndes.
Substitutes: Ferguson McAnespie (for O'Halloran, Connolly (for Lowndes), Whiteford, and Parker.
Attendance: 10,575 (still a record for McDiarmid Park).

Scottish League Cup, Group Three
Partick Thistle 1, St Johnstone 8
Firhill, Saturday 16th August 1969

"Firhill for thrills" is one of the best-known slogans in Scottish football. It originated from an old advert in front of the north terrace at the ground, which read, *"Firhill for Thrills, Johnson's for Rolls."* And on a sunny day, in the preliminary group stages of the 1969 Scottish League Cup, it most certainly proved true, although sadly not for the home supporters who had to watch their side roll over in the face of a sustained assault of attacking brilliance from Willie Ormond's stellar Saints.

Why was this Saints team so good? The Daily Record, in the days before stereotyping became a hate-crime, began a report on the club with a succession of paragraphs that, while setting the scene for a volte-face, are nonetheless very much indicative of a particular mindset, viz,

"St Johnstone as a club, Muirton Park as a ground and Perth as a town, all gave the impression that soccer had passed them by.

"Success to St Johnstone then was to keep clear of relegation. Their ambitions went no further.

"Yet now all that has changed. Sure the ground still has a sleepy air about it. The Perthshire hills rise gently to form a backdrop for the far terracing and weeds sprout lavishly on the terracings behind the goals. There are even cobwebs clinging stubbornly to the rails guarding the players' tunnel…"

To be fair, the Record's reporter then uses this to make the point that, in their play so far that season, *"the cobwebs that once clouded the club's thinking and clogged their ambitions have been swept away."*

The reason for this, according to the Record, was simple: it was because Willie Ormond wanted to make it happen. The manager was quoted as saying, *"This isn't a flash in the pan. I knew at the end of last season that things were beginning to come right with the team. I knew what I wanted from them and now it is all happening right for us. We have a system which we stick to – you have to have a system for any team – but we also have players with individuality. Not only that, the players are thinking for themselves now. They know what to do in certain circumstances without having to be told all the time. That's when you really know you are making headway."*

Even the most optimistic of the away fans turning up at Firhill that afternoon would not have put any money on the final score being what it was. Saints wasted no time in getting ahead. In the first minute, Kenny Aird's corner was laid off by John Connolly to Ian McPhee, who crashed the ball home from about 10 yards.

Although Buck McCarry then headed narrowly over, there were no more goals for a quarter of an hour, and when the next came it was an equaliser for the home side. There were two former Saints in the Jags' line-up, Dan McLindon and John Flanagan. The latter fed the ball to outside left Arthur Duncan, who was faced by the onrushing Jimmy Donaldson. Duncan - who later went on to greater fame with Hibs and Scotland - coolly slotted the ball home. Another quarter of an hour passed before Hall restored Saints' lead. The PA described this as follows: *"he latched onto a long punt upfield and gave Ritchie no chance as he prodded the ball into the net."* Then, a few minutes later (some reports say two minutes, others three), John Connolly got Saints' third. The PA described just what a good goal this was: *"the tall ex-Glasgow United Juvenile player expertly swept past two players before unleashing a low, sizzling 20-yarder which looked a winner all the way."*

Two minutes from the interval and the match was as good as over when Aitken notched St Johnstone's fourth, turning in a nice ball from Connolly.

At half-time a group of Saints' fans turned up, having missed all the action in the first half. Their bus had caught fire in Stirling, which delayed them somewhat. On the bus was a friend of Jim Masson's who came running into the ground to look for him. Jim was at the pie stall, in the queue, when his mate dashed up to ask what was the score. On being told it was 4-1 Saints, he responded, *"dinnae be daft,"* and when Jim insisted that was indeed the score his friend

turned to a Thistle fan in the queue and asked him the score. The Jags' supporter, thinking this was a wind-up – and not too pleased as a result – promptly decked Jim's mate, who responded in kind until the police intervened and both supporters were removed from the ground. It was probably the shortest time anyone has spent in a football ground and failed to see any one of nine goals scored in a match. Unfortunately, this was the same friend who had an even more truncated view of the League Cup final later that season, as we described in Part I, Chapter 21.

Having scored in the first minute of the first half, Saints then proceeded to do the same in the second half. This time, it was Henry Hall who fired home. Here's the PA again, and in passing we should note that this goal more than explains that Hall was not just a goal-scorer – he had a lot of skill too. "(Hall) *raced to intercept a short pass back from McKinnon. He lobbed the ball over the advancing keeper's head and ran round to nod it into the open net."*

Two minutes later and it was six, with Kenny Aird getting in on the act. His left-wing counterpart, Fred Aitken, fired the ball over, low and hard, and Kenny was in the middle to knock it home.

Any Thistle fans who were contemplating leaving early would have been well advised to do so. While Saints were excellent, Thistle were bewitched by their opponents. Ex-Rangers' keeper Ritchie, in the home goal, *"had a nightmare game"* according to the PA, *"although most of the blame must rest on slipshod defence work."* It would be a few years before that defence was bolstered by the young Alan Hansen, but playing that day was his brother, John. Later in their report, the PA tells us, *"Partick Thistle had no answer to this jet-paced soccer from the Muirton team, and only on a few occasions did they manage to move into attack. Their efforts, however, were easily dealt with by a competent Perth defence. Ritchie did well to stop a McPhee thunderbolt in the 65th minute, but a further score was only delayed four minutes. McPhee slipped the ball to Hall and it looked as if the latter had lost the chance when he hit the ball just a shade too far ahead. The inside-man quickly regained control and touched it past Ritchie before angling the ball into the net for his hat-trick."*

John Connolly then finished the scoring, knocking in an easy finish after Ritchie had denied Hall his fourth goal of the game.

Henry was then substituted by Gordon Whitelaw. Despite being brought up 50 yards from Firhill in Springbank Street, then being a ball boy for Thistle before starting his career with them, Gordon came very close to making it double figures for Saints, with two powerful shots being repelled by Ritchie in the Thistle goal.

Saints team: Donaldson; Lambie, Coburn, Gordon, Rooney, McPhee, Aird, Hall, McCarry, Connolly, Aitken. Substitute: Whitelaw (for Hall).
Attendance: 3,500.

No. 27
Full of action, suspense, and clever football

Scottish League B Division
St Johnstone 2, Airdrieonians 2
Muirton Park, Saturday, 4ᵗʰ December 1954

SATURDAY, DECEMBER 4, 1954   5

A Penalty Each In Muirton Thriller

Expectations of a promotion thriller are entertained at Muirton by both Airdrie's large contingent of supporters and Saints' "faithful."

Headline: The Sporting Post

In its introductory paragraph to the match report for this game, the PA bemoaned the problem clubs had in getting fans to turn out for games. However, they noted that if all games were like this one, the fans would soon flock back...

"A big drop in attendance is B Division's major problem these days, but if all games were in similar mould to Saturday's thriller at Muirton Park the crowds would not be slow to come back."

In fact, the attendance wasn't exactly terribly small and those who were there saw a fabulous match, in which, as the PA's match report described it, *"Perth's best encounter of the season kept the 8,000 spectators on tenterhooks from start to finish, and perhaps the most encouraging feature from Saints' viewpoint was the tremendous vocal encouragement which they received from their supporters. There has been nothing like it at the Dunkeld Road stadium for a long time. But then it was that kind of match – full of action, suspense, and clever football."*

The Sporting Post's heading (above) noted that many of the spectators had travelled from the west, while the Airdrie and Coatbridge Advertiser tells us that some of these fans came on a *"Special Football Excursion"* on Scottish Omnibuses, paying a return fare of 7/- (seven shillings - £11.62 today) for the privilege.

Although this was a B Division match, there was some real talent on display, notably the visitors' Ian McMillan, revered by many Diamonds' fans as their greatest ever midfielder. Known as *"the Wee Prime Minister,"* because he shared his name with an incumbent of No. 10 Downing Street, McMillan played for Airdrie from 1948 to 1958, before going to Rangers for six years and then returning to Broomfield for another two years between 1964 and 1966. He also had six caps for Scotland during that time.

Another well-known name was Doug Baillie, then a teenage centre-half whom many older readers will remember as a football reporter for The Sunday Post.

Cartoon: The Courier

The referee was another very famous name - Jack Mowat - who would go on to officiate at the celebrated 1960 European Cup final at Hampden when Real Madrid defeated Eintracht Frankfurt 7-3.

The strength of this Airdrie team was reflected in the fact that they went on to win the B Division that season, scoring 103 goals from 30 games. Saints, in contrast, finished in seventh place, 14 points behind Airdrie's total of 46 and scoring only 60 goals from their 30 League matches.

On the St Johnstone side, there were also some fine players, especially Ian Rodger, the club's second top scorer of all-time. In that 1954-55 season, Ian scored 30 times - over one third of St Johnstone's 80 goals in all games, at an average of nearly one per game. Meanwhile, at the centre of the home defence there was Jimmy Clarkson, like Baillie, a giant of a man, who featured with his Airdrie counterpart in one of the celebrated Courier cartoons of the day.

This period of the 1950s was when Saints were battling hard under their relatively new manager, Johnny Pattillo, to regain their top flight status, cruelly taken away after the war. It was also a period of financial insecurity, with the directors struggling at times to pay the players their full wages. Despite this, they were considered one of the teams that had a chance of promotion. When Airdrie came calling for this match in early December, the Diamonds were undefeated at the top of the table, with 17 points as a result of seven wins and three draws from their ten matches. Saints, in contrast, were fifth, with 13 points from 11 games.

The Airdrie and Coatbridge Advertiser, in their preview of the match, said, *"Airdrie's undefeated record is at stake, but, more than that, their promotion and championship prospects might be jeopardised by the loss of any points at all at the present time. St Johnstone are worthy challengers and the Airdrie defence will require to tighten up and the whole team to put in 100 per cent effort."*

The first half ended goalless, but not for want of trying, especially on the part of the St Johnstone forwards. Interestingly, all the local papers – both east and west - took a similar view about the game. Here's the Airdrie and Coatbridge Advertiser on the first half: *"St Johnstone showed early on that they were out to knock Airdrie off their pedestal,"* while the PA recorded that, *"First half especially they stretched the Broomfield defence to the limit"* and the Courier stated, *"A draw was just about right, yet if only for that brilliant first-half display no-one would have grudged St Johnstone full points."*

The key difference between the teams this day seems to have been that, as we say today, Saints wanted it more. The PA put it like this: *"The equal of Airdrie in skill, Saints were ahead in enthusiasm."*

The Sporting Post, reporting live, provides the best account of the game. The opening paragraphs of their report give an indication of just how to-and-fro the action was and how exciting it must have been for the watching fans of both clubs. After telling us that Airdrie won the toss and decided to shoot with the wind, we read…

"McLaren is in action right away to a softish Price attempt.

"McMillan is difficult to dispossess in a mazy run in the middle, but Ewen is there when the danger arises.

"Airdrie's Baird performs a quick dash up the left, but Clarkson outwits him with a pass-back which causes McLaren to look lively.

"Saints have hard lines when a snap 40-yarder from Rodger is deflected by Rice. Walker just manages to save and a corner it is.

"There is quite a scramble in the visitors' goalmouth, but Baillie eases the situation with a hefty clearance.

"Airdrie's turn now and McCulloch rounds big Clarkson. McLaren brings off a first-class save. Again he saves the home bacon when he dives at the feet of Baird and Reid to stop a certain score (see photo below).

McLaren saves from Baird: The Courier

"Airdrie don't look secure in defence.

"Walker saves a Rodger header, and then doesn't see a Carr drive which touches a defender as it flies over the bar.

"Clarkson slips as McCulloch intercepts a Woodcock pass, but the winger is yards wide.

"Hodgson and Landles execute a clever move, but Rodger shoots past.

"Saints are every bit as good as the league leaders and look to have a penalty claim when Gordon handles, but the referee says 'no'."

And so the match report goes on, with paragraph after paragraph describing one exciting moment after another before the Sporting Post's reporter called the half-time score, with neither side having managed to breach their opponents' defence. His reflections on that first 45 minutes state, *"it's been a real thriller, with Saints unlucky not to be ahead. A good defence has blanketed out Airdrie's forward stars."*

With such constant attacking play, it was inevitable that the second half would see some goals. In the 59th minute, Saints opened the scoring. The PA described it as, *"the culmination of a Hodgson-Rodger move which brought Robertson tearing in from the wing to screw the ball in at the post with his left foot."*

Airdrie's equaliser came from what the PA described as a 'soft' penalty, when a cross-shot hit Clarkson on the hand. Both the Airdrie and Perth papers say the ball struck him rather than his moving his hand to the ball, but Mr Mowat, obviously anticipating the nonsensical handball law we are saddled with in 2023, pointed to the spot. The 17-year-old Doug Baillie put his laces through it and the scores were then level. The Airdrie and Coatbridge Advertiser commented, *"Had McLaren got in the way of the spot kick, it would probably have taken him into the goal as well."*

That Airdrie equaliser came in the 72nd minute. Five minutes later and the league leaders were ahead. Again, it was a rocket-shot, albeit this time from open play. The Sporting Post described this as follows, *"Airdrie, however, get their second with seven minutes left and it's a good goal. After some lovely play on the right, McCulloch cracks a right-footer well and truly home."*

Bizarrely, the Airdrie and Coatbridge Advertiser said that it wasn't Airdrie but Saints who went in front when the score was 1-1. After describing how *"Referee Mowat ... pointed to the spot. Ewan (sic) didn't give Walker much chance and St Johnstone were in the lead again. It was one of those situations which only McCulloch can solve ... and he secured the equaliser seven minutes from the end."* If the Airdrie historians are reading this and

then banging their head against a wall, we sympathise: it only goes to show how hard it can be to get basic facts right – something of which we are only too aware when it comes to St Johnstone as well…

What actually happened is that with the Diamonds having taken the lead with only seven minutes of normal time left, Saints threw themselves forward. Given that Clarkson and Baillie were both, in different ways, involved in Airdrie's penalty, it seemed apt that they would also be the key figures in the penalty that resulted in the final goal of the game. The PA again provides the best description…

"It was fitting that Clarkson was instrumental in bringing about the equaliser. The big fellow went forward to lend his height to a Robertson corner, and as the ball came over he was nudged by Baillie who, physically is something of a big boy himself. The referee pointed to the spot, and the uneasy silence of the home fans was broken with a great cheer as Ewen maintained his reputation for converting penalties."

None of the papers records precisely how long was left after Saints' equaliser, but it must have only been minutes. The Sporting Post tells us that Saints then went all out to try to grab a winner, but *"Airdrie managed to keep them out."*

Although Saints didn't win this game, the final 20 or so minutes seem to have been every bit as exciting as the famous 1990 Airdrie game at McDiarmid Park.

We are fortunate that Donald Paton was at this match and he shared his reminiscences of it with us…

"Back in those days, you went to the game wearing a collar and tie and few went in an open neck shirt. Very often people came straight from their work, because, of

course, many worked on Saturday mornings. Also, there were no floodlights, so kick off times were usually 2.00 pm or 2.15 pm. There was no enclosure then, so men were standing out in all weathers, but I remember some would bring golf umbrellas to shelter from the rain.

"The draw with Airdrie in 1954, was a real thriller - on a par with the 1990 Airdrie game. Both sides were battling for promotion. I remember the Monday cartoons in the Courier, and in particular the focus on the fact that both teams had gigantic centre halves.

"There was no crowd segregation in those days and you could have a good blether with the opposition fans and generally wish them the best - not like today. Fans were never frisked before going into the ground: everyone was more trusting. And because we all tended to have our favourite places to stand on the terracing, you'd meet the same people every other week and get to know them. This even applied to some of the away fans. There was a father and son who came from Hamilton to watch the Accies at Perth and we almost became pals. And all older fans will remember there was also the ritual of changing ends at half-time; something that's not possible nowadays."

While the 1950s was not the finest period in St Johnstone's history and the club was in dire straits financially (with a £12,000 overdraft causing serious concern to the St Johnstone board), there is no doubt that - as Donald Paton recalls and the match reports make clear - this was an outstanding football match. We'll leave the last word to the Courier…

"Here we had two teams full of football craft and plenty of running, and spectators urging them on with shouts that haven't been heard in Perth for years… I have seldom seen a crowd leave the ground so thoroughly satisfied."

Saints team: McLaren; Woodcock, Clark; Ewen, Clarkson, Baird, Robertson, Landles, Rodger, Hodgson, Carr. Attendance: 8,000.

Of the forward lines the Saints five were far and away the prettiest

Perthshire Cup, Second Round,
Fair City Athletic 4, St Johnstone 9,
Balhousie Park, Saturday, 16th November 1895

As we have mentioned previously, during their formative years St Johnstone's principal rivals in Perth were Fair City Athletic. If things had gone differently, it might have been Fair City that we follow today, and it would be black and white scarves and striped replica kits that adorn the necks and torsos of the current generation of Perth fans.

As the nineteenth century wound to its close, some of the smaller local teams dropped out of the picture, leaving Saints and Fair City as the city's two principal clubs. As noted above (Part I, Chapter 3), they became great rivals, playing each other 71 times, with Saints winning 30, Fair City 27 and 14 matches drawn.

As football in Perthshire evolved, so too did the Perthshire Cup, becoming the major local knock-out contest and the highlight of most seasons for the city and county clubs. In 1895-96, when Fair City were drawn at home in the second round against the then Cup-holders, St Johnstone, the press played up the prospect of the match, highlighting the rivalry between the two clubs - although also demonstrating that west-coast patronising of teams from Perth is not a modern phenomenon. To illustrate the point, The Scottish Referee began their preview thus, *"Perth will be as excited tomorrow in its own small way over the meeting of St Johnstone and Fair City Athletics for the Perthshire Cup as Glasgow will be in its larger way."*

To be fair, this report went on to put the match in its local context, *"For the past two or three years St Johnstone have far outshone its rival. More than ever*

pronounced has this been the case this season. Up to the present, the St Johnstone has had as successful, as their opponents have had a disastrous, season. Never in the history of the Fair City club have matters been at so low an ebb as regards success in the field. With St Johnstone it has been a gratifying opposite. Left to the ordinary players of each club there would be little doubt as to the result. Fair City are, however, to make a strong effort tomorrow, not only to pull over their rivals, but also to put their team on a stronger playing footing. St Johnstone will, no doubt, play their hardest to retain the county pot which they presently hold. There is a strong feeling in St Johnstone circles that, notwithstanding the outside aid arrayed against them, the Edinburgh Road team will pull through."

Anyone reading this will have been none the wiser as to what Fair City were doing, although there is a strong hint that they were drafting in new players for the match. A more detailed answer as to what was happening came in the Evening Telegraph's preview of the game. It's fair to say that the Telegraph's reporter was not so confident of a St Johnstone victory as the man from the Scottish Referee. This is what the Evening Telegraph said…

"The local Derby comes off tomorrow, when the City meet the Saints and Dalhousie (sic – they meant 'Balhousie') Park is sure to be crowded with the supporters of the two Clubs. The question of who will win is a very open one. The Saints certainly have the better record, but their out and in form is not to be relied upon in the least degree. The 'City' have been

rather unfortunate in losing Arnott, their goalkeeper, and latterly Hill and Moir (the last two had gone to Saints). Last Saturday, however, they tried a team, which performed well, and tomorrow the eleven will very likely be much the same, the new men – Ferguson, Morris, McKnight, and Crawford – taking the places vacated by the old members. The Saints may have the pull in goal, but Crawford and Neilson are stronger at back, and the halves of the 'City' are every whit as good, if not better than the Saints. The front rank is the doubtful part, and with Buttar not playing, and Moir in his place, the 'City' are level nearly at every point. Hill and Moir will be well watched by their old clubmates if they play for the Saints. Both teams are keeping their players in training. The match will be a hot one, and although the 'City,' with the advantage of the ground, should win, it will likely be close up to the end of the 90 minutes."

Thus, on the one hand we have a local paper saying Fair City were favourites, and a national one saying Saints were favourites. They couldn't both be right…

The two clubs had not played each other so far that season, but in the preceding season it had taken three matches in the final of the Reid Charity Cup to separate them. The first two of these both resulted in a 2-2 draw, but St Johnstone won the second replay 6-1. However, as the local newspaper reports suggest, Fair City were not having such a good time of it in the first few months of the 1895-96 season, so, despite the Evening Telegraph's view, Saints were regarded by many as the favourites going into this game.

That this was a very big match with a lot of local interest is borne out by the size of the crowd. We have very little information of the numbers attending Saints' matches from 1885 until after the First World War, when more match reports began to give the estimated size of the crowd. Where we do

have figures in the nineteenth century, they are generally about 1,000, 2,000 or, occasionally, 3,000. This game seems to have exceeded all others, with the Dundee Courier commenting that, *"A very large crowd witnessed this fixture,"* while according to the Scottish Referee's report there were some 4,000 spectators, a higher number than for any previous match in Saints' history for which we have figures. To put this in context, the city's population at the 1891 census was 29,902.

Further evidence of the importance of the game comes in the match report in the Scottish Referee. Under the heading *"Championship of Perth,"* we can read that, *"This tie has been the talk of Perth all week."* The match itself was played in difficult conditions, as the Dundee Courier reported: *"Owing to the heavy rains the ground was very heavy…"*

The inclement weather and wet pitch don't seem to have dampened the enthusiasm of the fans or the players. Fair City had the aforementioned Crawford in their ranks. A Glaswegian, he had previously played for Morton. A second *"stranger"* (as the Scottish Referee put it) in the home side was McGregor, another Glaswegian.

The game was even in the first half. St Johnstone scored first, within the first five minutes. None of the match reports tells us who scored this goal, but (again from the Scottish Referee) we do know that Ben Waddell got the second soon after the first, *"amid great cheers."* Then, *"a bad miss by the St Johnstone defence enabled D. Crawford to score, and immediately after Scully made the game level."* Thereafter, it seems to have continued to be end-to-end stuff (*"corners in plenty fell to both sides"*) but there was no further scoring before half-time.

In the second half, Fair City started the stronger. The Dundee Courier tells us, *"On resuming, play was in the Saints' territory* and *Tulloch was called upon."* However (the Scottish Referee again), *"From a dirty bit of play, St Johnstone were granted a penalty, which Robertson converted."* Fair City then equalised once more, but Saints scored twice more. Once again, the home side returned to the attack and were awarded *"a doubtful penalty,"* but they failed to score from the spot-kick. Had they scored, it might have been a significant turning point in the match, but instead St Johnstone went further ahead, once more through Robertson. He went on to secure his hat-trick, as did Waddell. The other Saints' scorer we know of was Andrew Moir, while the identities of the final St Johnstone and Fair City's fourth goalscorers are unknown.

The way football was played in 1895 was very different from the structured and methodical approach we are used to today. For a start, each side had five forwards.

To help paint a picture of what a game was like at this time, the Perthshire Constitutional's match report records that the difference between the two teams was largely in the forwards. This is also borne out by the preview in the Evening Telegraph quoted above, where it is noted that although Saints had a better keeper, the full-backs and half-backs of each team were well-matched. However, the Constitutional also recorded that, *"Where the St Johnstone far outstripped them was in their smartness on the ball, their playing of a better passing game, and in their persistent habit of shooting for goal whenever they saw the slightest chance to score. Of the forward lines the Saints five were far and away the prettiest and most effective players. Waddell and Cairncross combined well, McFarlane was a capital centre, and Moir and Anderson played much better than was expected."*

We can also get a good impression of the aggressive nature of nineteenth century football from some of the other comments

in the Constitutional's report, where they described the Fair City Athletic's right wing and centre forward as being *"too rough in their play, and* (they) *had a bad habit of using their hands when charging."*

Overall, this seems to have been a cracking match, with an enormous amount of local interest from the supporters of both clubs. The fact that two St Johnstone players scored hat-tricks – the first time in the club's history that had happened in the same match (there have been two other instances of this – Rodger and Steel in 1955 and Liddell and Haughey in 1959) – on its own justifies the inclusion of this game here, but in addition the reports from the media also emphasise, as if it is needed, just what a fabulous footballer Johnny Robertson was for St Johnstone – and, if he had had more luck in the Scottish international trial matches, he might well have been our first international player.

As the Perthshire Constitutional noted, *"For the Saints, Robertson towered head and shoulders above everybody for his accuracy of judgment in putting the ball into the goal. No-one would be far wrong in stating that few backs can take place kicks like Johnny Robertson. Robertson is, indeed, Perthshire's greatest back."*

The Scottish Referee's summary of the game, shown below, concludes that although the home side had made a stern effort to compete, on the day they were no match for their visitors and St Johnstone *"deserved their great victory."*

Notwithstanding their strongest efforts Fair City fell a terrible victim to their townsmen, St. Johnstone.

A result of 9-4 must have made not a few people imagine that Perth had got early started to cricket.

Fair City's Glasgow importations were no better nor no worse than the home article, and St. Johnstone from the start played with a dash begat of confidence.

Fair City made a fair show, but a team gathered within a fortnight from the four winds of heaven was no match for the St. Johnstone, who from start to finish went solid, and well deserved their great victory.

Fair City Athletic continued to play for only another seven seasons. A disastrous move to a new ground at Muirton Bank created a substantial debt and they then made this even larger by commissioning a new grandstand. Their last full season was 1901-02, after which they went bust and stopped playing. By this time, Saints had left them far behind, but in a generous gesture had played a friendly against Fair City in order to try to raise funds to keep the latter going. It was the last game that Fair City Athletic ever played, but for St Johnstone the future – albeit with many slings, arrows and the occasional burst of outrageous misfortune lying in wait – was far more promising…

Saints team: Tulloch; Robertson and Dakers; G Burnfield, White and Hill; Cairncross, Waddell, McFarlane, Moir and Anderson.
Attendance: 4,000.

A piece of skill Brazilian ace Ronaldinho would have been proud of...

CIS/Scottish League Cup Quarter-Final
Rangers 0, St Johnstone 2
Ibrox Stadium, Wednesday, 8th November 2006

Milne nets twice as super Saints stun Rangers

Headline: The Courier

The 2006-07 season saw St Johnstone, under manager Owen Coyle, focused on trying to regain the Premier League status they had lost in 2002. As described elsewhere in this book, they came within a whisker of doing so, but in the course of the season they also had two outstanding Cup runs, reaching the semi-finals of the CIS Insurance/League Cup (where they lost after extra time to Hibs) and the Scottish Cup (where they were overcome by Celtic). Coyle's impact as manager was evident in the purposeful way St Johnstone approached matches, seeking to out-gun their opponents and attack where possible, but with the safety-net of a solid defence, centred on the veteran and man-of-many-clubs, Allan McManus, and the emerging talent of Steven Anderson.

Saints had reached the quarter-final by beating East Fife, Elgin City and Premier League Dundee United – the latter going down 3-0 at McDiarmid in what should have been advance warning for Rangers that, despite their lower league status,

St Johnstone would be no pushover. Moreover, going into the game, Saints were top of the First Division table but despite this not many gave the Perth men much hope, especially at Ibrox.

Owen Coyle played it safe in his pre-match comments, telling the press that, irrespective of their poor form in the league at that point, Rangers were obviously favourites. He did note, however, that if Saints played to the top of their form and Rangers had an off-day then a shock might be possible.

The St Johnstone fans who made the trip to the southside of Glasgow for the game, mostly travelled in hope rather than expectation. After all, Saints hadn't beaten Rangers at Ibrox for 35 years, with the last time being when Willie Ormond's team won 2-0, with John Connolly and Henry Hall scoring the goals.

This Saints' team was not a patch on Ormond's side, but they did have a similar esprit-de-corps and a charismatic, young manager who had created a well-drilled unit with a real goal threat, especially from Jason Scotland and Steven (Savo) Milne.

To no-one's surprise, Rangers took the game to St Johnstone in the opening stages of the match, but that did not mean the Perth men were out of it, as the Courier related: *"The hosts were out the traps first, with Sebo shooting just over the bar from distance with a couple of minutes on the clock. Thomas Buffel then found room at the back post but could only strike the side-netting.*

"The visitors came close on 14 minutes when a Paul Sheerin free-kick from the right was just missed by Martin Hardie's boot, then Scotland saw his shot comfortably saved just seconds later.

"It was promising stuff from the Perth men and when Milne and Scotland combined to carve open the Rangers' defence with a one-two on 25 minutes, it took a last-gasp challenge from Steven Smith to steal the ball off Milne's foot as he was poised to let fly."

A tendency to over-complicate things didn't help the home side's cause and, as the PA tell us, *"...the longer the first period went without a goal for the hosts, the more Owen Coyle's side believed they could nick a result from this daunting tie.*

"They nearly saw a return on their optimism after 30-minutes when Milne headed just over from a neat Sheerin set-piece on the left.

"The Perth side didn't look intimidated by their SPL rivals and only a few dubious offside calls prevented Scotland and Milne from springing through..."

Come half-time and the game was still scoreless. Getting through the first forty-five minutes without conceding is always a good thing against the Old Firm, but normally it's hard to sustain this throughout the second half. This evening, though, was different. The PA takes up the story again: *"...if the travelling Saints support had been impressed with their side's confident stroll inside Ibrox during the first half, they would be ecstatic when it broke into an outright swagger six-minutes after the restart.*

"A Paul Sheerin corner found Allan McMannus in the box, but he could only knock his header towards Milne.

"With the ball falling unkindly to the striker, he pulled a stunning overhead kick straight out of the fairytale goal handbook to put St Johnstone ahead."

The Courier's take on Savo's athleticism was much more enthusiastic...

"With a piece of skill Brazilian ace Ronaldinho would have been proud of, the former Dundee man leapt up and sent an overhead kick into the net after Mensing had headed on a Sheerin cross."

In the PA, Savo recounted this goal as follows: *"I can't remember who won the header at the corner for my first, I think it was Steven Anderson...*

"I managed to peel away from my marker and when I saw the ball coming I thought I'd try an overhead kick.

"When I heard the crowd and the other players coming over I knew it was in."

These different reports starkly illustrate the problem football historians have when trying to understand what happened in a match. Was it Mensing or McManus or Anderson who headed the ball on – and was it from a corner or from a cross by Sheerin? Looking at the grainy images of the match on YouTube, it's obviously a corner taken by Paul Sheerin; then it appears that it was McManus who headed the ball, but it's not clear. To try to solve the mystery, we spoke to Ando, who said it wasn't him. We looked at the video again and it does seem that it's more likely to be McManus than Mensing – so that's that cleared up…

Irrespective of who headed it on, in the corner of Ibrox where the Saints' fans were housed, bedlam ensued. In another corner, amongst the posh seats of the hospitality, Alastair Blair and his wife sensibly suppressed their excitement while all around them the Rangers' fans expressed their displeasure.

No matter who headed it on, Saints got a massive lift from that first goal, with Owen Coyle subsequently telling the PA, *"After we scored I thought we stepped up a level and you could see the players really grow in confidence."*

Rangers responded by bringing on some of their bigger name players who had been left on the bench, presumably because Paul Le Guen thought he had enough talent in his starting line-up to overcome a First Division outfit. Dado Prso was one of the substitutes and he had a great chance to level the score after an hour, but fortunately *"the striker put his finish into orbit when he should have had the net bustling."*

The likelihood is that if Prso had scored, Rangers would have gone on to win the game. His chance was not quite as clear cut as the press suggested, being a shot from the edge of the box, but irrespective of how good it was, not long after he scorned this opportunity Saints went two up.

In the 67th minute, what can only be described as a hopeful punt up the park from within his own half by Martin Hardie left Milne in a foot-race with Rangers' defender Brahim Hemdani. Given that Savo had been tormenting the Ibrox rearguard with his pace all evening, it was no surprise that he outdistanced his pursuer before firing home from just inside the box.

This is how he described it to the PA: *"The second was pretty good as well. Martin Hardie played the ball through for me and I held off a defender and put it away with my left foot, which was unusual.*

"I haven't scored too many with my left this season and I'm delighted to be in double figures before the turn of the year."

There is a video on YouTube of the end of this match, taken by one of the wildly celebrating crowd of Saints' fans. As well as the wild whistling to encourage the referee to end the match, the main feature is the loud shouts of *"yaahs!"* - while a final chorus of *"Easy, Easy"* sums up how it felt to be a St Johnstone fan that night and how well the team had played. This was no lucky victory, but well merited by dint of a superb performance by a team of players that would continue to attract plaudits for their cup exploits throughout the season.

In the hospitality seats, Alastair Blair had long abandoned any pretence at neutrality. Fortunately, most of the Rangers' fans in that area had long since departed. Alastair called Andrew, his younger son, who was working in Edinburgh. *"What was the score dad?"* his son asked. *"Listen to this and you'll find out,"* he replied, holding his phone up towards the still celebrating St Johnstone fans some 150 yards away. The sound came across loud and clear. *"I take it we won then?"* Andrew said…

As well as hundreds of celebrating Saintees, the video taken by a fan at the end of the game showed that Ibrox was largely void of home fans well before the final whistle. The Courier (and most other papers) gave the attendance as 31,074, with about 1,000 of them being St Johnstone supporters.

For Saints' managing director, Stewart Duff, the size of the crowd was another cause for celebration: not only had the team won but, because the gate was split, a decent amount of money would be coming to Perth. However, he reckoned without the Ibrox management's interesting approach to recording the match attendance, as he told us:

"In those days, you were paid by cheque, which came with a breakdown of the crowd. I was surprised to see that the gate was recorded as being only around 25,000. I can't remember the precise figure, but it was of that order. Anyway, I called Ibrox and asked why they had announced the crowd at over 31,000, as all the press subsequently reported, and requested to see the details from their computerised turnstiles. I also got in touch with Strathclyde Police and made a request under Freedom of Information for their figures on the match, but they wouldn't give them to me. Eventually, Rangers agreed to increase their figure for the attendance to 27,500, which meant a few thousand pounds more for St Johnstone, but it still rankled. To be fair, they weren't the only club who tried to do this to us, but there was a large gap between 31,000 and 25,000 compared to the few hundred difference we were occasionally faced with by First Division clubs."

Stewart also recalled the atmosphere in the Ibrox boardroom at the match: *"At that time, Rangers were not always the most welcoming club for our directors. Donald Findlay was always personable and affable, as were Campbell Ogilvie and the Treasurer, Donald McIntyre, but some of the others didn't go out or their way to speak to us. After the match though, we were in their boardroom, which is one level above the street, and we could hear the shouting and chants as the Rangers' fans demanded the head of the manager, Paul Le Guen. It's fair to say we were delighted at the result..."*

The match stats for the game illustrated just what Stewart Duff meant. The BBC website recorded that Rangers had only 51% possession, far less than for many matches at Ibrox against Premier teams, while they also had fewer shots on target (seven) than Saints (eight), albeit they had more shots off target (13 as opposed to five for St Johnstone). Unsurprisingly, Saints were guilty of more fouls than Rangers (17 compared to nine), and the Glasgow side also had more corners (nine as opposed to five). But interesting as all these figures are, the only statistic that really matters at the end of a football match is the final score. And on this particular Wednesday night, it was Rangers 0, St Johnstone 2. For Saints, a glorious victory, for Rangers, a humiliating defeat and one which their manager would not survive.

Paul Le Guen, frequently referred to by his initials as PLG, was the subject of much angry protest after the game. The Daily Record's headline expressed the feeling of many Rangers' fans – *"PLG = Please Leave Govan?"* The (Glasgow) Herald, as befits its status as a more cerebral broadsheet, was a bit more measured, heading their report, *"Le Guen plunges even further into misery after shock defeat,"* with a sub-headline reading, *"Manager facing battle to save his reputation and Rangers' season."* Within two months, he had gone.

In contrast to the luckless Le Guen, Owen Coyle's ability to forge a team capable of punching well above their weight was being noticed both north and, especially, south of the border. Within a year, he too was gone - to what was to prove to be a successful stint at Burnley. More importantly, Owen left behind the nucleus of a squad that Derek McInnes would further develop and take back to the Premier League in 2009.

Saints team: Halliwell, Lawrie, Stanic, Mensing, McManus, Anderson, Lawson, Hardie, Milne, Scotland, Sheerin.
Substitutes: Cuthbert, MacDonald (for Scotland), Sheridan (for Lawson), Jackson (for Milne), Dyer.
Attendance: 31,074 (at first count!).

No. 24
The climax was almost unbelievable

Scottish Football League, Division One
Dundee 3, St Johnstone 4
Dens Park, Monday, 2nd January 1978

Saints' turn to grab the late glory

By DON JOHN

DUNDEE 3, ST JOHNSTONE 4

Headline: The Courier

A few months before this particular 'New Year's Day' game, on 12th November 1977 to be precise, Saints had been on the wrong end of a 5-3 defeat at Dens. The loss to Dundee was painful enough, but what made it even worse was the fact that, having been 3-0 down at half-time, Saints clawed their way back into the game and the teams were level at 3-3 as the game moved into injury time. Then Dundee were awarded a very controversial penalty, which they converted in the 92nd minute before adding one more contentious counter two minutes later, with Dundee striker Pirie seemingly standing two yards offside when he received the ball.

Saints had also lost to Dundee at Muirton in September that year, beaten 2-1 by a visiting team that would eventually finish third at the end of the season, one point off the promotion places. All of which meant that the St Johnstone fans who travelled down the Tay could have been forgiven for fearing the worst. Yet despite those worries, they travelled in numbers, adding considerably to the home fans in a very large crowd with a real derby atmosphere.

However, once the dust settled, those fears had not been realised. In fact, they had witnessed a contest that the Courier described as, *"a roller-coaster of a game (where) the climax was almost unbelievable."* Derek O'Connor recalled that before the match the Saints' players were in fine fettle, looking forward to the game and, knowing it was the derby, wanting to put one over Dundee. Moreover, he added, *"I had never won at Dens, even when I was at East Fife, so I was looking forward to hopefully putting that right. We had a really good bunch of lads at Perth at that time. And the club did things properly and looked after the players. Every year, we'd get a Christmas hamper, but when I went to Tynecastle they had nothing like that. As for the game against Dundee, they had a very good team then. Alex Caldwell, who obviously came to Saints later, was a very difficult opponent so we knew it would be tough. Then when we ran out, the crowd was huge, with lots of Saints' fans getting right behind us."*

St Johnstone started the match well. In three minutes, they were a goal to the good, scored by the pocket dynamo that was John (Pop) Pelosi. However, as we discovered, Pelosi was somewhat surprised to be on the pitch, and even more surprised that he was actually able to score this goal. A 'reliable source' told us the following (subsequently verified) anecdote …

"John had only signed the previous March and up to that time had only made a few starts and sub appearances. He got a call from the club on the 1ˢᵗ of January, telling him that he had to travel to Dundee for the game. There was only one problem: he was going to a party in Glasgow that night…

"Thinking that there was no chance he would actually be in the squad, John went to the party, with inevitable consequences. He told me he could never have driven legally the next day, but fortunately he got a lift from one of the young lads in the squad and ended up in the Dens Park dressing room, still somewhat the worse for wear. Brogie said, 'are you no getting changed wee man?' to which Pop replied, 'what for?' only to be told that he was wearing the No. 7 shirt that day."

John Brogan remembers this well: *"Pop thought he was only coming to make up the numbers. I don't remember him being obviously hungover though, and it didn't seem to affect him in the match."*

Irrespective of hangovers, or indeed shirt numbers (he played on the left wing against Dundee, despite his No. 7 shirt), Pelosi had set the course of the game. As the Courier noted, *"though Dundee huffed and puffed and pressed, the finishing spark was absent. Saints showed confidence and composure in dealing with home attacks – and their own wind-assisted raids had the Dens defence floundering at times."*

The PA provides more detail about this early goal: *"Saints went into attack from the kick-off and in three minutes went into the lead. A two-pronged attack from Brogan and Pelosi saw the ex-Albion Rovers striker fire in a shot which Allan could only palm down. John Pelosi followed up on the rebound to touch into the net."*

John Pelosi's own description is a bit more mundane, although understandably so after all these years. He told us, *"Someone had a shot, I can't remember who, and it was deflected. I just hit it and it went in."*

Despite the alleged excess of alcohol that was swirling around inside him, Pelosi was quick to take a corner in the 34ᵗʰ minute, while the Dundee defence were still trying to get organised. The PA tells us what happened next: *"Brogan attempted a volley on the turn but didn't connect properly. The ball broke to Derek O'Connor who had only to side-foot it home."*

O'Connor had been hurt in a match a few weeks before this, but fortunately for Saints he kept on going, or rather, as he told us, *"I'd had a bad injury on my knee and was struggling. The week before I was due to go into hospital to get my knee done, but the manager asked if I could soldier on for a bit. I told him I'd try, but if my knee gave up then that was that and I'd have to have the op. Fortunately, it didn't, and I'd scored twice against Alloa in a 3-0 win at Muirton only a few days before* (on the 31ˢᵗ December). *I'd also missed a penalty against Alloa, which was annoying because the League had a sponsorship deal with a whisky company at that time and if anyone scored a hat-trick the team was presented with a case of their product."*

Although Saints had been dominant, Dundee came back into the match. In 22 minutes, Sinclair hit the post for the home side, then five minutes before the interval, Scott got one back. Then Dundee - through Williamson - hit the post again, just three minutes into the second half.

As all good derby matches tend to, the game proceeded to get testy, with the referee not helping matters when, as the PA described it, *"Bobby Thomson was booked for allegedly fouling Sinclair when the culprit was very obviously another St Johnstone player! Referee Cuthill did not have the* best of afternoons and gave Dave Clunie a stern lecture when John Mackay should have been on the receiving end."

Although Dundee were clearly striving hard to turn the game around, they were shocked when O'Connor scored his second. Ross and Mackay combined to create the chance, with the latter sending over a good cross which Derek finished off with a firm header (*"Derek was really good in the air,"* John Brogan told us).

As you'd expect in a new year derby, the home side threw themselves forward, trying to retrieve the situation. To the consternation of the visiting fans, Williamson first reduced the arrears in the 74th minute, before notching the equaliser (from a suspiciously offside position according to the Courier), in the 77th minute. The Dundee paper then described how the remainder of the match, from then to the end of the regulation 90 minutes was, *"Sheer pandemonium as Dundee went flat out for the winner. Pirie almost grabbed it and Saints tottered, but held out."*

While all this had been going on, John Pelosi had been substituted. This is what happened next: *"I was taken off when we were winning 3-1, so I headed straight into the bath, where I subsequently heard two roars – big roars, so I knew it was the home fans. I thought that was it and the game had ended 3-3, but then the door was flung open and someone rushed in and shouted 'Big Derek's scored the winner!'*

"Not only did that mean a win bonus, but it also meant a case of whisky for the team. Big Derek was a good target man who had a really effective partnership with Brogie:

he was really tough and no-one messed him about."

Derek O'Connor remembers this goal well. He told us, *"We were going quite well and Pelosi had scored early doors. Once we were 3-1 up, there was a Dundee barrage and they scored a couple of goals in a couple of minutes.*

"When we got the corner in the last minute, I just thought, 'I'll hold back rather than go to the front post.' Mickey Lawson took the kick, the ball came across and the Dundee defenders didn't seem to jump for it, so it fell nicely to me – it was, 'thanks very much, header, boom, goal!' The Saints' fans were going mad. It was fantastic."

Derek O'Connor had an impressive goalscoring record for Saints. His hat-trick against Dundee was part of a sequence of nine goals in six games and was the first scored by a Saints' player since Jim Pearson against Forfar in 1974 (see Part I above). It also took his tally for the season to 17, the most since Henry Hall had scored 19 in the old First Division in 1972-73. O'Connor ended the season on 20 goals and continued scoring in the early months of the following campaign, earning a move to Hearts in 1978, with £30,000 coming to Perth in return for his services. However, as he told us, *"… even though Hearts were always my favourite team, my time at Saints was the best and the most enjoyable of my career."*

Saints team: Geoghegan; Mackay, McBean, Rutherford, Houston, Clunie, Pelosi, Brogan, O'Connor, Thomson, Ross.
Substitutes: Lawson (for Pelosi), Wright.
Attendance: 12,785.

No. 23

As long as football is played at Muirton Park they will talk about this game

Scottish Cup, Fourth Round
St Johnstone 3, Rangers 3
Muirton Park, Saturday, 14ᵗʰ February 1981

By GRAHAM FULTON

ST. JOHNSTONE 3, RANGERS 3
(Half-time: 1-2)

attack. The scent of victory was in their nostrils and it looked like being achieved in 81 minutes when in a furious onslaught, Peter

Ian Redford got his head to the cross ball from Davie Cooper and Saints knew that they had it all to do again at Ibrox tomorrow. It

Headline: Perthshire Advertiser

The title of this chapter is the first sentence in legendary PA sports' editor (and lifelong Saints' fan) Graham Fulton's report on an extraordinary afternoon in which St Johnstone of the First Division (then the second tier of Scottish football) came within only a few seconds of knocking Glasgow Rangers out of the Scottish Cup.

Given Saints position relative to Rangers, a victory would have been a major shock on its own, but what really distinguishes this match is the way the Perth men overturned a two goal deficit to take the lead against the Ibrox giants with less than 10 minutes to go. Moreover, it wasn't just that turnaround – impressive as it was – but also the manner in which Saints took the game to Rangers for much of the match.

Having started well, Saints then went one behind against the run of play. As you'd expect, Rangers then set about trying to put the game to bed and when Ian Redford got their second in the 36ᵗʰ minute it seemed it was all over bar the sectarian shouting. In normal circumstances, lower league (and also most top league) teams just don't come back from two down against the Old Firm. The early problems for Saints were, as The Scotsman reported, in defence and, specifically, *"a lack of authority in the air."*

Consequently, *"a neat interchange between Johnston and Dawson set up McAdam for the simplest of diving headers in the 17th minute. Then Redford followed that one up in the 35ᵗʰ minute by taking advantage of a Jardine free-kick the Saints defence had completely misjudged."*

The Perth rearguard did look suspect at both Rangers' goals and it seemed as if it was game over, but again as recorded in The Scotsman, *"No-one, however, informed St Johnstone that they were on the way out of the Cup and by maintaining the measured rhythm of their play, Alex Rennie's side struck a vital blow before half-time."*

That goal was indeed vital. Two down, nine minutes before half time, certainly left little room for error at the back as a third goal would have utterly killed the tie, but, as the PA described it, *"Saints kept working away and got their reward in 41 minutes. After good leading up work from Drew Rutherford, John Brogan chipped a perfect ball right into the path of Jim Morton. The midfield man cut back from the bye-line and Jim Docherty had a simple task of prodding home from a couple of yards."*

John Brogan remembers that goal well and his description after all these years mirrors that of the PA: *"I dinked it to Jim Morton and he squared it nicely for Jim Docherty."*

Only one down at half time. How would Saints approach the second half – and how would Rangers respond? After the match, Alex Rennie told The Scotsman, *"We had given away two bad goals and I told the players at half-time that if they kept playing the breaks would come."*

John Pelosi's memory of that half-time talk is slightly different. He told us, *"We were 2-1 down and the manager told us to do our best and enjoy ourselves. As I am a Rangers' fan, I was really looking forward to the game beforehand. Mind you, I wasn't the only one in our team - McCoist comes to mind - but we were all out to win the match. It was such a great day, with a big crowd and it was a fantastic pity we didn't hang on."*

However, as it turned out, Rennie was right: the chances did come. Here's Graham Fulton in the PA again: *"The second half, with the exception of the final four minutes, belonged entirely to St Johnstone.*

"The build-up was tremendous, the football inspired and the crowd sensed that the home team were still in with a chance. They roared them on with a voice that hadn't been heard in Perth for many a year and the Rangers defence began to look decidedly suspect."

The Scotsman's report concurred, telling us, *"St Johnstone were in almost total control of the game after the interval. The promptings of Fleming, McCoist and Morton and the raiding of Docherty and Brogan created any number of convertible chances before Peter McCloy had something of a brainstorm in the last 15 minutes."*

Whether McCloy was at fault or not for both Saints' subsequent goals, it still remained the case that someone had to create the circumstances for him to make an error. That someone was John Brogan. Not for nothing was Brogie Saints' top scorer of all time. The PA description of the first goal was as follows…

"George Fleming took a free kick and Ally McCoist controlled the ball well to send it into the space on the right. John Brogan was on it in a flash and squeezed the ball past Peter McCloy's left-hand post.

"The striker did his familiar jig on the spot – the only real emotion he permits himself on the field – and the crowd was in a frenzy."

Once again, another paper's report causes a headache for the historian, with Mike Aitken in The Scotsman writing, *"In the 76th minute a Fleming free-kick was nicely controlled and laid off by centre-back Rutherford to Brogan. The striker got in a low shot which McCloy seemed to have covered but somehow the ball squirmed under the 'keeper's body."*

Fortunately, we can turn once again to YouTube for confirmation of what happened. From the video there, it seems that Rutherford made an initial header from Fleming's cross, but then McCoist pounced on the loose ball and played it through for Brogie to beat McCloy at his near post. Certainly, a poor goal to lose from the goalkeeper's perspective, but in fairness it was a firm shot from close in and not one St Johnstone fan in the crowd gave that 'error' a moment's thought.

If that equaliser sent the fans wild, the third took them into the stratosphere, if not several dimensions beyond. This time, it was clear that McCloy *was* very much to blame. Here's The Scotsman again…

"Worse was to follow for McCloy, ironically playing his 500th first-team game – five minutes later when he blundered in releasing the ball to allow Brogan to score his second."

Ally McCoist again played a key part in this goal, flighting in a free kick from a central position just outside the box. The ball broke, was fired towards the goal by John Pelosi only for McCloy to spill his shot and Brogan, following up, kicked the ball into the net from a few yards out. Here's John Pelosi's thoughts on the goal…

"I remember it well. I hit the ball with my left foot – I was, obviously, right-footed – so there was no power in it and I thought when I hit it that there was no chance of scoring. I couldn't believe it when the keeper spilled it. All Brogie had to do was knock it in!

"Brogie was like Ally McCoist; not the fastest but they both had a real eye for goal. To be honest, back then Ally was more of a midfield player and I didn't think he was going to be a centre forward, but he and John had this amazing gift of knowing when and where the ball was coming and then being in the right place for it."

Graham Fulton in the PA then described how, *"Muirton exploded in a cacophony of roaring the like of which I've never heard before."*

There were only nine minutes of regulation time remaining. Could Saints hold out? In the dying minutes, it seemed that their luck was out when Willie Johnston got the ball in the net, but it was ruled out for an infringement. There were seconds remaining. Then, the aforementioned *"lack of authority in the air"* proved St Johnstone's undoing…

The PA was matter-of-fact about Rangers' last-gasp equaliser, simply recording, *"Ian Redford got his head to the cross ball from Davie Cooper and Saints knew that they* had it all to do again at Ibrox…" The Scotsman, in contrast to the PA, provided a much fuller description of the denouement of the match: *"…in the final half minute of play, Cooper managed to swing over one last cross, the St Johnstone goalkeeper Tulloch made the basic error of coming off his line and Ian Redford glanced a header into the net."*

Almost every Saints' player from that team will tell you the same story – that to this day they are still shouting for Tulloch to stay on his line and, as John Pelosi pointed out, if he had done so, Drew Rutherford was actually poised to head the ball clear, *"however, George shouted for it so Drew left it for him…"*

The cliché of seizing victory from the jaws of defeat was stood on its head. It may not have been a defeat, but as Alex Rennie told the press afterwards, *"Suddenly, the bottom fell out of everything. It left everyone feeling flat after going so close to gaining a victory I think we deserved."*

One player who recalls this game well is Jim Morton. He told us: *"I can remember that match like it was yesterday. I got the Man of the Match award and I've still got the VHS (video) tape of the game.*

"For the players, it was the first time most of us had played at Muirton when it was really packed out. Back in the day, if you were in the lower Divisions you only played the Old Firm very occasionally and you were overawed when you did. Some players couldn't cope with their support. I remember coming out to warm-up and thinking 'wow!' – this is the noisiest, biggest crowd I've played in front of, so I felt this is a day to play out of your skin and show what you can do. Everyone's parents were there – my mum and dad and my gran.

"We didn't really do much different at training in the week beforehand. No-one really gave us any chance and when we

went two down most people probably thought it was all over.

"Their two goals came out of nothing really and both times we were left wondering 'how did that happen?'. Then when we scored, the place erupted. I thought, 'we can score again,' and at half-time we were buzzing to be back in the game and thinking to ourselves that despite having players like Jim Bett, Bobby Russell and Davie Cooper, Rangers weren't that great.

"This confidence showed in the second half. We went out and started to play a bit. While John Brogan's goals might have been a bit scrappy, once we were ahead, we felt we could go on and win. Then came that last minute equaliser. George (Tulloch) could have stayed on his line and just picked it up...

"After the game, we didn't really get a chance to speak to the Rangers' players. Having been on such a high, we then hit an even deeper low. It's fair to say we were very flat at the final whistle. Saints deserved to win and Rangers knew it. We weren't lucky: we had our chances to score more - I had a header at the back post - but we couldn't get over the line."

John Brogan told us that, in his view, Saints deservedly took the lead in the second half. As for his goals, *My first one was drilled in while the next was scrambled, but you take everything that's going ... it's about being in the right place at the right time. Then, when they equalised, I remember taking the ball back up to the centre-spot to kick off and asking the ref how long there was, only to be told, 'I'm about to blow for time now'."*

For the fans, this was a bitter-sweet day. Gordon Muir remembers it well: "What a game, what a memory. What a crowd... That was the first thing that got me. The crowd was, I think 17,000 and you couldnae move - it was beyond rammed.

"I kept thinking though that Muirton's record crowd was actually 10,000 more, and then trying to work out where exactly another 10,000 fitba fans could fit into a ground that was already bursting at the seams.

"The game itself was, at least to start with, a typical Saints game against the Old Firm: we were okay but they were all over us and nobody was surprised when they scored and then got a second. And then it all changed: we got one back and were in the game... I can't recall who got the first but clearly remember Brogie getting the next, then after the Girvan Lighthouse spilled a ball, Brogan got a second and it was mayhem. I could hardly breathe and I remember the Muirton Park 'goal-scored dust storm' as well as taunting the Rangers' support with shouts that would get you arrested these days.

"Time was nearly up. I was sweating, I kinda knew we wouldn't do it because that was (and remained for a long time) 'the Saints' way.'

"And then it happened... Wee George Tulloch, a great keeper in my eyes, came for a ball he was never getting, Redford got on the end of it and just like that it was over. I don't believe I had ever been as excited and then depressed at a fitba match before. As it turned out, it wasnae gonna be the last time..."

Meanwhile, Iain Smith was down south, working in Wellingborough. He recalled, "I was playing football that Saturday afternoon for Weavers' Old Boys. I can't remember the score in our game, but what I do remember was coming into the changing room where the radio was on and the announcer saying, 'and here is an incredible result from the Scottish Cup.' Obviously, I didn't know the score and I have to be honest and say I wasn't expecting much. However, those words 'incredible result' made me think we'd *won; then the final score was announced and I went from complete euphoria to total disappointment in a split-second."*

Although Saints went into the replay at Ibrox with all the outward confidence and bravado you might expect (manager Alex Rennie commented that *"if we get the breaks we can do it again"*), the bookmakers did not share their optimism. Saints were priced at 8-1 and Rangers at 3-1. The bookies tend to be right, more often than not. Ironically, the score was 3-1 to the Ibrox men.

One final point is worth recording. This was the last really big crowd in Muirton's history. With some 17,500 fans bringing gate receipts of £28,000 (contrast this with the c. £158 for the first ever Scottish Cup match with Rangers at Perth, back in 1909), it was far and away the largest number to attend a game at the old ground in the last decade of its existence. The only other time in the 1980s when there was a five-figure attendance was in August 1981, when 10,406 saw Ally McCoist and Jim Morton score the only two goals of the game against Celtic in the League Cup. On that occasion we, obviously, won the match. On this occasion, we really should have won, but, as Gordon Muir said, that's not *"the Saints' way"* of doing things…

Saints team: Tulloch, Mackay, McNeil, Fleming, Rutherford, Caldwell, Pelosi, McCoist, Docherty, Morton, Brogan. Substitutes: Kilgour and Weir (not used). Attendance:17,500.

Scottish League, First Division
Hamilton Academical 3, St Johnstone 4
New Douglas Park, Hamilton, Saturday, 28th April 2007

Ecstasy turns to agony

Headline: Perthshire Advertiser

In the club's official history, we described this game as *"The cruellest denouement to any football season ever."* It still is and, in our view, is unlikely to be challenged as such, even if football lasts for another millennium. Perhaps the only one that comes close is Sergio Aguero's title-winning goal in injury time for Manchester City against QPR, which snatched away the English Premier League Championship from their arch rivals, Manchester United.

Consider the circumstances. Gretna were top of the table on 63 points while Saints were second on 62 points. Both clubs were playing their last games of the season: Saints at Hamilton and Gretna at Ross County. Both games were scheduled to kick-off at 3.00 pm, but in the event the start was slightly delayed in Dingwall. With only one team being promoted, Saints had to win and hope that Gretna lost or drew. But what perhaps quite a lot of people forget is that County had to win their match to have a chance of avoiding relegation. Consequently, as the goals went in, the swings to-and-fro during the two matches meant that the results in both places affected the fortunes of not just two but

three of the clubs involved, thus making this beyond question the most sensational end to a season.

Saints were given 2,700 tickets. These soon went. On the day, it was estimated that over 3,000 Perth fans got into the ground – a substantial majority of the entire crowd. Both the authors of this book were there, sitting side-by-side in the away stand behind the goal. From that vantage point, and with the sun beating down, we had a perfect view of the drama unfolding in front of us…

This was the time before smartphones (the first iPhone was launched just a few months later). Fans got their news from pocket radios and many in the ground carried one, hoping for good news from the north. Early in the match, word spread through the Saints' fans that just such good news had arrived and Ross County had gone one up. It was fake-news, although of course that phrase hadn't been invented then.

Despite this false alarm, Saints took the game to Hamilton and could, perhaps should, have scored early on, with Simon Mensing and Paul Sheerin both having chances. They were not to be denied though and in 24 minutes, captain Kevin James rose at the back post to convert a Sheerin corner.

James's statuesque physique caused problems for almost every defence that tried to keep him quiet from dead-ball situations. Thus it proved when he knocked the ball down in the 32nd minute for Martin Hardie to turn it home. We were two up and heading for the finish line…

As if that wasn't exciting enough, County went ahead in Dingwall. This time it was no phantom goal, but within minutes Gretna had levelled. Saints could only play the game in front of them though and set about taking it as far away from Hamilton as possible, with the PA describing how Jason Scotland, who was expected to leave the club for pastures new in the summer, *"weighed in with a farewell gift, ghosting past the keeper to slide home number 25 (for the season) after being released brilliantly by Peter MacDonald."*

If there were any neutrals in the ground, they would have been impressed that the home side refused to lie down in the face of the all-out St Johnstone assault. On 40 minutes, McCarthy (who would go on to have a stellar career in the top flight in England) scored via the post. Then news of another goal in Dingwall filtered through – Gretna were winning. Thus, half-time came and went with the Borders' team in pole position for promotion.

Football matches are sometimes described as a 'roller-coaster," or, a 'roller-coaster of emotions.' Frequently, such descriptions are journalistic cliches, but if ever a game deserved this description this was it. You really had to be there to appreciate it – although 'appreciate' is probably not the best verb to describe how it felt as we nervously watched what was happening in front of us.

News from the north again told us that County had equalised. Whether this news reached the players or not, Saints seemed to wilt temporarily. We were still in the driving seat, but would it be enough? Of course, Hamilton could put a spoke in the St Johnstone wheel by scoring again, which is precisely what they did. With the Accies attacking the away end, the fans crowded behind Kevin Cuthbert's goal had a perfect view of Richard Offiong's superb 25-yarder as it sailed past the Saints' goalie. As Gordon Bannerman put it in the PA,

"for six tantalising minutes in the April sunshine time stood still at New Douglas Park and St Johnstone's five-year exile from the SPL was drawing to a close."

Cometh the hour, cometh the man. The man in question being Martin Hardie, one of the most popular players to don a St Johnstone jersey in living memory. Although Saints had fallen out of the contest a bit, Martin turned the tide in the 81st minute, as the PA tells us: *"...that man Hardie made his presence felt. Saints weren't flooding forward but the midfielder strode onto a Scotland touch to drill in a powerful shot from outside the area. It was a classic daisycutter but this was synthetic turf."*

While this might have restored all those frazzled nerve-ends in the Perth support, they were soon to be restored to an even more ragged state as the match ground on to its end. Although Jason Scotland came close with a lob, the key moment was virtually at the end, when Accies' sub, Wake, *"dinked home the seventh of the contest to further fray the Perth nerves."*

The last moments of this match were agony. As well as the possibility of Hamilton snatching an equaliser, there was the ever-present danger that Gretna would spoil the party by taking the lead. The final whistle at New Douglas Park blew and, as the cheers for the victory subsided, every Saints' supporter in the ground sought a fellow fan with a radio.

The Hamilton fans trooped out, passing the edge of the away stand. Some of the home supporters jeered, but a few applauded the Saints' fans. In the away dressing room, the Saints' players emulated their fans by clustering round a portable radio.

Managing Director Stewart Duff had a more direct line to the north, as he explained to us... *"I cadged Tommy Campbell's mobile phone and called*

Donnie McBean, the Ross County Secretary. He was as nervous as me. 'It's still two-all,' he said, then, 'oh, wait a minute... they're breaking, it's three on two'... He was as deflated as me... I remember the bus going home was very quiet. Just after the score came through from Dingwall, I was captured by a photographer kicking at a can in the dug-out. It's the proverbial picture that says more than a thousand words."

Gordon Muir described this as, "a great game of fitba with an ending that simply shouldn't have been allowed. To be fair I remember little of the game other than it was a ding-dong affair. What I do remember was the end, the waiting, the feeling that - as always - it was gonna go pear-shaped. We were up, promoted, but the other game wasnae done. No mobiles, internet or techno gadgets back then, just trannies (for the younger generation, these are radios!).

Gordon Muir forgives James Grady

"And we waited, on the edge of a massive party, a gargantuan celebration and then - bang - and I was back to going from hugely excited to totally depressed yet again. James Grady... I met him later and got my photo taken in the dug-out at McDiarmid (as shown here). I may have forgiven him, but I have never forgiven those Hamilton fans who took great joy out of our sorrow and taunted us as we left the ground.

Yet another almost but not quite..."

Kevin Heller recounted how he drove through to the game with his wife's nephew (who, he says, had been badly brought up to support Rangers but was now being re-educated) ...

"Obviously, I wasn't drinking, but we still went to the pub beforehand where we discussed how we were reasonably confident we'd win the game because we'd been playing well throughout most of the season. I particularly remember how we had a belief that in previous games, when things were looking ropey, someone, usually Martin Hardie, would drive the team forward to a victory.

"Then, when the game started, we scored a couple, they got one back, we scored another, they got back into it, basically it ebbed and flowed but we won in the end. That's when everyone crowded round a guy with the wireless. That period after the match seemed longer than the game: where I was, we could barely hear what was coming through the little, tinny speaker.

"The guy who owned the radio had it to his ear and I'm not sure even he could hear it properly, but then we saw his face drop. I couldn't believe it. The news spread round; the guy couldn't even speak. You could tell by his face. I was thinking, 'this shouldn't have happened.' Then the Hamilton fans who were left started cheering to wind us up. It was devastating; one of the worst days in my St Johnstone-supporting life.

"I just remember everyone silently walking back to their cars and buses. I thought about our relegation at Motherwell when Paul Sturrock was the manager: that was worse, possibly because I was younger and felt it more. However, after the Hamilton game I remember getting back to the car that day and I just sat and put my head on *the horn in frustration. It was terrible, but looking back on it now, it was just one of those days you get used to as a Saints' fan. More importantly, I believe it turned a corner in our story and made the 2014 Cup win even more special when it came. The joy of that success after so many, massive kicks in the teeth like that game at Hamilton was off-the-scale.*

"I can't remember if I had a night out when I got back to Perth. I do recall that people who weren't fans but knew what had happened, asked how I was. The tragedy was that we had actually won, and deservedly, but it felt as if we had been pumped. We had done our job, but we were pumped."

Colin McCredie was sitting in the right-hand side of the away stand at Hamilton…

"That Hamilton game was the proverbial roller coaster of emotions. I was enjoying it - we were winning - then they kept pegging us back. The last twenty minutes were hellish, but at last we'd won – but then the wait began. Many people didn't realise that the game had been delayed in Dingwall. There was a guy about three or four seats away: he just said, 'Gretna have scored.' This was the worst moment ever in my time following Saints, but in a strange way it made everything that came afterwards seem sweeter, starting with the Challenge Cup win later that year. It had all been going swimmingly; the momentum had been with us for the previous weeks while Gretna faltered. We'd done what we needed to; we'd won in real time. When you have victory so close and it's snatched away from you it's hard to take it in."

Similar sentiments were washing across the several thousand Saints' fans in the ground

- and elsewhere. We made our way slowly out of the stand and huddled in groups, looking for friends with whom we could share a moan and a groan about the unfairness of it all. Sympathy poured from the radio, with the peerless Richard Gordon on Sportsound expressing his view that no league campaign had ever finished in such dramatic fashion.

Earlier in the season, Geoff Brown had expressed his personal view that it would be better for Scottish football if Saints went up rather than Gretna. Some thought there was a degree of schadenfreude about the results that weekend, but Geoff was correct. Gretna were relegated at the end of the following season and in May 2008 they went into administration and were demoted to the Third Division. A few days later, on 2nd June, they went out of business.

What would have happened if St Johnstone and not Gretna had been promoted? Certainly, we would have been much more financially stable than Gretna and in no danger of going bust. Perhaps Owen Coyle would have stayed longer and not taken the money on offer at Burnley (unlikely), and we might have established ourselves more quickly in the top-flight. Or we could have been relegated again. We'll never know, but one thing we do know is that the Horror of Hamilton will never be forgotten by anyone who was there that day.

Saints team: Cuthbert, Anderson, Stanic, McInnes, Lawrie, James, Sheerin, Hardie, MacDonald, Scotland and Mensing. Substitutes: Halliwell, McLaren (for Sheerin), Lilley (for MacDonald), Jackson and Morais.
Attendance: 4,795.

Scottish Cup Quarter Final
Rangers 1, St Johnstone 1 aet (2-4 on penalties)
Ibrox Stadium, Sunday, 25th April 2021

Saints produce the unthinkable to advance to Scottish Cup semis

Headline: Perthshire Advertiser

When a Cup draw is made, there are two things a club wants. The first is a home game: the second is to avoid the Old Firm. Consequently, an away game at Ibrox in the quarter finals of the 2021 Scottish Cup was, no matter what was said publicly, not ideal, especially as Rangers were playing much better than they had done for some years. They were unbeaten at Ibrox in the league at that point and subsequently went on to win the Premiership that season. Given that Saints have only won seven times in 76 games at Rangers in our entire history (including this match), the bookies were not taking many bets on an away win. To make matters worse, with the Covid pandemic still in full swing, there would be no fans in the stadium, although in retrospect that might well have been to Saints' advantage at the end of the day.

Prior to the game, not many St Johnstone fans would have given their heroes much of a chance. Instead, many clustered around radios, listening in trepidation as the game progressed and taking heart from what sounded like some good Saints' chances and daring to believe that as time went on and Rangers failed to score that perhaps the miracle would happen…

Liam Craig remembers this night especially well. He told us, *"My favourite game was that quarter final against Rangers. Looking back, no-one had won at Ibrox that season domestically and what many people forget is we played them at McDiarmid on the Wednesday before the quarter final and I scored an injury time equaliser from the penalty spot. They had made seven changes for that game – something which we didn't have the luxury of doing. Going to Ibrox is never easy and, of course, they brought the boys they'd left out at McDiarmid back into the side. They knew we'd given them a good game in midweek and when I look back at the Cup game, I remember the elation on their bench when they went one up. They knew how big a goal that was, but then for us to score the equaliser was unbelievable. We got the ball back in our defensive third, worked it to Jamie McCart who hit a diagonal ball to Mick O'Halloran, who then did what he does and forced the corner. I remember standing over the corner to take the kick, thinking I needed to give the players something to attack. I put my hand up as if to indicate a planned set-piece but then, when I crossed it, I could see Zander attacking it and then that Kano had scored. I was looking along the line and was the only one who knew straight away it wasn't Zander's goal.*

"Looking back, what Zander does to maintain his composure after that excitement - to calm himself down to save the penalties - was amazing. His second save, from Kemar Roofe, was particularly good.

"In previous penalty shoot-outs I had taken part in, I took the fifth penalty. I did this against Dundee United and also against Dunfermline. When I walked over to where we were arranging who would take the pens, Macca said, 'you're going fifth.' However, I pointed out we had no regular penalty taker on the park, so I said I would go first, thinking it might not go as far as five. I had never seen Jason hit a pen and Ali McCann wasn't great at penalties in training. So, I wasn't actually feeling too confident, then I saw Jason leather his in and when Ali stepped up you can see Allan McGregor was actually telling the ref the ball was not on the spot to try to distract him. But his composure and his penalty were outstanding. We trooped off, dreaming of a Cup double. That game at Ibrox, how we did it after going a goal down so late in the game, epitomises everything that is good about St Johnstone."

Ali McCann admitted his track record with penalties in training wasn't the best. He told us, "I felt confident enough stepping up as I'd played well in the game. As Liam (Craig) ran across with the rest of the players he said, 'what were you doing taking that – you never score in training!' I didn't feel under as much pressure as you might think, because I knew that even if I missed, we had another chance to win with our next penalty. Nonetheless, I was delighted to see the ball hit the inside of the side-netting."

When Rangers scored, many of the Saints' fans who were tuning it thought the game was over. It wasn't just the fans who thought this: Jason Kerr said to us, "We went into the match full of confidence: after all, we'd already won the BetFred Cup. However, I'll be honest, when they scored, I thought it was done as it had been a long game and it was near the end. You always hope you can get something though and we stuck at it and we had that extraordinary ending when it looked like Zander had

scored but it was actually Kano. I think that Rangers lost a wee bit of confidence when we equalised, which then made it much more difficult for them in the penalty shoot-out. When they missed their first two penalties and we just kept scoring ours it seemed like it was written in the stars that we were going to win."

Callum Davidson told us how much he appreciated the role that Michael O'Halloran played in the equaliser…

"The Rangers quarter final was possibly the best performance of that Cup run. I put O'Halloran on and, although everyone remembers Zander coming up for the goal, Mickey was responsible for it because he chased down Barisic and got the corner.

"When you watch it back, Zander's header wasn't going in. We tell the strikers where to position themselves in these situations, to 'make the goal big' and Kano did just that. Zander was running up the park, pursued by the others, and Kano was running behind, pointing to himself and shouting, 'it was me!' Then, when it came to the shoot-out, Zander made the vital saves and we hit great penalties.

"Afterwards, Steven Gerrard was courteous and gracious in defeat, but for us it was a great night and the Cup double was now on."

Ali McCann also recalled how the Rangers players waited for the Saints' players to finish their celebrations before shaking hands. "They were obviously gutted, but there were no bad-natured comments.

"This was probably my favourite game for St Johnstone. We'd played well in midweek when we drew with Rangers at McDiarmid so we felt we were in with a chance. Callum had us so well set-up and kept at us during the match to keep our shape off the ball. Then when Tavernier scored, I thought, 'that's all our hard work gone for nothing.' But of course, Kano then got the equaliser. I don't think many people will realise just how much work he did for that goal. If you watch it back, he's keeping Alan McGregor pinned back on the line, then he moved off him and was in the right place to deflect Zander's header over the line. And, of course, it all came from a great corner from Liam. There is no-one else you'd want taking a corner in those circumstances than him."

As for the unlikely hero of the hour, Zander Clark told us that, "I had made a couple of decent saves, but I remember that after they scored, when I got the ball out of the net, I threw it – to Kerso I think – and said, 'we'll get one more chance.'

"When we got that last minute corner, I didn't wait to see if the manager would send me forward – I just went. As I got to the halfway line, I looked over and Callum signalled me to carry on. While I ran forward, I said to Liam Gordon, 'what's the routine for the corner?' and laughed, because goalkeepers aren't usually featured in corner routines, well, not when we're attacking.

"I knew right away that it hadn't gone in directly and that Kano had got a touch. However, there was no way I wasn't going to milk the moment, so I did. But when you look at the video, at the full-time whistle the camera pans to me and you can see me saying to Gordy that it was Kano's goal."

We wondered if it had occurred to Zander that he might have to take a penalty…

"Yes, it did – when we were huddled together after the final whistle, deciding who would take them … and I was thinking about faking a hamstring! My mind was more on the penalties I'd be facing. Paul Mathers (the goalkeeping coach) and I had done our homework on where we thought the Rangers' players penalties might go,

but in the moment they might change their minds and not do what you expect. It's just a lottery. Fortunately, a lottery we won.

"The day before, we'd practised taking penalties. It's fair to say that wee Ali wasn't the best, but in the moment, when there was so much pressure on him, he held his nerve brilliantly."

There were, of course, a few lucky Saints' fans there that night. They were at Ibrox to work, to disseminate social media updates and to provide commentary for Saints' TV. However, in the event, nothing went smoothly for Steven Watt and his companions - as he recounted …

"The first problem was that Midgey Millar was supposed to be doing co-comms with me, however, at very short notice, but for a genuine reason, he had to call off. What to do? It was a wee problem, but we immediately thought of Liam Doris, the McDiarmid stadium announcer, who lives in Glasgow…"

Liam was surprised to get a call at about 5.00 pm on the day of the game. Here's what he remembers…

"I got an 'are you free?' call asking if I could stand in for Chris Millar and, after about a nano-second of considering what else I might have been doing that night I replied, 'Of course, I'll see you at Ibrox.'

"When I got there and met the rest of the Saints' media team, we discovered that we had a major problem, namely that the ISDN line that would normally have carried our commentary, was down.

"While efforts were made to sort this, we also arranged a back-up, which was to take the Rangers' commentary feed. The problem couldn't be rectified, so that's what happened and Saints' fans across the world must have wondered why they were hearing a pro-Rangers' commentary.

"However, that wasn't the only one of our worries. As happened at all grounds during the pandemic, the pre-match stadium announcements went ahead as normal, as did the pre-match music. You'd have thought that, in the circumstances, they might have lowered the volume, but not a bit of it. Instead, they pumped out all the Rangers' music and announcements at the volume normally associated with a 50,000-strong crowd, which meant that Steven and I could hardly hear each other in the build-up to the game."

Steven Watt was slightly concerned that with the ISDN line down some official might question what they were actually doing and if they should even be in the ground if they weren't actually working. Although it is highly unlikely they would have been chucked out, they decided that discretion was the better part of valour, as Steven recalled for us…

"We pretended we were commentating, although the Rangers' TV boys alongside us must have thought we were off our heads, especially as we were shouting and dropping the occasional swear-word into our 'commentary.'

"When they scored, I just thought, that's it - a sterling effort boys but we can head to the car now. I obviously didn't envisage what came next…"

Liam Doris remembers that they were sufficiently over the top with their 'commentary' that Sam Porter, who was then working for Saints' media team, came across and told them to turn it down a bit.

Liam also recalls his feeling when Rangers scored in extra time: *"Like Steven, I remember thinking 'that's it, here we go, out of the Cup.' But then came those dramatic final minutes. When Zander loped upfield for that final corner, I turned to Steven and said something along the lines of 'wouldn't it be funny if Zander scored?'*

It was obviously the last throw of the dice. Funnily enough, I don't have a lot of memories of the rest of the game, although we had played well and as it went on, I thought we might have a chance, until Tavernier scored.

"At the time, I thought it was Zander who scored – it wasn't until the next day I realised that Chris Kane had actually turned it in. We could obviously see the TV feed, but there were no replays, so we couldn't see precisely what had happened."

Steven takes up the story again: *"At that point, when it went to pens, from the body language of Rangers players you could tell it was going our way, whereas Zander's adrenalin was pounding out of his pores."*

Liam, in contrast, wasn't so sure: *"I didn't know how many of the lads who stepped up had actually taken a penalty before. And I was acutely aware that, in my mind at least, our penalty record in the previous decade wasn't very good* (in fact, it was OK). *However, before we kicked a ball in anger in the shoot-out, Rangers went first.*

"Tavernier was, in theory, their absolute banker to score a penalty. So, when he missed, I thought 'we've got a chance.'

"If you watch the YouTube video of the game, you can actually hear me shouting 'Come on Zander!' as he saves it. At that point, I'd given up pretending I was on commentary and was a totally biased fan. That save threw the penalty shoot-out on its head; you could see it drained the momentum from Rangers, then when Zander saved the second one – a much better save as it happened because Tavernier's was, inexplicably, a poor penalty – and as we kept on scoring ours, I thought we were going to do it. Being privileged to have been at McDiarmid for the games during the pandemic, I'd seen just how good a player Ali MCann is, then when he calmly slotted it home that was it."

215

Masquerade – Steven Watt and Liam Doris pretend to commentate at an empty Ibrox.

After the penalties were over, Steven and Liam just sat there, drinking it in. Steven remembers that the Rangers' commentators were good with them, telling us, *"Tom, who works for Rangers' TV (and whose voice can famously be heard on the YouTube video saying 'what's the keeper doing?'), is a nice, amiable guy and, to be fair to the Rangers' TV team, although they were obviously really disappointed to be out of the Cup, they were fine with us."*

Another St Johnstone fan who was present thanks to his job with the media was the Courier's Eric Nicolson. Eric told us that one of the great advantages of attending games without fans was that he could hear the respective managers trying to coach their teams through games and make tactical changes as and when they thought them appropriate.

"It was a tactical masterclass from Callum that night. I'd been privileged enough to see and hear him do this previously, but I suspect that not many fans will have realised what a difference he made to the team in key games that season. I'd seen it against Hibs in the semi-final of the League Cup, where he easily outcoached Jack Ross and kept Saints in the game as Hibs battered us in the first half. Then, in the League Cup final, he really stood out. David Martindale was not managing the game at all, but in contrast Callum was far more aware of what was happening on the pitch and how to go about changing it.

"The same applied to this game at Ibrox. I could hear how he reacted to the way the game changed as it progressed. To be honest, given the season Rangers were having I didn't expect Saints to win. Rather, I felt that the momentum had slightly gone from our season: we had struggled to beat Dundee in the third round and although we'd drawn with Rangers just four days before the Cup quarter final, on that night at Ibrox none of the players played outstandingly well. However, the way Callum guided them meant that the overall performance was greater than sum of the individual parts. Ali McCann played well, Stevie May put in the maximum effort as usual, it wasn't really a 'Rooney game,' and then poor Scott Tanser got the injury that kept him out of the final. I felt for Tanser as he only made the bench in both finals that season: luck wasn't on his side."

Normally, extra-time and penalties are a nightmare for football reporters. With their deadline hovering, any game that goes over its expected duration leads to copy being ripped up, intro paragraphs hastily re-written and, occasionally, goals being missed out of the final report. Fortunately for Eric, because the game had kicked off over an hour earlier than the normal evening start-time of 7.45 pm, this was less of a problem than usual: *"I'm so glad it was a 6.30 pm start and not the usual 7.45 kick-off because, for a journalist, this game was the ultimate 'rip it up and start again.' As the game went into extra time, I was prepared for Rangers scoring – it's what most people thought would have happened.*

"Consequently, I think I had two, possibly three, different intros which, dependent on how the game ended, I could then use, but the early kick off meant it wasn't as crucial as it would normally have been.

"When Kane got the equaliser, in common with almost everyone else, I thought it was Zander that had scored. At that point, I put my pen down and thought, 'I'm going to

*watch this and not take any more notes.'
I felt that I just wanted to soak it up and that
something amazing was happening to our
team. At the end, it was bizarre; watching
Saints in a penalty shoot-out and expecting
them to win.*

*"Even without my notes, I knew I had
sufficient time to file my copy. Due to
Covid, there was a longer gap than usual
before we went to the Ibrox press room.
In common with most of the journalists
there, I thought Zander had scored. Saints
winning was already a huge story, but
Zander scoring made it even bigger. Sadly
for him, it wasn't to be, but that early kick-
off meant we all had time to tweak our copy
and give Chris Kane the credit he was due.*

*"If I was going to choose a game based on
the drama involved, this Rangers game
would be top of my list. I'm also so lucky
that I was there in person."*

Meanwhile, across the country (and indeed
across the world), St Johnstone fans were
pinching themselves. Some, doubtless had
switched off their radios when Rangers
scored, later to discover, to their delight,
that we had won.

Only two games to go and the dream of a
Cup double was on. One player, though,
was already confident it would happen.
Shaun Rooney told us, *"I remember
standing next to Jamie McCart while the
penalties were being taken against Rangers
and saying, 'if we win this, I think we'll go
on and win the Cup'."* Whether this was
simply bravado or a genuine premonition, it
proved correct. However, one thing Shaun
didn't know was the key part he would play
in the final…

*Saints team: Clark, Kerr, Gordon,
McCart, Rooney, McCann, Craig,
Wotherspoon, Tanser, May, Melamed.
Substitutes: Brown, Conway, Kane (for
Melamed), O'Halloran (for May), Parish,
Bryson (for Wotherspoon), Gilmour, Booth
(for Tanser), Ferguson.
Attendance: N/A due to Covid regulations.*

Grant was always up to harass the Celtic defence

Scottish League Cup, First Round, Section One
Celtic 0, St Johnstone 1
Celtic Park, Wednesday, 16th August 1961

GRANT GETS WINNER AFTER TAYLOR HEROICS

St. Johnstone's Scottish League Cup Shock for Celts

Celtic, 0; St Johnstone, 1

Half-time—0-0

Scorer—Grant (75 minutes)

ST Johnstone can thank their magnificent rearguard, in which Taylor was outstanding, for the win over Celtic at Parkhead

Headline: Perthshire Advertiser

The current generation of St Johnstone fans has become used to supporting a full-time team that holds its own in the top rank of Scottish football. As part of this success, we have, from time to time, been able to enjoy beating the Old Firm, even if it's not as often as we might wish. However, it was not always thus, especially in the days when Saints were a part-time side and the Glasgow giants might have been expected to stroll to victory without breaking too much sweat.

Having been promoted to the First Division in 1960, St Johnstone had two seasons in the top flight before being relegated again in 1962. However, that second season of 1961-62 did see the club have some superb victories in the round robin that then, as now, was the preliminary phase of the Scottish League Cup, played mainly in August before the League season kicked off in September.

Saints were drawn against Hibernian, Partick Thistle and Celtic – all First Division clubs. It has to be said that at this time none of them was any great shakes, with both Hibs and Thistle being mid-table teams in the preceding few seasons and even Celtic were well off the pace compared to their great Glasgow rivals. Indeed, the Parkhead men only finished ninth in 1959-60, 21 points behind champions Hearts, and fourth in 1960-61, 12 points behind Rangers who had only pipped Kilmarnock to the title by one point.

Today, in 2023, the League Cup seedings (theoretically) make it harder for the top flight teams to go out in the preliminary round, but back in the 1960s a slightly different system was used, albeit with the same intention of making it easier for the 'big' teams to progress to the latter stages of the tournament. In 1961, there were nine groups of four or five teams, which were seeded into two sets with the top 16 teams in Division 1 making up the first four groups. This meant that (again, theoretically), four top flight teams would probably play four lower Division teams in the quarter-finals.

The first match of this League Cup campaign was at home against Hibernian and ended in a 1-1 draw. That same Saturday, Partick Thistle lost 3-2 at Firhill to Celtic. Saints next game was a visit to Celtic Park on the Wednesday, where the home team were expected to win reasonably comfortably.

St Johnstone manager, Bobby Brown, made a number of changes in the forward line for the trip to Glasgow, although, wisely as it turned out, he made no alterations to the defensive positions.

Big Ian Gardiner was moved from inside left to inside right, taking the place of Jim Walker. Two other players were also dropped: outside right Jim Menzies, with Matt McVittie (who had been signed from Celtic in 1959) moving from the left wing to the right wing; and centre forward Bobby Gilfillan, with former Ranger, Bobby Grant, taking the No. 9 shirt in his place. John Bell came into the side at inside left, with Joe Henderson outside him.

There was a big crowd at Parkhead that night, some 25,000 or so, with a decent number travelling from Perth to support their favourites. Back in the 1950s and early 60s, as Saints' fan Bert McIntosh told us, if fans wanted to travel on the supporters' bus, many of them used to go to the Masonic Lodge on King Street, where the man with the tickets set up a table at the entrance and fans would queue up to buy them.

As you would have expected, Celtic sought to demonstrate their superiority by taking the game to the visitors from the outset. The PA tells us that, *"Right from the kick-off Celtic snapped into the attack and Hughes beat Ferguson out on the left touch line and raced up the wing."* Fortunately, he must have raced too fast, because the PA went on, *"There was no-one else to take advantage of the move, however, and by the time the centre got his cross over Saints defence had time to cover up and clear the danger."*

The PA then tells a story of further Celtic pressure and chances: *"Within minutes Chalmers hit the side netting when a bad pass from McFadyen went straight to the winger's feet and this was the pattern of play for the first 15 minutes, with only occasional St Johnstone breakaways easing the strain. In fact, the first 'save' Connor had to make was from a pass-back by McNeill after almost ten minutes play."* Younger readers might be surprised to learn that in those days players could pass back to the goalie, who could then pick up the ball rather than having to kick it to a teammate, or hastily sclaff it into the stands.

The Courier's match report tells a similar story, noting that, *"Celtic started off at a devastating pace. For a time it looked as if the Saints' defence was most certainly going to be completely overrun.*

"Celts had really only themselves to blame for not scoring at least a couple of goals in those opening 15 minutes."

This proved to be the story for much of the match: Celtic attacking and St Johnstone defending. However, this was the era of *"Taylor, McFadyen, Lachlan,"* one of the greatest combinations of goalkeeper and full-backs in St Johnstone's history. As the match reports make clear, ably supported by the half-back line, all three had to be on their toes, especially Billy Taylor in the Saints' goal.

That they were on top form is confirmed by the Perthshire Advertiser's first paragraph, which tells us that, *"St Johnstone can thank their magnificent rearguard, in which Taylor was outstanding, for the win over Celtic at Parkhead."*

Celtic did not help themselves. The Courier recorded that: *"Hughes and Chalmers missed two wonderful opportunities.*

"Hughes' miss must rank as the miss of the season. A neat flick by Chalmers let Divers

away on the left wing. The inside man cut the ball back from the by-line straight to the feet of Hughes, only seven yards out.

"His casual shot was easily parried by Taylor, but Hughes succeeded in hitting the rebound against centre-half Ferguson."

As we have noted, this was not a great Celtic side, but Jimmy McGrory, their manager at that time, had been giving opportunities to younger players, with some considerable success. A number of the squad – Pat Crerand, Frank Haffey, Duncan Mackay and Billy McNeill had already been capped, while John Hughes, who was then a teenager, had been capped at Under-23 level (there were no Under-21 teams in those days). Of this Celtic squad, McNeill, Clark and Chalmers would go on to win the European Cup with Celtic in 1967, while Crerand would do so with Manchester United in 1968.

Unfortunately for the Parkhead side, a young team is not always a consistent team, and although they dominated most of the play they were not able to breach the Saints' defensive line. In fact, the Courier noted that the home fans gave their team *"periodic bouts of slow handclapping."*

Slow handclapping has rather gone out of fashion these days, but back then it was a fairly common mark of disapproval from a team's supporters if they felt their heroes were not performing as they wished.

Bobby Brown's changes to the forward line took some time to have an impact. The PA tells us that *"Up front, Saints were still a bit slow and ponderous at times, with the left wing pair Bell and Henderson at first looking out of their depth."*

Bell had the only real chance for St Johnstone in the first half, but after half-time he and his fellow forwards had a better time of it. Although Celtic continued to press, the Courier tells us that, *"the quick*

attacks of the nippy St Johnstone attack seemed far more dangerous."

McVittie had two shots at the Celtic goal early in the second half. The game then seems to have got bogged down a bit, with *"minor infringements"* breaking up the flow of play. However, that changed when, with 15 minutes left on the clock, Saints scored what would prove to be the only goal of the game.

This goal was scored by Bobby Grant, father of current Saints' director (and no mean centre forward himself), Roddy Grant. Roddy wasn't born until several years after his dad scored at Parkhead, but he told us that, as well as passing on the sound advice that all good centre-forwards play with a degree of aggression, his father also occasionally reminded him, *"Listen son, you've never scored the winner at Celtic Park."*

The PA's excellent description of Grant's strike was as follows: *"The goal came 15 minutes from the end as Saints shook off another spell of Celtic pressure and came roaring back into the attack. Henderson beat Mackay and raced up the left wing, sending over a perfect cross, but McVittie, right in front of goal, just failed to connect.*

"The right winger, however, chased the ball out to the wing and crossed across the goal to Henderson. The latter back-headed to McKinven and from 30 yards the left-half crashed in a terrific drive which Connor could not hold. He palmed the ball on to the bar and it broke out to Grant who shot into the net from four yards with the 'keeper lying helpless on the ground."

The Courier's journalist didn't provide quite so many details and not only lops five yards off Ron McKinven's shot but gives the Celtic goalie a bit more credit. Nonetheless, between the two papers' descriptions we can get a very good mental picture of how the move played out. Here's the Courier… *"Grant scored a well-deserved and hard-worked for counter in 75 minutes. A long pass from McVittie on the right came to McKinven 25 yards out.*

"His magnificent shot was equally well saved by Connor but the keeper could only touch the ball on to the bar and Grant following up, netted."

Celtic kept plugging away in search of an equaliser. First Carroll, their right winger, put the ball miles over the bar when Bill Taylor was sprawled helplessly in front of him, then Chalmers missed two further chances before the referee brought the home side's agony to an end.

Back in Perth, Gordon Small told us how he was glued to his radio as the result came through. Later, on the Scottish news it was reported as a shock result at Parkhead. Gordon recalled how the next morning's papers, as they almost always do, looked for an Old Firm angle on the game, with most mentioning that it was an ex-Ranger who had downed the Celts.

This was an important result for Saints. With only two games played, the group was still anyone's to win. St Johnstone had two more games - away to both Partick Thistle and Hibernian - before they welcomed Celtic to Perth. As we shall see in the next chapter, by the time Celtic did come to Muirton, a few weeks after this match at Celtic Park, everything was still to play for; although for Saints another win against the Glasgow giants was going to be necessary if they were to have any hope of qualifying for the quarter-finals.

Saints team: Taylor; McFadyen and Lachlan; Little, Ferguson and McKinven; McVittie, Gardiner, Grant, Bell and Henderson.
Attendance: 25,000.

No. 19
Celtic bottle it

Scottish League Cup, First Round, Section One
St Johnstone 2, Celtic 0
Muirton Park, Wednesday, 30th August 1961

Headline: The Courier. Note the steel structure of the enclosure in construction.

Having won at Parkhead two weeks beforehand, it might have been expected that St Johnstone would struggle to contain a Celtic side that would, naturally, be looking for revenge. So far in the group stage, Saints had played four, won one, drawn two and lost one. More specifically, as well as the win in Glasgow, they had drawn at home to Hibs and away to Partick Thistle, before being soundly defeated 4-1 at Easter Road on the 26th of August, just four days before Celtic came to Perth. If they were to have any chance of progressing to the next round of the competition, Saints now needed to conjure up a win.

A huge crowd of 15,000 crammed into Muirton to see if they could do it. In the event, they more than did it, putting a poor Celtic team to the sword, with the Courier's sub-heading proclaiming (as you can see in the cutting above), *"Goal-hungry Saints run Celts ragged."*

The PA was similarly effusive, telling its readers that Saints *"outclassed Celtic by*

their almost non-stop attacks in the first half and broke their opponents' heart with an 'iron curtain' defence in the second."

As in the first match at Celtic Park some players really stood out, as the PA describes...

"Keeper Billy Taylor was in brilliant form then, but all through it was the Muirton mid-line of Little, Ferguson and McKinven which exerted the dominating influence. All three were immense, with Little really outstanding."

The Courier agreed, singling out Little in particular for praise, recording that, *"Right-half Little was a real giant for Saints. The half-back fetched and carried and started raid after raid."*

Saints' fan Gordon Small was at this match and he told us, *"A lot of people don't realise how good a team we had in those days. Jim Little was one of the best centre halves we've had, but, overall, it was a really good squad, with the likes of Johnny Bell and Ian*

222

Gardiner being particular favourites of mine."

Bert McIntosh, who was at the game, also remembers Gardiner, telling us, *"He was a proper, old-fashioned centre forward who could really hit the ball very hard."* To prove Bert and Gordon's point, Ian Gardiner scored Saints' first, courtesy of what is today called an 'assist' from Jim Little. Here's the PA again…

"It was the tall, rangy right-half who paved the way for Saints' opening goal in the 16th minute. A long crossfield ball, perfectly flighted, deceived pivot McNeill (this was Billy McNeill, later of Lisbon Lions' fame). *Centre-forward Ian Gardiner, positioned behind the Celtic player, brought the ball down in an instant and blasted it home with his right foot from 12 yards range."*

Nowadays, Gardiner's movement off the ball (a phrase that wasn't used in the early 1960s) would probably be described as *"getting goalside of the defender,"* and it seems that he completely outfoxed the normally sound McNeill. The Courier tells us that, *"A long probing ball from Little completely beat McNeill. Gardiner raced on to the ball and with the Celts appealing for offside* (as can be seen in the photo at the top of this chapter), *gave Connor no chance with a low drive."*

The home side's almost total control of the match up to this point meant that they had several good opportunities to add to Gardiner's opener, firstly when the centre-forward's neat flick released Henderson, who cut in from the left and fired in a great shot, which Connor in the Celtic goal managed to knock over the bar. Then, with the Celtic defence hesitating, Bell got on the end of a cross from Menzies but his driven shot was straight at Connor.

The PA noted, *"Such was Saints' continued superiority and Celtic's mediocrity that a second goal just had to come,"* as it

eventually did in the 36th minute when *"Inside-forward Wright slammed the ball into the roof of the net from the edge of the penalty area after nearly every Perth forward had had a shot at goal."*

Celtic were virtually non-existent as an attacking force in the first half, such was Saints' dominance. The PA tells us, *"Such was the stranglehold maintained by the home mid-line, backed up by stalwarts Lachlan and McFadyen at full-back, that 'keeper Taylor hadn't a worth-while shot to save all through the first half."*

The Courier was even more damning in its appraisal of the visitors' performance, noting that *"Celtic had little to commend them. In the first half only Chalmers and veteran Willie Fernie seemed to have any idea of how to penetrate the Saints' iron defence."*

Bill Taylor and his colleagues did have to earn their corn in the second half though, *"with Celtic throwing everything into the attack in a desperate bid not only to save the game but restore their reputation."* It was all to no avail. The PA recorded, *"And long before Celts mounted another frenzied 10-minute spell of pressure towards the end, their real challenge had faded in the face of magnificent saves by Taylor from Jackson and Fernie."*

Celtic's Mike Jackson (who went on to sign for Saints towards the end of the 1962-63 season) came the closest to getting his side back in the game with a shot that came back off the post.

As time petered out, Celtic, naturally, threw caution to the wind, but according to the Courier, *"they lacked the guile to split the defence."* When they did, they still had to beat Billy Taylor, which on this particular evening was beyond them.

In the last two minutes of the game, Fernie had a terrific daisy-cutter of an effort, but

Bill (just) managed to smother the ball at the post.

Saints' commitment to the cause was seemingly taken to the edge on occasions. The Courier talked about *"Saints rock-steady defence,"* before going on to tell us that, *"Lachan and McFadyen were like tigers and gobbled up every piece of loose play. Tension was running high and referee Crossman spoke to several of the players."*

The combativeness between the players seems to have transferred itself to the crowd and, sadly, the game was marred by a very small number of Celtic fans who took umbrage at their team's looming defeat and, more specifically, at two of the referee's decisions in the second half. The first was when Celtic were denied a penalty. This seems to have been the correct decision by the officials, with the Courier reporting that, *"The players accepted it, but the fans thought otherwise and two bottles flew onto the pitch. Play was held up while the referee removed a bottle from the penalty box. Minutes later police removed a youth wearing a Celtic scarf from another part of the terracing"*

The second incident came when Hughes had a goal disallowed. The game was held up as (the Courier tells us), *"In the 83rd minute Hughes had the ball in the net when Fernie beat Taylor and passed to the centre.*

"Mr Crossman said 'offside' and another bottle flew on to the pitch, as the crowd howled disapproval and play was again held up. Police went into the terracing behind the St Johnstone goal as fans pointed fingers and two men were removed."

Celtic fans (and they were not the only club who suffered in this respect) had a reputation for this sort of behaviour, notably some six years earlier when Stanley-based referee Duncan McKerchar officiated in the infamous 'Battle of Brockville,' where there was such serious fighting on the terraces that the police had to call for reinforcements and one of many bottles thrown felled the Falkirk goalkeeper.

Brian Doyle also remembers being at Muirton and, in particular, just what a great game Bill Taylor - and the rest of the defence – had that night. Bert McIntosh concurs with Brian, telling us that, *"Billy Taylor just stopped everything! Bill, Jim Lachlan and Charlie McFadyen were all really good players. They and the rest of the team were outstanding that day. We simply outplayed Celtic and deserved the win."*

The result meant that St Johnstone went into their final match of the Group stage level with Hibs on six points. The Edinburgh side had to play Celtic, who, as the table below shows, could still qualify if they won at Parkhead and Saints dropped points at home against Partick Thistle.

How the Clubs Stand This Morning

SCOTTISH LEAGUE — Section I.

	P.	W.	L.	D.	F.	A.	Pts.
Hibernian	5	2	1	2	10	7	6
St Johnstone ..	5	2	1	2	5	5	6
Celtic	5	2	2	1	8	9	5
Partick Thistle .	5	1	3	1	7	9	3

The match against Thistle was another cracker, as we'll describe in more detail in a chapter below…

Saints team: Taylor; McFadyen and Lachlan; Little, Ferguson and McKinven; Menzies, Wright, Gardiner, Bell and Henderson.
Attendance: 15,000.

224

No. 18
The coolness of a cucumber sandwich

Scottish League Cup, First Round, Section One
St Johnstone 2, Celtic 0,
Muirton Park, Wednesday, 12th August 1981

Headline: Daily Record

Some might look back to Owen Coyle's Saints win over Rangers in the same competition in 2006 as being Saints' best Cup win over either half of the Old Firm by dint of the fact that, a) Coyle's team was in the second tier of Scottish football and, b) the match was at Ibrox. However, the reason we believe this particular victory over Celtic was marginally more notable is that not only was this St Johnstone team in the second tier, but it was - unlike the 2006 side - also part-time.

To be fair, despite their part-time status, this Saints' team had one particular ace up their sleeve which was not available to Coyle's squad, namely the burgeoning talent that was the young Alistair McCoist.

If you weren't around at that time, it's easy to be unaware of just how good McCoist was, even at this early stage in his career. To illustrate this, it's worth looking at some of the comments about him in the match reports from this game...

The PA: *"And the toast of Perth must be Ally McCoist. He won't be 19 until*

September 24 yet he displayed a maturity far beyond his years as he notched the first goal for Saints."

The Daily Record: *"A glorious goal by Scotland's latest soccer sensation Ally McCoist pushed Celtic deeper into League Cup trouble at Muirton Park last night."*

The Courier: *"The brilliant solo goal by McCoist must add to his already huge transfer value. This 18-year-old outshone the more famous Celtic names, and his team mates had a cup-tie spirit and surge Celtic could never subdue."*

Those *"more famous Celtic names"* had won the Premier Division the previous season and included the likes of Pat Bonner, Tommy Burns, Danny McGrain, Roy Aitken, Frank McGarvey, Murdo McLeod, Davie Provan and (on the bench) Charlie Nicholas.

Saints had gone into the 1981-82 League Cup following a third place in the First Division the previous season. While Ally McCoist was the obvious star, the club had also spent money – some £20,000 (just over £100,000 today) to bring Stuart Beedie to Perth from Montrose as a 'replacement' for McCoist, whom everyone knew would sooner or later be heading for a big club in England.

Saints were drawn with three Premier sides, Celtic, St Mirren and Hibernian (the latter had only just been promoted as First Division champions in 1981). No-one expected the part-time, lower Division side to do much other than act as cannon-fodder for the big boys. However, in the first game of the group, Saints went to Easter Road and beat Hibs 2-1, with McCoist and Beedie scoring the goals. That might have been a surprise, but nothing like the shock that resulted from the next match…

Celtic were, as noted, the reigning Scottish champions and as such were expected comfortably to defeat little, part-time St Johnstone. Some 71 buses reportedly travelled from Glasgow, their fans expecting their heroes to sweep aside the wee team from Perth. In the event, it was little St Johnstone who swept aside Celtic.

Although play was fast and frantic in the opening forty-five minutes, with both sides having shots fly past, the Courier tells us that, *"The first direct shot in ten minutes came from Pelosi, his angled drive from the edge of the box forcing Bonner to fingertip over the bar."* Minutes later, it was the Saints' keeper's turn to impress… *"A tremendous Tulloch save kept out an Aitken shot from 12 yards. Celtic claimed, in vain, that a St Johnstone defender's arm also helped."*

The PA was a bit less sure about the penalty claim, suggesting that it had some merit: *"Roy Aitken hit a fine shot which appeared to be diverted by a Perth arm. In the event, the referee said no."* Nowadays, we'd doubtless have a five minute wait while the VAR officials watched the incident in super-slow motion, sucking the joy out of the game before electing to send the referee to the video screen to change his decision… Aitken also played a key part in the first goal, albeit not one to his liking, as the PA described…

"Roy Aitken, dismayed at his team's lack of progress, decided to take a hand upfield. He surged through with the ball to be met by a resolute midfield.

"The central defender was dispossessed and John Pelosi set up a perfect ball for McCoist. It landed between Danny McGrain and Willie Garner and the Scottish Youth international showed both a clean pair of heels.

"Keeper Pat Bonner raced from his goal to narrow the angle; McCoist steadied and rounded the big man to slot the ball home from 12 yards with the coolness of a cucumber sandwich."

John Pelosi remembers this goal well, telling us, *"As a Rangers fan this was my first game against Celtic, so it was awesome. I'd been surprised when Celtic signed Willie Garner as I never thought he was the fastest and, while I may be exaggerating, I reckon McCoist gave him ten yards of a start and still took him."*

Both sides had other chances in the first half and Saints, arguably, should have gone two up, with the Daily Record noting that, *"In 20 minutes McCoist had a shot saved by Bonner and a minute later Bonner smothered a snap shot from John Brogan.*

The Courier was a bit more enthused about Brogie's chance, telling its readers, *"The biggest let-off so far came in 23 minutes when Pelosi crossed from the right and Brogan, just a few yards out, first-timed a shot which Bonner smothered brilliantly."*

The Courier then tells us of a further excitement for Saints' fans when, *"Before half time Beedie almost made it 2-0 with a snap shot from fully thirty yards which Bonner saved at the second attempt."*

It wasn't all one-way traffic though, with the Record observing that, *"Celtic's best try arrived just before half time when a Garner header was cleared by Rab Kilgour with Tulloch beaten."*

We can only presume that Billy McNeill, the Celtic manager, read the riot act to his players at half time because they came out forcefully at the start of the second half.

Only two minutes after the restart, Frank McGarvey carved his way into the box but put his cut-back behind the onrushing Celtic forwards and John Weir guided the ball to safety. The Courier recounted how, *"...there were a few heart-stopping scrambles in front of Tulloch ... For the opening ten minutes the home side took a pummelling and lost some of the composure which had been a feature of their defensive play. But they survived."*

Celtic continued to press, with Garner heading narrowly over on the hour mark. As you would expect, with the players growing tired and the atmosphere growing more tense, several players were booked – Caldwell for a body check on McCluskey, McAdam for *"an illegal tackle"* on Mackay, and Rab Kilgour for time-wasting.

Despite all Celtic's pressure, the Courier noted that, *"Tulloch was never required to perform heroics. In fact, the danger was at the other end as McCoist burst through again in 75 minutes. This time Bonner dived to push his shot round the post."*

With ten minutes remaining, Jim Morton came on for Beedie. Barely 60 seconds had elapsed when Saints won a penalty. Mind you, you wouldn't have known this if you were a Celtic fan who bought the Daily Record the next day. Clearly under pressure of a rapidly shortening deadline, their reporter didn't even record the fact of the penalty, simply finishing his report in

bold capital letters that said, "IN 81 MINUTES ST JOHNSTONE WENT TWO GOALS AHEAD." That was it: no mention of the penalty or what happened to cause it or what happened thereafter. It's no surprise that the one thing sports reporters hate almost above all else is a late goal in an evening match.

Fortunately, the local press provides more details. The PA told how, *"It was that man McCoist again who was brought down in full running order for the Celtic goal* (sic) *by Danny McGrain. Consternation as Bob Valentine indicated the penalty spot."*

Having not yet kicked the ball, Jim Morton stepped up to the spot. He takes up the story for us at this point: *"I had been on holiday abroad when we signed Stuart Beedie and he had scored in the win in our first League Cup match at Hibs. Consequently, when I came back from my holiday, I was told I was on the bench for the Celtic match.*

"It was an evening match and I remember hearing the noise sweeping down from the big crowd. As the light faded and darkness crept over the ground, you couldn't see the fans so well but you could sense the excitement building as we went ahead. The boys played very well that night and deserved to be in front. Then Stuart was injured and I was told, 'on you go, see what you can do.'

"Of course, the first thing I could do was take the penalty, but that wasn't quite so simple as it might have seemed. The Celtic players had crowded around referee Bob Valentine and while that was going on I think that both Brogie and McCoist thought they were going to take the penalty. However, George Fleming took the ball and gave it to me, telling me to go and play keepie-uppie while the referee sorted the Celtic players out.

It all eventually calmed down and George said to me, 'just go and stick it away.' I put the ball down on the penalty spot and faced up to Pat Bonner. My run-up was meant to deceive him and it did. He went one way and the ball went the other.

"That moment is one of those things that stay with you. It's the kind of thing that so many people wish they could experience – and I was fortunate enough to be able to – and the feeling when the ball went into the net was just unbelievable. The place erupted. It was a brilliant night."

John Brogan's memory is – more or less – the same as Jim's but with some additional information: "Alistair had scored earlier and when we got the pen Jimmy Morton was warming up to come on. He was the penalty taker, so I went up to McCoist who had grabbed the ball and said, 'what are you doing?' He replied, 'Hitting the pen,'

and I said, "No you're no,' and took the ball off him. I think I handed it to Jim, but I may have handed it to George who then gave it to him. Either way, he scored!"

At the final whistle, a standing ovation broke out from the home support. The Celtic fans, meanwhile, made their way back to all those 71 buses for an unhappy journey back home. Doubtless, they would not have agreed with the PA's final summary of the match, which read, "It was a great night for Perth and, it must be said also, for Scottish football."

Saints team: Tulloch, Mackay, Kilgour, Weir, Rutherford, Caldwell, Pelosi, McCoist, Beedie, Fleming, Brogan.
Substitutes: Docherty (not used), Morton (for Beedie).
Attendance: 10,406.

No. 17
Ten goals – with nine men

Eastern League
St Johnstone 10, Brechin City 1
Recreation Grounds, Saturday 6th December 1919

GOAL-SCORING GLUTTONY.

St Johnstone Merciless Against Brechin.

Headline: The (Dundee) Courier

At the time of writing, and almost certainly for many years, if not decades, to come, this is St Johnstone's record win in any league match. It's also only one of the very few times that we have scored double figures in any competitive game.

Brechin City were only 13 years old when this game took place, having been formed by the merger of two local teams, Brechin Hearts and Brechin Harp. Moreover, Glebe Park had only just opened in 1919, and Saints had played their first match there a few months earlier that season, on 11th October, winning 3-1. Going into the return match in Perth at the beginning of December, it was recognised that Saints' main issues were in the backs. The Dundee Courier of 5th December, commenting on their defeat the previous weekend, noted, *"At Arbroath the Saints were much below strength, particularly in the defence, in which division the management's troubles during the season have generally lain. At right back a new player is being tried."*

The PA of 6th December previewed the match thus, *"Today St Johnstone have Brechin on St Johnstone Recreation Grounds in the Eastern League at 2.30 p.m. It will be remembered that some two months ago St Johnstone defeated Brechin in the same competition at Brechin by a narrow margin. St Johnstone will endeavour to add other* (sic) *two points to their score as a result of today's match. An interesting experiment is being tried in the formation of today's St Johnstone team."* The paper then listed the team that was expected to play, with *"Newman"* lining up at right-back; this being the commonly used term for someone who was being given a trial. In this case, it was Walker (forename unknown), whom the Dundee Courier of 6th December revealed was from Fife and *"is being introduced by Pitt, the Saints' goalkeeper, and is a brother of Rod Walker, who played for the Heart of Midlothian."*

The Courier also reveals that Aitken, St Johnstone's left-back, had missed the previous game, *"due to his losing the train connection from Edinburgh."* The arrangements for travel and the means by which players turned up for training and matches were very different back then.

The PA's report is brief, consisting of only one paragraph, under the heading, *"St Johnstone play cricket with Brechin"*

"St Johnstone were both fortunate and unfortunate on Saturday. They put on a record score against Brechin before the poorest gate of the season. After the usual 'blaw' by the Pipe Band the game started, and Brechin showed good all-round play. Then St Johnstone began to score, and such scoring. The home team re-arranged front rank were in romping form, the half-backs held the opposing attack, and Aitken and new back Walker had little to do. There were two hat-tricks, the goals being scored by Williams (4), T. McCulloch (3), and Linn, Robertson, and Taylor one each. Stewart scored for Brechin. The visiting half-backs were fair, and Cruickshank, outside-right, and Stewart, centre, best forward."

The Dundee Courier carried a longer report, under the headline, *"Goal-Scoring Gluttony - St Johnstone Merciless Against Brechin."*

"St Johnstone have been a strange team this season. Against Brechin City, the unfortunates of the Eastern League, Saints outstripped all previous performances and came out victors by ten goals to one. Williams claimed four, T. McCulloch three, and the other forwards – Taylor, Robertson, and Linn – had one each. Stewart scored the City's only goal.

"While the visitors were plucky throughout and their early play gave good promise, it was evident after the first ten minutes that the homesters had 'a soft thing.' But the spectators – a mere handful – called for goals, and goals they got. The most popular was the tenth, which was secured in the closing minutes by Linn, one of the smartest forwards on the field.

"Saints had out a new back, Walker, a brother of Rod Walker, but he was not altogether safe. Aitken was the strength of the defence and R. McCulloch the best half, with Queen a good second. The forwards had a day out, and while all were good, T. McCulloch, for his judicious passing out to the wings, and Linn, for absolute trickiness and fine returning, were outstanding."

One staggering thing about this match, which isn't mentioned in the PA or the Courier's reports, is that for much of the second half Saints played with only nine men. This is revealed by The Scotsman, whose short report explains…

"Brechin City were completely outclassed by St Johnstone at Perth. The St Johnstone forward line, which had been reorganised, combined well, and before half-time had netted the ball on five occasions. On resuming, the Saints again swarmed around the visitors' goal, and although playing with only nine men during the greater part of the time again registered five goals."

Further digging, this time in the Angus papers, allowed us to discover more about this, with the Montrose Standard recording, *"The Saints took the game in hand, and all the home forwards registered goals… Brechin City were plucky, but completely outplayed. For a considerable portion of the second half the Saints were without Aitken and Galloway, but notwithstanding, they registered five goals during this period. Prominent Saint* (sic) *players were Aitken, McCulloch, and the forwards."*

This was also noted by the Evening Telegraph, which additionally claimed that at times the fans weren't even sure how many goals had been scored.

And interestingly, the Telegraph's report of the match suggests that, even back in 1919, there was thought and method applied by players in specific circumstances, viz,

"Against Brechin City, St Johnstone piled on the goals, and at times during the progress of the game spectators debated as to what the actual number was. But the game was not so extremely one-sided as the score of ten goals to one indicates. The City lads were game, and despite the mounting of the odds against them they introduced considerable vigour and dash. They came away with a bang, but the Saints, apparently weighing the weakness of the opposition, resorted to close combination, and in this style the inside men played to each other with excellent effect. Five goals were scored in each half, despite the fact that during a large portion of the second period there were only nine Saints, Aitken and Galloway having walked off ... The Brechin lads frequently attacked, but they had not sufficient strength to push home their desultory invasions. The Saints, on the other hand, shot well – with force and good directness."

The implication here is that the two St Johnstone players simply left the field as there is no reference to their being injured. This seems almost as unlikely as nine men scoring five times against eleven, however, it is not beyond the bounds of possibilities for we know of at least one friendly match in Perthshire in the nineteenth century when a team was so dominant that one of their defenders and the goalkeeper engaged in races against each other for their own entertainment and to keep warm.

Finally, the Telegraph also suggested that Saints might have been more generous to their opponents, *"It would have been a gracious act if Pitt had made more slips than the one which gave City their goal."* Somehow, even in 1919 never mind 2023, we can't see that happening...

Following this stunning win, the PA reported that for their next match, against then Eastern League leaders, *"St Johnstone, for once in a while, have decided upon making no change from their eleven to meet Dundee Hibs at Recreation Ground today (Saturday)."* Similarly, the Evening Telegraph noted there would be *"no change in the eleven which swamped Brechin City,"* although they did add, *"strengthening in the half-back and rear divisions is necessary."* One can only imagine what the players would have thought - and said - if one of them had been dropped after such a win...

Saints team: Pitt: Walker, Aitken, Queen, Galloway, R. McCulloch, Linn, Taylor, T. McCulloch, Williams, and Robertson. Attendance: unknown.

It wasn't all one-way traffic, even Chris Millar had a shot!

Europa League, Second Round Qualifier, first leg
Rosenborg 0, St Johnstone 1
Lerkendal Stadion, Trondheim, Thursday 18th July 2013

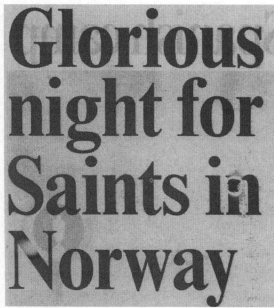

Headline: The Courier

The first competitive match for Tommy Wright as manager of St Johnstone was, on paper, more than intimidating. Having finished third in the Premier Division under Steve Lomas, who had been made an offer he should have refused to become manager of Millwall, Saints began their new European adventure in the second round of the Europa League away to Rosenborg, the most successful team in Norwegian football and a regular competitor in the group stages of the Champions League. In fact, regular competitor does them an injustice: between 1995 and 2007 they participated 11 times, eight of which were consecutive from 1995 to 2002. This was a record until Manchester United qualified for the group phase for a record ninth time in 2004. The joint record holder of the Norwegian championship, with 26 titles, and 12 Norwegian Cup successes, to say nothing of having actually won a European competition - the InterToto Cup - even if it was a relatively minor one

and they were joint winners. Just to rub it in, they went into the match in the middle of the Norwegian season, undefeated after 15 games. Unsurprisingly, they were very strong favourites to win against Saints.

Several players told us that the manger's pre-match team-talk was one of the best they'd heard. Steven Anderson told us, *"I walked out of the meeting thinking we could beat Barcelona."* David Wotherspoon concurred, telling us, *"It was one of the very best and we left the dressing room feeling very positive."*

Tommy himself gave us a unique insight into how he went about motivating the players: *"When I go in to a pre-arranged football meeting, whether it's a press conference or a pre-match talk to the players, I always have a few 'what ifs?' in mind – by which I mean I think about what the response might be to what I say and then consider how to handle it. For team-talks, you obviously have the tactical side and all the things you've practised in training, but it's how you go about presenting it that makes a difference. You have to try to motivate the players and make them share your confidence that we can win. I'd always have some ideas about what I wanted to say, but when I went into the dressing room, I'd then do it more or less off-the-cuff.*

For a big game, like Rosenborg, or the Cup final, it was usually on the basis of 'no-one expects you to do anything, but this is what you started playing the game for – to win trophies.' Like many managers, I'd mention the sacrifices their families made to help them succeed and the sacrifices they were making for their own families. It's a mix of confidence and determination underpinned by a human touch. I looked at every one of them individually, stressing that they were all good players who deserved to be there, making them believe that I believed we could win. Having worked with that squad of players, I genuinely did believe they could win every game, and for the Rosenborg match there really was no pressure because no one gave us a hope. The main thing was to sound confident, but not over-confident."

Alan Mannus recalls the manager telling him before the match, *"Use your experience, slow the game down when you have to,"* adding, *"That was common sense thinking for a goalkeeper away from home, but Tommy stressed how important it was that we got a good result to take back to Perth."*

One thing that did make a difference to the result was that Rosenborg were, as noted, part of the way through their season. That meant Tommy Wright was able to watch them beforehand, as he told us: *"We were quite lucky with Rosenborg because their season had already started. At that time, St Johnstone didn't have the technology to get videos of European opponents, so in some games we were playing it by ear. However, I'd seen Rosenborg twice, which helped with our game plan. I saw how they pushed their full backs high and left space in behind. I also felt we could challenge them at set plays. We knew they were good but I had seen how Crusaders of the Irish League, even though they lost heavily, had previously caused them problems.*

"Stevie May didn't play in the first leg because he had a wee hamstring problem, although if he had been fit, I'd have had him in the side in Norway for his runs in behind. That apart, anyone looking at our squad from outside will have seen how everyone was relaxed: I was relaxed, the staff were relaxed, the planning was done, we'd
trained well and given the players everything we believed would give them a chance of causing an upset.

"You could see how the training worked at the goal. We'd worked on Frazer Wright attacking the area, so it was not off the cuff - it was planned – and we were delighted when it worked.

"Another thing that did make a difference was that Alan Mannus had an outstanding game: when you see clips of the game you can see he made some incredible saves.

"It's also important to remember that it wasn't all one-way traffic, even Chris Millar had a shot! For that first game, it couldn't have gone any better, and it was all down to the players.

Some 450 Saints' fans descended on Norway from Perth and much further afield. On one flight, after another rendition of *"Oh When the Saints Go Marching In,"* the captain came on the intercom to ask, *"please stop singing…"*

The heaviest subs bench ever? Photo: B. Doyle

Upon arrival, as well as heading for the nearest pub, some fans, including Brian Doyle and his son, Philip, took the opportunity to see round the ground, posing for a photo in the dugout as 'the heaviest subs' bench that Saints have ever had.'

On the afternoon of the game, all the Saints' fans gathered in Trondheim city centre and - as had been done in Monaco - marched to the stadium, waving their scarves, banners and singing their songs. This time, there was no airline captain to ask them to put a sock in it and Brian Doyle recounts that the locals seem both bemused and amused at their good-natured visitors.

Saints' media team's Steven Watt and Liam Doris travelled together to Norway. Liam told us, *"I didn't appreciate at the time just how big and successful a club Rosenborg were. Unlike, say, when we played Galatasaray, it didn't register just what an achievement this was. The game itself showed our defensive qualities: we were definitely on the back-foot for some time but we were dogged and determined. Although they were the better team, it was by no means a smash and grab, rather a well-planned and resolute performance where the result was what mattered."*

For Graeme Buchan, this was a stunning performance, which more than justified the cost of getting there... *"The week before, I remember shelling out about £400 for flights to Norway. In the end it was worth it though as that was the best result I've seen Saints have in all my years of watching them."*

Initially, the players were perhaps relieved more than impressed with their performance. Steven Anderson told us how, as he and Steven MacLean were walking off the pitch at the end of the game, he turned to Macca and said (words along the lines of...) *"how on earth did we win that match?"* To be fair, Ando did also add that it was the result that mattered more than whether Saints were lucky or not.

The game itself was memorable not just because Saints unexpectedly won, but because they played at a level that most fans watching would not have thought them capable of – and also because the sole goal-scorer on the night was Frazer Wright, this being one of his only five goals in 131 appearances for the club.

The Courier noted that Tommy Wright, unsurprisingly in their view, had opted for a cautious approach, playing only one up front. However, that lone striker was Steven MacLean, whose game intelligence and awareness were second to none in this Saints' squad. Also featuring in the side was a new signing, local Perth boy David Wotherspoon, who had just joined from Hibs a few weeks before. Gordon Bannerman, in the PA, was more positive about how Saints approached the game, telling his readers, *"...suited boss Wright showed an admirable sense of adventure for his first game in charge since taking over from Lomas, with debutants David Wotherspoon and Gary McDonald in offensive midfield roles."*

Spoony (David Wotherspoon) had grown up supporting Saints and dreaming of playing at McDiarmid. He told us, *"I had played abroad in the Scotland Youth side, and been in a few European games at Hibs, but not all the other lads had played in Europe. Despite that, in the dressing room before the game, I was on edge. I remember Nigel Hasselbaink, who is a really laid-back guy, telling me, 'Just relax.' I did what he suggested and felt ready for the game."*

Rosenborg opened strongly, winning two corners in the early minutes, but nothing came of them despite the notes on the set-pieces being missing from the dug-out, as Callum Davidson recalled: *"It was Tommy and my first game in charge and when they got the first corner he shouted at me, 'What's Ando doing – where are the set-pieces (book)?' I had forgotten to bring it out and Tommy Campbell had to go and get it. Fortunately, they didn't score..."*

Saints then gradually grew into the game, with Wotherspoon hitting a long-range pot-shot that, according to the Courier *"flew just wide."* The PA described this as *"Wotherspoon fired a speculative 25-yarder wide."*

Next, the Courier described how *"in the 15th minute, MacLean cut in from the left and hit an angled drive which was saved at his near post by Daniel Orlund ... Just three minutes later, Saints took their shock lead. Wotherspoon swung in a corner from the left, which sailed all the way through to Frazer Wright lurking at the back post. The centre half made no mistake with his close-range shot to the delight of the travelling support."*

The PA's take on this was brief and to the point... *"Perth fans exploded in joy as central defender Wright charged into the six-yard box and rammed a perfect connection into the gaping net."*

The Courier said, *"It was a remarkable triumph for the entire team and for Wright personally, especially as he conceded an own goal against Turkish side Eskisehirspor at the same stage of the same competition last year."*

While he probably wasn't too happy to be reminded of that own goal, when interviewed by the Courier after the game he did make the point about his goalscoring prowess in Europe, noting that, *"That's me scored twice in Europe now."*

After the goal, Rosenborg were stunned into action and Alan Mannus in the Saints' goal pulled off a stupendous save to keep them in the lead; as described in the PA, *"... it required a quite breathtaking reflex Mannus save, spreading himself and extending his legs to thwart Nielsen six minutes later when the striker seemed certain to guide home a Svensson cross from point blank range."*

The Courier were similarly enthusiastic, describing it as *"a stunning unorthodox save with his foot."* Alan himself was, as usual, modest about his efforts, telling us, *"I do remember that one save but not many of the others that day. It was a sort of cross/cut-back and their player ran across*

the front post-area, between me and the near post. I thought, 'this is a bit awkward for me to get my hand to,' so I stuck my right leg out as straight as it could go and fortunately got my right foot to the ball."

It wasn't all one-way traffic however, with Nigel Hasselbaink keeping the home defenders on their toes – as the Courier put it, *"proving a persistent thorn with his dangerous runs."* Crucially, St Johnstone maintained their composure for the rest of the first half, although there was also a deserved yellow card for Steven Anderson when he *"chopped down Chibuike in full flight."*

The second half began with a loose back-pass from Rosenborg that Steven MacLean failed to latch onto, and just after this David Wotherspoon tested the keeper again with a 22-yard, curling shot. Saints kept at it, trying to attack rather than withdraw into a shell. In the 49th minute, Chris Millar put MacLean in the clear but, as the PA told us, *"... his instinctive strike veered agonisingly wide of the target."*

Ando recalled that the team rode their luck, *"but then again, you need to ride your luck to win any game against a really good team. We were definitely hanging on towards the end, but we kept our shape really well and kept them out. Big Al* (Mannus) *was brilliant. They had quality players, especially Cristian Gamboa* (who went to play for Celtic)*, the Costa-Rican right back. He was some athlete and the best player on the pitch. I made a point of swopping strips with him after the match."*

Several of the newspapers made the point that Rosenborg had underestimated Saints. The Daily Record and the Courier both quoted Frazer Wright as saying *"The Norwegians paid the price for failing to take Saints seriously,"* while the Courier also noted that he knew the tie was far from over, with Frazer saying, *"We'll see what happens next week now. They will aim to* give us a backlash ... we need to have another performance like this."

The final words on this match - the first ever away win in Europe for Saints - should go to the architect of the victory.

Tommy Wright told us, *"The win out there gave the players the confidence to believe they could also come through the second leg successfully. Our training went well for the home leg, but, when we were practising penalties, I noticed Chris Millar hadn't taken one so I asked him 'What's up?' and he replied, 'My groin's tight.' With Chris not going to be fit, I had to make the choice between bringing in another midfielder or dropping Macca back. We opted for the latter, which we did when we didn't have the ball. Of course, we didn't need to win,* so we could afford for Steven to drop into midfield. Rosenborg had signed a big striker between the two games, but we got the perfect start with Stevie's goal which gave us the confidence to hold on, even after conceding the equaliser. The 8,000 fans created a great atmosphere, and our performances against Rosenborg set the tone for the rest of the season and, of course, the Cup win at the end of it."

Saints team: Mannus, Mackay, Scobbie, Cregg, Wright, Anderson, Millar, McDonald, MacLean, Wotherspoon, Hasselbaink.
Substitutes: Banks, Edwards (for Hasselbaink) Caddis, May, Miller (for Wotherspoon), B. Easton, Fallon
Attendance: 5,952.

Schoolboy fantasy stuff in a thrill-a-minute encounter

Scottish Premier Division
St Johnstone 3, Celtic 2
McDiarmid Park, Saturday, 22nd December 1990

Sporting Post headline

The more eagle-eyed readers may have noticed that quite a lot of the games in this book took place around Christmas and the New Year. This is probably just coincidence, but nonetheless it meant that the St Johnstone support could frequently enjoy their turkey and/or Hogmanay drinks/New Year's Day dinner with even more relish than usual. As the PA put it in Graham Fulton's match report, *"The win over Celtic ensures that supporters Christmas stockings are now brimful with 21 Premier league points at the halfway stage of the competition."*

As well as another two points (three points for a win wasn't introduced until 1994 in Scotland) this game was undoubtedly one of the most entertaining and – being Saints – nail-biting in recent decades. And all this for an entry fee of only six pounds – which, in an indication of how much admission fees have inflated in recent years, is equivalent to only £17.76 at the time of writing in 2023.

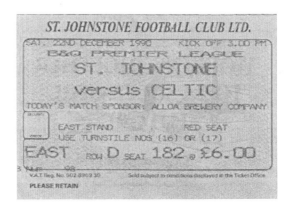

Saints went into the match in good fettle, with what was widely regarded as their strongest line-up taking the field. Ironically, this meant there was no place for the then record-signing, the £165,000 midfielder John Davies who, along with Don McVicar, started on the bench.

This Celtic team were not having a great season. In fact, they were three points behind Saints when the match kicked-off. That said, they were no slouches, with the team containing, as it did, players of the calibre of Charlie Nicholas, John Collins, Tommy Coyne, Pat Bonner and the Pauls Elliott and McStay. However, they had lost their two previous games, the last one to Dunfermline, and Nicholas had started that one on the bench. He was restored to the starting eleven for Perth, along with several others who had previously been sidelined. No matter, they, and indeed no-one in the large crowd, could have anticipated the whirlwind start that had all those of a blue-and-white persuasion out of their seats twice in the first six minutes.

The standard kick-off for Saints in those days was for the ball to be touched forward (as was the law then) and then knocked back, before being floated out to the right wing where, hopefully, Roddy Grant would get his head on it and flick it on to Allan Moore. After that, the idea was that Moorie would do something wonderful and we'd score. On this particular afternoon, this is what happened… (from the PA):

"The (Celtic) new men had hardly got themselves sorted out when they were a goal behind. Allan Moore did the trick on the right as he left Dariusz Wdowczyk stranded and cut a fine ball across the face of the goal. The quiet but splendidly efficient Harry Curran gave the ball a change of direction and Steve Maskrey headed home from close range."

The Sporting Post, in its 'as live' report, provides an additional, crucial detail about Curran's part in the goal, telling us, *"Moore gets behind the defence on the right and crosses to the back post, where Curran heads the ball back for Maskrey to head home from point-range."*

However, it's the Sunday Post that provides the missing piece of the jigsaw, explaining that it was indeed Grant who linked with Moore…

"A Baltacha free-kick was played through to Moore by Grant. The winger wriggled to

the by-line and crossed deep. Curran returned it and, with the visiting defence in total disarray, Steve Maskrey easily headed home from inside the six-yard box."

Saints were getting huge crowds in that first season back in the Premier – demonstrating the potential support that does lie (unfortunately dormant most of the time) in Perthshire for its local team. The home fans were, in the modern vernacular, 'buzzing' (although that word wasn't in common use in 1990) and the excitement had barely abated when we went two up. This time, it was the turn of the *"quiet but splendidly efficient Harry Curran…"* Here's The Sporting Post again…

"Baillie fouls Maskrey 25 yards out, and Curran blasts the free kick through the defensive wall. Bonner is completely deceived, and the ball ends up in the back of the net."

This time, it's the PA that provides more detail…

"Baillie gave away a foul 25 yards from goal. The wall was set up and Tommy Turner ran over the ball to leave Curran to actually take the kick which found a gap that left Pat Bonner hopelessly lost."

Cue, once more, bedlam in the home stands. We could hardly believe what we were watching. Graham Fulton in the PA summed it up well, *"To score in 90 seconds and then be two up against an Old Firm side after only six minutes is schoolboy fantasy stuff."* While most schoolboys would probably have other things further up their list of great fantasies, the Saints' support in general were hugging themselves in a gleeful mix of disbelief and ecstasy. The more pessimistic and/or realistic (depending on your point of view) were looking at their watches and wondering if Saints could withstand the inevitable and doubtless prolonged assault that Celtic would make on Lindsay

238

Hamilton's goal for the remaining 84 minutes. However, in the event, the closest the Parkhead side came to a goal at this stage was when Tommy Turner back-headed a pass from Baltacha and was relieved to see the ball slip narrowly past the post.

Having successfully negotiated the first half without conceding, the last thing Saints wanted was to lose a goal fairly quickly in the second half. So, of course, that's what we did. But first, this being an Alex Totten team that was based on attack rather than defence, we nearly went further ahead. Once again, it was Allan Moore as provider, sending over a cross for Roddy Grant to smack a header firmly off the base of Bonner's post.

Unfortunately, Moore's next 'assist' was at the wrong end of the park. As the PA tells us, after he had hit a shot that went past the upright and subsequently had Bonner turn one over the bar, *the wee man then attempted to be clever by dribbling in defence and lost possession to John Collins. The midfielder bored on to net with a low grounder that gave Hamilton no chance.*

Charlie Nicholas may have been restored to the Celtic team to provide a stronger attacking threat, but he was not doing anything to live up to this expectation and he was replaced by Dziekanowski. The PA recorded the swing in the match thereafter, noting, *With Collins turning in a power of work, Celtic sensed the game was far from lost and it was Hamilton who came to Saints rescue in 61 minutes with a brilliant stop from substitute Dziekanowski.*

The Sporting Post described this as *the save of the match* but it was only one of several outstanding saves that Lindsay Hamilton made throughout the game. In the view of many of those present that day, Lindsay had one of his best games for St Johnstone. But before that, the balance swung again…

Showing a total disregard for all the Celtic effort, that cult figure Roddy Grant took on Paul Elliott with a smart bit of footwork. He defeated the Celtic defender twice before sweeping a perfect ball for Turner to lash past Bonner."

Tommy Turner was about 16 yards out, but the ferocity of his shot was such that it simply zipped past Pat Bonner, rising all the way into the net. And for those who were there, the quote immediately above hardly does justice to Grant's skill. For anyone who is too young to have seen Roddy Grant play, his touch, with his feet and with his head, was exquisitely delicate, yet deadly and purposeful.

The third Saints' goal was in the 65th minute and from then until the final whistle both sides served up a memorable feast of attacking football, with near misses at both ends. For those pessimists who had been fretting since the seventh minute, this was the time to reduce their nails to the quick whilst also prematurely ageing years in a matter of minutes.

With 17 minutes left on the clock, Tommy Coyne got one back when he ran away from the St Johnstone defence and coolly flicked the ball over Hamilton as the keeper came out to try to block the ball. This, naturally, galvanised the Glasgow side. The Sporting Post's description details the excitement perfectly…

"Within seconds (of the goal) *Fulton shaves the outside of the post with a blistering 18-yarder.*

"Elliott goes even closer when he rattles the bar with a header from 12 yards. "Thirteen minutes from time, Roddy Grant and Chris Morris are booked after an off-the-ball tussle.

"A minute later Coyne has the ball in the net for Celts, but the flag is up and the 'goal' is chalked off.

"Steve Maskrey is the next player to go close when he chips the advancing Bonner, only to see the ball drop on the wrong side of the post.

"It's real end-to-end stuff now, and only a great one-handed save by Hamilton denies Coyne his second.

"Next, the big keeper does well to smother a back-heel from the same player after Collins and McStay combine well on the left.

"With six minutes to go St Johnstone send on McVicar for Curran, and three minutes later Davies replaces Grant, who has run himself into the ground.

"In the last few minutes Celtic move Elliott to centre-forward, but there is no denying Saints their victory."

As well as big Lindsay Hamilton performing heroics, Saints were well marshalled in defence by Baltacha in what The Sunday Post described as, *"A top-class act who held Saints together, especially when Celtic threatened to snatch a point."* That was their raison d'être for making Sergei Baltacha their man of the match.

For Kevin Heller, this was a memorable game for a number of reasons…

"My first season watching Saints was in 1983-84, when we got relegated from the Premier. It had taken some time to get back and this was Celtic's first visit to McDiarmid Park. Alex Totten had really turned Saints around and I remember thinking how big we were compared to when I first went. Because it was Celtic, there was a bit of fear before the game, but then we blew them apart in the first ten minutes. Zorro, who was one of my favourites, scored the first, then Harry Curran, who was one of the new boys Totten had brought in, then they came back into it only for Tommy Turner to score our

third. Strangely, given that everyone tells me what a great strike it was, I'm afraid I can't actually remember Turner's goal.

"I was 14 at the time and, as a Saints' fan, in the minority at my Perth school, where there were a lot of Celtic fans in my year. You have no idea how much I was looking forward to going into school and lording it over these guys…

"I was in the Ormond stand for the first two seasons at McDiarmid and in those days the opposition fans were allowed in as it was ostensibly a 'family-friendly' stand. The Celtic fans in the Ormond were not really that friendly, noising us up when they scored their first – 'that's us back in the game, watch out now,' but we held on and they were strangely subdued at the end."

This was indeed a spectacular game and, as the Sporting Post implied, St Johnstone thoroughly deserved to win. The Sunday Post concurred, saying, *"In fairness, Saints just deserved to win a thrill-a-minute encounter."*

Once the dust settled, and as the weeks and months rolled on into 1991, the other teams began to work out how to play against St Johnstone. The initial flush of post-promotion enthusiasm and vigour, underpinned by a big home support that drove the team forward on days like this one, dissipated and good results were less frequent. Saints may have finished this match on 21 points, but they only put on another 10 in the rest of the season. Still, for a newly promoted team, 31 points was more than acceptable. Celtic, in contrast, finished in third place, 12 points behind Aberdeen and 14 behind Rangers.

Saints team: Hamilton, Treanor, Baltacha, Cherry, Inglis, McGinnis, Moore, Turner, Maskrey, Grant, Curran. Substitutes: McVicar (for Curran), Davies (for Grant) Attendance: 10,267.

240

No. 14
More feckless play

Scottish League Cup, First Round, Section One
St Johnstone 4, Partick Thistle 3,
Muirton Park, Saturday, 2nd September 1961

Photo: St Johnstone FC – note the training lights in front of the part-finished enclosure.

Having beaten Celtic in the previous Group match, there was, understandably, huge local interest in this tie. The picture here, taken in the aftermath of Johnny Bell scoring his second goal, in the 74th minute (and also showing the ongoing construction of the enclosure roof and the training lights, which some older fans will remember), shows the size of the crowd, which was recorded at just under 10,000.

Those who did attend knew that Saints' destiny was still not entirely in their own hands. It wasn't simply enough to beat Partick Thistle, who had no hope themselves of qualifying: they had to pray

that Hibernian would, at best, draw at Celtic Park. In the event that Celtic won and Saints lost or (depending on the number of goals Celtic scored) even only drew, then Celtic would progress to the quarter finals. Of course, this being St Johnstone, we had to do it the hard way, but fortunately for those attending this meant they saw a match of high drama, where the scoreline ebbed and flowed and the fans, at both grounds, were on tenterhooks as reports of goals elsewhere filtered through to the terraces.

By half-time, Thistle were in the driving seat. It seems that big match nerves had got to the home side, for the PA tells us that,

"... far from gaining confidence from their midweek win against the mighty Celtic, Saints played a shaky, loose game which found them labouring under a two-goal deficit at half-time."

This was despite Saints dominating the first fifteen minutes of the match. Unfortunately, this dominance was not turned into goals, with the PA noting, *"even during this period chances were squandered by poor work in front of goal."*

Inevitably, it was Thistle that broke the deadlock, with a cute run up the right by McParland, whose chip into the box was headered in via the post by McBride.

We've noted before how earlier generations of sports' reporters tended to be far less restrained in their comments than today's journalists. The PA's (unnamed) reporter was forthright in his criticism, stating baldly that, *"Ian Gardiner was the only forward who was really worth his salt during this period, but he didn't get much support from his colleagues, whose shooting was pitiful."*

This was despite Partick being reduced to 10 men for part of the half. There were no substitutes in those days, so when their full-back, Dougie Wright, sustained a bad injury to his arm, soon after Thistle's first goal, he had to leave the field for running repairs. He returned *"after ten minutes with his left arm heavily bandaged."*

Just after the half hour mark, Thistle went two ahead. The resolve that the St Johnstone defence had shown in the games against Celtic seemed to have gone, with the PA telling us that *"A cross from half-back Cunningham found Charlie McFadyen unprepared, and outside-left Ewing literally ran a ring around him before slamming the ball into the left-hand corner ... Now two goals down, St Johnstone's play took on a desperate look. There was no cool appraisal of the*

situation and a determined rally, only more feckless play from all divisions."

There was only one thing for it: the home crowd gave the team the dreaded slow handclap *"as the dejected St Johnstone trudged from the field."*

It seems we really were at sixes and sevens in this period of the game. The Sporting Post tells us that at the interval, *"Saints are shaky and struggling."*

The only good news at half time was that Hibs were one down at Celtic. The mood in the ground changed, albeit only briefly, just after the resumption, when Ian Gardiner took a pass from Bell and fired home, only for a linesman's raised flag to rule it out.

Having crocked the visitors full-back Wright in the first half, Saints' combative approach to the game led to another Jags' player being removed temporarily from the field. Inside forward McParland had to be helped to the touchline in the 55th minute, *"the next victim of robust St Johnstone tackling."* Fortunately, after five minutes attention he was able to return to the fray.

With two-thirds of the game gone, Saints eventually got the goal that they hoped might signal the start of a fightback. John Bell scored from a tight angle, following a neat move between Gardiner and McVittie. The Sporting Post describes this as follows: *"Gardiner does all the spade work out on the right before passing to McVittie. He crosses for Bell to slam home an angular shot."*

Unsurprisingly, Saints turned the screw, and intense pressure on the Thistle defence paid off just two minutes after Bell's goal when Charlie McFadyen atoned for his earlier mistake by drawing his side level. Freebairn in the Jags' goal managed to get his fingers to McFadyen's lob, but only succeeded in diverting it over his own head and into the goal. The Sporting Post tells us that this was partly because the keeper had come too far off his line, giving McFadyen the opportunity to chip the ball over him.

The home fans turned up the volume. Saints pushed forward again, buoyed by *"a continuous roar of support."* The defence pressed up to help the forward line and, inevitably, were caught out by a Thistle breakaway. In the 72nd minute, outside right Williamson ran on to a pass from Duffy to lob the ball deftly over Billy Taylor and put his side back in the lead.

Brian Doyle remembers the intensity of the home support that day. However, as Brian said, *"having clawed our way back into the match, it seemed like we were going to have it snatched away from us. However, we didn't have long to wait, because John Bell got our second equaliser only two minutes after Williamson's goal."*

The excitement, which had been at boiling point, now went off the scale as Saints pursued a winner. It came in the last ten minutes of regulation time. Here's the Sporting Post again… *"Saints got their noses in front for the first time nine minutes from the end. Wright beat two men before calmly shooting past Freebairn."*

In its summary, the Sporting Post celebrated the goalscoring efforts of both teams: *"What a sizzler of a cup-tie this turned out to be… Five goals in 16 minutes from the time Saints first scored gave the fans all the excitement they could ask for."*

Meanwhile, back at Parkhead, the Celtic players thought for a short while that they were through to the quarter finals. Gordon Small tells a (possibly apocryphal?) story that the Celtic fans were chairing John Hughes – the scorer of their game's winning goal – off the park on their shoulders when news came through that St Johnstone had won in the last ten minutes. Hughes was, reputedly, dumped on his backside by the disgruntled Celtic fans…

It's fair to say that one of the reasons why this was such a stupendously exciting game, with both sides' supporters undergoing an emotional roller-coaster, was that Thistle put just as much effort into trying to achieve victory as St Johnstone. The PA concluded that, *"It's only fair to say the result could have gone either way."*

Fortunately for Saints, it didn't, and they went on to the quarter finals, winning 4-3 on aggregate over two legs to a fine Motherwell side before losing 3-2 (aet) to Rangers, the eventual winners of the competition, in the semi-final.

Sadly, this cup run was the only highlight of a season which ended somewhat dismally, with Saints being relegated in the infamous, last-day-of-the-season match in which Dundee clinched the First Division Championship with a 3-0 win at Muirton. The excitement engendered by this early season cup run in no way made up for that traumatising defeat, however, Saints bounced straight back up again the following season, thus beginning a lengthy period in the top flight which reached its peak with Willie Ormond's superb team of the late 1960s and early 1970s – several of whose performances merit inclusion elsewhere in this book…

Saints team: Taylor; McFadyen and Lachlan; Little, Ferguson and McKinven; McVittie, Wright, Gardiner, Bell and Henderson.
Attendance: 9,767.

No. 13
The slickest bit of marksmanship in his scoring career …

Southern League Cup
St Johnstone 9, Albion Rovers 0
Muirton Park, Saturday 9th March, 1946

Six goal Willie M'Intosh, St Johnstone leader, in a merry dance in front of goal with M'Innes, Albion Rovers back.

Picture: The Courier (imagine trying to play in those boots!)

In our book on the 60 Greatest Saints, some people might have been surprised that Ally McCoist only featured on the bench in our all-time team. The main reason he didn't (other than Henry Hall), is because Willie McIntosh was almost certainly a better goal-scorer than Super Ally, not just for Saints but also in his brief war-time stint at Ibrox. Certainly, his goals-per-game was better for both clubs, and, to the best of our knowledge, Mr McCoist has never scored a competitive double hat-trick. For that's what Willie McIntosh did in an astounding rout of Albion Rovers in the final season of the Southern League Cup, a competition that began in 1940 during the Second World War and finished at the end of the 1945-46 season, with the Scottish League Cup then being introduced the following season.

The Southern League Cup was played for on a regional basis, with the A and B Divisions (effectively the First and Second Divisions) playing in a round robin of groups of four. In 1945-46, Saints were drawn with Airdrie, Albion Rovers and Dunfermline. The third game of the group was played at Muirton, with Albion Rovers the visitors. In January that year, Saints had beaten the Wee Rovers 3-0 at Perth and the previous October they had won 6-1 at Cliftonhill, so there would have been a reasonable degree of confidence going into the match.

That confidence was not misplaced. Under a heading, *"Saints Best Ever"* the Courier told of *"a personal triumph for Willie McIntosh, who had a double 'hat-trick'."* However, despite the size of victory, the Courier' reporter did not think the visitors had played too badly, commenting, *"Rovers, perhaps, did not deserve to be beaten by such a margin, but no disputing Saints' superiority."*

Strangely though, and perhaps reflecting the fact that the crowd had all very recently been through the war together, the Courier also reported that, *"Rovers' supporters were loud in their acclamation of McIntosh as Scotland's best leader at the moment."* We are not sure the current St Johnstone (or indeed any club's) support would be so generous in the wake of a nine-goal defeat…

Even more strangely, the Courier didn't even think McIntosh was Saints' best player on the day, telling its readers, *"In the matter of class and polish the best man on view at Muirton on Saturday was Alfie Boyd. In breaking-up tactics and in forward support Boyd's play is delightful to watch. Clean in a tackle and resourceful in recovery, his efforts are seldom wasted."*

And yes, just in case you've forgotten, this is the same game in which Willie McIntosh scored six goals…

To be fair, Alfie Boyd did score the first, after 19 minutes. The local Coatbridge paper, The Coatbridge Express, disagreed with that timing, noting that *"Boyd scored the first goal after twenty minutes, when he let loose a terrific drive which Mackie could not hope to save."*

Up to that point in the game, Albion Rovers were seemingly as good as Saints. Then the roof fell in for the visitors, as the PA recorded for us, *"But once pierced their defence was ripped to ribbons. Inside sixteen minutes St Johnstone rattled on five goals. McIntosh's three in eight minutes probably being the slickest bit of marksmanship in his scoring career."*

The PA's report also helps explain just how – and why – McIntosh was such a good striker. His ability to find space and be in the right place at the right time were memorably described thus, *"The centre-forward's genius for taking a chance from any angle was chiefly responsible for the glut of goals. Twice he was on the right spot to collect as the ball came off the crossbar – in the other cases he acted too quickly or too subtly for goalkeeper Mackie, who had the unhappy experience of being too late in covering up not once but several times."*

All this, despite playing – as the photo above shows - in heavy leather boots, weighing c. one kilogram (over 2lb) a pair, which in turn required players to seek the protection of enormous shin-guards.

Even after his stellar career in England, Willie McIntosh was – and is - not as well-known as he should be, largely because he would have been at his peak during the years of the Second World War. That cannot be said for the man who was his immediate opponent that afternoon. Here's the PA again…

"No one on the Rovers' side worked harder than Stein but he could not counter the needle-like thrusts of the Perth centre-forward." Yes, it was indeed the legendary Celtic manager who was put through the wringer that day, albeit he seems to have made a better fist of it than most of his colleagues.

Jock Stein was not the only one of Albion Rovers' side who suffered that afternoon.

The Coatbridge Express reported that this was *"one of the most humiliating defeats they have ever suffered. Except for the first few minutes of the first half and a period in the second half, St Johnstone were in complete control of the game and were ever striving to increase their lead.*

"While Rovers' players watched and waited for the ball coming their way, the homesters would move forward to meet the ball, carry it upfield and make scoring look ridiculously easy...

"Rovers' defenders made a poor attempt to mark their men, and the St Johnstone forwards, well fed by a dominant half-back line, could do practically as they pleased.

"McIntosh was in devastating form. He was irresistible on the ball as his double hat-trick proves."

Even though the final score was then described as a record for Saints in higher grade football (it is not the highest score in any competitive match, nor is it the only occasion on which Saints have won by a nine - or more - goal margin), it seems that they could easily have scored far more. For one thing, the PA said that Hird, the outside right, had to play with an injury for over an hour. In fact, the Coatbridge Express suggests it was even longer than that, reporting, *"For the greater part of the game St Johnstone had to play with virtually ten men. In the opening minutes Hird received an ankle injury, and although he returned to the field after attention he took little part in the game."*

To be fair, it wasn't just Saints who suffered in this way: Albion Rovers too had their injury problems. According to the Coatbridge Express, in the second half their new outside left, Willie McClure, who had only just joined the club the week before, *"received a leg injury which forced him to leave the field fifteen minutes before the end."*

Despite each side's injury woes, the PA commented that, *"if Saints had not been content to play on the soft pedal for long periods in the second half, the tally might well have run into double figures."*

For the record, Willie McIntosh's goals were as follows (all details from the PA).

(1) *"Two minutes later McIntosh seized a Boyd pass and netted from close range and* (2) *two minutes after that he surprised Mackie with an angled header from Hird's cross."*
3) *"in 29 minutes McIntosh raced through with a pass from Robbie to register his hat-trick and the half was 35 minutes old when..."*
4) *"he received a gift of his fourth, and Saints' fifth from Robbie, whose long-range shot hit the crossbar."*
5) *"Nine minutes from the end...Phillips put Cook in possession, the winger crossed accurately and McIntosh, with all the nonchalance of the practised performer, placed the ball into the corner of the net."*
6) *"With a minute to go Phillips whacked one against the crossbar and McIntosh was up and doing for the sixth and last time."*

The Coatbridge Express gives us more details of some of these goals. For example, McIntosh's fourth goal (Saints' fifth) came about when *"Robbie smacked a lovely ball against the crossbar and McIntosh, collecting the rebound, walked the ball into the net with Mackie lying (on the ground."* His final strike (Saints' ninth) came after not one but two shots had hit the crossbar.

Interspersed with McIntosh's goals, Robbie had headed the sixth some six minutes into the second half. The Coatbridge Express gives us some more detail on this, telling us it came after *"Stein was cautioned* (i.e. a yellow card today) *by the referee for a rough tackle on McIntosh. From the free kick which was awarded in respect of this foul, Robbie scored a sixth goal. His header struck the crossbar and rebounded off Mackie's upstretched hands into the net."*

The other goal – the eighth, came when Cook drove home, with the ball deflecting off a defender's head.

This goal-scoring frenzy was another of the most intensive in the club's top-flight history. With five goals scored in only 16 minutes, an average of one goal every three minutes 12 seconds, it is not quite as rapid as the four goals in 11 minutes against Leith Athletic in the Cup in 1950 (as described above), but neither can hold a candle to another match which we'll feature below.

We were fortunate to speak to Donnie McPhee, a mere 92 years' young in 2023, who recalled being at this match as a youngster. Donnie told us that before 1947 he did watch other teams and it wasn't until he returned to Perth after his National Service and started working in the Waverley Hotel that he really got the bug and started going to as many Saints' matches as he could, getting his first season ticket in 1952. Even though it is over three-quarters of a century ago, he remembers just what a great player McIntosh was, telling us, *"Willie was the star of that post-war team. I was fortunate not only to see his double hat-trick, but also Ian Rodger and John Brogan scoring five goals in one game, in 1955 and 1982 respectively."*

The other big name in that Saints' team was Sandy McLaren, although he was well past his best and his wartime service on the Russian convoys had clearly aged him and sadly contributed to his early death. Donnie remembers Sandy playing in the late 1940s and also that he was employed at RN Almondbank, where Donnie also worked in the 1950s and 60s, along with Sandy's son Garrow and a number of Saints' players of that era.

A few weeks after their humiliation at Perth, the final group game took place at Cliftonhill. Albion Rovers put in a much stronger performance and the match ended goalless. Despite their goal-blitz against the Wee Rovers, Saints didn't actually qualify out of their group. McIntosh who scored 42 goals in his 49 games for Saints, was snapped up by Preston, where he made his debut the same day as the legendary Tom Finney and subsequently went on to have an outstanding career in England, including playing at Blackpool with the other all-time great of that era, Stanley Matthews. He was indeed one of the greatest goalscorers in our club's history.

Saints team: McKay; Anderson and Johnstone; McGeachie, Blyth and Boyd; Hird, Robbie, McIntosh, Phillips and Cook.
Attendance: 6,000.

No. 12

He had time to compose himself and spear the most precise shot of his life

Scottish League Cup Semi-Final
St Johnstone 3, Hearts 0
Easter Road, Tuesday, 27th October 1998

The final countdown

Headline: Perthshire Advertiser

As in 1969, St Johnstone's progress to the semi-final of the League Cup had been flawless, with the team scoring freely while conceding none. Partly, this was due to the rock-solid defence that Paul Sturrock had assembled, but there were also two crucial additions made by him earlier in the season, with additional skill and firepower being added in the shapes of Miguel Simao and Nathan Lowndes. When Sturrock then left for Dundee United, Sandy Clark came in and one of his most immediate tasks was to see if he could build on the success in the earlier rounds and take his new team to the later stages of this competition.

There were far fewer rounds to negotiate in those days and a 3-0 win at home against Stranraer was followed by a 1-0 victory at Falkirk. The quarter final was a much tougher prospect, with Hibs being the visitors to Perth, but with Lowndes starting for the first time the Edinburgh side were sent homewards to lick their wounds after a highly impressive 4-0 drubbing. In addition to Saints, there were three other teams left now – Airdrie, Hearts and Rangers. While everyone else would have wanted to play First Division Airdrie, they, of course, got drawn against Rangers, leaving St Johnstone to tackle Hearts.

Hearts had won the Scottish Cup the previous season. By any reckoning, the Edinburgh side are a far bigger and wealthier club than St Johnstone; albeit arguably not so well managed as the Perth club at various times in the recent past.

At this particular juncture, it ought to be noted that St Johnstone were a better team than Hearts, as was amply demonstrated at the end of the season when the Jam Tarts finished in sixth place in the ten-team Premier League, on 42 points, while Saints were third with 57 points. Moreover, the two clubs had drawn 1-1 at Tynecastle a few weeks before the semi-final and Saints would not lose to Hearts in any of the four league matches that campaign – drawing three and winning one. Nonetheless, Hearts' history and tradition, plus the choice of an Edinburgh venue (even if it was the ground of their arch rivals) gave them a not insignificant advantage. This was reflected in the ratio of the opposing fans on the night: some 2,200 from Perth in a crowd of just over 12,000. However, the game was being shown live on the BBC that evening, which possibly accounted for the relatively low turnout.

The last time Saints had played Hearts in a League Cup semi-final at Easter Road was in 1962. On that occasion, the Jambos won 4-0. However, Saints were then in the Second Division while Hearts were in the First and as a result the PA's account of that match, whilst reporting that *"the Perth side were magnificent in defeat,"* also acknowledged that they *"were power-played out of* (the tournament) ... *by a superbly fit, clever Hearts team."*

In 1998, there was no obvious gap in fitness or in the 'cleverness' or otherwise of each team. Saints began the game well, with

Miguel Simao having the first chance in the ninth minute, but, as the Courier reported, *"Having outstripped Dave McPherson to reach a chipped pass from Dasovic, he then lifted the ball high over the bar as well as the advancing Giles Rousset."* This is slightly unfair because Miguel was bearing in on goal at an angle and at some pace, but nevertheless it set the scene for how Saints were going to approach the game.

This is another of those matches we can watch on YouTube and, allowing for the partiality of whoever posted it there, it's evident that Saints were by far the more dangerous team in the first half. That said, the PA wasn't entirely wrong when it noted that there was *"a rather turgid opening half hour."* After that, things looked up, for Saints at least. As the Courier recounted, *"The breakthrough came in the midst of a spell of sustained pressing by Saints. A neat 1-2 between O'Boyle and John O'Neil left the latter clean through on Rousset but having rounded the keeper O'Neil was thwarted by a great recovery from Rousset who got down to block his netbound effort for a corner.*

"From the flag kick, taken by Preston, Dasovic knocked the ball down for Alan Kernaghan to wheel and turn it goalward, only for Vincent Guerin to block on the line and Rousset to clutch the loose ball.

"With four minutes remaining, Saints struck a glorious first blow as another Preston corner was headed into the path of the un-marked Dasovic, who drilled the ball right foot (sic) *across Rousset and into the far corner from 16 yards."*

The Saints' fans were housed in the away end of Easter Road and unfortunately this goal was at the other end. That didn't stop everyone going nuts – and most of us just thinking, now let's get to half-time.

Given that there were only a few minutes till the break, that seemed a not unreasonable hope. However, with fourth official John Rowbotham signalling a further minute of playing time, Hearts' fan Allan Preston took it upon himself to deal a serious blow to his boyhood favourites before referee Willie Young did blow for the end of the first half. Here's the indefatigable Gordon Bannerman's lyrical description of the goal in the PA…

"Preston found himself unguarded 30 yards out, with Gary Bollan sweeping past his shoulder. No challenge was forthcoming and he had time to compose himself and spear the most precise shot of his life beyond the reach of an Eiffel Tower-like keeper. It ripped into the postage corner and but for the netting Her Majesty's Head would have landed in Leith Walk."

In contrast, Steve Bruce, the Courier's reporter, was somewhat reserved, although he too deployed the obvious philatelic metaphor in describing where the ball ended up…

"…Preston effectively put the tie beyond his former club planting the ball in Rousset's postage stamp corner from what, on the angle, was a distance of fully 30 yards."

For Jim Mackintosh, Biscuits' wonder-strike was a cause of celebration – but also some pain…

"My son, who was about 10 at the time, somehow jumped on my shoulder, literally straddling me with his legs, and bounced up and down with excitement. That shoulder still isn't right today…."

No matter who recounts it, it is one of the great St Johnstone goals. There is no doubt that the overused term 'wonder strike' is appropriate here and it sent the two teams into their dressing rooms with wildly differing responses from their respective sets of supporters. In the blue corner, all was sweetness and light, but in the three stands of the maroons there was considerable disquiet and grumbling.

Hearts made two half-time substitutions and although they strove mightily to get back into the match, other than a few scary moments, the St Johnstone defence held firm. Firm is perhaps too mild a term for Paul Kane's tackle on Guerin (*"a wild, two-footed lunge"* according to the PA) and he, like Alan Kernaghan, who committed robust challenges on Quitongo and Hamilton, might be considered lucky to have escaped a red card. Fortunately, in those days, referees (and Willie Young was a first-class exponent of this) ran the game sensibly, without having to be cross-examined by the spy-cameras of the VAR.

Despite Hearts pressure and their occasional chances, it was St Johnstone who looked more threatening on the break. Two efforts nearly brought a third goal: the first when, as the Courier described it, *"Paul Kane released George O'Boyle down the right only for David Weir to pip Simao to the Ulsterman's cut-back"* and the second when, *"Nathan Lowndes ... embarked on a terrific run, surviving challenges by Steve Fulton and Dave McPherson, but he couldn't supply the necessary finish."*

Lowndes did, however, have one last trick up his sleeve. As time ran out, and with the Saints' fans looking at their watches, Allan Preston sent Nathan free down the left in the 87th minute. The ball was recycled into the middle and Nick Dasovic played a precision pass into the box for Lowndes to run on to. He bore down towards the line before pulling the ball back just beyond the six-yard line for his fellow striker, George O'Boyle, to fire into the net.

We have no recollection if there was a man of the match award made that night, but if there had been it undoubtedly ought to have gone to Allan Preston. Not only was he involved in all three goals, his own strike is

still remembered as one of the most spectacular goals in St Johnstone's history. Here are Biscuits' own recollections of the match…

"Sandy Clark (the manager) was not long in at the club, and he took us to stay at a hotel in North Berwick the night before the game. Hearts had a team that had just won the Scottish Cup the season before, but we knew that we also had a great side, full of top pros who could run their own dressing room and we really believed in ourselves and our ability to get the job done.

"I remember that I took the corner for Nick Dasovic's goal and also my pass to Nathan for the move in which George scored, but overall it was just a brilliant night. There was a good crowd from Perth, filling the top tier and some of the lower section behind the goal and they gave us great backing.

"Yes, it was certainly the best goal I've ever scored – and the timing of it was almost equally important. To go in one nil at half time would have been good, but to go in two up, well, we just sat in the changing room and said 'we just need to keep a clean sheet and we're there.' As for the strike itself, it was one of those 'once in a blue moon ones.' I knew the moment I'd hit it that it was going in."

There is a famous story which Allan had recounted publicly several times, but which still bears re-telling for those who haven't heard it. After the game, the Saints' players were lapping up the hospitality in a well-known Edinburgh establishment. A young lady approached Biscuits and asked if there was anything she could do for him… *"Aye, there is,"* he said, *"you can switch the telly on and pass me the remote – my goal will be coming on soon – and after you've done that, can you get Roddy 20 fags?"*

After the match was over, the PA interviewed a number of the Saints' players, including John McQuillan, who revealed that he'd had a £10 bet with Allan Preston about which of them would score more goals that season. In the event, Biscuits did, but he can't remember if John ever paid up.

When O'Boyle scored, the Saints' fans, many of whom, naturally, had been pessimistically wondering when Hearts would score and get back in the match, now realised that we had done it. Jack Findlay told us that, *"We had three buses from the St Leonards Bar but most of us weren't travelling with any high hopes. However, it turned out to be an incredible night. Then came Biscuits' amazing goal but even then I kept thinking Hearts would come back. Then O'Boyle scored and we knew we'd done it. The sheer euphoria that washed over the fans as we headed back to the buses reflected the excitement of the game and the scale of the achievement. It was a marvellous night."*

For those Saints' fans watching on the telly, commentator Archie McPherson, in a classic case of stating the obvious, opined, *"That's it, St Johnstone are in the final, without the slightest doubt."*

And we were. Even the most pessimistic St Johnstone fan would not have expected Hearts to come back, and indeed they could not. The Hearts' fans may have outnumbered the St Johnstone support by nearly five to one at the start of the night, but in the final minutes the maroon-clad horde fled the scene, leaving far more blue-and-white fans than Edinburgh ones in the ground at the final whistle. Then it was time to head for the cars and buses for a very happy return to Perth and elsewhere, listening in to the radio as the commentators extolled the virtues of this excellent St Johnstone team. The PA summed it up well when they noted, *"There wasn't a failure in this St Johnstone team."* This was a team on the way up and although Rangers (and a hard-fought defeat) awaited them in the final, they had played an important part in putting St Johnstone another notch higher in the Scottish football firmament.

Saints team: Main, McQuillan, Preston, Dasovic, Kernaghan, O'Neil, O'Boyle, Kane, Bollan, Dods, Simao. Substitutes: McMahon (for Preston), Grant (for O'Boyle), Lowndes (for Simao). Attendance: 12,027.

No. 11

An emotionally charged evening laced with drama boundless courage and no little flair

UEFA Cup, First Round, Second Leg
St Johnstone 3, Monaco 3,
McDiarmid Park, Thursday, 30th September 1999

Headline: Perthshire Advertiser

Having (eventually) overcome VPS Vaasa of Finland in the Qualifying Round, Saints were given an entirely different level of challenge when the draw paired them with Monaco, the millionaires of the little principality that lies in southern France.

The quirks of the draw at that time meant that the players knew they were either going to be facing West Ham or Monaco. Danny Griffin, who played in both matches against the French League club, told us, that, *"in my opinion, the club would have preferred to go to London, but the players were all hoping for Monaco. When the draw was being made, we were all in the players' lounge and then when we found who we'd got it was 'wow, we're playing Monaco.' Everyone was on a high because at time getting Monaco was a really big deal. They were, rightly, seen as one of the biggest European teams, spending big cash on some great players, but in all our minds there was always the thought that we might have a chance to cause an upset what would put Saints on the world map."*

"At that time, Monaco were a team chock-full of expensively purchased talent, including the likes of World-Cup winner

Fabian Barthez and well as other fabulous players in the shape of Trezeguet, the young Riise, Simone, Prso, Giuly and Gallardo – amongst others.

With the first leg away in Monaco, Saints were reckoned to be on a hiding to nothing, but in the event, they performed very creditably, keeping the match scoreless at half-time before going under in the second half. Alan Main's performance in that game was one of the greatest by a St Johnstone goalkeeper before or since. Described in the PA by Gordon Bannerman as *"a one-man resistance campaign,"* he had kept Monaco's star-studded forward line at bay until the 69th minute before being beaten twice more, in the 72nd and, cruelly, the 90th minute.

The Daily Record's preview of the match consisted of an interview with Claude Puel, the Monaco manager, in which, after noting that his side's performance in the second half of the first leg *"was near our best,"* he commented on the differing styles of the two teams, saying *"It's hard to situate them in Europe because they don't play the same type of game. They are more direct,"* adding, *"You only need to look at last*

252

season's table in Scotland to see they are not far behind Celtic and even Rangers." Moreover, he "insisted the biggest problem his squad of millionaires face at McDiarmid Park tonight is taking St Johnstone seriously," before concluding that, "We must be very combative because we know the Scots' mentality – they will come at us from the start."

If the millionaires had any doubts that Saints would come at them from the very start they were soon dispelled. Within the first minute, Miguel Simao had scampered down the right and cut the ball back for Nathan Lowndes, whose first shot was saved by Barthez but when the ball came back to the Saints' striker, with the goal at his mercy he fired over the bar.

However, as the Courier reported, "It mattered little for barely had the sighs subsided than Saints took the lead courtesy of a bizarre own goal. This time John O'Neil was the man who found a space in the Monaco defence, finding Simao 10 yards out. The Portuguese made a hash of his shot but it struck Phillippe Leonard on the back and sneaked in at the back post."

Hash or not, at this point Saints were deservedly in the lead. Unfortunately, as tends to happen against high quality teams, Monaco struck back almost immediately, through Dado Prso. It was the first goal St Johnstone had conceded at home in European football and, it must be said, it was a thing of beauty, even if we didn't think that at the time. Here's the PA's description …

"And what a strike it was as Saints' proud record was shattered.

"The Frenchman took on Alan Kernaghan at the angle of the box, made space and, with the briefest of targets, thrashed home an unstoppable shot high to the left of astonished keeper Alan Main."

Many years later, Alan Kernaghan told us that this incident was the main thing he remembered about the match.

While Main might have been helpless to prevent Prso's goal, he was still sufficiently on his toes to turn away a long-range, netbound effort from John Riise a few minutes later. However, in the 24th minute, Simone crossed into the St Johnstone box. Alan Main, for once, hesitated, unsure of whether to come for the cross or stay on his line. In the event, he caused confusion, with Danny Griffin then left to try to cover two attackers. Unsurprisingly, neither Saints' player got the ball, but John Arne Riise, free at the back post, did, angling it into the net with relative ease.

The Daily Record's take on the game was, sadly, patronisingly true to type. The back page of the paper majored on an Old Firm story, with a smaller piece telling readers that both Saints and Kilmarnock had been knocked out of Europe. The match report itself (situated alongside their 'hotline' column for fans – which was solely about the Old Firm) claimed that the second half was "no more than a training exercise for Monaco," before going on to say that while Saints pressed hard for a winner, "Monaco had still to break sweat." It is hard to believe that if this had been either Celtic or Rangers drawing 3-3 with the millionaires of Monaco that the Record would have taken a similar line. For those who were at the match, including both the authors of this book, Monaco did have to break sweat from the first minute to the last, while Saints' performance against a team that outmuscled them financially by a massive margin was one of their most dogged and determined in the club's history.

Nick Dasovic thinks that Monaco certainly got a fright. He told us, "What a game that was. We could have been two or three up in the first 15 minutes. Their team was full of World Cup stars but even though they might have thought the tie was over after the first leg, both teams tried to play football. Scoring against Barthez was a highlight for me personally, but afterwards there was a bitter-sweet atmosphere in our locker room. Some of the players had exchanged jerseys with the French lads: Nathan Lowndes had Marco Simone's shirt and we were amazed when he came into our dressing room and asked Nathan to sign his shirt.

"They were top players, as good as I'd played against, but it never fazed me because I'd played against some of the very best for Canada. It was, for me, 'let's see how you deal with the big boys' And the good thing is that when you come off the pitch and get to know them, they are just ordinary, like you or me."

Danny Griffin, agreed with Nick and recalled that Monaco had to work hard to get the result. Although they won 3-0 in Monaco, that result was, Danny said, "a bit harsh. We played terrifically well that night. It was Alan Main's best game for the club – he was unbelievable - and Miguel missed three one-on-ones with Barthez."

The fans who travelled to Monaco had had a ball and their ironic rendition of "In your Monaco slums" is still remembered with laughter today. However, despite the defeat, Danny said, "We gave them a fright over there, but we still knew it would be tough at McDiarmid. A lot of people had, I think, written us off, but when you think about how we played over there, we were prepared to do whatever we could to try to win at home. No matter what, we knew the fans would turn out in Perth."

"When we were preparing for the game at McDiarmid, we knew they were going to make changes, but although they did, they still were able to bring in other world class players. Things didn't change for us: we still had a game plan and wanted to go and show them what sort of a team we were. The boys rolled up their sleeves and we caught them off guard and gave them a wee dunt in the first minute.

"I think they were probably thinking the game was over. That's football; players switch off, even when the manager says not to. But knowing we had lost the first game the pressure was off to some extent. I remember the pitch was in good condition and it was an end-to-end game, like a boxing match: we'd attack, they'd attack, we'd score, they'd score.

"They had great players, I had played against players at that level in international games, but for many of the others it was a new experience. What made the difference was our teamwork, but we could play as well and I think the recognition we received afterwards for our performance was well deserved."

Danny was right about the fans' appreciation of the efforts of the Saints' team that night. The players were cheered to the echo as they left the field. We, and they, knew they had given their all and while they fell short, it had been a hugely enjoyable adventure for the fans and the club at large. It should be remembered that this was only St Johnstone's second season in European competition and in the minds of many, if not probably most, of the fans it was unlikely that we would have many, if any, more. How wrong we were…

Saints team: Main, McQuillan, Bollan, Dasovic, Griffin, Kernaghan, Simao, O'Neil, Lowndes, O'Halloran, Kane. Substitutes: Ferguson, O'Boyle (for Lowndes), McAnespie (for Kane), Grant (for O'Halloran), Thomas, McCluskey and McBride.
Attendance: 7,706.

He had sneaked into Hampden and hidden in the men's toilets

The Scottish League Cup Final
St Johnstone 1, Livingston 0,
Hampden Park, Sunday, 28th February 2021

Saints win the League Cup for the first time: The Courier

At the time of writing, this match – and the same season's Scottish Cup final - is still fresh in the memories of all Saints' fans. Both games are, of course, covered in depth in Ed Hodge's book on the Cup Double season. As with the 2014 final, finding fresh insights and information is therefore difficult, however, in keeping with the general theme of this book, we can look to the press coverage of these two amazing games to see what the media thought and wrote about what is, without a shadow of doubt, the greatest season in St Johnstone's history.

The background to this final was, of course, the Covid-19 pandemic that totally disrupted everyone's life during 2020-22. Scottish football stopped for a short period at the end of the 2019-20 season, before eventually resuming behind closed-doors on 1st August 2020. For the players, this meant a strenuous regime of semi-isolation and training, interspersed with competitive matches in soulless stadia where a handful of club officials were present but no-one else was allowed anywhere near the action.

For the fans (of both clubs), the fact of having got through to the BetFred League Cup final was somewhat tempered by the continuing public health emergency which meant no-one, other than the players, match officials and the smallest possible number of club officials, could attend the game. Instead, we were forced to sit in front of our televisions, in many cases surrounded by friends, family and beer cans - and cheer, curse and cajole our un-hearing heroes as they strove to win the Cup in the vast emptiness of Scotland's national stadium, Hampden Park.

The game itself was, it's fair to say, not a classic, not that anyone in St Johnstone colours cared overmuch. The prevailing mood was summed up by Matt Gallagher's report in the PA. It began by planting the author's colours firmly on the page…

"Legends. Forever Legends. St Johnstone are the 2021 Scottish League Cup champions. The trophy sits proudly in the Perth cabinet for the first time in its history."

He went on, *"Manager Callum Davidson, in his first season, will never be forgotten. He didn't care how this game of football was won."*

The way in which it was won is, of course, well known, but this is how the PA recorded it – interestingly, setting a different time for the goal to the one that was finally agreed, *"With 31 minutes on the clock, Rooney wrestled in front of his man to nod Conway's corner into the bottom corner.*

"He wheeled away in celebration, joined by jubilant mates. Those on the bench and sitting in the stand punched the air in delight."

Rooney might have made it two before half-time. With the gallus swagger that characterises his approach to football, he advanced on goal from midway inside their half and unleashed a piledriver from around 35 yards that had McCrorie in the Livy goal scrambling to grasp it.

Early in the second half, Saints had another chance to double their lead when Ali McCann cut the ball back for Wotherspoon, who steered the ball towards the net, only to see McCrorie block his shot, with Chris Kane *"only inches from turning in the rebound."*

As in 2014, much of the strength of this St Johnstone team lay in defence, where the three-man enterprise of Kerr, Gordon and McCart formed a tough layer of protection that, when it was breached, had the final security of Zander Clark's immense shot-stopping skills. That said, other than a few instances, notably early in the game when Clark, at full stretch, turned away a Josh Mullin strike, and then as the game moved into its later stages as Livingston, naturally, threw themselves forward, Saints had a relatively comfortable afternoon.

The whole team got over the line, but there were mixed emotions for some in the Perth squad. Murray Davidson, in particular, who had missed out on the 2014 triumph through injury, was again side-lined due to a calf strain. On the other hand, Liam Craig, who had missed out in 2014 because, having left McDiarmid in 2013, he was being relegated with Hibernian, was able to come in for Murray and add all his experience and ability to help guide more youthful colleagues through the match.

However, the real man of the match was, undoubtedly, the phenomenon that is Shaun Rooney. His goal that day was his third in four games and the previous three were the principal reason that Livy's manager, David Martindale, had re-arranged his team to put Marvin Bartley into a man-marking role on Rooney.

As the Daily Record said, *"He went from strength to strength. Had his long-ranger found the net before the break it would have been some strike. The Bellshill Cafu indeed."*

The Courier agreed with the Record's assessment, writing, *"Saints' man of the match – again. His pace, strength and directness was* (sic) *on display from the start, despite the close attentions of Marvin Bartley. Rooney outfought the man tasked with shutting him down and outmuscled Jon Guthrie to notch the winner."*

Interviewed after the game by Eric Nicolson for The Courier, Callum

Davidson presciently noted that this victory might be *"the start of something special, rather than the end ... hopefully we can now hold on to the players we have and build on it. We have some huge games coming up and we can't take our eye off the ball."*

We suspect that not even in his wildest dreams would Callum have been thinking that Saints would go on to complete a Cup double in the next few months, but at the time he also realised that, amidst the players' excitement, the fans were missing out on what should have been one of the best days of their lives. He told The Courier, *"It's disappointing the supporters from Perth are not here to enjoy the occasion and make it even more special, but it means just as much to me just now and to my family and friends and everyone involved downstairs."*

When we spoke to Callum in 2023, he said that in his view the League Cup semi-final against Hibs was a better match than the final (it was!), but for him the player who made the big difference in the final against Livingston was Shaun Rooney.

"There had been pressure for us to play with two strikers, but I resisted this. That said, it took us a little time to work out their strategy of putting Bartley on Rooney. As well as Shaun, Kano was brilliant and Conway was at his peak at that time for us. We believed in what we were doing and the course of the game proved we were right.

"Naturally, we had an enormous pride in having made history, but Covid was a massive issue – both before and after the match, although it is possible that a few players and a club official or two (not, we stress, including Callum himself) might have inadvertently broken the government regulations on close proximity to others after the match..."

Of course, winning the final didn't just mean glory, but also a substantial financial boost to the coffers, with £300,000 in prize money from sponsors BetFred coming Saints' way as a result of their success in the final. And of course, that wasn't the only source of much needed, additional revenue. In an enterprising move, the club produced 'virtual' tickets for the fans, so even if we couldn't be there then there was (as shown here) a unique memento of the occasion, while soon after the final whistle, 'League Cup Winners' T-shirts and other commemorative items were available on the club's website.

There were, of course, a tiny number of fans who did make it to Hampden, because their work took them there. One of those lucky few was Saints' TV commentator, Steven Watt...

"When football restarted behind closed-doors, there was almost a pre-season feel to it. I remember my first exposure to the empty stadiums: it wasn't like a normal football experience and it seemed very alien to the little Saints' TV crew. We'd been at Hampden for the semi-final, but on the day of the final I felt like we were in a theatre with an empty stage and no audience.

"As a result, I actually did more preparation than I would normally do. In particular, I picked up quite a lot from Rory Hamilton, the lead commentator for Premier Sports, who were broadcasting the League Cup.

Steven Watt's notes on what to say if Saints lost the League Cup final against Livington

Rory was very helpful and gave me good advice, but when we turned up for the Hibs semi-final I was surprised to hear him rehearsing his commentary before the match started and I then twigged that all that good stuff he rattled out at the end of games was scripted.

"I remember sitting at the breakfast bar in our house, writing up my notes and my wife came in and asked what I was doing. She was surprised when I said I was prepping for the game. While I always do some work before a commentary, this was far above my normal. I spent more time than usual learning about the Livy players. It's fair to say that I made good use of Wikipedia. Unfortunately, when push came to shove, I hardly referred to it during the commentary!

However, I did think about what I'd say if we won the Cup. What I did was to try and put myself in the shoes of all the supporters, who would, of course, have given their eye teeth to have been there, and talk up the magnitude of the victory while also trying to stay humble and curtail my own excitement. I also wrote a page of what I'd say if we failed. When I prepared both the scripts in the week leading up to the game, I noticed that my handwriting was really neat compared to normal – like it was for an exam."

Steven has kept his commentary notes from the final and he kindly let us have a copy of

what he was going to say if we had lost, as shown above.

In the event, he didn't have to worry about what to say if Livingston won. Instead, along with the rest of the Saints' media team and their guest pundit, he had a day that, as he said, every other fan would have happily given several limbs to experience in person…

"When we arrived the day of the final, we were welcomed by Louis Irons of the SFA's media team. I knew him because he does Motherwell TV, but until that day I didn't know he is the former Saints' player Davie Irons' son.

"We were situated right beside the Livy TV guys: we could hear what each other was saying. All the different clubs' TV teams know each other and the Livy boys are fine lads and we always got on well with them."

Usually, a former player or well-known Saints' fan provided the colour and punditry to support Steven. However, for the final, he was supported by perhaps the best-known Saints' fan of the modern media age, Stuart Cosgrove. Stuart has been a Saints' fan almost since the egg, and is a very public cheerleader for our club and the fans. Like any Saints' fan would have been in the circumstances, he was really looking forward to the match. Stuart's excitement was contagious, as Steven Watt recalls…

"We'd just exchanged the niceties with the Livy guys, then Stuart turned up and he was wired with excitement. He was the loudest in the crowd by some distance. Even young Sam Porter, the Saints' media rep, was taken aback...

"When the Livy TV boys saw we had Stuart Cosgrove, with us it was like two opposition teams in the tunnel before the game, eyeing up their opponents. During commentary his excitement occasionally took over and he was doing the commentary as well as the punditry, until I gently pointed out that he was doing me out of a job!

"After the semi-final with Hibs, I had a weird air of confidence. In the final with Livy, when we scored it had a feeling of inevitability. Saints seemed to master the big stage better than Livy, who got their tactics wrong, especially trying to get Marvin Bartley to mark Shaun Rooney. Speaking to the Livy commentators afterwards, they were resigned, with no sour grapes on show. 'You deserved it,' was their final verdict."

For Stuart Cosgrove, the day was everything he hoped it would be – and more. He told us, *"Having disposed of Hibernian in the semi-finals, St Johnstone went to the delayed final against Livingston with high hopes.*

"What was significant about the Saints team on the day was that the spine of the side had graduated from the club's academy system. Goalkeeper Zander Clark, captain Jason Kerr, midfield dynamo Ali McCann and striker Chris Kane all started the match, with Stevie May – a winner in 2014 - on the bench. Furthermore, two Perth born players were also in the starting eleven: Liam Gordon and the peerless David Wotherspoon, who, like May, had starred in our previous cup final victory.

"Although David Martindale's Livingston had a reputation as a stuffy and dogged side, there was nothing about them that proved either daunting or insurmountable. Tricky but beatable summed it up.

"My friend, the St Johnstone director Stan Harris, had arranged for me to be a guest commentator on Saints TV. The national stadium was like a ghost town and even the routes to the normally bustling ground were deathly silent.

"To access the media platform, I had to walk through countless empty checkpoints to the North Stand, passing the other camera crews dotted along the way. Ally McCoist was there on co-commentator duty and shouted his best wishes, as did another former Saints' player, James McFadden, at the BBC production unit.

"I have since fanned the myth that I was the only Saints fan in the stadium but that was not actually true: The Saints TV crew numbered four and we excitedly began to broadcast in the knowledge that another trophy was – potentially - there for the taking. When Shaun Rooney headed what proved to be the winning goal in the 32nd minute, I took off, screamed down the microphone and jumped back on to the concourse of the North Stand. There, in the corner of my eye, I saw a lad dancing behind me. He was dressed in full dungarees but was too joyful to be anything but a Saints fan. I found out later he had sneaked into Hampden in a lorry delivering advertising hoardings and hidden in the men's toilets, undiscovered for three hours.

"When the trophy was presented, I managed to get down to the pitch-side and gathered up the blue and white confetti that had been fired up above the victorious Saints. I keep them in a wee jar at home, a souvenir of another cup victory."

Stuart might not have fancied Livingston's chances, but the players were well aware of the challenge that lay ahead. Jason Kerr told us, *"Livy are always tough and very* well-drilled. No-one in Scotland, not even the Old Firm, enjoys playing against them.

"It didn't help that there were no fans in the stadium. In some ways, not having the pressure of fans watching meant the game had more of a pre-season feel, except that it was anything but that. It was such a big event in our lives and the club's history so naturally it would have been much better if the supporters could have been there. By this time, we had got used to the fact that the absence of fans meant we could hear what the manager was shouting. Even so, most of the time you're that focused, so you just get on and it can be hard to take in what's being said from the touchline.

"It took a bit of time for us to adjust to Marvin Bartley matching up against Shaun, but as the game went on it was clear that that wasn't really Marvin's position and Shaun was too much for him.

"We knew if we went one up we were hard to beat, so when Shaun scored we took a lot of confidence from the goal.

As for the goal-scoring hero, he remembers that Marvin Bartley did have some success initially in his man-marking role, *"but as the game went on, I knew I could keep on going whereas he was older and couldn't keep up with me... Then came that corner in the first half and we scored.*

"Macca used to organise our corner routines for when we were attacking. I was usually on the front post, with Jason at the back stick. Craig Conway put a great ball across and I just got my head on it."

There was a bit more to it than that. Watching the goal back on YouTube, it's clear just how strong Rooney is, as he holds off Livy's Guthrie and bullets a really strong header in off the post.

In midfield, Ali McCann added to his growing reputation with another sound performance, against, as he noted, doughty opponents, telling us: *"Livy are brilliant at what they do; they are so well organised and drilled. However, we were equally well set-up and although it was what I'd call a tough, standard-sort of game against them, we knew that if we went one up our defence, who had been brilliant all season, would get us over the line."*

Shaun Rooney's goal was the first of a double-header, if you'll pardon the pun, to be repeated within a few months in the Scottish Cup. But on this day, it was the difference between the teams. Thereafter, the resolute and organised performance from his team-mates was enough. The final whistle sounded and, for the first time in our history, St Johnstone had won the Scottish League Cup.

There was one thing remaining to be done: the players had to pick up the medals and the captain had to lift the trophy. Jason Kerr recalled the moment for us: *"In that instant, I am thinking, 'I'm the captain, I've got to go and pick up this trophy. I was so happy, so caught up in the moment, but it didn't really hit me until a few months later when I realised the significance of what I and the team had achieved. Not many captains get to lift a major trophy..."*

After having finished his Saints' TV duties and his wholesale plundering of souvenirs, Steven Watt had a Zoom call with his mates in Auchterarder: *"It was all getting quite boozy, so I sent a message to Zander Clark asking if he'd like to join us. Zander is a great guy, very friendly, and he came on to the call, sitting there, still in his playing kit and with his medal round his neck. We had about half an hour of really good craic with him."*

Zander remembers this well...

"In the aftermath of the final, what with Covid, there wasn't much that could be

done in the way of extended celebrations. This was partly because we had a re-arranged game with Hamilton coming up in a few days, but I still managed to join their Zoom session, sitting downstairs in my house with a crate of beer, somewhat the worse for wear. I think my fiancée had gone up to her bed, but I really enjoyed being with the fans for that moment."

Zander also pointed out something else unusual about the post-match celebrations…

"Normally, when a team goes up to collect a Cup, each player lifts it high up to show it to the fans. The lads all started to do this, but as there were no fans there, once we got to the fourth of fifth person, we were, like, what are we doing this for? – it was a strange atmosphere."

Like Stuart Cosgrove, Steven Watt also has a jar of confetti, which he keeps in his garage. He collected a few other unusual mementos of the match, although inadvertently this got him into a spot of trouble…

"We were told we could keep some of the marketing paraphernalia, so I went around ripping down any banners I could find. I also took the dugout sign, but I tore the whole thing off the wall and got a row from the Hampden management team: apparently, I was just supposed to take the laminate, not the whole thing!"

While all this was going on, Saints fans the length and breadth of the country (and further-flung Perth exiles) were celebrating in their own way. In Glasgow, Colin McCredie, like the rest of the country, was stuck in his house, watching the game on the telly…

"Like everyone else, I'd paid for the Premier Sports package to watch our progress to the final. On the day, I had a

Zoom call with some mates and we all watched it 'virtually' together - it was the nearest we could get to being in a crowd, but still not the same, although of course we were able to have a beer while watching it.

A friend who is also a Saints' fan and who lives round the corner from me came round to my house and we had a glass of fizz in the front garden – socially distanced of course!"

Back in Perth, Maggie Anderson had been watching on the TV with her husband. She is perhaps unique amongst Saints' fans because her very first memory of anything in her life is about St Johnstone. More specifically, it was eating the cinders on the terraces at Muirton when she was only three years old. Her mum thought her dad was simply taking her for a long walk on Saturday afternoons, but instead he would take her into Muirton and she'd happily sit there snacking away. She is such a die-hard fan that once, when going to Edinburgh to see Saints at Hibs, she fell in Leith Walk and refused all offers of an ambulance, telling those who were trying to help that there was no way she was going to miss the game. She then hobbled to Easter Road, climbed up to her seat in the second back row, where she had to stand for the entire game because the FCU were in front of her, and "by the time I got home I couldn't actually walk…"

As for the League Cup final, "I was so upset we couldn't be there, I actually cried. After the game, my husband, Bob, and I were having a glass of champagne and I just found myself in tears."

Saints team: Clark, Rooney, Kerr, Gordon, McCart, Booth, McCann, Craig, Conway, Kane, Wotherspoon.
Substitutes: May (for Conway), Parish, Brown, Tanser, Bryson, Gilmour, Melamed, O'Halloran.
Attendance: N/A due to Covid regulations.

Europa League, Third Qualifying Round
Galatasaray 1, St Johnstone 1
Istanbul Basakshehir Fatih Terim Stadium, Istanbul, Thursday, 5th August 2021

54 SPORT FOOTBALL

THE COURIER & ADVERTISER
Friday, August 6, 2021

Saints hog the limelight again after denying Turkish giants

Headline: The Courier

Saints have played against some big names in European competitions. Monaco, Hamburg, Rosenborg, Lucerne all had an impressive track record of success when we came up against them, and only Monaco managed to subdue us. So when we were drawn against Galatasaray – the most successful team in Turkey and known as the 'Conqueror of Europe' by their fans (they won the UEFA Cup and Super Cup in 1999–2000) – not many people gave us a chance. Especially when we were drawn away in the first leg of the tie...

Galatasaray's Nef Stadium is famous for the "Welcome to Hell" banners sported by their fans and the fact that the local Turkish fans in the 52,000 capacity ground set a record for the loudest crowd roar at a sports stadium when, on 18th March 2011 a peak level of 140.76 decibels (dbA) was recorded. To put that in context, most rock concerts are about 120 dbA, while even the

real heavy-rock monsters – the likes of AC/DC, Motorhead and Led Zeppelin - aren't in the same league, having only been clocked at a paltry 130 dbA.

Unfortunately, the Nef was out of commission for Saints' visit and the game was played at a smaller ground in Istanbul. Due to restrictions caused by the Covid pandemic, only around 6,000 were allowed in to this game. Spoony recalled that despite the small crowd, the noise and the atmosphere were incredible, telling us, *"The shouting and especially the whistling were so loud that you couldn't hear yourself speak at times."* It's just as well they weren't at the Nef Stadium…

Sadly, almost none of the fans in the ground were from Perth. However, the BBC, reflecting Saints' high status in Scottish football at this time, did broadcast the entire game live.

This was the background for what was (at time of writing), Saints' penultimate European adventure. Having just enjoyed the most successful season in the club's history in 2020-21, St Johnstone still had almost all the key players who had been the driving force when they became only the fourth team in Scotland to win the Cup Double. That said, and despite the fact that Galatasaray were not quite the force that they once were, the expectation was that, as Saints' manager Callum Davidson said after the match, *"If you'd asked people beforehand what they thought would happen here most would say Galatasaray will score four or five."*

That they didn't, was down to Davidson's Saints who continued to show the team spirit, drive and commitment, allied to some moments of genuine class from the likes of David Wotherspoon and the burgeoning talent of Ali McCann. It was also a product of the care and attention put in pre-match by the management, as Callum Davidson told us…

"Galatasaray was one of my favourite games. Not only are they a big club in Europe, they had a very different style from us. Tommy and I loved Europe as it gave us a chance to compete tactically in a very different way from the Scottish game. I'm not normally one for keeping mementos, but I took a photo of the scoreboard at 1-1. The second leg was a great game too. Over the two matches we had 180 minutes toe-to-toe with a huge club and often more than matched them".

Jason Kerr remembers that everyone was excited when the draw was made. Like David Wotherspoon, he also remembered the noise, telling us, *"Although I wanted to play against the best, I also wanted to qualify for the next round. We were full of confidence: we had the same team that had won both Cups and we were going hopefully to cause a shock. Then, when we arrived at the stadium, we went out to see the pitch. Normally at that time, there's hardly anyone in the ground, but there were a couple of hundred Galatasaray fans already there and they all started whistling when we appeared. The noise was incredible: it was like there were thousands rather than hundreds."*

The game began with the home side firmly on the front foot, as if Galatasaray intended to put as much clear water between them and their visitors as soon as possible. As the Courier noted, *"It was straight for the jugular.*

"Attacking down their left flank was a clear early strategy and twice it should have produced an early opening goal.

"Quite how Mostafa Mohamed managed to miss from seven yards with not a soul near him is a mystery for a striker of his quality."

For those watching at home, or listening on the radio, the early minutes were stressful. Mostafa's close-in attempt was skied over the bar in the third minute and then five minutes later Kerem Atkürkoglu hit the post and (as the Courier reported) when the ball pinged back off the woodwork Zander Clark *"made a magnificent reflex save to deny Mosatafa from the rebound and wasn't to know a flag was going to be raised for offside."*

Slowly, Saints got a foot in the match. Matthew Gallagher's PA report told of a Murray Davidson shot that *"was sweet but … not wide enough to evade the grasp of an outstretched Muslera,"* before, *"an even better opportunity for the men in blue arrived just shy of the half-hour mark, carved out by tenacious and direct running from star man Ali McCann.*

"He breezed beyond a couple of challenges before slipping the ball to David Wotherspoon. Everyone knew what was coming next. Everyone bar the Galatasaray rearguard.

"The former Perth High School student chopped inside on his right foot and suddenly the goal opened up."

"The visiting bench rose to their feet but the strike was weak and was scooped up by Muslera."

As Tommy Wright said to us, with such talent on the ball, if Spoony finished all these chances he would have departed St Johnstone for a bigger club long ago, although that does nothing to diminish the phenomenal contribution he has made over the last decade or so at Perth.

A key factor in the game was the temperature, which was approaching a sweltering 30C. In such heat, most people head for the beach or the bar, but the St Johnstone players metaphorically rolled their sleeves up and ground on. Jason Kerr recalled that it was really hard to play in that temperature, especially at the start of the game and given that the Turkish players were far more used to the heat than the Saints' team. However, *"we were so well drilled we got through the opening phase but we found it hard and I'll admit we rode our luck a bit."*

Half-time came and the game was still scoreless. Twelve minutes into the second half and we had one of the moments that St Johnstone fans will remember forever. The PA described what happened next…

"A short back pass had Muslera scrambling under pressure from Kane. The pressure was too much and he pulled the hard-working striker to the floor. Penalty and a red card … Captain Kerr took full responsibility and, while his spot kick was not the cleanest of hits, it bounced into the bottom corner. Dreamland."

The Courier was less than sympathetic to the Turkish keeper: *"Muslera was given a tricky and underhit back pass to deal with but nothing he won't have seen a thousand*

times or more before. That a goalie with more than 100 caps for his country proceeded to kneel down, take the ball clumsily on his thigh and then drag Chris Kane down when it got away from him was a series of chaotic errors.

"He was sent off and it took an eternity (about three minutes) for the replacement, Berk Balaban, to get between the posts and for the Swiss referee to let Kerr take his spot-kick…The captain didn't make the cleanest connection but it was low, hard and a goal."

Jason's own recollection is that the press were right, telling us, *"I'd said to the gaffer before the game that I'd take any penalties. Ali McCann had taken the last one at Ross County and missed. When Kano won the penalty, he was all for taking it, but I just ran up and took the ball. It's fair to say I didn't connect as well as I might have, but at the time I actually thought I'd hit it well. It went into the net, which was what mattered, but when I watched it back, I could see that I'd actually hit the ball into the ground. That might even have helped me score, but I certainly didn't mean to do it. It was only the second penalty I'd taken: the first, against Rangers in the quarter final of the Scottish Cup, was much better!"*

Zander Clark recalled that there was a lot of pressure on Jason: *"it was similar to the situation Ali McCann found himself in at Ibrox in the Scottish Cup quarter final. The Turkish players were in his ear as he went up to take the kick. As a goalkeeper, I know that it's often the mis-hits that go in…and fortunately it went in!"*

Saints going one up away to Galatasaray was one of those 'pinch-me' moments. Like the famous time when Raith Rovers were one up away to Bayern Munich, someone (Jim Mackintosh) managed to get a shot of the scoreboard, taking a quick photo on his mobile phone while it flashed up in front of him on his TV screen.

Photo: Jim McIntosh/Bob Murison

Sadly, the joy loudly expressed in homes across Perth and beyond was short-lived. Barely two minutes later, Galatasaray had equalised. On-loan full back Reece Devine, from Manchester United, was caught out by a swift break down the right. In two minds about whether to cut out a pass or fall back, he fell between these two stools, and Galatasaray's Boey drilled the ball past Zander Clark.

For the remaining minutes, Saints played it mostly safe, looking to secure a draw with which to give themselves a chance in the return leg, but despite being down to ten men, the Turks continued to prove a threat, with Clark making a crucial save from Christian Luyindama. At the other end, Saints had one more (difficult) chance, as described by The Courier, *"Scrambled decision-making by Galatasaray keepers was contagious and Balaban inexplicably came far too far out of his box to contest a*

ball with Stevie May. He was in no man's land when the substitute Saint curled a shot goalwards from a narrow angle but there was a man on the line to clear."

Liam Craig says this was, *"A game I always talk about, one of my favourites. As one of the older players in the squad, I was better able to remember how good a side Galatasaray were in the 1990s and their great performances in the Champions League.*

"When Jason scored, I looked at the scoreboard to see Saints leading one of the giants of European football, even if it was only for a few minutes. It was the whole performance that was so good, especially given the heat that night. I think it was the night that many people realised just how good Ali McCann was – he was sensational against a team that was full of internationalists. And although we

265

ultimately went out, it was great that the fans got to see just how good Galatasaray were when we played them at Perth."

Jason agreed with Liam's assessment of his young colleague, saying to us, "*He was amazing, reading the game so well and so strong with it - physically matching up to the Galatasaray players. He was the same in the home leg - unbelievably good."*

As for Ali McCann himself, he told us that this was up there with his favourite matches for the club: "*On a personal level, it is one of the best I've played. At that point, I had had a few experiences with Northern Ireland of going to play abroad, but to go with your club team-mates was just great. Everything about it – the flight, getting to the hotel, going into the ground and walking on to the pitch to be met by hostile booing from the Turkish fans – was absolutely brilliant.*

"*We should have won. Their players were very good – probably about the same standard as the Old Firm – but even though it ended in a draw I really enjoyed it and we came away knowing we still had a chance to go through."*

To finish his report in the PA, Matt Gallagher wrote, "*If it was possible, Perth has become even prouder of this football club."*

Indeed we had. The return leg, as we know, did not have the happy ending we all wanted (although it too was a very exciting game), but Saints performed admirably, never giving up as they lost 4-2 on the night. The European dream was nearly over, or at least the Europa League element. Having lost to Galatasaray, Saints then went into the qualifying rounds for the Europa Conference League, where they sadly lost to LASK of Austria. It had been great fun while it lasted, but when, we wonder, will St Johnstone next play in European competition?

Saints team: Clark, Gordon, Kerr, McCart, Wotherspoon, Davidson, Rooney, McCann, Devine, O'Halloran, Kane.
Substitutes: Parish, Brown (for Rooney), Booth (for Devine), Hendry (for O'Halloran), May (for Kane), Sinclair, Denham, Muller, Craig, Ballantyne, Moreland and Northcott.
Attendance: 6,216.

**Only the fourth team in Scotland to do the Cup double
St Johnstone 1, Hibernian 0, Scottish Cup Final,
Hampden Park, 22nd May 2021**

Shaun makes sure fans are ordering doubles

Headline: Perthshire Advertiser

Having won the League Cup only a few months previously, no-one in Scotland, including, it should be said, probably every St Johnstone supporter, would have expected them to have any chance of winning the other major cup competition in the same season. Saints' journey in the Scottish Cup began at the home of our favourite enemy, Dens Park, Dundee.

Dundee at that time were in the Championship, but they still proved tough opponents. Saints won courtesy of the only goal of the game, by Guy Melamed, but it should also be remembered that Zander Clark saved a penalty from Charlie Adam that helped secure the tie.

Clark recalled that save as being particularly important, *"because I'd given the penalty away! Mind you, when I watch it back, I'm still not sure it was a pen. I genuinely don't know how I save it. It looks as if the ball is by me, but I've touched it and it came off the post and came back to my hands... Even if I hadn't got it, Spoony was on hand and if I hadn't got it, he was going to clear the ball."*

A comfortable 2-0 home win against Clyde in the next round led to a quarter final pairing with Rangers in Glasgow. The story of that match is told in more detail elsewhere in this book, but as everyone knows, Zander Clark was again the hero, coming up for the final corner kick and heading on for Chris Kane to steer home from a yard out, before saving two of Rangers' sudden-death penalties while all the Saints' players scored theirs.

After the excitement at Ibrox, the semi-final with St Mirren was (slightly) more low-key, with the Perth Saints two goals up midway through the second half before conceding one but holding out to make the final. However, it could all have been very different, because, like every club at that time, St Johnstone were badly affected by Covid.

Obviously, the threat of Covid was the same for all sides, but to what extent it made a substantial difference to the outcome of games it is very hard to tell. Certainly, from St Johnstone's point of view, the strange circumstances did not impair their progress in the League Cup although, as Callum Davidson and Ali McCann revealed to us, it might easily have done. Here's Callum's version...

"At the time of the semi with St Mirren the measures we had to take against Covid were really difficult. As well as all the regular testing, we had to take the players to the matches in separate buses, then we had lots of the lads testing positive. There

267

was also scrutiny of how the players celebrated goals. This applied to those who had just had Covid but were able to play due to having had sufficient days' gap from the onset of the illness. For the Celtic game before the semi-final, we only had 11 players available. I was happy to take a 4-0 defeat in those circumstances. On the Wednesday before St Mirren, at one point we had only half a team. It was one of the longest weeks of my life.

"Ali was one of those who had gone down with Covid, but he was out of the period when he wasn't able to play. Then, when we scored, I was so pleased that when Chris Kane scored the first, Ali just tapped him on the head. That was what the protocols demanded and I was relieved he'd remembered what he had to do."

Ali McCann has a slightly different recollection of what happened…

"We were down to the bare bones that week, but I have to be honest and say that I didn't even think about what to do when Kano scored. I made no deliberate attempt not to join in the celebration. If you'd had Covid, you had to talk to someone from Test and Trace and this lady asked me 'were you in close contact with anyone when your team scored?' I remember thinking, 'Oh no!' but then I watched the video and saw – to my relief – that I'd just tapped Kano on the head and was in the clear."

While Saints were working their way through Covid and on to the final, on the other side of the draw, Hibs had beaten Queen of the South, Stranraer, Motherwell and Dundee United. With their pedigree, bigger support, larger budget and, on paper, more talented squad they were favourites. Although Saints had beaten Hibs twice in the League, and also lost once and drawn, it was the Edinburgh side that finished higher up the Premiership table at the end of the campaign, in third place with 63 points, 18 points ahead of fifth-placed St Johnstone.

With the Covid pandemic still dictating most aspects of life and causing earlier rounds to be re-scheduled, the date of the final was delayed from 8th to 22nd May. There was a small hope that some fans might be able to attend, but with building works taking place at Hampden prior to the Euro 2020 tournament that summer, and despite offers from Aberdeen to allow Pittodrie to be used, allowing 500 fans to attend, the Scottish Government rules meant that, as with the League Cup final, no fans were able to see the game.

However, one fan did actually get his hands on the trophy, and that was even before the game started. Dave McPhee, who as well as being a die-hard Saints' fan is also the Chair of the Scottish Mental Health and Wellbeing Football League, had received an invitation to attend an event in Edinburgh the day before the match. This was all cloaked in secrecy, because the principal guest was the then Duke of Cambridge, and now heir to the throne, Prince William. Dave takes up the story…

"With Covid, the teams in our league had not been able to have any games and teams couldn't do much in the way of training and the pandemic was obviously having a serious impact on many people's mental health. Prince William was on a visit to Scotland that week and is extensively involved in work around mental health in general but also, as the Head of the English FA, in football. We had been invited by the Scottish FA to put on a showcase game for him involving our Saints Community Trust Mental Wellbeing Squad at Spartans ground in Edinburgh. It was terrible weather, but he clearly was very interested and spent a lot of time with everyone. In another wee highlight for me, the 2014 Saints' Cup winner Chris Iwelumo was there for the BBC and I got my photo taken with him and got to touch the Scottish Cup itself which was also on display. Afterwards, I had to say a few words to the assembled crowd and I remember telling

them that I hoped this was the last time the Cup was in Edinburgh that weekend…"

One of the few fans who did get to Hampden was Saints' TV commentator Steven Watt. This was his fourth trip to the national stadium that season, however, as he told us, things had changed slightly compared to the League Cup semi and final ties…

"There was definitely a different air to the Scottish Cup final. For a start, the weather was more like a traditional, sunny, Cup final day. Also, compared to the BetFred (League) Cup, there were more people in the stadium: there were a few dignitaries, albeit spaced out around the ground, plus there were definitely more media folk about. Ally McCoist was doing the punditry for Premier Sports who were broadcasting the final and when he saw us with our Saints' jackets he came right across – 'You're the St Johnstone boys? Nice to see you…I cannae wait for the game…any idea where the pies are?' It was obvious which side he wanted to win.

"Then the Hibs players came onto pitch and some of their staff unfurled a banner near the corner flag. I felt it was a bit cocky and that they obviously believed they were going to win. I remember thinking, 'That's a bit off, because if they don't win that will come back to bite them.' Which it did!"

For any neutral watching, the game itself was not a wonderful spectacle, although at the final whistle no-one from Perth cared about that. The PA, naturally, and correctly, took the view that, *"this team will never be forgotten,"* and suggested, again correctly in our view, that although Hibs had, *"A bigger squad, bigger budget, bigger fanbase…on Saturday is was the Perth club that had the biggest heart."*

Ali McCann recalled that because Saints had beaten Hibs more often than not in the league, and also won the crucial semi-final against them in the League Cup, the players were reasonably confident. That said, he also noted, *"Hibs were a good side then, with some excellent players, like Martin Boyle. However, once we scored, we knew our defence was so strong that they'd struggle to break us down. That's what happened, and we should have added another goal."*

Jason Kerr agrees, telling us, *"We were confident going into the final. We had Hibs' number that season and having beaten them in the semi of the League Cup we were probably more confident than they were. I saw a few things on Twitter, Hibs' fans' comments and posts, which suggested they were worried about us. Still, it was a Cup final and like any game you treat the opposition with respect, but we knew that if we got the first goal we should have enough to see it out. We'd proved that over many games that season.*

"When we were one up, we enjoyed the way Hibs came at us. They probably played to our strengths, humping balls up the middle, which we'd head away all day. Then when we got the penalty, I thought that was it - if we score the game's done. But of course we didn't score: their keeper saved the first shot and also the rebound. Hibs obviously put us under pressure towards the end. That was to be expected, but we knew we were strong enough at the back – and at the front, where Kano was great at holding the ball and drawing fouls – to get over the line."

Zander Clark also thought that Saints were looking forward to the match perhaps more than Hibs. He said, *"inside our camp we were confident; we had a wee hold over Hibs that season, especially after beating them 3-0 in the semi-final of the BetFred Cup, Like that final, against Livingston, we knew it would be cagey and it panned out that way in that they had the early pressure, but once we were in front we knew we'd probably win. I did have a wee scare with Boyle's chance early on and then when we* missed the penalty, they got a lift. It wasn't enough though as our team was so solid in defence: the boys knew what they were doing and they also knew that anyone who came on during the match would fit in seamlessly and not let anyone down."

The man of the match was lifelong Saints' supporter - and former Hibernian player - David Wotherspoon…

"Being a former Hibs player didn't make any difference. We had a good record against them at that time and had beaten them in a great game in the League Cup semi-final: we looked forward to playing them every time. The only thing that took away from the occasion was that with Covid there were no fans there, so the celebrations were not as extensive as they would normally have been. At the end of the game I was totally drained, physically and mentally. Although we were all over the moon, I think being a fan made a difference to me personally and my family. The fact I now have three Cup medals and a man of the match trophy to show my kids is very special."

Spoony was characteristically modest about his part in the goal. The way he turned Alex Gogic inside out before flighting the inch-perfect cross for Shaun Rooney's headed goal will stay forever in the memories of all who saw it.

Callum Booth also played a vital role, winning the ball in two crunching tackles, before it broke to Wotherspoon who duly performed his magic, deceiving Hibs defender Alex Gogic with his trademark 'Spoony chop' – cutting back and flighting over a perfect ball for Rooney at the back post to bullet past Macey in the Hibs goal. Yet there was an outside chance that Rooney might not even have been on the park, as he told us: "I did my ankle in training during the week. I remember big Jason and Gordy telling me to make sure I was alright for the final. I took it easy and

had two paracetamols beforehand, but on the day I was fine. Then, when we went up 1-0, we knew we could go on to win.

From a Hibernian perspective, the Edinburgh Evening News probably summed up the tenor of the match better than most. Here's how they began their report…

"Hibs tried to make an impression in the early stages as Jackson Irvine hooked a ball over from the byline on the left. As the ball dropped for Martin Boyle on the other side of the area, he shaped up to volley but could only manage a fresh air shot. It summed up what was to come for the remainder of the 90 minutes. Hibs had no end product… A side who have struggled to get the better of Davidson' men, they huffed and puffed but there was no real response. Not one that worried their rivals, anyway."

The players' anecdotes pretty much sum up the course of the game, but of course there were two key moments. The first was the poetry-in-motion wing play from Spoony that led to the only goal of the game. It has famously been recorded that Shaun Rooney scored a goal in the 32nd minute of each final that season. However, we studied the videos on YouTube, both of which show the game time clock, and we reckon that, based on when the ball crosses the line, the goal against Livingston was scored in 31.05 minutes, in other words the 32nd minute, while the goal against Hibs came in 30.50 minutes – that is in the 31st minute. Irrespective of the actual time, the story of two crucial goals within 15 seconds of each other in two Cup finals still makes Shaun's feat one that must be celebrated for as long as St Johnstone FC exists…

The second key moment was the missed penalty. Chris Kane got the better of the Hibs' defence and burst through in the 75th minute, forcing McGinn to concede the penalty. Macey saved Middleton's spot kick and then quickly scrambled up to block

Kane's follow up with his feet. It could have been a pivotal moment that sparked hope for Hibs, but as the Saints' players quoted here said, they were confident of their defensive abilities and together held firm. Equally, Hibernian could not grasp the opportunity they had been offered. That missed penalty should have given Hibs a shot in the arm, yet although they tried to up their game, as the PA recorded, *"Hibs had a lifeline, yet they still did not look up to the challenge. Like we have witnessed so often, Saints pulled together again. They defended remarkably well through to the last kick of the football."*

The pressure on the players at that penalty kick - and in the remaining 15 or so minutes afterwards - must have been both intense and immense. Meanwhile, up on the gantry, the Saints' TV commentator was, strangely, still moderately relaxed. Here's Steven Watt explaining why: *"I never felt Hibs were putting us under any great pressure. It was a one-goal game in my head, but then when we got the penalty I thought 'this is the clincher.' Even after we'd missed, I still felt pretty optimistic that it was going to prove a one-goal game, although then I wished that the ref had played an advantage and Kano had gone on to score without the penalty being given."*

While Steven and his colleagues were doing their stuff at Hampden, back in Perth, the big party was just beginning. At the Cherrybank Inn, some 300 fans had bought tickets to watch the final on a big screen. The logistical challenges of doing this when there were still severe restrictions thanks to the pandemic were daunting, as Jack Findlay, the owner of this famous Perth pub explained to us: *"We had started opening up for business again, but still weren't allowed inside, so we'd created a bar underneath the balcony of the lounge. The Council were, understandably, very nervous about all this and we had to get special security in to police the event and make sure the tables, chairs and loos were kept spotlessly clean. Then we organised a friend of mine who has a Spitfire to fly over before the game and do a victory roll over Craigie Hill, plus we got some pipers in to play 'When the Saints go marching in.' We had to sell tickets so we could track and trace everyone, but in the event it all went really well as could be seen when the BBC ran a programme from our car park.*

"There were 300 people there and everyone was meant to be seated at tables, but when we scored it was impossible to contain all the excitement. The stewards did their best, but what could they do as everyone leapt to their feet?

"I only saw bits of it, because I was obviously busy, making sure table service was working because obviously people weren't allowed to go to the bar. However, I kept glancing at the screen out of the corner of my eye to see how we were doing. When I got home, at 10 o'clock that night, I watched the entire game. The whole day was a wonderful experience..."

Although all the St Johnstone players were heroes, for one, perhaps, this was a day that meant more to him than anyone else. Murray Davidson, who had missed the 2014 triumph and then the League Cup through injury), came on in the 64th minute to replace Craig Bryson. Murray's wholehearted approach to the game meant he had suffered many injuries and lay-offs during his career, but like Captain Scarlett from the 1960s children's TV show, he was indestructible. As the PA put it, *"He battled, scrapped and put his body on the line to keep the capital club at bay."*

Saints team: Clark, Kerr, Gordon, McCart, Rooney, McCann, Bryson, Booth, Middleton, Wotherspoon, Kane.
Substitutes: Parish, Brown (for Rooney), Davidson (for Bryson), O'Halloran (for Middleton, Conway, Tanser, May, Melamed, Craig.
Attendance: N/A due to Covid regulations.

A wonderful match that will be very hard to better

Scottish League Division One
Celtic 2, St Johnstone 2
Celtic Park, Saturday 30th August 1969

CELTIC MATCHED FOR SKILL AND DASH

St. Johnstone Do Perth Proud in Parkhead Thriller

CELTIC 2, ST JOHNSTONE 2.

(Half-time: 1-1).

Headline: Perthshire Advertiser

It is hard to imagine, but once upon a time, football supporters were capable of applauding their opponents. It still happens nowadays, but not as frequently as in the past, and it was pretty rare even then. However, at the end of this match, which was the league opener for both sides after the League Cup group stages had been dispensed with, the PA tells us that not once but twice, the fans of both teams cheered both sets of players off the park. This is the second paragraph of their report, *"Both sides received a tremendous ovation at the end of this 90-minute soccer spectacular from the massive crowd of 60,000, and never have two teams so richly deserved it."* Then, as if to drive home just what a sensational match this was, their final sentence says, *"As the final whistle blew, this Glasgow crowd gave both sides a wonderful ovation as they left the field."*

That Glasgow crowd, some 60,000 strong, was the largest in Britain that day. They had come along to see the reigning Scottish champions begin their campaign to try to retain their title (they did, comfortably) and, for those from Perth who had seen their side finish sixth the previous season (some 17 points behind Celtic), to see if their club's

stupendous form in the League Cup could be carried on into the new league season.

John Litster, who (much) later became Saints' General Manager, attended as a neutral. He told us, *"I've watched an awful lot of football, but this was one of the best matches I've ever seen."*

What made it such a special game? Well, for a start, both sides were committed to trying to win by playing attacking football. It's very hard for those who have grown up watching Scottish football in the last decade or so to believe that there was once a time when teams played with four or five forwards as standard and set out to win games by attacking consistently rather setting out first to stop the opposition scoring while trying to sneak a goal themselves and then defend for their lives to the final whistle.

In particular, imagine a scenario in which Saints take the game to either half of the Old Firm from the first minute and then don't let up for the remainder of the match. If you don't believe us, consider the following quotes, all from the PA's report of this game…

"Both sides were brilliant, and the crowd were treated to a wonderful display of attacking football, goalmouth thrills, excellently executed moves and four picture book goals."

"St Johnstone played magnificently, and as manager Mr Willie Ormond had forecast before the game, attacked right from the word go. To single out anyone for special mention in this Saints side would be unfair for this was a team playing for one another and helping each other at all times."

In Aberdeen, the Evening Express was equally enthusiastic, although they did express slight surprise in their headline that, *"Saints hold Celtic to a draw."* After that, their admiration for the efforts of both teams was profound:

"St Johnstone were first on the attack and looked impressive... Play remained fast and exciting, fulfilling the pre-match expectations of this clash between the country's highest scoring sides... The fast-moving St Johnstone forwards were posing many problems for the home defence, which at times did not look too impressive ... There was no let up in the pace. A goal was always likely at either end."

The fact that both teams were going all out to score for the entire 90 minutes is what made this match so special. Imagine Saints are drawing at Celtic Park (or Ibrox) today and there is just under half an hour to go. Do we, a) try to shut up shop and keep a point, or b) go all out for a winner? In 1969, the only option they thought about was the latter. Here's the PA again…

"Both sides gave a great display of attacking for the last 15 minutes, but neither managed to get the much wanted winner."

The game was played in bright August sunshine, which gave the impression, according to the PA, of the ground being *"more like an American 'ball park' than a football stadium."*

Saints were first to threaten, when John Connolly took advantage of an error by Billy McNeill but unfortunately hit his shot wide of the post. This was in the second minute but it was Celtic who came close next when Harry Hood fired just over the bar in the eighth minute.

With both sides going for goal on every available opportunity, it was only a question of when, rather than if, the first goal was scored. It came in the 22nd minute, courtesy of the substantial presence of Bill McCarry, who headed home a typically brilliant corner from Fred Aitken. Jim Masson, former Evening Telegraph sports reporter and lifelong Saints' fan, recalled this was a really powerful header – *"Buck really slammed it into the net with his head."*

Celtic then strove mightily to get back to parity and did just that in the 38th minute. Steve Chalmers received the ball from Willie Wallace, who had run from inside his own half before playing an inch-perfect pass to his team-mate who, in turn, gave Jimmy Donaldson no chance from 15 yards.

Jimmy Johnstone had been operating on the left during the first half. The Saints' players of this era all believed that Jinky struggled when he came up against Willie Coburn, which is maybe why he started there, but as he was getting no change out of John Lambie either he moved to the right flank after the interval. He did have one great run which culminated in a powerful shot which Jimmy Donaldson saved, before John Connolly showed that anything Celtic could do Saints could do equally well, hitting a tremendous drive just over the bar.

Next, Henry Hall got clear but Fallon in the Celtic goal managed to flick his shot away from his goal. Play surged to the other end and Donaldson punched a difficult corner away before Jimmy Johnstone missed an easy chance. The PA described this in detail, telling its readers, *"A cross from Gemmell came right across the Saints goal about three yards out. Wallace failed to get a foot to it, then Jimmy Johnstone, taken completely by surprise, missed altogether from almost on the St Johnstone line."* Even the greats are human, but Johnstone should have taken it, because in their next attack Saints went ahead again.

Although he doesn't recall all his games and, unlike some strikers, is not really able to remember all his goals, Henry Hall does remember this game well.

"I enjoyed this match more than the League Cup final," he told us, adding, *"it was one of the most exciting games I've played in, up there with the game against Hamburg at Muirton. It was a glorious sunny day and both teams tried to attack throughout the match. We were up against one of the best Scottish teams of all time and went head-to-head with them. Both teams had great wingers. Wee Kenny Aird always used to tell us that he was the best, but we'd say that Jimmy Johnstone was and Kenny was the next best. Kenny wasn't having this, but at the time it was probably just about right."*

Jimmy Donaldson also remembers this match, showing how much it must have stuck in the memory after all these decades. He told us, *"It was a real end-to-end game. We were under pressure in the early stages, but then came back and scored first, then they equalised, then we went ahead again and they fought back.*

"They were a really good side, but they didn't take us lightly as they knew we were as well. I think they appreciated the challenge we gave them. The match went by in a flash, it was so quick there was hardly time to stop and think as the action happened in front of me – sometimes right in front of me!

"I think we could have finished second in the league that year: we had great performances against the top teams but unfortunately let ourselves down against the smaller teams."

Our second goal was made by John Connolly, who played it in and Freddie Aitken was on hand to drive the ball home. This was in the 57th minute but, given the to-and-fro nature of the contest, it was no surprise when Celtic came back again to equalise. That was in the 62nd minute, with Harry Hood heading in from short range a cross from Chalmers.

Back the game swung, with Ian McPhee next to ping one over the Celtic bar from around 18 yards. That was in the 68th minute, and then seven minutes after this Celtic went close again through Hood.

Try as they might, neither side could land a knock-out blow as the game sped on to its conclusion. Afterwards, a Celtic fan was heard to say, *"St Johnstone beat us at our own game,"* causing the PA reporter who heard the remark to add, *"Never have truer words been said."*

Saints team: Donaldson; Lambie and Coburn, Gordon, Rooney and McPhee; Aird, Hall, McCarry, Connolly and Aitken. Substitute: Whitelaw (not used). Attendance: 60,000 (the largest in the UK that day).

No. 6
Paul Sturrock said, "I wasn't happy about the two goals we conceded…"

Scottish League Division One
St Johnstone 7, Dundee 2
McDiarmid Park, Wednesday 1ˢᵗ January 1997

Dazzling Saints in seventh heaven

St Johnstone 7, Dundee 2

ST JOHNSTONE stretched their lead at the top of the first division to 13 points with a scintillating victory in the Tayside derby at McDiarmid Park.

It was the Perth side's 10th straight league win, their biggest ever against Dundee, courtesy of doubles from Roddy Grant and Leigh Jenkinson plus singles from Philip Scott, Steve Tosh and sub George O'Boyle, and contained what Paul Sturrock

allowed a 60th minute header from Tosh to squirm between his legs.

"To be honest I missed the incident so I will have to wait for the referee's report and talk to the players concerned before deciding what action to take. I have to say, though, the question of how you deal with a player with so much skill but such disciplinary problems is a hard one."

The sending off was insignificant in terms of the result because by that stage Saints were leading 6-1 and had the game won thanks to a five-

Headline: The Courier

Some think that Saints' rivalry with Dundee stems principally from the 1962 match where Dundee won the First Division championship at Muirton, beating Saints 3-0 and relegating them at the same time. However, the antipathy goes back much further than this. As is frequently the case between any two Scottish towns that are in reasonable proximity to each other – whether Stirling and Falkirk, Glasgow and Edinburgh, Coatbridge and Airdrie, Kilmarnock and Ayr and, of course, Perth and Dundee – local rivalries and a desire to be demonstrably better than your neighbours have existed for eons. You can see little hints of antagonism in the press reports of games between Dundee and St Johnstone over many years, but in truth, the Dark Blues were in different Divisions from Saints for much of the 20ᵗʰ and 21ˢᵗ centuries (and entirely for the 19ᵗʰ) and in many ways it would make more sense for our rivalry to be greater with Dundee United rather than their near neighbours.

After all, it was Dundee Hibernian (as United were initially called) who, after only one year of existence (they were founded in

1909), were given the coveted Scottish League place in 1910 when St Johnstone, by virtue of their Consolation Cup success (see Part I, Chapter 8) and established track record, believed they should have been the preferred candidate. However, that's not the way it is and future generations of St Johnstone fans yet unborn will doubtless be raised with an awareness that beating Dundee is one of the highlights of any season. And on this particular occasion, it was most definitely *the* highlight of the 1996-97 promotion season, which, given that we were promoted, was a season of many highs.

Back in the good old days, New Year's Day games were just what they said on the tin: matches played on the first day of the New Year. Nowadays, 'New Year's Day' games are invariably on the 2ⁿᵈ of January, or sometimes even later. This is a shame, because a major part of the pleasure of the old, 1ˢᵗ January games was the herculean effort that had to be made after the excesses of Hogmanay to actually get to the ground. Then, once you got there, there was an enormous, hungover camaraderie amongst

275

all the fans (well, at least your own fans), the Happy New Year hand-shakes and, of course, a huge fug of alcoholic vapour washing over the stands and terraces. Happy daze.

One fan who was certainly in a happy daze in 1997 was Kevin Heller: *"I was very hungover. I had been out at my mate Sandy's house and woke up too late to go for a pint before the game. I remember there was the feel of a constant party in the build-up to the game and I wasn't feeling either good or bad about the outcome. Unusually, and unlike almost every other Saints' fan, I view Dundee United as the bigger game. This is because I grew up with more Dundee United fans at a time when they were successful in Europe – as they constantly reminded me.*

As for the game itself, it wasn't till the second half that it came to life. I remember Leigh Jenkinson's performance, especially the magic free kick and his thunderous shot. Roddy was brilliant too that day. My hangover is my excuse for not having a perfect memory of it all, but I remember feeling brilliant, thinking, 'we're not going to get many days like this.' At the end, there was the farce of Chic Charnley getting sent off for fighting with his own player.

After the game, David McPhee and I made up a song, based on the old 'The game had only just begun' song, then had it printed on T-shirts, with the lyrics on the back and the Dundee manager (John McCormack) on the front looking despondent."

While many of the fans were feeling the effects of the night before, one of the players was also tired, but not because he had been hitting the sauce. Let Nick Dasovic explain: *"I had only joined the club a few months before, in November 1996, so this was my first experience of what happens at a Scottish New Year. I'd gone to my bed, but was then woken up by pots and pans being banged and people*

obviously having a good time. Where I'd played before, there was always a winter break, so there was no football at New Year. It wasn't the best preparation...

"Before the game, Paul Sturrock warned me about Chick Charnley. 'He'll try and get into your ribs,' he told me. Chick did indeed 'try and get into my ribs,' but I simply told him, 'Is that the best you've got?' and that was an end to it."

For obvious reasons, this particular New Year's Day game will live long in the memory of the majority of the 7,087 fans who saw it and those who played in it. As the PA noted in the introductory paragraph of its report of the match, *"They'll talk of New Year's Day 1997 for years to come. Grandchildren will be bored to tears well into the 21st century as Saints' fans in their dotage recount a well-worn tale of derring-do and This Perfect Day. When the teleprinter taps out the number in letters, confirming the scale of a score-line, it's always an occasion for raising a glass to your team."*

Given the final score, it might surprise anyone who doesn't know the story of the match to find that at half-time the teams went into their dressing rooms with the score at 1-1. It might also surprise even those Saints' fans who were there to discover that Dundee were in second place in the league and unbeaten on the road that season. However, according (correctly) to the PA, St Johnstone were *"simply a class apart from the rest of the contenders for Premier League status."*

Nonetheless, although Roddy Grant had put Saints in front in the 26th minute with a trade-mark header from a Leigh Jenkinson cross, Dundee then equalised only six minutes later, courtesy of their enfant terrible Chic Charnley, who swept home a 20-yarder. Although undoubtedly one of the more gifted Scottish footballers of his generation, Chic had received a total of 14 red cards in his career up to this match and his booking in the second half, for a kick on Nick Dasovic, was hardly a surprise. However, after a first half when the visitors gave as good as they got and, to quote the PA again, *"...the Dens side had matched Saints every step of the way, peppering Alan Main's charge with long-range shots. All were dealt with by a goalkeeper who must rank among the top three Scots currently plying their trade between the sticks."*

The Courier quoted Roddy Grant as saying, *"Paul Sturrock rightly gave us a row when we went into the dressing room at 1-1 and it made all the difference."*

Leaving on one side the rather quaint image of the manager telling the team they had jolly well better pull their socks up in the second half (we suspect it may have been a slightly more colourful *"row"*), whatever Sturrock (and probably John Blackley too) said certainly did the trick. The Daily Record's report rather confirms this, quoting Paul Sturrock as saying, *"I had a few words at half time and the players realised they cannot coast through games."* As we all know, *"a few words"* is football-speak for an absolute bollocking. And even once the dust had settled, the manager was still not entirely happy about every aspect of his side's performance, telling the Courier, *"I don't want to get too carried away...Despite the fact that we won by a comfortable margin, I wasn't happy about the two goals we conceded."*

Regardless of the manager's post-match caution, whatever was said at half time soon had the desired effect. Within a few minutes of the second half starting (six to be precise), the same double-act that had conjured up Saints' first were at it again. The PA described it thus: *"Jenkinson suckers Adamczuk on the touchline and makes space for a sublime near-post cross. Grant heads home his 21st goal of the season, eclipsing his previous career best."*

In the stands, Jim Mackintosh and his pal John Lamb were, like every other Saints' fan, going daft. John, who sadly died in 2023, went a bit further than Jim, bounding down the steps three at a time and jumping up and down with excitement at the exit gate to the pitch. *"I can clearly remember his beaming smile,"* Jim told us, *"Although for a moment I was worried he was going to stage his own mini pitch invasion."*

With Roddy's goal the course of the game changed. The PA told its readers, *"...it was the signal for one of the most exhilarating 45 minutes produced by a St Johnstone team of this or any other era. This was up there with the drubbing of the Dons and the Grant-aided surge to the 1990 championship, when Airdrie were disposed of at McDiarmid Park."*

Having got going, it didn't take Saints long to add to their tally. Here's the PA again... *"Steve Tosh releases Philip Scott and the midfielder, who was denied a first half goal when a header crashed off the underside of the bar, coolly lobs advancing keeper Billy Thomson."* At this point, *"the visitors' stand is emptying faster than a Ne'er Day bottle."*

There were only four minutes between the second and third goals and only another five minutes before Steven Tosh secured the fourth, perhaps with a bit of help from the Dundee goalkeeper: *"John O'Neil bides his time to release overlapping John McQuillan and Steve Tosh sees his header squirming underneath Thomson."*

Saints generously waited a full twelve minutes before scoring again. This time, it was man-of-the-match Leigh Jenkinson who weighed up his options at a free-kick before planting the ball *"past a bewildered keeper. Sublime stuff."*

Leigh wasn't finished yet. If his first had been sublime, his second, seven minutes later, was ridiculous – taking the ball after it was tapped sideways by Attila Sekerlioglu and unleashing a thunderbolt of a shot that flew into the net with Billy Thomson grasping at thin air as it flew past him, brushing a post on the way into the net. Hangovers now well forgotten, the Saints' fans rose as one to acclaim what their heroes were doing to their favourite enemy. It was going to take something spectacular in the next 364 days for this to be overtaken as the best day of 1997. And just to add to the excitement, in the aftermath of St Johnstone's sixth goal, the linesman, flagged an off-the-ball incident to referee Willie Young, who promptly dismissed Chic Charnley. There are contradictory accounts of what actually happened. According to the Courier, *"Charnley himself appeared to be struck by teammate Robbie Raeside in the recriminations ... the seeming injustice of the decision prompted Saints' Grant to appeal to the official on Charnley's behalf to save him from the ordering off (no action was taken against Raeside)."*

The PA, in contrast, said Charnley was dismissed, *"for the umpteenth time in his colourful – as in red and yellow – career ... for a flare-up with his own captain."*

When we spoke to Roddy for this book, his recollection was that his intervention was perhaps because he had played with Chic at Partick Thistle, but *"Chic had lost it – but these things happen in football."*

As if all this wasn't enough, George O'Boyle came off the bench minutes later to score from close-in after Sekerlioglu's shot was blocked. And on another day, we might even have seen Saints reach double-figures, with Willie Young *"lambasted for ignoring three tangible penalty claims."* Just imagine a 10-2 win over Dundee…!

The action wasn't finished yet and when Danny Griffin brought down Jerry O'Driscoll in the box a minute after O'Boyle's goal, the young Dundee striker took the penalty himself and gave Alan Main no chance. The PA described what happened next… *"With the Dundee end almost barren, it was left to celebrating Saints' supporters to mock the moment…"* with the home fans now, *"utterly convinced engravers could begin work on preparing the championship trophy."* The *"irony-laced acclaim"* as the Courier called it, put the seal on an extraordinary day.

The fans may have responded to Dundee's penalty goal with ironic mocking, but the loss of this late goal famously left assistant manager John Blackley fuming. So much so that his false teeth flew out in mid-tirade: he picked them up, wiped them clean, stuck them back in his mouth - and then carried on shouting at the players.

Philip (Fizzy) Scott, who had been substituted in the 71st minute, was sitting behind Sloop and to this day remembers this as one of the funniest things he's seen at a football match. Nick Dasovic told us that John Blackley's reaction was exactly what he would have expected, adding, *"That was the way he was. You could be winning easily but he was so focused on his back-four that he would snap when anything went wrong. He did it because he cared. I learned a lot from Sloop: he was a great communicator and an incredible coach. It was a moot point who shouted louder, him or Paul Sturrock, but they were both very personable and I consider myself very fortunate to have worked with them."*

Roddy Grant agrees with Nick, telling us, *"It wasn't a case of 'Good Cop – Bad Cop', it was "Two Bad Cops!"* However he also added, *"It was because they were perfectionists. But they also allowed us to voice our opinions. Luggy loved arguing but he was the boss and we had to just get on with it."*

At the end of the day, the score could easily have been more. Allan Preston recalled, *"I think Dundee were lucky to get away with* seven. I had been ill the night before the game and was then physically sick on the pitch and had to be taken off with about 15 minutes to go. Dundee were a good side but we were at the top of our form and had really good characters and the best team spirit I've experienced. Highly experienced pros like Jim Weir, Kerny (Alan Kernaghan) and Kano (Paul Kane) had been around the block and played for some great clubs, but they all say that Saints' changing room was the best. We self-policed ourselves, but when Saturday came we would all dig in and fight for each other for the full 90 minutes.

"At that time, I had a neighbour in Edinburgh who was a big Dundee fan. Every New Year's Day from then on, I used to wish him 'Happy 7-2 day!' He hated it..."

Fizzy agreed with Biscuits that Saints could have scored more. For a start, there was his header that hit the bar in the first half and – in his view – crossed the line, but, as he said, "there was no VAR in those days so we just had to get on with it. However, after we'd scored the second goal, we just went on and on: it could easily have been double digits. We played well in the first half and then even better in the second half. It was one of those days when almost everything went in."

After the dust had settled, Saints were on 47 points, with Dundee still second on only 39 and Airdrie third on 32, It looked as if the PA's prediction that the engravers could start working on adding St Johnstone's name to the trophy would be proved correct – and indeed they were able to do so at the end of the season, when St Johnstone were promoted with 80 points, 20 ahead of second-placed Airdrie and 22 ahead of third-placed Dundee. Unsurprisingly, and considerably helped by this New Year's Day thrashing of our local rivals, Saints' goal difference at the end of the campaign was +51, with 74 scored and only 23 conceded. Happy Daze indeed!

Saints team: Main; McQuillan, Preston, O'Neil, Weir, Griffin, Dasovic, Tosh, Grant, Scott and Jenkinson. Substitutes: Donaldson (for Preston), O'Boyle (for Tosh) Sekerlioglu (for Scott).
Attendance: 7,087.

No. 5
Hot Rod's Red Alert

Scottish Premier Division
St Johnstone 5, Aberdeen 0
McDiarmid Park, Saturday 29th September 1990

The Aberdeen morning newspaper, the Press and Journal, in its pre-match musings on the day of this game, commented, *"Aberdeen must expect to win this one and, though Saints will battle, it will be a major shock if they don't pocket the points."* Two days later, in its Monday edition, the P&J ran a top-of-the-front-page article (shown above), surrounded by a heavy black border, of the type normally used for the death of a monarch…

The Aberdeen paper was scathing in its denouncement of their local favourites' performance. Celebrated North-East journalist Jack Webster was quoted as saying, *"I cannot recall a clear 5-0 scoreline in 48 years of following the Dons. It is the most astonishing result I can remember."*

After their phenomenal success in the 1980s, Aberdeen were rightly regarded as one of Scotland's very best teams and, sad to say, some of their followers had assumed the arrogant sense of entitlement that many of them currently (and previously) associate with Old Firm's fans. In the P&J's front-page piece, a Mr Brian Rae, the vice-chairman of the Aberdeen Supporters' Association said, *"I am shocked, horrified and ashamed…There is something far wrong when you get beaten 5-0 by teams you should be beating by that margin."*

Those watching the scores come in on the BBC's teleprinter (for younger readers, this was the way you got the results in those days – a rolling stream of typed scores, filmed as they were punched out onto paper), were equally astonished. The BBC had a policy of spelling out the actual number of goals when there were a lot of goals in a game or a shock result and in this case the letters "F-I-V-E" appeared after the number 5, just in case anyone thought it was a mistake. It wasn't. It was a stunning result.

Other fans at games across Scotland were equally stupefied as the Tannoy announcer at each ground read out that afternoon's scores. It's fair to say that there were a goodly number of St Johnstone fans who were pinching themselves after the final whistle too, before heading for a celebratory beer or five (or quite possibly many more) at the first available opportunity. Certainly, in the hospitality lounges, the drink flowed freely…

Going into the match, Aberdeen were second in the table, behind Dundee United. Saints, who had only just been promoted the previous season, were 'finding their feet,' or, to put it another way, had only three points from five games – from a 3-2 home win against Dunfermline and a 2-2 draw at St Mirren. The Dons had just lost to Rangers in the Skol (League) Cup semi-final but, as Alex Totten pointed out to every journalist who would listen, the entire St Johnstone team cost only £500,000, or less than Aberdeen had paid for just one player – Hans Gilhaus. The disparity between the two clubs was laid bare when the Saturday P&J listed the Aberdeen squad, which was as follows: Snelders, McKimmie, D. Robertson, Watson, McLeish, Irvine, Van de Ven, Grant, Bett, Connor, Mason, Jess, Gilhaus, Harvie.

Unsurprisingly, Aberdeen, as always, brought a lot of fans, all expecting a fairly easy afternoon. Some, it must be said, were not there just for the football. Jack Findlay, who at that time owned the St Leonard's Bar, one of the nearest hostelries to the railway station, recalled that his pub was invaded by a horde of Aberdeen football casuals, seemingly intent on mayhem. However, as he told us, *"Fortunately, the police had been following them from the station and they pursued them into our pub and promptly moved them on."*

Elsewhere in the hospitality industry, those in the one of the upstairs suites at McDiarmid Park were intrigued - not to mention relieved - to see Alex McLeish walk in and take a seat at an Aberdeen fans' table. He clearly wasn't playing, which, in the minds of some there, gave Saints a slight glimmer of hope. This was confirmed when the team-lines were distributed round the tables. But even without McLeish, the Dons were still, on paper a far, far stronger side than the Premier newbies.

The game began with, as expected, Aberdeen in the ascendant for the first ten or so minutes. With Willie Miller, like McLeish, also out with an injury, the Dons paired Brian Irvine and Stewart McKimmie in central defence. It was not to prove a successful combination…

Saints' first came from an error from Scottish international McKimmie. As the Press and Journal reported it, this merely seemed to be a blip in proceedings: *"When McKimmie unbelievably sent a clearance rolling gently to Maskrey for him to tap to Grant, who fired home the opener, there appeared still little to worry about."*

The Sporting Post seemed somewhat startled to find that Saints had taken the lead, although their description of the players involved is not the same as the P&J's. Reporting in real time down the wire, the Post said that, *"A mistake by captain McKimmie leads to Saints taking a surprise lead in 17 minutes. The defender takes too long to clear in his own penalty box, and Turner gains possession to cross for Maskrey. The striker's shot is deflected into the path of Grant, who fires a shot beyond Snelders from eight yards."*

Having committed one foolish error, Aberdeen compounded things by a second preventable mistake. Full back David Robertson was sent from the field just past the half hour mark for what the P&J said was *"a mime-kick at Allan Moore"* but the Daily Record called, *"a frustrated, fresh-air swipe at winger Alan (sic) Moore."* The Sporting Post reported, *"Aberdeen receive a further blow in 32 minutes with a sensational sending-off of young full-back David Robertson. The youngster aims a wild kick at Moore as the striker advances, but makes no contact. To the surprise of the crowd, referee Thow sees the offence as being worthy of a red card."*

At this point, Saints' fans began to wonder if perhaps the footballing gods were smiling on them. Those from the North-East were, as always, loud in their support of their heroes, but as the game went on even the most optimistic Aberdonian must have wondered if they were hallucinating.

That they most certainly were not was demonstrated emphatically when Mark Treanor took advantage of a lay-off from Roddy Grant to burst through the middle of the Aberdeen defence and fire home St Johnstone's second.

In the 42nd minute, Robert Connor handled the ball in the Aberdeen box. Louis Thow gave the penalty, which didn't go down well with the Dons' keeper. Louis later told us, *"There is a photo in my archives of me running to position for the kick and Theo Snelders snarling at me while I'm doing my best to ignore him."*

Mark Treanor, one of Saints' most dependable penalty-takers of all time, stepped up to send the ball beyond Snelders and send Saints into the break three goals to the good. In the stands, the home fans in the crowd of 8,711 were drunk on a heady mixture of joy and amazement. Bizarrely, the P&J reported that *"even with the score at 3-0 to the Saints at half time, Dons fans were still confident their team would pull the game round."*

Meanwhile, in the hospitality, Saints' fan Iain Smith, who was then working at Perth Leisure Pool, was entertaining a supplier of swimming pool equipment from Aberdeen. Iain told us, *"This chap was a die-hard Dons' fan and before the game, he was quite optimistic. It was a really good Dons side, so we understood why. It was one of those days when everything goes right and, because we were his client, he had to grin and bear it. It's fair to say we probably didn't hold back, especially at full-time..."*

The red army may have been confident, but their confidence was misplaced. After only three minutes of the second half, Harry

Curran should have scored. Here's how The Sporting Post described it: *"Grant sends Moore clear on the right, the winger beats (Aberdeen defender) Grant and sends over a cross which is missed by both Maskrey and Snelders at the near post. With the goal gaping, Curran blazes over..."*

Roddy Grant added a fourth, bamboozling Brian Irvine before shooting home. The Sporting Post's description tells us that the goal came from another Aberdeen error, this time from Gilhaus, which led to Gary McGinnis feeding the ball to Roddy some 45 yards from the goal. Running past a few defenders, he hammered the ball past Snelders from the edge of the box. His famous, post-match quote of *"I beat a few defenders but I was too knackered to go on so I just hit it,"* - combining all his qualities of skill, lack of pace and great goalscoring ability - sums up just why the big man is one of Saints' all-time legends.

With 10-man Aberdeen reduced to firing long-range shots at Lindsay Hamilton, to no avail, Saints nearly got their fifth only a minute after the fourth when Harry Curran sent over a fine cross from the left, finding Allan Moore in space, but the winger took the shot on first-time and it went over.

With only ten minutes left on the clock, the rout was completed by Steve Maskrey, whose near-post drive deceived Snelders and sent many of the away fans flooding from the ground. It was a famous victory and one whose echoes reverberated across Scottish football for some weeks.

For Ian McLaren, on holiday in Corfu, the result was communicated in a topsy-turvy manner. He had lent his season ticket to a friend, who then messaged Ian at his hotel. He was out, but when he returned, the receptionist passed on the message that read something like, *"Abelene 5, St Johns 0 – phone home."* So Ian phoned home, where his mum told him the real score.

Linda Henderson had been at the match with her husband, Eddie. For her, it was a special day: not only had we won 5-0, but it was also her birthday. While they were leaving the park after the match, they noticed a man and his son alongside. The man's face seemed familiar, then they realised it was Alex McLeish and, as Linda recounted, *"the son was saying to his dad, 'was it really 5-0?' – and Alex was none too pleased!"*

d in 1990; the Oracle report of one of the shock results of the season.

The margin of victory created waves throughout Scottish football. And in another example of the way in which technology has changed how we get to see scores and match reports, we reproduce ITV's Oracle Service report on the game. As you can see, compared to the interface of the modern-day smart phone, this was basic in the extreme, but the sense of shock is almost tangible…

Interestingly, this wasn't the only St Johnstone side to beat Aberdeen that day. The Sporting Post tells us that the respective 'A' teams of both clubs played in Aberdeen that afternoon. Saints had a number of trialists alongside a few better-known names, such as Don McVicar, Dougie Barron, David Bingham and, on the bench, Bobby Mann. After a goal-less first half, *"Saints trialist Dick, opens the scoring when he turns past two defenders and slips the ball beyond Watt. In 89 minutes,*

McVicar scores a second with a free kick from 20 yards." An aggregate score of 7-0 between the two matches put the seal on a good day for Perth and a bad day for Aberdeen.

The following Saturday, Saints were away at Celtic. A larger than expected number travelled to Glasgow, to be met by a number of local 'entrepreneurs' selling hastily made-up T-shirts, emblazoned with the headlines from the previous weekend. Saints drew 0-0 with Celtic, putting down a marker and raising the traditional fingers of contempt to those who thought the drubbing of the Dons was a one-off.

Photo: Alastair Blair

These first few months of the 1990-91 season were a time of great excitement for Saints' fans, with the team performing well above expectations. That said, it should also be admitted that the rest of the season was a mixed offering, seasoned by an excellent run in the Scottish Cup that culminated, perhaps unfairly, in a 2-1 defeat to Dundee United in the semi-final. When the dust settled, St Johnstone were 7th in the 10-team League table. And there is no doubt that the catalyst that sparked their season into life and set the club on its first solid run in the Premier Division, was that afternoon in late September 1990 when the Dons were put to the sword. In fact, the team's performances were such that pressure mounted for further league reconstruction.

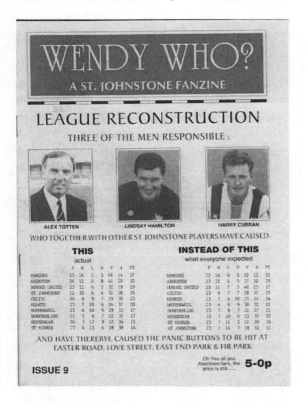

This was satirically noted by the Saints' fanzine, the wonderful *"Wendy Who?"* in the cover of their ninth issue, which also featured a dig at the Dons for the score-line that afternoon. League reconstruction did in fact come about, with none of the teams in the Premier being relegated and the top two in the First Division being promoted to make the top flight a league of 12 rather than 10 teams. Would this have happened if Saints had been at the bottom? This 5-0 win had a significance way beyond the result on the day…

Saints team: Hamilton; Treanor, Baltacha, Cherry, Inglis, McGinnis, Moore, Turner, Maskrey, Grant and Curran.
Substitutes: Lee (for Curran), Deas (for Turner)
Attendance: 8,711.

No. 4
The greatest day of my life

The first major national trophy
St Johnstone 2, Dundee United 0, Scottish Cup Final,
Celtic Park, Saturday, 17th May 2014

Headline: Perthshire Advertiser

Given that this particular match has been extensively covered elsewhere, notably by the official club video and Ed Hodge's excellent book, *'Our Day in May,'* it's quite hard to go over such familiar ground. However, we'll try, with as many interesting quotations from the media, players and fans as we can fit in…

In retrospect, most Saints' fans look back at the 2014 Cup final and think that we were almost guaranteed a win, given how well we'd performed against Dundee United that season. In the four previous competitive matches, St Johnstone had won three. Perhaps that's why, on the day of the final, Tommy Wright seemed to have an advantage over his United counterpart, Jackie McNamara, even before a ball was kicked… Roddy Forsyth, writing in the Daily Telegraph, noted, *"Certainly, the managers' demeanour beforehand provided an intriguing contrast. On encountering both men in the tunnel area a few minutes prior to kick-off, it was this correspondent's impression that Wright was discernibly more relaxed than McNamara."*

There was a good reason why Tommy seemed more relaxed because, as he told us, *"I enjoyed every minute, from waking up in the morning until I eventually got to my bed late at night. I had total confidence in my team. I couldn't see a way in which United would beat us, although obviously at the time I didn't say this to the players. From a sporting point of view, it was the greatest day of my life."*

Tommy Wright also gives short shrift to those who say that Saints won the Cup without beating either half of the Old Firm. United had beaten Rangers in the semi-final and despite the fact that the Ibrox team were in a lower Division at that time they still had a budget bigger than anyone else in Scottish football bar Celtic. As Tommy pointed out, as Saints progressed, in the quarter final they had to beat Raith, who had defeated Hibs in the previous round and, of course, Aberdeen were big favourites in the semi-final, given that they had pasted Saints at the corresponding stage in the League Cup a few months earlier. Dundee United too were many people's favourites in the final and it ought to be remembered that both the

285

Dons and United finished higher - 3rd and 4th respectively and 15 points and five points ahead of St Johnstone (who were 6th) in the final Premiership table.

Moreover, as Tommy noted, *"Aberdeen had the Indian sign over us that season: we'd drawn twice and lost twice to them and, of course, lost the League Cup semi. United, had a number of very gifted players, probably some better individuals than us with the likes of Robertson, Armstrong and Mackay-Steven. After Celtic, who had lost to Aberdeen in the fifth round, Aberdeen and United were the second and third favourites, so it's hogwash to suggest we were somehow or other fortunate to win the Cup."*

As the match approached, the managerial mind games began. David Wotherspoon told us how Tommy kept the players away from the press in the lead-up to the game, whilst also dropping in the rumour that Dundee United had already booked their open-top bus and planned their victory tour. However, as Spoony also said, *"Given we'd won most of the games, we felt we had something over them that season so we were not fazed by all that sort of stuff…"*

Steven Anderson recalled that the United manager had described him and his defensive partner Frazer Wright as *"ugly centre-halves."* By that, Ando explained, *"he meant that we were out-and-out defenders who would do anything to protect our goal. Going into the game, we knew that United had quality individuals – after all, they had beaten us 4-0 the first time we met them that season, but we had their number after that game. We had a bit of quality too and we all knew our roles because Tommy and the coaching team had drilled them into us. I should also say that his (Tommy's) lead-up to the final was spot-on. As he had done with Aberdeen before the semi-final, in his interviews with the media he put all the pressure on United,* saying they were favourites. This took all the pressure off us."*

The game was played at Celtic Park because Hampden Park was being used for the Commonwealth Games, taking place later that summer in Glasgow. For a number of the older Saints' fans, who had watched their team lose at both these venues, this was a third shot at seeing their team lift a major trophy. Some, like Ian McLaren, had been at the 1969 League Cup final at Hampden as small boys and had also experienced the disappointment of losing out to Rangers at Celtic Park in the 1998 final of the same trophy. Consequently, Ian and his mates went through to Glasgow the day before the game to soak up the atmosphere and do their best to enjoy the trip, no matter the result. They went to the Griffin, a famous Glasgow pub, only to find that the lounge there had been booked by United fans…

"The banter between the fans was good," Ian told us, *"Although it was clear that the United fans thought that they only had to turn up to win. I remember speaking to someone I thought I recognised and realised sometime later it was the former United player Craig Brewster. I also remember this guy in an orange boiler suit with black arrows on it and thinking, if we win then he's not going to have any hiding place on the way back to Dundee.*

"On the day of the match, we got the train from Central Station out to Hampden. The Saints' fans had to get off at a stop before the ground, with the United fans staying on to the next station. The United supporters were saying, 'you guys need to get off here because this train is going to Europe and you won't be on it'."

The BBC's website described the game as being between *"two well-matched teams and moments of inspiration were restricted, as much by familiarity as any overbearing sense of occasion … St Johnstone were the* more composed side. United often relying on the counter-attack rather than establishing rhythm or control, but while Ciftci was intermittently involved, the trio of attackers behind him - Dow, Stuart Armstrong and Gary Mackay-Steven - struggled to deliver their usual swift incisiveness."

One moment of swift incisiveness came from James Dunne, who "was deft and agile enough to react when the ball broke to him at the edge of the United penalty area. He arched his body so that he could meet the ball with a stinging volley, but the effort was matched by the ability of goalkeeper Radoslaw Cierzniak to tip the ball over with a stretching save."

A few minutes later, United's Polish keeper blocked a shot from David Wotherspoon which spun off Gavin Gunning. Although Saints had the early ascendancy, United, with the quality of player they had at their disposal, were still dangerous though and they came very close to scoring in 30 minutes, as described by Roddy Forsyth in the Daily Telegraph: "...there had been no show from Robertson, whose surges upfield from full back are such a key component in United's counter-attacking game. When he did start to make ground along the left flank, United immediately looked dangerous and, bang on the half-hour, Robertson delivered a dangerous cross into the box which was met by Dow with a delightful flick off the outside of the boot which beat Mannus, but skipped off the upright."

Alan Mannus's recollection is that this was more of a worry to him than the other time United hit the woodwork (in the second half) because, "I had dived and was at full stretch, but in these situations you turn your head to see what's happened. I could actually see the ball come off the post and I thought it was going to hit my back and go in. Fortunately, it skimmed by me and Ando hacked it clear."

Initially, Ando also believed it was a goal, telling us, "I just thought ... that's going in. Then it came back to me and I just cleared it as far away as I could. I didn't have time to think about it: when you are playing you just deal with what's in front of you..."

For Tommy Wright, watching from the sidelines, "When that one hit the post, it was one of those moments in the game when you know it's your day."

Other papers' reports give us different insights as to how they regarded this historic day. The Guardian - which, it's fair to say, was probably disinterested in the final result - had a live stream of written updates on its website and its penultimate note, published at 5.00 pm, probably sums up the match perfectly for anyone who was just tuning in rather than for the committed football fan...

"So in a tussle between two well-matched positive sides, it was Saints' superior know-how and tenacity in defence that, on balance, provided the decisive factor in bringing the old trophy to Perth for the first time. Dundee United showed regular flickerings of the flair for which they have become renowned, but they were mostly flickerings, against a defence that did its job doughtily. For that, and for taking their chances ruthlessly, Saints deserved to win, even if luck was with them too, with United suffering unkind rebounds off post (first half) and bar (second half.)"

Then, just before half-time (actually in the first minute after the regulation 45 minutes to be precise) it happened. Saints forced a corner; David Wotherspoon's right boot lofted a consummate delivery across the penalty box. The United keeper misjudged its flight – and there was Ando, peeling off to the back post and bulleting his header into the net.

Iain Smith, who was there with his daughters, remembers that when Ando's header hit the net, *"there was a brief second when we all looked at each other and no-one seemed to know what to do. I remember the look on their faces – it was a 'have we really scored?' kind of look. Then it kicked-in and we joined in the huge, ecstatic wave of joy that surged through the Saints' support."*

Tommy Wright recalled that this was not the first time that Saints had done this to United, telling us, *"They never learned: we did them with the same corner/free kick about three times that season."*

The teams went in for the break and the Saints' fans slowly got their breath back. Could we - would we - hold out in the second half?

Dundee United obviously had to come out and try to turn the game around. With only one goal in it the match was still in the balance. Consequently, it became a bit more frantic at times as the anxiety levels on both sides rose. Mind you, they were nothing like the anxiety in the Saints' end, where the collective blood pressure of our fans was probably at A&E levels.

That blood pressure was pushed even higher when United won a free kick inside the first ten minutes of the second half. Nadir Ciftci's perfectly flighted strike hit the bar, bounced down and, instead of, as would have happened nine times out of ten, hitting the goalkeeper and going in, the ball nestled under Alan Mannus's back and he swivelled on the ground to gratefully pull it into his grasp.

Stevie May (sadly, but, it has to be said, correctly) had a goal disallowed for punching the ball over the line. Then there was Spoony's amazing, mesmerising run from well inside his own half, culminating in a shot from just inside the box that, unfortunately, although perhaps understandably given the distance and pace with which he'd just run, lacked the power and direction to beat Cierzniak.

David's own recollection of this was that, *"When I got the ball, I expected to pass it, but the space opened up and as I got to the edge of the box I was one-on-one with their defender, so I thought I'd take him on. My legs were feeling it by this stage, so the shot wasn't quite as good as I'd have wanted."*

If Spoony had managed to beat Cierzniak it would have been one of the best goals ever scored in a Scottish Cup final. It's worth seeking it out on YouTube to see the way he rolls his foot over the ball and then drops his shoulder and waltzes round the United defenders in their box: it was sublime, classic David Wotherspoon.

Finally, with six minutes on the clock, the ball broke to Steven MacLean. As the keeper came out, Macca got there first; the two collided, the ball broke free and the Saints striker reacted first to knock the ball forward and over the line from about eight yards out.

Even then, given this was St Johnstone, there were still a lot of nerves to be shredded before the final whistle. Fan Andrew Tulloch told us, *"I was working out how United could win the 2014 final even when we were 2-0 up."* Ian McLaren was similarly afflicted, recollecting that he was virtually reciting a mantra throughout all the minutes after Macca's goal along the lines of *"it's not over till it's over."* Iain Smith said, *"I wasn't able to relax until there were only about 30 seconds to go…"*

Then there were no seconds to go. Referee Craig Thomson blew the final whistle and many of the Saints' players sank to their knees, punched the air, ran to embrace their comrades in arms and the management team and generally went daft. In the stands, the Perth fans let out a bellow of joyful euphoria, tinged perhaps in many cases with more than a soupcon of relief. It was indeed third time lucky, albeit there was absolutely nothing lucky about the final result: St Johnstone, although they rode their luck at times, were deserved winners.

On the pitch, the players queued up excitedly to get their medals. For the first time ever, the captain of the winning team was fitted with a body camera, to capture the moment when he lifted the trophy. As a result, Dave Mackay mounted the podium with a strange black contrivance strapped around his torso. He didn't let it bother him though as he raised the oldest trophy in world football into the Glasgow sky. Blue and white confetti rained down and the party – for players and fans - was about to begin in earnest.

Ando's 2014 Scottish Cup Winners' medal: photo, Steven Anderson

Andrew Tulloch had come to Glasgow in one of the four Saints' buses that left Edinburgh for the final. His bus was the last to leave Glasgow, *"because two of the guys went into Glasgow to celebrate and we had to find them. When we got to Edinburgh, we went to the Polwarth Arms. After a night of singing every Saints' song we knew, we got a night bus to Musselburgh. There were some United fans on that bus, trying to be good sports and congratulating us, but you could tell they were really gutted."*

Jack Findlay went through to the final on one of the numerous Saints' buses:

"The buses were all organised by the wonderful Bev Mayer and there was a brilliant atmosphere all the way there. On the way back, it was even better, then when we got to the Cherrybank the pub was full to bursting at the seams. There was a hilarious moment when we were trying to get in. A man inside said to my wife, 'you'll not get in there, lass' only to meet the reply, 'I think I will, I'm one of the owners!'"

Former player Danny Griffin was on a supporters' bus with his family and mother-in-law. He told us, *"United weren't ready for us that day and Saints were outstanding. When Ando scored that header the place erupted, then when Macca got the second there was almost a sense of relief because we felt that was the game done.*

"On the way home, all the Saints' buses were bouncing. I remember we were passing the United buses and my son, who was five at the time and had those foam fingers, was sticking a foam finger up to them. We said, 'tell them it was two nil,' and a second foam finger appeared."

Ian McLaren got the train back with lots of other Saints' fans, only to discover it took a meandering journey via Edinburgh and Fife before reaching home. His abiding memory of that journey was that it was strangely subdued, almost as if the magnitude of what had happened had not sunk in.

His story about the quietness of the train journey may seem strange, but Maggie Anderson, another life-long fan, remembers exactly the same thing: *"All our family had travelled through to Glasgow on the train. It was a lovely sunny day and, oh, we couldn't believe it when Ando scored, then Steven MacLean scored and we'd won the Cup. I always remember coming home on the train though; it was quiet, like we were all in shock. When we got off the train at Perth one person started up with, 'Oh when the Saints go marching in' and we all joined in."*

Ian McLaren also remembers that more normal football behaviour kicked in once they go back to Perth. He and his friends made their way to the Foundry before ending up in Greyfriars, where the band was playing, *"What shall we do with the drunken Saintee?'* to the tune of *'What shall we do with the drunken sailor?'."* It's a fair bet that many pub staff were still counting the takings well into the wee small hours.

The Cup-Winners' bus turns into Unity Terrace: photo, Derek McIntosh

As the dust settled, a celebratory, open-top bus tour around Perth was organised. Some thought that it might prove to be a bit of a damp squib: although some 15,000 had gone to Celtic Park, fewer than a third of that number were regular or even semi-regular attenders at McDiarmid Park. The doubters were proved wrong and thousands and thousands turned out to fill the Fair City's streets and salute their heroes.

For one man, it was an opportunity to hold his dad to a promise made nearly 45 years earlier. Derek McIntosh takes up the story: *"I was just a boy when we moved into Unity Terrace and in 1971 we discovered a number of flags behind some shelves in the house. I asked my dad if we could fly them out of the windows and he said, 'aye, when Saints win a Cup and drive an open-top bus down our road.'*

"It's fair to say he probably never thought this would happen, but I have the photos to prove that it did - and he kept his word."

Many of those watching the procession - probably the vast majority - thought this would be the only occasion in their lives when they would see St Johnstone lift a major trophy, so they celebrated loud and long into the night. How little we knew…

Saints team: Mannus, Mackay, Easton, Dunne, Wright, Anderson, Millar, Wotherspoon, MacLean, May, O'Halloran Substitutes: Banks, Cregg, McDonald (for Wotherspoon), Hasselbaink, Miller, Croft (for O'Halloran), Iwelumo.
Attendance: 47,345.

In those days, the only time you didn't play was if you were in hospital

Scottish League, Division Two
Stenhousemuir 5, St Johnstone 5
Ochilview Park, Saturday, 22nd September, 1962

A FANTASTIC FINISH AT OCHILVIEW

St Johnstone Wipe Out Four-Goal Deficit in Six Sensational Minutes

STENHOUSEMUIR 5, ST JOHNSTONE 5.

(Half-time—3-1)

In 2016, it was calculated that in over 1,000 games in the English Premier League the team that was two goals ahead only lost on 22 occasions; that is 2.1% of the time. What the odds are of a team that is 5-1 down with only twenty minutes remaining then staging the mother of all comebacks to get a draw is unknown, to us, but it's likely to be quite high…

In the course of our long history, Saints have staged a (small) number of impressive come-backs. Alex Totten's Saints were 2-0 down with twenty minutes to go at Cliftonhill on 10th March 1990, but, after changing to what was effectively an old-fashioned 2-3-5 formation, they ended up 5-2 winners. The amazing turnaround against Rangers in the Scottish Cup in 1981, when the team came back from two down and were 3-2 ahead, only to surrender a last gasp equaliser, was also notable, as was the turnaround at Kilmarnock in 2021 when three, second half goals shattered the 2-0 lead the home side had at the break.

However, none of these can match the amazing day in 1962 when Saints were being trounced 5-1 in an away match at Stenhousemuir with only 20 minutes left on the clock. Rather than accepting defeat, they stormed back to draw 5-5, thanks to an astonishing blitzkrieg of attacking football that brought four goals in six stupefying minutes.

For the small, select band of fans who are still alive and remember being at that game there are fond memories, not just of a stunning fight back, but of a typically lion-hearted performance from Billy Taylor in the Saints' goal.

There was a problem for the visitors even before the match kicked-off. John Bell, who was to go on to become one of the heroes that day, had only just made the team. While he was getting changed before the game, John dropped one of his contact lenses. With 12th man George Rankin ordered to strip to replace him, Ron McKinven found John's lens on the dressing room floor. Of course, there were no substitutes in those days – which, as we'll see, was to have a significant impact on Saints in the first half - but it would have been permissible for the team to have been changed prior to the kick-off.

291

With Bell restored, Saints went ahead in the fourth minute, courtesy of a slightly fortuitous goal, when, as the PA described it, *"the wind swirled a 40 yard lob from McFadyen out of the 'keeper's reach."*

Then, in the 12th minute, came a pivotal moment. Billy Taylor was injured when dashing from his goal to throw himself at the feet of the Stenny centre-forward Richardson, who was trying to capitalise on a loose pass-back from Ashley Booth. As a result of receiving a boot in the face for his bravery, Bill was stretchered from the field with a nasty gash on his forehead.

As we noted, in those days there were no substitutes, so Jim Lachlan took over in goal. To add insult to Bill's injury, a Saints' player was deemed to have handled the ball in the immediate aftermath of the Taylor/Richardson clash, so the first thing Jim Lachlan had to do was pick the ball out of the net from the ensuing penalty.

However, his tenure in the yellow jersey was relatively brief as some four minutes later he was retrieving the ball from the net again, although this time he did, at least, get his fingers to the shot. Nevertheless, it was deemed expedient that Jim return to his left back berth, with the 17-year-old Jim Townsend taking his place between the sticks. Bill Taylor then came on to play on the left wing for the remainder of the half. Despite these tribulations, Saints actually played some good football. The PA reported that *It must have been frustrating for manager Brown to sit on the sidelines and watch his forwards play slick, clever football without tangible result. For there was no doubt that the Perth attack was the better line-up."*

That said, there was no further scoring before half-time and the teams went into their dressing rooms with Stenhousemuir 3-1 ahead. Fortunately, big Bill Taylor was deemed to have recovered sufficiently to resume his normal place between the uprights and Saints were then back to full strength.

We took the game to the home team early in the second half and a Kemp shot and a Bell header both came close, but not long after Stenhousemuir got another penalty. The PA described how Charlie McFadyen *"charged Richardson to the ground in the box in the 58th minute and spot-kick expert Jenkins gave Taylor no chance."*

With just over half an hour to play, Saints were now 4-1 down. In 63 minutes, the score was 5-1. It was a goal that a fully-fit Bill Taylor would normally have been expected to save, but at the time it seemed the final nail in the Saints' coffin, as the PA reported…

"And the last shred of hope was hammered out of Saints' supporters five minutes later when Richardson ran on to a ball rolling to the left and rattled it in off the right-hand post, behind the advancing Taylor. This was one goal, though, which an uninjured Taylor would never have conceded."

Normally, in these circumstances, the team on the receiving end is content to draw the game out and try not to concede any more, while hoping that a consolation goal might come their way. On this particular day, that's not what happened. Here's how the PA described what happened…

"If their supporters' hopes faded, Saints' efforts certainly never showed any signs of flagging at this stage.

"They kept peppering the 'Muir goal with shots from all angles, hoping and knowing all the time that their luck was about to change.

"And in six spectacular minutes it did. Jim Townsend started it off in the 70th minute when he beat three defenders and netted the shot of the match a 20-yarder. The score – 5-2.

"Ron McKinven started an attack two minutes later which culminated in his trapping a cross from McIntyre on the right and bulging the back of the net from a few yards out. The score – 5-3.

"Bell got his first in the 75th minute off a cross from Kemp on the bye-line, and within a minute Townsend had beaten two defenders and pushed the ball through to Bell, who equalised from all of 15 yards. The score – 5-5.

"Excitement was at fever pitch among the visitors' supporters who had witnessed one of the greatest recoveries in the history of the Second Division."

Fever pitch is one way to describe it. Gordon Small, who was about 15 years old at the time, told us there was a mini pitch invasion after the fourth Saints' goal, and a much bigger one after the fifth: *"It was the first time I'd seen - or taken part in – a pitch invasion. I remember ducking under the solid metal barriers and running on the pitch after the fourth, then when it went to 5-5 we did the same again!"*

Not content with having levelled the scores, Saints still had nearly quarter of an hour to try to do even better. And they came very close to snatching an improbable win…

"In the dying minutes of the game, John Bell sent a screaming 10-yard drive through a defender's legs. But the unsighted 'keeper brought off the save of the match."

Unsurprisingly, the result was extensively reported in newspapers the length and breadth of the kingdom as being the highest aggregate score that day, while the unprecedented feat of scoring four goals in six minutes is, we believe, the most intense burst of goalscoring in St Johnstone's history and unlikely to be repeated any day soon. Several other goal bonanzas are recounted in this book, but this is the best.

As well as Gordon Small, there are still some other Saints' fans around today who were at this game. Amongst them was Tom McLaughlan, who was only 11 years old when he went to Stenhousemuir - for his first away game…

"We stayed in Glover Street and we went through to the game in an old Post Office van. My cousin drove, with his two boys alongside me and my brother on the benches in the back and Bert Alexander, a real Muirton stalwart who was the newsagent in Glover Street, in the front beside him. We were expecting to win because Saints had just been relegated the season before so we thought we'd be able to get straight back up, which we eventually did, but not before we watched this amazing game.

"We were with the other Saints' fans, behind the goal that we were defending in the first half. I remember that in those days there were far more men wearing bunnets than now, as well as the occasional blue-and-white knitted toorie. Billy Taylor took a real kick to the head and had to go off, so we were down to ten men – and at half-time we were 3-1 down. I remember Jim Lachlan going in goal, then Bill Taylor came back on with a bandage on his head and played on the wing. In those days, the only way you didn't play was if you were taken to the hospital. Jim Townsend took over as goalkeeper from Lachlan and in the second half Bill Taylor went back in goal, so we were back to 11-a-side. Then the fight-back started.

"I don't actually recall who scored all the goals, just that they got another one and we got one back, so it was 5-2, but in the last ten minutes we just kept scoring. You could see the players were cock-a-hoop and for us it felt like a win. We crammed back into that wee van and went home, fair chuffed."

Gus Stewart, who would go on to become a St Johnstone director many years later, was also one of the lucky ones. He told us, *"I was at Stenhousemuir as a young laddie and remember Billy Taylor limping along the wing. As a youngster, I didn't realise the significance of that result and how unusual it was for us to come back like that."*

The atmosphere and the way fans dressed was very different in those days. As Gus recalled, *"Back in those days, we used to go to away games and there was no segregation; there'd be a bit of banter, but there were never any real problems. At that Stenhousemuir game, people weren't going nuts the way they would today: there was not the same chanting and shouting.*

"We used to have Saints' scarves in those days, but there were no replica strips. I do remember having a rattle, but you wouldn't be allowed in with one of those nowadays. It took all your strength to get it to revolve. The clothes people wore to games were very different. There was no casual clothing. Lots of men wore hats and many would also wear a tie: my dad would always wear a jacket and tie as well as a hat, which he would tip to the ladies."

Gordon Small has similar memories to Gus about the clothing fans wore in those days, telling us, *"It was common to see men in their jackets and ties and for games immediately after Christmas they would often have new ties and suits, but it was also the case that people worked shifts on Saturday mornings back then so often they would come straight to the ground from their work without having changed into smarter clothes.*

"For example, I remember John Kaylor's dad, whom I used to know, would turn up at Muirton after his morning's work with his work rucksack over his shoulder, ready for the game to begin."

Donnie McPhee remembers the impact that Bill Taylor had throughout the game: *"When we lost Billy Taylor, after he went off injured, we were really stretched and conceding goals left right and centre. I remember Bill went on the wing, with his head swathed in bandages, which at least gave us the same number of players as Stenhousemuir, but when he went back in goal in the second half we were much better. I don't think anyone imagined we would come back from 5-1 down though, but we did - we scored the goals that made it a much happier journey back home than it looked like it was going to be when there were only 20 minutes to go."*

After the game, Saints' chairman, Alex Lamond, commented, *"I've never seen anything to match this performance. It was quite extraordinary."* He was not wrong: this was indeed an extraordinary match - and the most extraordinary – and brilliant - come-back in St Johnstone's history.

Saints team: Taylor, McFadyen and Lachlan, Little, Booth and McKinven; McIntyre, Townsend, Young, Bell and Kemp.
Attendance: unknown.

Scottish League Division One
St Johnstone 3, Airdrie 1
McDiarmid Park, Saturday 31ˢᵗ March 1990

The Courier and Advertiser, Monday, April 2, 1990.

Super Saints take Airdrie apart

Headline: The Courier

In the PA of Friday, 30ᵗʰ March, Graham Fulton wrote, *"This is it! The eyes of Scottish football turn to Perth tomorrow for not just the game of the day but the match of the season. And the stakes have never been higher. A win for league leaders Airdrie – a point ahead and a game in hand – will almost certainly give them the First Division championship. St Johnstone need outright victory if they hope to clinch that single place that will give them entry to the Premier League. With Rangers and Celtic playing their game on Sunday, media attention will most certainly focus on McDiarmid for the great showdown."*

Graham's last point was important: with the Old Firm not playing on Saturday, all the attention was, unusually, on a lower Division fixture. As a result, once the dust settled, the match reached a far wider audience than it would have otherwise and the fact that it was on Sportscene that night helped cement it – and St Johnstone's performance – in the minds of the thousands watching. The Sportscene presenter, Dougie Donnelly, described it as, *"a match which had everyone reaching for the superlatives. It was, quite simply, one of the best games* we've covered for a very long time."

We'd go further and say it was one of the best games that anyone could hope to see, ever. The fact that it's available on

YouTube makes that possible, but for those who were actually there, the atmosphere, the almost ceaseless excitement and the unabashed delirium that accompanied the final whistle will live in their minds for ever.

Alex Totten went into the game with some injury concerns in his squad. Harry Curran was expected to be out, but, on the plus side, Stevie Maskrey was told he was playing from the start. In total, it was estimated that the Saints' squad had cost only £231,000, whereas Airdrie's manager Jimmy Bone had spent over £440,000 on his players. The bulk of that money – some £175,000 – was spent on just one player, the former Clydebank forward (and future Saints' manager) Owen Coyle, who was at that time Scotland's top goal-scorer, with 23 goals. Moreover, Airdrie were full-time, while Saints were part-time. The two sides had scored 139 goals in the league between them that season

Alex Cameron in the Daily Record, displaying the lack of audience awareness and insensitivity that, unfortunately, can be the default setting of many a Glasgow-based newspaper hack, referred to McDiarmid Park as a *"little-Ibrox,"* adding, with equal condescension, *"The boom-place of soccer's lesser lights is engaged in a fight with Airdrie for a place in the Premier League."* To be fair to

Cameron, he did go on to say that Saints were *"exceptional candidates"* and that the match was *"the most exciting game I've seen all season."*

There are many things that come to mind when fans remember *"the Airdrie game"* (other Airdrie games are available, but not so consequential), including the weather, which was as good as could possibly be hoped for, with blue skies and a sunlit park providing the perfect backdrop for a game of such significance. Saints' fan Maggie Anderson remembers, *"I nearly wasn't there. My friend and I were planning a trip to Amsterdam to seen the bulb fields, but because of the importance of the game there was no way I was going to miss it. I've still not seen any tulips from Amsterdam, but I have seen Saints beat Airdrie 3-1 in the most glorious sunshine imaginable."*

The other main memories most of us who were there will have are of the noise and enthusiasm of the crowd, the unrelenting pressure applied by St Johnstone throughout the entire contest, the 69th minute goal by Airdrie's Steve Gray, which momentarily burst the home side's bubble – or, more aptly, applied a flame-thrower to it - and, of course, Saints' refusal to concede defeat that culminated in the most glorious of comebacks in the last 20 minutes. In addition, looking at the highlights of the game on YouTube, the other things that stand out are the very short shorts that were then fashionable, the fact that all the players wore black boots rather than today's explosions in a paint factory – as well as the traditional, square-faced wooden goalposts that Saints had brought from Muirton to McDiarmid. These posts were to play a significant part in the game.

It wasn't just the occasion and the result that makes this match stand out. It was the way the Saints' players approached their task. Sadly, we don't see this kind of bravura nowadays, but in 1990, with a winger on each flank, a big, amazingly

gifted (yet, it must be said, even by Roddy himself, not very speedy) centre forward, all aided by a powerhouse yet skilful midfield and a robust defence, the only way for Saints to play was to go forward. And that's what they did.

We hit the woodwork three times during the course of the match and, in addition, John Martin in the Airdrie goal made a string of truly splendid saves. Yet when it came to the crunch, it was the incessant pressure that St Johnstone applied that got them through the match.

After conceding the first goal, there was a very brief lull in the ground (other than at the Airdrie end, where, to be fair, they were pretty ecstatic) but within a few seconds the home fans found their voice and a roar of encouragement swelled across the home stands. Within seven minutes, we were level. Steve Maskrey was clipped inside the box and the ever-dependable Mark Treanor, one of the best penalty-takers Saints have had, coolly rolled the ball home.

With time marching on, Maskrey was clattered on the right, well inside the Airdrie half. There were only four minutes of regulation time on the clock and then Treanor stepped up, flighted in a perfect ball and Roddy Grant got in ahead of his marker to bullet home. The response from the home supporters was phenomenal - possibly the noisiest McDiarmid Park has ever been.

Then, to make siccar, with time virtually done, Roddy Grant got the ball wide on the left. Rather than holding it up, playing it back and trying to use up time, he juggled the ball to give himself space to make the pass that sent Ian Heddle haring away down the wing and into the Airdrie box, where he crossed for sub Kenny Ward to drill home.

Here's how the PA described the coup-de-grace: *"...any lingering doubts were destroyed when Heddle made a great run down the left just before the final whistle. His low cross found Ward who scored with a low drive from 10 yards."*

Ian Heddle would perhaps have expected to start this game as he had been a regular in the matches leading up to it. Unfortunately, on this occasion, Alex Totten decided to alter his starting line-up, which meant that Ian watched most of the match from the bench, before his decisive moment late on in the proceedings: *"When you watch it back it was a fabulous game. It was end to end and we were so dominant but simply couldn't score. We seemed to hit the post and bar every time, then we went down to Stevie Gray's brilliant goal.*

"I am really proud of my part in the move where we got the third goal. It's one of those things that, as a midfielder, I'd had drummed into me by my coaches – to run past your striker. Roddy had the ball and was holding it up: I ran past and he released me to run down the line and cut in. I saw Kenny coming in and played him in. It was one of the best games I've ever watched and/or played in."

This final goal was the cue for yet more bedlam in the stands and, more importantly, the result broke Airdrie's resolve over the remainder of the season, while galvanizing Saints to go on to lift the title. Despite having a game in hand, the Diamonds could not sustain their thrust on the title and, as we describe elsewhere in this book, Saints went to Ayr and came away with a famous, championship-winning victory.

In the Courier, Alex Totten described his feelings in the aftermath of the victory: *"I've said all season that I have the best team in the league and they proved it against Airdrie ... Sometimes the heads go down when you dominate a match yet find yourself trailing but my players refused to let that happen and their never-say-die attitude and superb fitness saw us through to a tremendous result."*

For the Diamonds, Jimmy Bone, their manager, was honest about the course of the game, telling the Courier, *"To have played so badly and taken the lead – I thought it was Christmas.*

"At 1-0 I felt we'd got the win because it didn't seem St Johnstone would score but in all honesty we didn't deserve to take anything from the game.

"I've no complaints at the outcome as Saints were the better side on the day."

For the Saints' fans, this was one of the best days: for the Airdrieonians, one of the worst. However, for one, theoretically neutral visitor, it was a real eye opener. A subsequent edition of fanzine *"Wendy Who?"* included an article taken from the Charlton Athletic fanzine *"Voice of the Valley."* Writer Richard Hunt was in Perth with his work and decided to take in the game. This is some of what he wrote: *"I took my top price seat (£5) and surveyed my immediate neighbours. Home and away supporters cheek by jowl, plenty of women and children. If this sounds twee to you, you should have heard the racket as the teams took the field.*

"As for football, it was the best match I've seen all season. It had everything. Misses galore, a psychopathic goalkeeper, a glorious comeback, all played out to a background of deafening noise...

"St Johnstone stormed forward, surfing towards the Airdrie goal on a billowing wave of sound. And with six minutes (sic - it was four minutes) *left, big Roddy Grant powered in a header...*

"Demonstrating the delightful naivety that obviously characterises Scottish part-time football, a glorious sweeping move involving Moore and Maskrey (sic – he was wrong about the players involved) *saw substitute Kenny Ward roar into the penalty area to plant the ball in the corner of the*

net, causing an eruption that set off avalanches in Aviemore. I was on my feet with the rest of them, I can tell you."

We are fortunate in that Bev Mayer, the St Johnstone Supporters' Liaison Officer, has TV commentator David Begg's notes from the game. These are shown on the following pages. Begg said that in his long career of commenting on football matches this was the best game he saw - as confirmed at the top of the second page here, which shows the team-lines, with the comment in his handwriting, "The Best Game Ever."

It wasn't just David Begg who thought this. For many other St Johnstone fans this was an equally memorable game. Graeme Buchan, one of the founders of the Wendy Who? fanzine, told us that the day started early: *"The Airdrie game started in the morning for me, because 15 guys from Hull came up and our Saints supporters team played them on the morning of the game. They called themselves the Sassenach Saintees and they were subscribers to Wendy Who? We played on the Inch, but in truth I can't remember if we won or they did. But I do know they had a great weekend in Perth. Some had seen Saints at Muirton and a few still go occasionally. For me, the Airdrie game was just the greatest game of football a Saints' fan will ever see."*

Saints team: Balavage, Treanor, McVicar, Barron, Hegarty, Johnston, Moore, Cherry, Maskrey, Grant and McGinnis. Substitutes: Heddle (For Johnston), Ward (for McGinnis). Attendance: 10,170.

THE LAST GAME EVER   1994

ST JOHNSTONE   AIRDRIE
(ALEX TOTTEN)   (JIMMY BONE)

1 JOHN BALAVAGE   1 JOHN MARTIN

2 (30) MARK TREANOR   2 (16) JIMMY BOYLE

3 (32) DON McVICAR   3 (26) ~~SANDY COWN~~
   (CAPT)   (CAPT) BRIAN McKEOWN

4 (06) DOUG BARRON   4 BRIAN McKEOWN

5 (16) PAUL HEGARTY   5 (16) DEREK GRANT

6 (76) ~~KEVIN JOHNSTON~~   6 (16) JOHN BUTLER

7 (126) ALAN MOORE   7 (-30) STEVE GRAY

8 (36) PAUL CHERRY   8 JOHN WATSON

9 (96) STEVE MASKREY   9 (76) EVAN BALFOUR

10 (166) RODDY GRANT   10 (01) OWEN COYLE

11 OG GARY ~~CONNELL~~   11 (46) ~~INNES McDONALD~~

14 (10) KENNY WARD   14 (66) GRAHAM HARVEY

12 (C) (156) IAN HEDDLE   12 ALAN LAWRENCE

77 - TREANOR (IN)
87 - RODDY GRANT
90 - KENNY WARD

Match notes: courtesy of David Begg and Bev Mayer

No. 1

If Saints had scored six goals this would have been a truer reflection of the play

UEFA Cup, First Round, Second Leg
St Johnstone 3, SV Hamburg 0
Muirton Park, Wednesday 29th September 1971

Saints humble German stars

ST JOHNSTONE 3, S.V. HAMBURG 0.

(Aggregate 4-2)

Scorers: St. Johnstone—Hall (15 mins.), Pearson (63), Whitelaw (78).

In deciding in which St Johnstone match the team's performance should be considered the club's greatest ever, there is no doubt that we shall upset a few people and delight quite a lot of others.

It's not hard to agree that many of the other games listed in this section of the book were incredibly exciting, packed with drama, sensational denouements and some stunning individual moments of brilliance, yet when we look at the overall levels of skill and commitment and the level of the opposition faced, this game against SV Hamburg stands out – albeit marginally - above the rest.

Of course, the Cup wins and the performance of the various teams in the last decade or so have been without equal in the club's history, and we are well aware that for those too young to have seen this game – the majority of today's supporters – there

will be not unreasonable questions about whether age has imparted a rose-tinted glow to our memories. But for those old enough to have been at Muirton that night, their steadily advancing years and the countless Saints matches they have seen allow a sense of perspective not available to those younger generations who never experienced just what a special team Willie Ormond's Saints were at their peak. They reached their zenith in this game against SV Hamburg and it was, in our view, the best overall performance and the highest quality display of attacking football by any St Johnstone team before or since. And just how good this Saints team was can be judged by the fact that only three days after beating Hamburg, they went to Celtic Park and beat the outstanding team that were the current Scottish Champions by one (John Connolly) goal to nil; once again demonstrating the skill and drive that characterised Ormond's great team.

In those days, there was nothing like the amount of European football played as there is now. Rather than having preliminary rounds to weed out the hundreds of teams who qualify for any of the various Cup competitions, followed by a league format of games designed to try and ensure the biggest clubs don't go out at the first available opportunity, in 1971 the new UEFA Cup involved only 64 teams at the outset, drawn into 32, winner-takes all, ties played home and away. Saints, as we know, progressed to the third round: if they had beaten ZEL Sarajevo, they would have been in the quarter finals after playing only six matches. Today, it could take six matches just to get out of the qualifying rounds before a European competition properly begins with a round-robin of group matches.

Consequently, as the contest drew closer, the excitement in and around Perth built to a crescendo which climaxed on the night of the game. Today, it would be an all-ticket affair, but back then, standing in a huge queue, all of whom were there to support Saints, was a novel experience. Then there was the thrill of purchasing – for only the third time in the club's history - a programme that was completely different from the usual, blue and white, four-page affair that did duty for normal Scottish games. For a start, it had more than one colour, and more than one photo…

Then there was the crowd. The evening temperature was coolish and slightly damp and with the nights drawing in the floodlights were on from the start, helping create a special atmosphere. For most of those present that evening it was the largest number of Saints' fans they'd ever seen in the old ground. Estimates varied from 12,000 to 14,000 but from our own personal recollections we reckon it seemed nearer the higher figure.

For the players, this was a novel experience. Gordon Whitelaw told us, *"I recall how well the support got behind us. The Saints support weren't the most vociferous normally, but while it might not have been the biggest crowd I played in front of, it certainly was the biggest I played 'with'."*

The young fans, the predecessors (often the grandfathers) of today's Fair City Unity, massed in the centre of the enclosure and bellowed out their songs. It was a fabulous, hair-up-on-the-back-of-the-neck moment, even before a ball was kicked in anger.

Jim Pearson agrees with Gordon Whitelaw's assessment of the way the fans got behind St Johnstone, telling us, *"I was on the bench at the start and looking*

around the ground we could see it was packed. The atmosphere was incredible: I normally took games in my stride, but that night was special.

"Before the game, Willie Ormond continued where he'd left off in his pre-match talk in Hamburg. He told us, 'What we did there was good and we can do it again.' Willie, like most managers in those days, was not particularly tactical in his approach, but as a man manager he was second to none. I always say that the four years I had with St Johnstone were the best in my career, even though I played for Everton and Newcastle in the top flight in England, and I also always say that having Willie Ormond as my first manager ruined me, because no subsequent manager was as good as he was. He was the best man-manager I've ever had."

The principal reason why we have ranked this game number one in our list of greatest matches is due to the exceptional standard of the two teams involved and, in particular, to the way St Johnstone set about their task of overturning Hamburg's 2-1 lead from the first leg with outstanding skill and precision play, abetted by thunderous commitment and an unquenchable will to win.

That commitment was exemplified by John Lambie, standing in as captain in place of the injured Benny Rooney. The PA's report summed up Lambie brilliantly – telling us that, *"Lambie was certainly an inspiring skipper, roaring instructions to his fellow defenders and always ready to lend a hand to help out his forwards down the right flank.*

"The former Falkirk bargain-buy became slightly over-enthusiastic as the game progressed, however, and the only black mark against him can be that he allowed himself to become involved in a personal feud with winger Volkert."

In John's defence, he was severely

provoked. As the Courier noted, Saints so demoralised their visitors that the Germans *"resorted to rough tactics and got away with it for a long time."* The PA was equally harsh in its criticism, and in its disdain for Hamburg's tactics, telling its readers, *"So frustrated were the Germans by St Johnstone's brilliant performance that they displayed a petulance reminiscent of the Latin temperament rather than the traditionally dour and workmanlike Teutons. The Hamburg players incensed the Muirton crowd by their shady tactics off the ball, which seemed to leave the Swiss referee, Mr Pius Kamber, quite unworried ... The Germans did not endear themselves to Perth's public and were the first team to visit Muirton that I have ever seen to be booed and cat-called from the field at the interval."*

Gordon Whitelaw agrees that the Germans dished out some *"rough treatment."* He told us, *"They certainly did that, but I didn't find Hamburg too bad. They were nothing like as bad as Sarajevo mind; they kicked us to pieces. Henry and John got the worst of it but it was quite a few games later before I could play properly* (Gordon didn't play for four matches after the game in Sarajevo).

"Hamburg could play: they had a few internationalists and the rest of the team were good players. However, in my mind, I don't remember it being too different from Scottish football. We had some good players too. I think John Connolly's performance against Hamburg was his best ever – and he played a lot of good games."

Gordon was right. Hamburg were an exceptional side. Throughout the 1960s, they had been a major force in West German football, winning the national championship and the German Cup as well as getting to the final of the European Cup Winners Cup in 1968. Two of their players – Willi Schulz and Uwe Seeler - had played for West Germany in the 1966 World Cup

final in London, with Seeler captaining his country that day. Moreover, Uwe Seeler is recognised as one of the all-time great German footballers, scoring 507 goals in 587 matches. By any standard, this was a formidable team and their angry response to being given the run-around by St Johnstone almost certainly reflects their assumption that this wee Scottish team, making their first ever appearance in European football, would present little or no challenge to their rightful progress.

Gordon Whitelaw was also right about John Connolly's performance that night - and he wasn't the only one who thought this.

The PA, in noting his contribution, had a dig at the Scottish football authorities, suggesting that it was high time the young Saints' player was capped by Scotland...

"The Saint who did most to upset the German defence was John Connolly, whose exploits must soon reach the deaf ears of the Scottish selectors and Tommy Docherty. The centre-forward had an outstanding match and finally exploded the myth which surrounds the legendary and supposedly immaculate West German internationalist defender, Willi Schulz. Schulz could not get the better of Connolly and neither could any of the other Hamburg defenders without resorting to fouls."

Not only did Schulz not get the better of Connolly, but he was gracious enough to recognise the quality of his Scottish opponent by swopping shirts with him after the game. John still has the shirt and kindly took a photo of it for us.

As for the man himself, John believes this was the best game he had in a St Johnstone shirt, although as he noted in the earlier chapter on the 8-1 defeat of Partick Thistle in the League Cup in 1969, there were other matches where he reached similar levels. Bearing in mind that we ranked John as the greatest St Johnstone player of all time, his bar for great performances is set very high…

John told us, *"Personally, the best way I could describe the night would be to say that I rate it as my best ever game in a Saints shirt: the atmosphere was amazing, the fans were brilliant and the team performance was excellent and needed to be to beat one of the top teams in Europe at the time."*

"When a game starts, you soon get into it and get a feel for how you're going to play. My game was getting on the ball and running at defenders, then getting a shot in or passing to someone else to have a chance to score. Against Hamburg, I was fortunate enough to get on the ball early in the match and I had a couple of good runs which gave me confidence. It was just the way it went on the night."

Willi Schulz's shirt from the game at Muirton: photo courtesy of John Connolly.

The game – and the result – provoked much comment across the UK. Even the Belfast Telegraph carried a paragraph, telling its readers, *"Pride of place in Scotland's*

UEFA Cup hat-trick goes to European 'Babes' St Johnstone. In their very first big tie at Muirton they gave Hamburg a goal of a start (they meant after the first leg) *and a licking. Henry Hall levelled the aggregate in the first half and Jim Pearson and Gordon Whitelaw hammered home the victory goals in the second. Two of the Hamburg defenders were booked."*

Slightly nearer to Perth than Belfast, the Aberdeen Press and Journal also carried a full match report of the game in Perth. If anything, the P&J was even more enthusiastic than the PA and the Courier. The first paragraph of their article began thus, *"This was European football played at its very best by a St Johnstone side who, despite some rough treatment from the Germans, stuck to their task and shattered the mighty men of Hamburg by three great goals."*

The writer went on… *"The Saints men were everywhere and by the end of the match had the Germans on their knees begging for mercy. In fact, if Saints had scored six goals this would have been a truer reflection of the play."*

In the event, we 'only' scored three. The pictures shown here (all from the Courier) are well-known, but we make no apology for including them again. The first might have come as early as the first minute. With Saints attacking the Ice Rink End, Hamburg kicked off, but Saints gained possession and Connolly sent Hall away, although Henry's shot was well saved by Ozcan in the Hamburg goal.

Saints were not to be denied though. Hall and Connolly had a further three shots in the first six minutes of the match, then in 15 minutes came the breakthrough. Ian McPhee, whose passing ability was second to none in the Saints' midfield, lofted a perfect ball forward into the penalty box. It was aimed precisely at Henry Hall, who promptly demonstrated why he is

St Johnstone's record goalscorer at the top level, as he deftly turned away from his marker and hit it first-time into the net. Cue, as they say, pandemonium!

Henry remembers this goal. *"I scored a lot like that,"* he said, *"where I swivelled on the half-turn past the defender and hit it. The pass from Ian McPhee helped though: Ian was a master at seeing a pass and I just had to try to get on the end of it. I always made a point of running to whoever made the goal and thanking them."*

Barely two minutes after Hall's goal, Connolly had the ball in the net again, squeezing it in but clashing with the goalkeeper as he did so and the goal was disallowed.

Although Saints continued to dominate, such was the quality of the Germans that an equaliser could not be ruled out. A Winkler header on 25 minutes just cleared the bar and then just before the interval Hamburg had a great chance. The PA described how *"Danish internationalist Bjornmose raced in on goal with only the 'keeper to beat. The tall Hamburg player crashed in a shot from point-blank range but the ball, by some quirk of fate, cannoned off Donaldson's body and was deflected for a corner."*

Quirk of fate or not, at half-time, with the score at 1-0, St Johnstone were going through on the 'away goals' rule. This had been introduced by UEFA in 1965, but of course Saints hadn't been in any European competition until 1971, so there was some discussion among the fans on the terracing that night about how this all worked and

what it would mean if the scores changed as the match went on.

The German team's exasperation continued to manifest itself in some outrageous fouling. Volkert, in particular, was guilty of some heinous kicks on Saints' players. Right at the start of the second half, he tackled Henry Hall, injuring the Saints' man so badly he had to leave the field, with Jim Pearson coming on as a substitute.

Nozly then kicked Kenny Aird almost off the pitch. In the 59th minute, his team-mate, Volkert, turned his attention to the wee right winger, but this time the referee had had enough and, as the PA explained to its readers, he *"was finally shown a yellow card (the UEFA system of booking)."* Yellow and red cards had only been introduced a year earlier, at the 1970 World Cup and were not in use in Scotland until the late 1970s, so like the 'away goals' rule, this – the first 'card' in a game involving St Johnstone - was a subject of much comment in the stands and terracing.

Jim Pearson was also on the receiving end of the rough stuff, with Bjornmose kicking out after the Saints' youngster had beaten him fair and square. In those, far more lenient, days, the referee merely had a word with the Hamburg centre-forward: today, a yellow card, at the least, would almost certainly be shown.

However, Jim was to have the last laugh when, in the 62nd minute, he displayed all his striker's instincts to get on the end of a cross from John Connolly and, as shown above, steer the ball past Ozcan from only a few yards out. If the fans were ecstatic at the first goal, they were even more so as Saints took the overall lead in the tie. But, at the back of our minds there remained the nagging doubt of what might happen if the Germans equalised...

That prospect did raise its ugly head when Bjornmose had the ball in the net for Hamburg in 68 minutes, but to sighs of relief all-round, the referee had already blown for a previous infringement.

Some five minutes later, Saints might have scored again. The PA tells us that, *"Connolly ghosted past two German defenders on the left wing and hit the ball across the face of the goal. Keeper Ozcan failed to cut out the cross but Whitelaw was a shade too slow to connect properly with the fast-moving cross and the chance was lost."*

Muirton saw its second ever yellow card in the 75th minute when the visitor's captain, Kurbjuhn, fouled Jimmy Donaldson.

The pick of the goals, or certainly the most spectacular, was the last. You wouldn't have known it from the PA though. Their report merely recorded that, *"Whitelaw made amends for his previous miss in the 78th minute when he put Saints three goals ahead."* A glorious, sweetly-taken goal that put the game beyond Hamburg - and that was all it got!

In contrast, here's the Courier's description: *"An Aitken corner was back-headed by Connolly to Whitelaw, who took deliberate aim before smashing the ball into the net from 16 yards."*

Better, but neither of these does justice to the excitement that came from a corner, taken by that master of the dead-ball, Fred Aitken. From Freddie's corner, there was first a clever header to steer the ball into a danger area and then a well-controlled strike that, as shown here, simply fizzed into the net, leading to mayhem on the terracing as the Saints' fans went wild.

It must be said that at least one of the author's memories of this goal was that it was from the edge of the box, rather than 'only' 16 yards out. This is corroborated to some extent by Gordon's own recollection. He told us, *"Because I was not so tall, I used to hang about outside the box, hoping to pick something up. That's what happened. It helped that it was such a great corner. Freddie Aitken was one of the best dead-ball kickers I've seen. We used to say he could cross the ball even if he was facing the stand."*

After the match, the press was in no doubt about why this was a unique performance. The PA's reporter's second paragraph summed it up nicely: *"Perth was a proud city after the game and little wonder. The home fans had watched Saints display a fine blend of all-out attacking football and hard, uncompromising defence and eventually transform the tie into a one-sided contest. The Germans were made to look a very ordinary bunch indeed."*

The Courier was equally impressed. Their opening paragraph didn't hold back: *"Saints played the game of their lives at Muirton to thrash Hamburg 3-0 and qualify on aggregate 4-2 for the next round of the UEFA Cup"* before going on to add, *"The Perth team, given no chance when the initial draw was made, outplayed and outmanoeuvred their experienced opponents."*

Jim Pearson recalled the atmosphere after the final whistle sounded, telling us that, *"In the dressing room afterwards, we were delighted, but we always thought we could beat them. We had a couple of beers and it all made for a night I'll never forget."*

John Connolly believes that the Germans had gone into the match, 2-1 up from the first leg, thinking they would win in Perth. *"Given the talent they had in their team, that's understandable, but of course we had some talent in our team too. Once it was over, in the dressing room after the game, we were all congratulating each other, amazed and proud of what we had just done: it was a fabulous performance and a great night for everyone who was there."*

Jimmy Donaldson also remembers the game well and agrees with John's view of the Germans' expectations. *"They had expected to walk all over us as they were one of the favourites for the tournament,"* he said, adding, *"It was difficult not to get caught up in the atmosphere. I had a few one-on-ones which I managed to block, but we pounded them for much of the match. It was one of the best games ever. John Connolly was at his very best that night. He actually had an amazing game against Dunfermline where he was probably as good as he was that night, but to be fair, he had quite a few outstanding games for St Johnstone.*

"After the match, the boys were jubilant. Most of them had to stay over – I think they stayed in a B&B on the Dundee Road – but I was living on the Dunkeld Road at the time so I simply walked home."

Today, we would say the players and the fans were 'buzzing.' However, that expression - at least in its modern sense - was not in use in the 1970s, but the excitement at the final whistle was nonetheless palpable. While many fans milled around Muirton in the aftermath of the game, the majority of us who were there slowly began to wend our way homewards, the conversations filled with superlatives at what we had just witnessed.

This really was a special night. Jack Findlay recalled walking with Alastair Blair along Feus Road towards Muirton Park…

"I remember you and I walking along the Feus Road; we were so excited to be seeing our team playing in Europe for the first time at Perth. Then, when we got to Muirton, there were these enormous queues and once in we made our way to the middle of the enclosure and joined in the singing. The ground was packed and the fact that it was misty and dark and the game was under the floodlights made the whole experience seem even more magical. Coming out of the ground after we'd won, there were the street lights shining on thousands of euphoric supporters.

"It was a fabulous match and the best Saints' performance I've ever seen. John Connolly was something else that evening, but the entire team had a wealth of talent and the way we played that night will live with me forever."

One fan was not quite so relaxed. Bert McIntosh, now (in 2023) a mere 86 years young, then worked at Perth Yarns on Arran Road. Unfortunately, that Wednesday he had a night shift starting at 10.00 pm. Despite the excitement, and even allowing for the fact that the game kicked off at 7.30 pm, he had to cycle home to Unity Terrace, get changed and then whizz back to Arran Road for his work. However, as he told us, *"I always told them they couldn't start the shift until I got there in case anything went wrong with the machinery. Although they would have carried on without me, fortunately, I made it on time!"*

It is, as we noted at the start of this chapter, very hard - some would say almost impossible - to decide which is the greatest match in St Johnstone's history. Let's leave the last word to Bert. When we asked him which was the best game he's ever seen, he did not hesitate for a second…

"It was the game against SV Hamburg. I was in awe of our performance that night. We outplayed one of the very best teams in Germany at that time. It was, without doubt, the greatest game I've seen St Johnstone play in all the years I've watched the club, going all the way back from my very first match as a 10-year-old in 1947 up to the present day."

Bert is right. This is indeed the greatest match in St Johnstone's history to date.

Saints team: Donaldson; Lambie and Coburn; Rennie, Gordon, McPhee; Aird, Whitelaw, Connolly, Hall, Aitken. Substitutes: Pearson (for Hall), Muir, Argue, Mercer. Attendance: c. 14,000.

Printed in Great Britain
by Amazon